FROM
EVE
TO
DAWN

Other Books by Marilyn French

Fiction
The Women's Room (1977)
The Bleeding Heart (1980)
Her Mother's Daughter (1987)
Our Father (1994)
My Summer with George (1996)

Nonfiction
Beyond Power. On Women, Men and Morals (1988)
Women in India (1990)
The War Against Women (1992)
A Season in Hell. A Memoir (1998)

FROM
EVE
TO
DAWN

A HISTORY OF WOMEN

VOLUME 2:
THE MASCULINE MYSTIQUE

MARILYN FRENCH

Foreword by
Margaret Atwood

The Feminist Press
at the City University of New York

Published in 2008 by The Feminist Press at the City University of New York
The Graduate Center
365 Fifth Avenue, Suite 5406
New York, NY 10016
www.feministpress.org

The Library of Congress provided the following Cataloguing-in-Publication Data for all
four volumes of this series:

Library of Congress Cataloging-in-Publication Data

French, Marilyn, 1929-
  From eve to dawn / Marilyn French ; foreword by Margaret Atwood.
    p. cm.
  "Originally published: Toronto : McArthur, 2002.

  ISBN 978-155861-567- 0 (trade paper)

  1. Women—History. I. Title.
  HQ1121.F74 2008
  305.4209—dc22

                                2007033836

This publication was made possible, in part, by the Lawrence W. Levine Foundation,
Inc., and by Florence Howe, Joanne Markell, and Eileen Bonnie Schaefer.

Cover design by Black Cat Design
Cover illustration by Carole Hoff
Printed on acid-free paper in Canada by Transcontinental

12 11 10 09 08   5 4 3 2 1

"As if from Eve to Dawn
Your own name changes."
— Barbara Greenberg

To Barbara Greenberg and Margaret Atwood

CONTENTS

FOREWORD

FROM *EVE TO DAWN* is Marilyn French's enormous four-volume, nearly two-thousand-page history of women. It runs from prehistory until the present, and is global in scope: the first volume alone covers Peru, Egypt, Sumer, China, India, Mexico, Greece, and Rome, as well as religions from Judaism to Christianity and Islam. It examines not only actions and laws, but also the thinking behind them. It's sometimes annoying, in the same way that Fielding's *Amelia* is annoying—enough suffering!—and it's sometimes maddeningly reductionist; but it can't be dismissed. As a reference work it's invaluable: the bibliographies alone are worth the price. And as a warning about the appalling extremes of human behavior and male weirdness, it's indispensable.

Especially now. There was a moment in the 1990s when, it was believed, history was over and Utopia had arrived, looking very much like a shopping mall, and "feminist issues" were supposed dead. But that moment was brief. Islamic and American right-wing fundamentalists are on the rise, and one of the first aims of both is the suppression of women: their bodies, their minds, the results of their labors—women, it appears, do most of the work around this planet—and last but not least, their wardrobes.

From Eve to Dawn has a point of view, one that will be familiar to the readers of French's best-selling 1977 novel, *The Women's Room.* "The people who oppressed women were men," French claims. "Not all men oppressed women, but most benefited (or thought they benefited) from this domination, and most contributed to it, if only by doing nothing to stop or ease it."

Women who read this book will do so with horror and growing anger: *From Eve to Dawn* is to Simone de Beauvoir's *The Second Sex* as wolf is to poodle. Men who read it might be put off by the depiction of the collective male as brutal psychopath, or puzzled by French's idea that men should "take responsibility for what their sex has done." (How responsible can you be for Sumerian monarchs, Egyptian pharaohs, or Napoleon Bonaparte?) However, no one will be able to avoid the relentless piling up of detail and event—the bizarre customs, the woman-hating legal structures, the gynecological absurdities, the child abuse, the sanctioned violence, the sexual outrages—millennium after millennium. How to explain them? Are all men twisted? Are all women doomed? Is there hope? French is ambivalent about the twisted part, but, being a peculiarly American kind of activist, she insists on hope.

Her project started out as a sweeping television series. It would have made riveting viewing. Think of the visuals—witch-burnings, rapes, stonings-to-death, Jack the Ripper clones, bedizened courtesans, and martyrs from Joan of Arc to

Rebecca Nurse. The television series fell off the rails, but French kept on, writing and researching with ferocious dedication, consulting hundreds of sources and dozens of specialists and scholars, although she was interrupted by a battle with cancer that almost killed her. The whole thing took her 20 years.

Her intention was to put together a narrative answer to a question that had bothered her for a long time: how had men ended up with all the power—specifically, with all the power over women? Had it always been like that? If not, how was such power grasped and then enforced? Nothing she had read had addressed this issue directly. In most conventional histories, women simply aren't there. Or they're there as footnotes. Their absence is like the shadowy corner in a painting where there's something going on that you can't quite see.

French aimed to throw some light into that corner. Her first volume—*Origins*—is the shortest. It starts with speculations about the kind of egalitarian hunter-gatherer societies also described by Jared Diamond in his classic *Guns, Germs and Steel*. No society, says French, has ever been a matriarchy—that is, a society in which women are all-powerful and do dastardly things to men. But societies were once matrilineal: that is, children were thought to descend from the mother, not the father. Many have wondered why that state of affairs changed, but change it did; and as agriculture took over, and patriarchy set in, women and children came to be viewed as property—men's property, to be bought, sold, traded, stolen, or killed.

As psychologists have told us, the more you mistreat people, the more pressing your need to explain why your victims deserve their fate. A great deal has been written about the "natural" inferiority of women, much of it by the philosophers and religionmakers whose ideas underpin Western society. Much of this thinking was grounded in what French calls, with wondrous understatement, "men's insistent concern with female reproduction." Male self-esteem, it seemed, depended on men not being women. All the more necessary that women should be forced to be as "female" as possible, even when—especially when—the male-created definition of "female" included the power to pollute, seduce, and weaken men.

With the advent of larger kingdoms and complex and structured religions, the costumes and interior decoration got better, but things got worse for women. Priests—having arguably displaced priestesses—came up with decrees from the gods who had arguably replaced goddesses, and kings obliged with legal codes and penalties. There were conflicts between spiritual and temporal power brokers, but the main tendency of both was the same: men good, women bad, by definition. Some of French's information boggles the mind: the "horse sacrifice" of ancient India, for instance, during which the priests forced the raja's wife to copulate with a dead horse. The account of the creation of Islam is particularly fascinating: like Christianity, it was woman-friendly at the start, and supported and spread by women. But not for long.

The Masculine Mystique (Volume Two) is no more cheerful. Two kinds of feudalism are briskly dealt with: the European and the Japanese. Then it's on to the appropriations by Europeans of Africa, of Latin America, of North America, and thence to the American enslavement of blacks, with women at the bottom of the heap in all cases. You'd think the Enlightenment would have loosened things up, at least theoretically, but at the salons run by educated and intelligent women the philosophers were still debating—while hoovering up the refreshments—whether women had souls, or were just a kind of more advanced animal. In the 18th century, however, women were beginning to find their voices. Also they took to writing, a habit they have not yet given up.

Then came the French Revolution. At first, women as a caste were crushed by the Jacobins despite the key role they had played in the aristocracy-toppling action. As far as the male revolutionaries were concerned, "Revolution was possible only if women were utterly excluded from power."

Liberty, equality, and fraternity did not include sorority. When Napoleon got control "he reversed every right women had won." Yet after this point, says French, "women were never again silent." Having participated in the overthrow of the old order, they wanted a few rights of their own.

Infernos and Paradises, the third volume, and *Revolution and the Struggles for Justice*, the fourth volume, take us through the growing movement for the emancipation of women in the in the 19th and 20th centuries, with the gains and reverses, the triumphs and the backlashes, played out against a background of imperialism, capitalism, and world wars. The Russian Revolution is particularly gripping—women were essential to its success—and particularly dispiriting as to the results. "Sexual freedom meant liberty for men and maternity for women," says French. "Wanting sex without responsibility, men charged women who rejected them with 'bourgeois prudery.' . . . To treat women as men's equals without reference to women's reproduction . . . is to place women in the impossible situation of being expected to do everything men do, and to reproduce society and maintain it, all at the same time and alone."

It's in the final three chapters of the fourth volume that French comes into her home territory, the realm of her most personal knowledge and her deepest enthusiasms. "The History of Feminism," "The Political Is Personal, The Personal Is Political," and "The Future of Feminism" make up the promised "dawn" of the general title. These sections are thorough and thoughtful. In them, French covers the contemporary ground, including the views of antifeminist and conservative women—who, she argues, see the world much as feminists do—one half of humanity acting as predators on the other half—but differ in the degree of their idealism or hope. (If gender differences are "natural," nothing to be done but to manipulate the morally inferior male with your feminine wiles, if any.) But almost all women, she believes—feminist or not—are "moving in the same direction along different paths."

Whether you share this optimism or not will depend on whether you believe Earth Titanic is already sinking. A fair chance and a fun time on the dance floor for all would be nice, in theory. In practice, it may be a scramble for the lifeboats. But whatever you think of French's conclusions, the issues she raises cannot be ignored. Women, it seems, are not a footnote after all: they are the necessary center around which the wheel of power revolves; or, seen another way, they are the broad base of the triangle that sustains a few oligarchs at the top. No history you will read, post-French, will ever look the same again.

Margaret Atwood
Canada
August 2004

INTRODUCTION

FROM *EVE TO DAWN* was first published in Canada in 2002–2003, but it was written over a decade earlier. Publishers bought it, but procrastinated, intimidated by its length. Each one finally declined to print. The book, which took me more than fifteen years to research and write, was 10,000 pages long. Initially I refused the publishers' pleas to cut it, but eventually, I had to do so. Removing so much material harmed the book. For instance, in recounting women's battle for education, I described the awesome daily schedule of the first young women in England to attend college. I provided the onerous schedules of the first young women to study nursing with Florence Nightingale. In removing detail like this, I diminished the richness of the story, and the reader's admiration for these women. Unfortunately, I did not keep careful records of these removals, and can no longer retrieve them. The information can still be found, but only in my sources, the books or articles from which I gleaned my material.

The world has changed since I finished writing the book, but none of the changes alters the history of women very much. For instance, I had predicted that Serbia, in rabid Christian zeal, would mount military action against the other Yugoslavian states. But I had to remove this bit, since, by the time the book was published in 2002, the wars in Yugoslavia, initiated by Serbia, had not only begun but ended. Originally, I predicted that "fundamentalist" Islamic movements in the Middle East would grow; by the time the book was published, this forecast was a fait accompli.

The major change affecting women during the last three decades is this proliferation of fundamentalisms. These religious movements are widespread, occurring within every world religion: Christianity (the born-again Christian movement in the United States, the drive to criminalize abortion centered in the Catholic Church); Islam (militant brotherhoods like the Taliban in most Muslim states), and even Judaism (e.g., Gush Emunim in Israel) and Hinduism, which are both historically non-proselytizing. The politics of these movements are not new, but the emotions of the men involved in them intensified to the point of fanaticism after the1970s. Thus, whatever their claims, they were not only responses to Western colonization or industrialization, but a backlash against spreading feminism.

Another major change that occurred during this period was the demise of the USSR and the shift from socialism to a kind of capitalism, in Russia and its satellite states, without in most cases much movement toward democratization. China too has shifted in the direction of capitalism without moderating its dictatorial government. It has also experienced considerable industrialization and Westernization. Economic changes like these, globalization, and the emergence of "free trade" thinking, have increased the gap between the very rich and everyone else, and affect women and men similarly. Economic changes hit the most vulnerable people hardest, and everywhere in the world, women and children are the most vulnerable. Women and children make up four-fifths of the poorest people on earth. One consequence of these economic developments is a huge increase in slavery, trade in human beings, which particularly affects women, who are nowadays bought and sold across the globe for use as prostitutes and slave laborers—and in China, as slave-wives. Unlike earlier forms of slavery, this form is illegal, yet thrives everywhere.

But women continue to fight for egalitarian treatment: despite the double-standards, women in Iran (a religious dictatorship) and Egypt (a secular dictatorship) try to work within the law. The Iranian government frequently imprisons, whips, and even kills women who challenge its standards; Egypt imprisons them. Government does not get involved in Pakistan, Afghanistan, or the former Soviet republics, where women who appear to deviate from the oppressive moral code are punished and killed by their own families—their fathers or brothers—or their village councils. Yet women go on protesting.

Men involved in fundamentalist movements see feminism as a threat. Feminism is simply the belief that women are human beings with human rights. Human rights are not radical claims, but merely basic rights—the right to walk around in the world at will, to breathe the air and drink water and eat food sufficient to maintain life, to speak at will and control one's own body and its movements, including its sexuality. Fundamentalists deny women this status, treating them as if they were nonhuman beings created by a deity to serve men, who own them. Fundamentalist movements thrust the history of women into a tragic new phase. Across the globe, men who see feminism as a threat to their dominance are clamping down with religious fervor on women in order to maintain their dominance.

Control over a woman is the only form of dominance most men possess, for most men are merely subjects of more powerful men. But so unanimous is the drive for dominance in male cultures that men can abuse women across the board with impunity. A man in India who burns his wife to death in a dowry dispute has no trouble obtaining a second wife from another family that allegedly loves its daughter.[1] Latin American and Muslim men who kill their wives under the guise of an "honor" killing have no trouble finding replacements.

Misogyny is not an adequate term for this behavior. It is rooted not in hatred of women, but in a belief that women are not human beings, but animals designed to serve men and men's ends, with no other purpose in life. Men in such cultures see women who resist such service as perverse, godless creatures who deny the purpose for which they were created. In light of the ubiquity and self-righteousness of such men, we need to consider the origins of their beliefs.

In the original Preface to this book I said, "I wrote this history because I needed a story to make sense of what I knew of the past and what I saw in the present." In fact, I began with a vision. The first time I had the vision, it was a dream, but it recurred many times over my lifetime, and in its later reincarnations I was awake when I saw it—although always in bed, on the verge of sleep. I never consciously summoned this vision. In it, I am tortured by not-knowing, and one day I awaken to find an angel sitting on the side of my bed. It is a male angel, and gold from head to toe, like an Oscar—although the first time I had it, I was a young girl and knew nothing about Oscars. I welcome the angel and plead my case: please, please explain to me how things got to be the way they are, I say. Things make no sense. I don't understand how they came about. The angel agrees, and proceeds to explain. He talks for a long time and at the end I understand everything. It all makes sense. I am filled with gratitude. Yes, the angel says, but now that you know, you are not permitted to live. You must die. Okay, I say. I don't mind. He embraces me and together we magically ascend to heaven. I am in bliss because I understand everything.

This dream, or vision, is what drove me throughout the years of work. I did not start with a belief; the story emerged from the material as I did the research, especially after I started work on Africa, where the process of patriarchic organization was still occurring when Arab traders arrived there. I let the explanation filter into the text as I discovered it. The argument is thus threaded through the text, and is not readily abstracted from it. I am taking the opportunity in this new Introduction to offer the explanation separately.

Humans of some form have lived on the planet for almost four million years, although our own species, homo sapiens sapiens, is only about 100,000 years old. We do not know how earlier hominids lived, but we can study our nearest relatives, chimpanzees, to get some idea. Chimpanzees live in heterosocial groups, males and females, young and old, together. (Other animals do not live this way. Many mammals—lions, and elephants, for instance, live in homosocial groups—related females together, along with their young, and males in isolation.) Dominance hierarchies are also unisexual: those among males affect only males; those among females affect only females. Moreover, dominance has a narrow meaning for animals: a dominant male has first dibs over food and sexual access to females. Inferior males are expected to defer to the alpha male in disputes over food or sex. But his dominance can be and regularly is challenged or evaded; it also shifts from one animal to another. In no animal species do dominant males or females dictate the behavior of other animals. They do not rule each other, as humans try to do. An animal may have authority because of her status in the group, but does not possess the right to command other animals to do or not do anything.

But, females regularly intervene in male affairs. Within chimpanzee society, a particular animal may be loved or respected, usually because she has offered others comfort, grooming, or care. This gives her the authority to intervene when males are fighting among themselves, or picking on a particular animal. Her authority resides solely in the willingness of the other animals to hearken to her. Females regularly disregard male status, having sex with whom they choose, often with low-status chimps.[2]

Chimpanzees live in family groups of 20 to 30 in the forest. Females migrate to other groups to mate, but may return to their natal group afterward. Females take total responsibility for socializing the young. A mother teaches her child what is good as food and medicine, to make a bed each night, to make and use tools, and to communicate with other chimps through calls and expressive sound. She feeds her baby until it is five years old, but chimps usually remain with their mothers for a decade. If a mother dies, her baby often dies of grief, unless other family members take care of it. Fatherhood is of course unknown— as is the case with most animals—but males are heavily involved in tending the young.[3]

Chimpanzees often display empathetic behavior, even for beings of different species.[4] Their ability to feel empathy leads them occasionally to perform seemingly altruistic acts, in what is the foundation of a moral sense. Because chimp young, like human babies, require years of parental care to survive, they have a need to be loved. From the mother-child bond of love arises the bond unifying the chimpanzee community.

Scientists assume that early hominids lived in much the same way, in groups made up of sisters and brothers, the women's children, and their mates. This form of society is called matricentry. It is important to distinguish this from matriarchy, a term many people use in error. Matriarchy means "ruled by mothers." There has never been a matriarchal state, so far as we know, although there may be matriarchal families. Matricentry means centered around the mother, a form found in most families.

Female chimpanzees produce only about 3 infants in a lifetime, one every 5 or 6 years. Hominids may have done the same. Fatherhood was unknown and remained so during most of the three-plus millennia of human existence. For hundreds of years, people lived by gathering fruits, vegetables, and grains, which was done almost entirely by females. Males gather, when they do, only for themselves; females feed the entire clan. Both sexes hunted small animals with their hands. Around 10,000 BCE, people—probably women—started to plant crops, perhaps wheat. The move to horticulture caused a major change in human life because it entailed living in settled communities.

Women being central in the group, and being the ones who fed the group, were also the ones considered to have rights in the land. All early societies in Africa and North America believed land could not be owned, but that those who settled it had the right to use it. In prehistory, women had rights to use the land, which passed to their daughters. This system was still pervasive when foreigners penetrated indigenous societies. Women remained on the land they inherited, and men migrated from other clans to mate with them. Children belonged to the mother, the only known parent, and were named for her. If a mating was unhappy, a man could leave his wife but could not take the children, who were part of her matriline. All babies were accepted in their mother's clan from birth. There was no such thing as illegitimacy. Nor, in such societies, could men abuse their wives, who were surrounded by family members who would protect them.

Anthropologists who studied the remaining matrilineal groups in earlier decades reported that they were harmonious. They are now usually male-dominant, although men derive their importance from their sisters. Children inherit from their uncles. In hunting-gathering societies, men remain at the village when the women go to gather; they gamble, they play, and they watch the children. Only occasionally do they hunt. Male-female groups may hunt together with nets and spears.[5] When a clan discovered weaving or pottery-making, it was usually women who did this work too. But men's sociability and playfulness gave them an advantage when politics—negotiations among different clans—began. The women, who gathered singly although they went out together, were more bound to their own family units because they took responsibility for them.

Hominids and early humans lived this way for nearly four million years. They lived in peace; there are no signs of weapons until about 10,000 years ago. Some communities left traces behind, like Catal Hüyük in Turkey. This Anatolian community thrived from about 10,000 BCE until 8,000 BCE—surviving longer than ancient Greece or Sumer or any European nation. Its people lived in connected houses entered from the top by a ladder. (Houses of early periods were often shaped like internal female organs: they had a vaginal passage leading to a room shaped like the uterus—like igloos). In Catal Hüyük, many houses had shrines attached to them. Their wall paintings showed that they were devoted to animals and hunting. Later, when the supply of animals had dwindled, they were devoted to goddesses. The people of Catal Hüyük traveled far—their middens contained jewels, mirrors, stones, and woods from thousands of miles away. They had a rich and varied diet including alcoholic drinks, they had weaving and pottery and painting and made female figurines.[6] Their paintings depict a dangerous game played by young men and women: leaping the bull, and showed both sexes in lovely, sexy clothes.[7]

The ruins of Knossos are even more impressive, containing paved streets, houses with roof gardens, gutters, toilets, and baths. It seems to have been an egalitarian society with writing, a very high standard of living and a love of art. In their paintings, women sit in the front and men in the rear at public events. Women are depicted as hunters, farmers, merchants, chariot drivers; one is even commander of a ship. The city was probably destroyed by a volcano.

Not only these towns but this entire political structure perished. People went on living in matricentric, matrilineal clans—they still exist in Africa—but some clans changed their political structure. The first states arose in Egypt and Sumer, toward the end of the 4th millennium. The beginnings of a move toward patriarchy are reflected in Egyptian art, which depicts human beings of equal size until the end of the 4th millennium, when artists began to paint one man taller amid a crowd of others of normal height. This change reflects a political change in African societies that was occurring when the first Arab merchants infiltrated it and observed the process. It is the shift to patriarchy.

Patriarchy was the result of a revolution, the world's first. It occurred after men had realized they had a part in procreation, knowledge that triggered their discontent. They may have wanted to own the young they fathered, in order to control their labor, but it appears their main objective was to obtain more power over women. They raided villages to obtain captive women. (Many societies—like Rome, for instance—have founding myths based on men's rape of women.) Once removed from their clan, women had no claim to land or labor in their home villages, and were freed of their obligation to their families. Having no rights, they were essentially slaves.[8] Men mated with them, keeping them under surveillance, but because they were unsure how long it took for a fetus to mature, or how to prove fatherhood, they killed the firstborn child. Murder of firstborn children is a regular mark of patrilineal groups.

Men kept these women under surveillance in their villages to assure their paternity, and began to make rules that applied only to women. Thus, the first criminals were women. Men declared it a crime (adultery) for women to have sex with anyone but their owners, and for women to abort children, although men had the right in every ancient society, to murder their own children (infanticide). Men declared that children belonged to their fathers and named them for the fathers. Children whose fathers were unknown were decreed illegitimate, bastards.

Women, kidnapped from various villages, often could not speak the language of their captors, nor those spoken by other women in the village. Forever alien, they were probably unhappy. Most patrilineal groups allowed them to leave, but forbade their taking the children with them, so few women left. Children belonged to their patriliny, which disposed of them as it chose. Doubtless women's unhappiness communicated itself to the men, because in most patrilinies, men do not live with women. In past and present patrilinies, men use women for sex and require women to feed them, but live in separate men's houses. Some require great subservience, bowing and other forms of obeisance, from the enslaved women.

The society in men's houses, according to anthropologists who have studied them, is miserable—contentious and bickering. Women live with their children in women's houses until boys are taken from them at adolescence. Girls remain until they are grown enough to be used as barter to other clans in a search for wives. It is in these clans that the most cruel male puberty rites occur, when boys are taken from their mothers and introduced into the men's houses. Many of these clans have myths referring to a time when women had powers that they have lost—sometimes symbolized by flutes or other instruments. The message of puberty rites is the same whether a boy is being initiated by the Chaka, by British public (private) schools, or by the Catholic Church: the first birth, through women, is merely nature, a lowly state. To become a human being, a boy must be born again through men. Many puberty rites force boys to simulate crawling through the birth canal, and inflict pain supposedly caused by birth. Sometimes the penis is cut to draw blood, simulating women's menstruation. A boy learns through this process that the important parent is the father, whom he must obey. He learns the power structure he must live within and he learns to reject his mother as an inferior being, and emotion as an unworthy state. He learns to bear pain stoically and to isolate himself emotionally.

Matrilineal and patrilineal clans coexisted for thousands of years—indeed, they still do. The clans found in many Arab, Asian, and African states and in South America are descendants of these ancient clans. Some people consider clans egalitarian, because all the clans are equal in importance. But they are not egalitarian, they are male-dominant. Few matrilineal clans still exist, and even they have become male-dominant.

During the fourth millennium, in certain places, however,

men grew ambitious and built a larger structure, the state. A state is a property ruled by a particular government. States are supposed to be bound by fixed geographical features, are supposed to contain people related by genetic background and the same language, but none of these is actually the case. What we call the state arose first in Sumer and Egypt, and soon afterward, in China. It arose because certain men, not satisfied with dominance over women, wanted to dominate men. To this end, they introduced the two major instruments of patriarchy: war and religion.

A different form of religion had long existed everywhere, as is attested to by the ubiquity of female figurines. People implored the female principle, a goddess, for corn and oil and babies. If a goddess did not come through, her adherents turned their backs on her. She was powerful but not fearsome. Her main worshippers were priestesses, who also guarded the communal granary. (In American Indian groups like the Iroquois, women controlled stored food. Thus, the clan could not go to war without female approval.)

Myths of many peoples describe the long struggle by a particular male god to unseat a goddess. The god uses various methods of attack, but invariably fails. The goddess is invincible. Then one day he discovers weapons. When he attacks the goddess with weapons, he is able to overthrow her. He becomes supreme and immediately names subsidiary gods (and sometimes, a few goddesses): hierarchy is born. In some societies, myths describe a time when women owned the flutes—or other magical instruments—until men found a way to trick them out of them, or to steal them. We can deduce from clan structure to a state, and the shift from matricentry, matrilinearity, and matrilocal marriage to patriarchy.

Unlike the goddesses, male gods made decrees: they dictated rules and punishments for breaking the rules. All present world religions are patriarchal and male-dominant, and willfully deny godhead to women, from the early and very harsh Laws of Manu, which form Hindu law, to the Jewish man's daily prayer thanking god for not making him a woman, to the founding mystery of the Catholic Church, a Trinity made up of a father who alone creates a son, who together with him creates the Holy Ghost. Mohammed, who started out treating women as almost equal to men, himself changed as he aged, and the Hadith, the books commenting on the Koran, present a long record of Muslim leaders increasingly confining women and denying their humanity.[9]

From a largely anarchic world, humankind moved to patriarchy, authoritarian rule by the fathers. Early states were formed by one warrior who set himself up as king, general (leader in war), and head priest. The ruler and his entire family claimed to be humanly superior to all others by virtue of their relationship to deity. This was the beginning of a class system. Some early class systems may have been related to color. Caste, the Indian word for class, means color in Portuguese.

In the beginning, upper-class women may not have been bound by rules binding other women. Egyptian women were governed by the fairly egalitarian laws of their own land until Alexander ushered in a Greek dynasty that followed Greek law (which was extremely discriminating against women). There are records of women pharaohs (although they have been partly erased): women were rulers and military generals in China, empresses in Japan, and the heads of households in Egypt. But over time, as the goddesses were demoted into barmaids and prostitutes, women were all treated as servants, whatever their class—consider Athena, waiting on Achilles in *The Odessey*.

Early states were ruled by men who filled the position of

chief general, head of state, and head priest. Sargon, for example, who lived around 2,350 BCE, was a warrior said to make rivers run red with blood. A Semite from Akkad, as a general, he ruled a unified Sumer and Akkad, and named himself head priest. His daughter, Enheduanna, head priestess of Inanna, was also a great poet (the first poet we know about), and a philosopher. Her work celebrates her father's connection to the goddess Ishtar/Inanna. For millennia, Chinese and Japanese emperors maintained that they were related to deity or received their power from a deity. Witness the "divine right" of European kings. In early periods, humans might be sacrificed when such a ruler died, even if the group still worshipped a goddess.

Increasingly, rulers required the supremacy of a male god. The people demurred, they liked their goddesses and would not switch. As late as the Roman Empire, governments tried various stratagems to displace goddesses. The conflict is apparent in inadvertent slips in the sacred books—in the Vedas, the Old Testament, and Persian history. These volumes of women's history trace this movement in many societies. There are local variations, and some heroines along the way, but the picture is similar throughout history. I urge you to read a chapter at a time, pausing between them. Reading the books will alert you to the many ways women can be—and have been—constricted, and on what grounds. The great moment comes in the twentieth century, when women joined together to end this oppression.

Since there is a concerted movement worldwide to retract the progress women have made in the last three or four decades, it is essential that we be aware of what can happen—what has happened—and what is happening now. Women have made progress but only in certain geographical areas, and only in some classes. That is, women in the West who are educated have won great battles for rights. Yet even educated Western women continue to suffer from double standards, and there is much remaining to be done even here. But our sisters in the East require the most help. The American government claimed, when we first invaded Afghanistan, that part of the purpose was to liberate Afghan women—just as the British claimed, when they invaded India, that their purpose was to end the practice of suttee. In fact, the British did not give a damn about Indian women, just as the American government doesn't give a damn about Afghan women. A fine book by Ann Jones presents Afghan women as they live today.[10]

We are facing a long battle. Many of us are unaware that the war is even engaged, but if you watch television, or pay attention to the way the sexes are depicted in any medium, if you pay attention to history, and know what has happened in the past, you will realize that the rights we have so arduously won in the United States slowly but surely can be rescinded by a right-wing Supreme Court combined with a right-wing government. And are.

Acknowledgments

Although only I bear responsibility for the statements and point of view of this book, as well as the errors it must contain, I have not written it alone. Tens of scholars helped me, with essays summarizing the important points about their periods, bibliographies, and in some cases, articles or books. They helped me generously, even when they disagreed with my approach to historiography or disapproved of using anthropological information in a history. I thank them all.

First, I thank Claudia Koonz, who helped organize the subject matter and found most of the historian contributors. Jo Ann McNamara gave me information about Europe over an amazing period—from the Roman Empire all the way through to the late Christian period; Marcia Wright and Susan Hall patiently guided me through the thicket of Africa, the history of a continent. In addition, I thank Françoise Basch, Jon-Christian Billigmeier, Charlotte Bunch, Rebecca Cann, Blanche Cook, Elizabeth Croll, Ann Farnsworth, Kirsten Fischer, Jean Franco, Martha Gimenez, Karen Gottshang, Carol Hochstedler, Anne Holmes, Nikki Keddie, Renate Klein, Johanna Lessinger, Susan Mann, Marjorie Mbilinyi, John Mencher, Carol Meyers, Marysa Navarro, Karen Nussbaum, Veena Oldenburg, Leslie Peirce, Cathy Rakowski, Nan Rothschild, Kumkum Roy, Karen

Rubinson, Irene Silverblatt, and Stephanie Urdang. Help was also given by Alice Kessler-Harris, Catherine Pellissier, Carroll Smith-Rosenberg, Ann Snitow, Amy Swerdlow, Romila Thapur, and Alice Valentine. Researchers included Judith Byfield, Binnur Ercen, Tikva Frymer-Kensky, Rivka Harris, Kathi Kern, Stella Maloof, Linda Mitchell, Lisa Norling, Claire Potter, Gisela Shue, Temma Kaplan, and Tracey Weis. Other notable assistance came from Fadwa al Guindi, Beatrice Campbell, Donna Haraway, Barbara Lesko, Lynn Mally, Rayna Rapp, Judith Tucker, and Ann Volks. My incalculably important assistants over this fifteen-year period were Betsy Chalfin, Isabelle de Cordier, Hana Elwell, and Judi Silverman.

Marilyn French
New York, New York
June 2007

PART ONE

REACHING FOR ORDER AND CONTROL

A MAJOR PROBLEM OF PATRIARCHY is that, because it values and rewards competitiveness and aggressiveness, male-dominated societies are often at war. Constant war was a problem in two places on the globe at roughly the same time: Europe and Japan. These cultures found a partial solution, a political organization called feudalism, which involves mutually binding obligations and rewards on all classes of society. Feudalism did not stop war, but by fixing everyone in rigid relationships and placing both obligations and rewards on each class (much as the old kin-groups had), it allowed society to endure the constant upheavals.

CHAPTER 1

FEUDALISM IN EUROPE

FEUDALISM IS A POLITICAL, economic, and social structure devised to enable men to delegate control. Men conquered more territory than they could rule, and they feared their subordinates' ambition. They devised a system in which parcels of land (fiefs) and the income from this land were granted to vassals, male military aides who managed the fief (maintaining peace, justice, and public works), collected taxes, and offered deferential hospitality and advice to the grantor. This system arose in the militaristic societies of Europe and Japan, where both conquerors and vassals were called lords. A great lord like the king of England granted fiefs in some areas and took them in others; in turn, the vassal of one lord granted fiefs to his vassals, dividing his land. Fiefs could be voluntary: a small landholder in need of protection might ask a more powerful noble to provide it. In return, he would "pay court" to his overlord (or overlords) at least once a year, attend ceremonies, hold trials, and offer counsel. The system became extremely complex as more and more land was subdivided.

Feudalism is a contractual exchange, with two kinds of contracts—voluntary and hereditary. Before feudalism was established, the two basic classes were free and bound (slaves); afterward, all were bound and all had rights. All lords were vassals of other lords; serfs were bound to their lord and to the land they worked and lived on. The main distinction lay between dignified service, entered by voluntary oaths of fealty to a lord, and hereditary service, being born into bondage. In addition to the static landed community, other large segments of the population—clergy, merchants, and Jews—lived under special laws in a system called "personality of law," which was tied to the feudal system.

As always, the lowest rank of society supported the higher ones. In the manorial system that sometimes accompanied feudalism, farmers were bound to their land. Serfs (or villeins) could not legally leave their land; they were required to work for the lord several days a week and were subject to the jurisdiction of the lord's courts—and, sometimes, to humiliating interventions in their private lives (e.g., the lord might claim the right to deflower all brides). Their lot was hard, but they had advantages that slaves and wageworkers did not possess: the land was bound to them, was theirs to work, and could not be taken from them, as it was from peasants in England in a later age. Serfs had a place to go, a place where they belonged. Only much later, and only in Russia, did lords separate serf families. Most families settled their land on one son and dowered one daughter to marry advantageously, sending the rest out to find a living. After 1100, most daughters went into domestic service. If there were no sons, a daughter could inherit the holding, which enabled her to make a good marriage.

Origins

The dominant peoples in Europe during the Early Middle Ages were Visigoths in Spain, Franks in France, Germany, and the Lowlands, Anglo-Saxons in Britain, and Ostrogoths and Lombards in Italy (the name Lombard may be derived from "Longbeards," women who tied their long hair under their chins to simulate beards when they fought in battle). The Scandinavian Vikings were isolated from Europe until they invaded it in the ninth and tenth centuries. Many of these peoples had traditionally lived in landholding patrilineal communities that allotted land to all households. Women were often prophets, consulted about major decisions like wars or raids. Hannibal had to negotiate with a women's council before his armies could pass through Gaul. Women led armies. The most famous, Boudica (Boadicea), queen of the Iceni, went to war against the Romans in Britain. Until they saw Boudica standing with her four daughters in a war chariot, red hair flying, sword raised, the Romans had considered the inhabitants slaves. Boudica nearly drove Rome off the island, but, outfought, she died with 80,000 followers. In the tenth century Queen Aethelflaed commanded her own armies, built fortresses, and repaired them.

Customs varied widely in a decentralized Europe of small kingdoms and duchies, but in most places marriage was a partnership: grooms gave brides oxen, a plow, and armor; brides gave grooms weapons. Both plowed fields, went to war, and were supposed to be chaste until they were twenty. From the fourth to the seventh centuries, Franks, then Danes and Anglo-Saxons, hired landless men in units of a hundred as soldier-colonists. The king/chief granted his soldiers citizenship and land: they owed him taxes, labor, and military service; he owed them and their dependents protection. The bond between chief and retinue became the base of a new system that eroded women's independence.

War was constant; military retinues (of nonclan men) grew more important than clan councils. Because women no longer did military service, chiefs granted land only to men. Such grants antiquated clan functions. Unlike clans, retinues only fought, leaving plowing to women and old men. The retinues grew, eroding the lineages. Chiefs forbade soldiers to marry—and possibly shift loyalty—while in service. Lords responsible for protecting vassals claimed fines for harm to their bodies; a man who raped a woman had to indemnify her lord. Women who married non-kin lost their tie to their clans and claims to their land. By the seventh century, wives were dependent; in Wessex, they had to call their husbands "lord." Peasants were property. Because the church banned polygyny, men took concubines, who had no inheritance rights. Only a few elite women still owned large tracts of land and serfs. Chiefs and their retainers became manor-holders, kings, and nobles. This arrangement became feudalism.

A new, elaborate set of incest regulations barred marriages the church had previously accepted: if Adam had had sexual congress with Lilith, Eve's second cousin, Eve could not marry Adam. The dissolution of kin-groups, which respected women's claims to land, and the celibacy demanded of soldiers left many women destitute. Unmarried mothers had an especially hard time. Earlier, kin-groups raised all the children: in some, a mother had only to name the father to win his material support for the child. It became easier in Anglo-Saxon kingdoms for fathers to deny paternity, and destitute mothers often had to sell themselves and their young into slavery. Men's kin-groups began to disown "illegitimate" children, even if they were acknowledged by their fathers.

England, Germany, and France accomplished in a few hundred years what Mesopotamia, China, and India took thousands of years to achieve: turning women into property. Once kin-groups were gone, only men had rights or property; women were subject to men and to male rules. In most of Europe, female adultery was severely punished: women were stripped of property, publicly flogged, exiled, or executed, according to the region. In Burgundy, husbands could kill adulterous wives or give them to the king as slaves. Male adultery was of course accepted. Aristocratic women kept their rights a bit longer. As late as the ninth century, elite continental women made trial marriages without exchanging gifts or harming their reputations. Royal Anglo-Saxon women still received kingdoms at marriage and determined their children's marriages and inheritances. Elite Celtic and German women kept their family status: more men than women were hypergamic, improving their social status through marriage.

In the ninth century the pope, in need of military assistance, gave a successful Frankish soldier, Charlemagne, the title of Holy Roman Emperor. In return, Charlemagne barred nuns from many activities and tried to conform secular to canon (church) law. He virtually ended bride purchase when he decreed that grooms should give brides, not their families, a gift, usually of land, over which they had full rights. But he also barred women from power in their own right and placed noblewomen in guardianship, in absolute subjection to husbands who controlled their wealth. (He himself married four times but never let his daughters marry. They had lovers and large inheritances to keep them independent after he died.) Wives shared husbands' power, however. While in principle the entire kingdom belonged to the king, his wealth and power were rooted in his fiefs, which were managed by the queen. She ran his estates and controlled the finances and domestic affairs in his domain. As in Sparta, women did business while men did the more important thing—making war.

Charlemagne made marriage indissoluble: a man could not repudiate his wife except for adultery. According to the church, even adultery was not cause for divorce. A system of no divorce may seem to us a dubious benefit, but women in that era appreciated it. Barred from supporting themselves, they feared being repudiated by husbands who resented being limited to one wife. Laws forbidding divorce gave them some security, although there were always men who simply killed unwanted wives. Whatever the law, men with power could override it.

European Women from the Tenth to the Thirteenth Centuries

The Carolingian Empire collapsed in the late ninth century, ushering in a century so strife torn that historians call it "the age of iron." Noblemen of this period were goons who preferred to raid defenceless villages than attack the precincts of a rival noble, and they did little but fight. They lived on meat from their forests and fish from their streams, and their serfs were forbidden to take either. In the early years, their wooden manor houses, which frequently burned down, consisted of a broad central hall, a large semidetached kitchen, and outbuildings. Some noble couples had a bedroom, but most slept in the hall with the rest of the family, servants, and retainers. They pushed back the furniture—trestle tables, benches, maybe a clothes press, loom, and spinning tools—to lay sleeping pallets on the floor.

As prosperity increased, lords built stone castles with several rooms, furnished with couches, beds, chests, and hangings. They dressed more elegantly and fought less. But from the eleventh to the thirteenth century, they went on crusades. The first crusade (the only successful one) lasted from 1095 to 1099. At home, men held jousts, competitions in which they could display their skill with horses, lances, and other weapons. Early tournaments were brutal, but they were refined over the twelfth and thirteenth centuries into courts of courtesy. Women, who frequently ruled in this era, usually as surrogates for absent husbands or as regents for minor sons, refined the culture and favored literature presenting a new image—the "gentil parfit knight."

The most stable institution in this contentious time was the family, where women are always strong. As chatelaines of castles and estates, wealthy women held tremendous power; they acted as judicial authorities, participated in political assemblies both ecclesiastical and secular, and led armies. In Germany, nuns turned great monasteries into flourishing centers of learning; in Italy, noblewomen held huge influence over the church. Abbesses sent knights to war, while noblewomen acted as judges and defended their castles when men were away. The Countess Almodis of Barcelona co-authored an early written law code in this era.

By the twelfth century, queens no longer automatically controlled finance, but royal women with authority and strength still wielded personal power, especially in small courts. Adelaide of Maurienne, queen of Louis VI of France, shared his power—her name appears with his on royal documents. She appointed ecclesiastics, proferred benefactions, settled cases brought before the king's court, gave charters of privilege, and issued safe-conducts in her own name. Matilda, wife of Henry I of England, though she separated from him after bearing two children, lived alone in great splendor and ruled as regent when Henry was in Normandy. She supported writers and musicians and founded the leper hospital of St. Giles, a priory, and one of the first public baths.

Reforms made under Pope Gregory forced priests to give up their wives, ended lay influence over church offices, confined nuns, and subordinated the Holy Roman Emperor to church authority (see volume 1, chapter 10). By the thirteenth century the church had centralized its hold on Europe. Bureaucratic courts and churches enforced laws governing women's inheritance. The properties that queens brought to marriage were swallowed by the crown and thereafter managed by the king's clerks. Even the great twelfth-century Eleanor of Aquitaine could not annul this new ruling.

Eleanor's life was extraordinary.[1] Extremely intelligent, well educated, and a patron of literature, she was heir to Aquitaine, an important province that she governed herself. Married young to Louis VII of France, she found him dull and in fifteen years of marriage produced only two children—both daughters, to Louis' and his advisers' sorrow. In 1147 Louis decided to lead a crusade; he refused Eleanor's request to be regent in his absence, so she went with him. In the east she enjoyed herself and her uncle, Raymond of Antioch, who was eight years older than she. When Louis objected, Eleanor divorced him. The divorce was eased by the church's incest regulations (she was a distant relative of Louis) and by the French bishops, who wanted Louis to marry someone who would produce a male heir.

The moment she was divorced, Eleanor rode to Poitiers to tell Henry Plantagenet she wanted to marry him: they had met earlier, with sparks. Eleanor was thirty, Henry nineteen; she was the richest, most powerful woman in Europe; and he was ambitious. To reach him, Eleanor sneaked out of her lodgings in the middle of the night to avoid two ambushes on the journey. First she had to evade Count Thibaut of Blois, then Henry's brother, Geoffrey of Anjou, both of whom planned to kidnap her and force her into marriage, for they wanted control of her property. She reached Henry safely and they married; she bore him four sons and a daughter in the first five years, and three more children in the next decade. When Henry attained the English throne, she ruled with him in the early years of their marriage and as regent when he was away. But a quarrel sprang up between them and became irrevocable: she wanted a younger son to inherit Aquitaine, but Henry was adamant that her property was his and should pass to his chosen heir. She encouraged her sons to rebel against him: he defeated and pardoned them but kept Eleanor locked up for the rest of his life.

When Henry died after fifteen years, Eleanor was freed and, indeed, her favorite son, Richard, Coeur de Lion, succeeded Henry. He was imprisoned as he returned from a crusade, and the sixty-seven-year-old queen ran the kingdom, holding her ambitious younger son John at bay until she could reconcile the brothers. At seventy-two she retired to a convent but emerged five years later when Richard died and John became king. Foiling his rival (her grandson Arthur), she ensured Aquitaine's loyalty to John. At seventy-eight, having outlived eight of her ten children, she crossed the Pyrenees in winter to visit her daughter at the court of Castile and arrange a marriage between her granddaughter Blanche and the French dauphin, to seal peace between John and the French. Over the strong opposition of the French nobility, Blanche—a foreigner, Spaniard, and woman—ruled France. She became regent for her son, and when he came of age, she handed him a kingdom unified by her diplomacy and brilliant military strategy. When he was captured on a crusade, she raised the money to ransom him. She was, throughout her life, the strongest influence on him.

Generally, loss of control over property meant loss of power for women. Clever queens with strong personalities could subtly move kings, but most limited themselves to patronizing the arts and doing good works. A royal mistress had as much chance as a queen to influence policy.[2]

Nonroyal noblewomen had busy, responsible lives. A medium-sized barony had a staff of about twenty-five, not counting attendant knights and squires. Husbands were absent, sometimes for years at a time; women had to be good administrators for families to prosper. Wives oversaw production on the manor and managed food, goods, money, and staff. Since women were married very young, a fifteen- or sixteen-year-old girl often had responsibility for adjudicating quarrels among staff and servants and for managing a castle that was also a small industry, with a mill, textile workshop, and ale-making facilities. With the lord away, the lady had to oversee bailiffs and stewards, represent the family in local litigation, appoint attorneys to handle court matters, and ensure that rents were paid. Many lords owned several manors, each with a castle: families traveled (made a "progress") from one to another. Each time they moved they took all their belongings with them: household linens, furniture, kitchen utensils, food, plate, dishes, candles, books, household accounts, wall hangings, rugs, as well as the clothes and personal property of the family and its retainers.

Women also bore and raised children, educating them in religion, foreign languages, and basic skills. A smaller household, or fewer of them, meant less staff to worry about, but more labor. Yet women read and collected books, did fancy needlework, and endowed convents, monasteries, and hospitals. Throughout this period women took almost all the responsibility for tending the poor and the sick. Like early Christian women, they did this automatically—in Europe, women had always tended the sick, brewed medicines, and overseen medical care. Medieval romances depict ladies entertaining heroes with lays (sung verses) and fables, inspecting their fighting gear, and tending their horses.

Life was perilous. When lords were away, other men attacked their castles, which noblewomen aggressively defended. They went to war and supervised military defence. Queens, princesses, even children, were taken hostage. After Eustace de Breteuil put out the eyes of the son of one of Henry I of England's vassals, Henry gave the father permission to blind Eustace's daughter. Travel was fraught with danger: people had to carry their valuables with them. Women were often robbed and abandoned or held hostage, sometimes by the very men sent to guard them.

Most noblewomen were married by the time they were twenty, sometimes as young as thirteen, to men five to ten years older. Elite marriage was a property exchange: the more important the family in the social structure, the less individual desire mattered. The church required mutual consent to marriage, but church courts were unsympathetic to women who claimed coercion by threatened violence or disinheritance. They were roused only by actual violence: many parents beat their daughters and even allowed their rape to force them into unwanted marriages. Grooms gave brides substantial dowers—usually one-third to one-half of their land, along with serfs, buildings, animals, and abbeys. Property given as a dower at the time of marriage or as a jointure after the husband's death was, however, absolutely controlled by the husband during the marriage, even in regions where the law gave conjugal partners joint control of property. Women managed property when their husbands were away, but they did not originate major transactions concerning it.

As governments grew increasingly stable and effective, they steadily reinforced male control. Most nobles opposed subdividing holdings and supported primogeniture, but some chose to keep financial control over all their children. The right of a female to inherit if there were no sons was restricted in regions where it existed: an orphaned heiress became the ward of a lord who controlled her property and took its entire income during the wardship. If he became destitute, he could sell the wardship or the woman in marriage. Widows could live alone or could choose another husband, so long as they had a lord's permission and had paid a fine, but they were still regulated. By the thirteenth century all of France barred widows from inheriting unless they maintained strict moral standards. Italian law confined widows and their dowries in the husband's family.

Widows were a problem for feudal lords, especially in England, where common law granted them the use of one-third of their husbands' property for life, even if they remarried. English widows had full legal standing and did not have to be under a man's guardianship. The Magna Carta decreed that a widow receive her jointure within forty days of her husband's death, without being forced to remarry or pay a fine to get it. As a result, by the end of the thirteenth century, English widows could purchase their children's wardship and marriage rights from the king or lord and be their children's legally competent guardians. Some mothers, though, were as cruel as any guardian: the mother of twelfth-century Christina of Markyate (who was later sainted) beat her to force her to marry; when the bride persuaded her husband to respect her vow of chastity, her mother tried to induce him to rape her.

A widow who was an heiress (a common occurrence) controlled both her dower and her inheritance: so thirteenth-century Isabel de Fortibus became the owner of one of England's wealthiest baronies. A widow in Europe could not sell, give away, or waste her property or remarry without her lord's permission—a provision often ignored. It was harder for a woman to inherit in France than in England, but if she did, like Eleanor of Aquitaine, she wielded extraordinary political power.

Life on the Land

Women's main contribution in this era was to farming. Peasant men and women made two major innovations: crop rotation and the use of nonhuman energy—horses, mules, watermills, and windmills. As these changes transformed seasonal yields to surplus (where something was left over that could be stored or sold), they created a major agricultural revolution in Europe.

Into the early 1800s, 90 percent of Europe's women worked on the land. Tasks and conditions varied slightly from area to area, climate to climate. Peasant women, bound to their husbands as well as the land, were respected because their work was essential. They were expected to work much harder than men: first up, last to bed, they were never idle. A Sicilian proverb read, "If the father is dead, the family suffers; if the mother is dead, the family cannot exist."[3]

Serfs worked land together and shared tools and oxen. Few owned more than two oxen and some had none, but six to eight oxen were needed to pull a plow. Lords, always in need of money, charged for the use of their mills and made it illegal to own a hand mill to grind grain. Bread-baking ovens were communal. Most folks had a croft—a wattle and daub cottage made with mud and braided twigs, heated by a fireplace when there was fuel, with a stamped-earth floor and a kitchen garden. Only the well-off had more than 20 or 30 acres. Furniture was simple: a table and benches, pallets or piled leaves and ferns for sleeping, and a kettle and a few kitchen utensils hanging over the hearth. These serfs ate mainly oatmeal or other cereal and vegetable soup. The women raised onions, leeks, turnips, and cabbages in their gardens; in summer, the soup might contain peas, beans, radishes, or beets.

Women were responsible for three laborious tasks (the same ones they perform today in rural India and Africa): they gathered fuel, found fodder for animals, and fetched water. All three required carrying heavy loads over long distances. Women fed, watered, and milked animals and mucked out their stalls; they cooked, gardened, carded and combed wool, spun fabric, made clothes, and mended them. They found and brewed herbs to treat humans and animals, gave birth, nursed babies, and watched the children grow—or starve when the crops failed. Whatever the conditions, the lord demanded the same income. They had to surrender it even if their babies—or, indeed, the whole family—perished.

The agricultural revolution raised farm yields, making life a bit more comfortable. People built wood or stone houses and had more possessions—which in turn increased women's work. Now they also made candles, soap, beer, mead, and wine, raised chickens, sold geese and eggs, and reserved a goose for each feast day. They plucked and saved the feathers: twenty-four geese made a feather bed. As they roasted the goose, they saved the drippings for a pie crust or for coating the pig in summer. Wings became feather dusters; nipples, spigots. Women raised pigs on nuts they collected in the woods and slaughtered all but the sow in the fall; if the sow died, there was no meat the next year. They saved the blood from the pig's slit throat and added grain to make blood pudding. They boiled the carcass, picking out the hairs to make brushes or to plaster the walls, saved the bladder to store lard, and stewed the trotters for gelatin. They cut up the meat and stored it in salt or hung it from rafters over the hearth to smoke it. It provided meat throughout the winter.

During the cold months, women hung the washing from the ceiling and worked fleeces from the summer's shearing—cleaning, beating, and re-oiling each fleece, picking it clean, carding it, and making fluffy balls to spin into thread. Forty rolls made a skein, and five skeins a sweater. They made linen from flax, another laborious task. They collected vegetables for dye, dyed thread, then wove fabric or knitted it. They cut fabric and sewed it. Well-off women embroidered linens and wove woolen rugs; rich ones embroidered linen sheets and towels. Forty percent of a family's assets in the eighteenth century consisted of women's linens and feather beds.

Women worked for extra income, dairying, thatching roofs, hiring themselves out for day wages on neighboring farms, and picking grapes in winemaking regions. They sold eggs, fowl, or other animals, made butter and cheese for prosperous farmers, did laundry, and waited table at inns and rich houses. They gathered herbs for medicines and sold them, as well as beer and thread they had made. Everywhere, whatever their work, they earned half of men's wages.

Reproduction, work only women did, was time and energy consuming. A fertile woman with a normal lifespan was pregnant five to seven times in her life. Childless women were considered worthless. In Ireland, women not pregnant six months after marriage were abused. Barren women made herbal tonics to aid fertility. A pregnant woman might get privileges—a little of the fruit she was picking, a fish from the lord's stream, a hen she was supposed to pay him at Shrovetide. But pregnancy was dangerous: labor lasting over twenty-four hours could kill; after forty-eight hours, the woman was dehydrated, her heart might fail, or she could bleed to death. To extract the baby, a midwife used an instrument that could kill the mother. Women miscarried, hemorrhaged, and had stillbirths, blood clots, and puerperal fever; malnutrition could cause toxemia. Some went to work a week or less after parturition, and many died.

Couples wanting to limit their families despite church law made love nonprocreatively, a practice the church called "abominable sin." If husbands did not cooperate, women used instruments and potions to abort themselves. Women accused of abortion were punished, yet in some places fathers could condemn newborn infants (especially girls) to die. A Scandinavian baby would be abandoned unless a father took it in his arms, sprinkled water on it, and named it.

In some regions, babies were baptized immediately: godparents were summoned and a ceremony was held at the church door. The baby was immersed in the font, placed in a special white christening garment, and named. The font water was changed only when a baby defecated in it, not merely peed. In England, children could be given either parent's surname; a mother's name was used mainly when she owned or would inherit land.

Babies were swaddled: each limb was wrapped in cloth, then the whole body, totally confining it. Poor women nursed babies, believing that nursing prevented conception, and some local churches supported women who refused sex in the months after childbirth. Wet-nurses were hired when a mother died and were often used by wealthy women. Men demanded them, impatient with the sexual abstinence required for nursing (sex was thought to sour milk).[4] But most babies sent to wet-nurses died: in the nineteenth century the casualty rate was 75 percent. They died at home too: in France and England, women lost three of every five babies. A quarter of the children died in their first year, and another quarter before they were twenty. The lyrics to most lullabies speak of sorrow, threat, and death, all constants in the medieval world.[5]

There were also accidents. Mothers had to work and leave babies unattended. The major cause of accidental death in newborns was fire. A mother would nurse her baby, wrap it snugly and put the cradle near a warm fire, then go to the fields. The fire might spit a cinder, chickens near the hearth might pick up a burning twig or straw and drop it in the cradle, or a candle might tip and catch straw, igniting the house.

Mothers with many children often gave responsibility for a newborn to a daughter of four or five—the only children put to work that early. Most had no regular chores until they were about eight. Still, the loving childhood nurturing of simple societies had vanished. Children were chastised often and brutally (with the approval of the church), and were even killed. A French shopkeeper saw a boy steal a parcel of wool from her shop and struck him under his ear, killing him. In the trial, the jurors found the punishment just. Parents sometimes beat children to death.

The poor had more freedom in marriage than the rich, since little or no property was involved. Young villagers played together and flirted. Medieval society celebrated tens of feast days; older people left work to carouse, and the young were allowed to make merry. Some lords fined women for pregnancy or for having intercourse before marriage, but in many regions it was usual to defer marriage until a woman was pregnant. Some young women went from man to man and then had no problem marrying, whatever people said. Many couples did not bother to marry but simply lived together, because lords fined women when they married. In a few regions "illegitimate" children were not considered shameful. Sometimes parents chose a daughter's first husband, but generally girls acted independently.

Among the lower classes, bourgeois or peasant, free or bound, status was dictated by local practice, but some customs were general: propertied women needed male guardians and were excluded from most public positions, whether holding office or administrative jobs on manors. Girls could not inherit over male siblings. Widows received portions on a husband's death and, often, guardianship of their children. Lower-class widows often supplemented their income with outside work—most spun thread or brewed ale. Peasant women sometimes sued their husband's heirs for their dowers, which in England could tie up other inheritances for years. Young women worked and bought land, creating their own dowries.

In the thirteenth century, serfdom gradually disappeared from central Europe. Many serfs bought their freedom with surplus produce sold at free markets and were hired—or lured to escape—by free men with new land grants. Landlords now charged rent for land, rather than labor and a percentage of the produce. Emancipation occurred at different rates in different areas; it made lords rich, as serfs had to pay large sums for their freedom. The lords, who were no longer overseeing production, could live on rents and idle at court in accordance with their kings' demands. A class of absentee landlords developed.

The prosperity of the twelfth and thirteenth centuries generated larger families and a rise in the population. Men's lives were easier than women's. Free men did not have to do labor service for a lord or pay so many fines; they could explore new territories, go on crusades to seek their fortune, or move into the cities for work. Educated men took holy orders and became monks, priests, or professionals. Graduates specializing in law or administration could advance if they did not marry and endanger their chance for a job that required ordination. Men did not need wives, tended as they were by concubines, prostitutes, and servants.

Because of the different laws applied to them, women had so many problems that they began to constitute a class of their own—superfluous people. Few women inherited. Lords, who disliked the bother of squabbles over inheritance or conflicting claims to land and use rights, urged primogeniture on peasants. But settling all property on eldest sons left the remaining children destitute and unable to marry—and lords still controlled peasant women's marriage. Italy, following the Roman custom of marrying very young girls to older men, had a plethora of young widows. Guild regulations forbade women to marry outside a guild, so women barred from independent land grants had to move to cities, which had little work for them. These factors combined to create a huge class of single women who were excluded from most enterprises.

Life in Town

Episcopal centers grew into marketplaces, then cities. Cities built in strings fostered long-distance trade, and marketplaces sprang up on every river, coast, and hub of overland routes. Trade brought exotic luxuries to rich nobles and generated the commercial mechanisms that were the equivalent of our bank wires and credit cards (money was rare until several hundred years later): letters of credit, business partnerships, and accounting techniques. Artisans, landless folk, and escaped serfs settled in towns, where serfs became free if they stayed for a year and a day. Medieval towns were not the quaint villages of our imagination. Houses and their surrounding gardens, stables, pigsties, and chicken yards sat on dirt or mud roads. There were few drains or sewers, and stinking excrement was poured directly into the street. Drinking water was contaminated; fire and contagious disease constantly threatened.

Town workers joined guilds. Merchant guilds restricted outsiders from trading in a town and imposed uniform prices to keep individuals from dominating a market. Craft guilds ranked masters, journeymen, and apprentices. Only master-craftsmen with their own shops could vote at meetings. Journeymen were artisans employed by masters; boys, apprenticed to masters for years, usually for their keep, learned a craft. Apprentices and journeymen were forbidden to marry until they were masters; they attained this status by producing a "masterpiece" approved by a committee of masters. Craft guilds set fixed prices and wages, as well as guidelines for methods of production and quality of materials. They forbade after-hours' work and tried to limit competition. Controlling production in this way guaranteed members both work and good wages.

Guilds were also important politically and socially. They collected money for members needing medical help, dowries, or burials. Eventually they controlled a town's affairs. Merchants craved prestige, but both the clergy and the nobility scorned them. Still, noble younger sons went into trade. In Italy, guilds so dominated civic life that nobles who wished to enter public life had to join one. The church condemned usury—lending money at interest—and forbade Christians to engage in it. Jews, who were barred from most trades and professions, began to lend money and were later condemned for it. When theologians redefined usury to exclude money that was lent for investment, they allowed Christians to enter that field; mercantile society redefined wealth to include jewels, cash, and other movables. By the thirteenth century, wealthy merchants made up an elite urban class and saw themselves as patricians.

Despite their fine clothes, jewels, and servants, patrician women worked hard. Medieval scholar Eileen Power cites a book written in 1392–94 by a man called the Menagier of Paris.[6] Past sixty himself, he had married a girl of fifteen, inexperienced and eager to please, who asked him to educate her. He hired a "housekeeper" to help her with her duties, but also to keep her under surveillance, and wrote this book for her edification. It was kindly meant, but what he expected from the girl is extraordinary. Part One deals with moral duties—how to say morning prayers, how to confess, and the proper demeanour when going to church (always accompanied by her duenna, she walks suitably dressed, with her head upright and her eyes downcast, and must not stop to speak to anyone along the road). Most important is her manner with her husband: she must be humble, obedient, careful, thoughtful for his person, silent about his secrets, and patient if he shows interest in other women.

The second part contains essays on household management: gardening, managing servants and a farm, horse buying, training, and breeding (though none of these tasks with horses were expected of her), detailed instructions on how to mend, air, and clean dresses and furs (which were worn by men more than women), how to get out grease spots, how to keep fleas and flies out of the house (the medieval housewife seems to have been constantly at war with fleas), and how to care for wine. She is above all to tend to her husband's comfort: to meet him at the door when he comes in, have a warm fire burning, and remove his shoes and wash his feet; fresh shoes and stockings must be waiting along with good food and drink. She must be sure he and his bed always have clean linen. If wives do not do these things, he implies, men turn to women who will. She should be "buxom at bed and board" no matter how she feels. He offers his child-bride a metaphor for proper wifely behavior:

> You see how a greyhound, or a mastiff, or a little dog, whether on the road or at table, or in bed, always keeps near to the person from whom he takes his food, and . . . is shy and fierce with all others; . . . if the dog is afar off, he always has his heart and his eye upon his master; even if his master whip him and throw stones at him, the dog follows, wagging his tail and lying down before his master, seeks to mollify him, and through rivers, through woods, through thieves and through battles follows him. . . . Wherefore for a better and stronger reason women, to whom God has given natural sense and who are reasonable, ought to have a perfect and solemn love for their husbands.

Whether wives or servants, women worked only at the menial level. Wives worked with their husbands in the market or the shop, ran the house, tended children and apprentices, spun, brewed, tatted, or took in lodgers to earn extra money. Single girls worked at crafts which, had they been men, would have prepared them for careers, but which were intended only to attract husbands—spinning silk or gold thread, sewing, and weaving. Most young women became domestic servants, earning only their keep or nothing at all until their employers died, when they left payment in their wills, or until they married, when employers provided a dowry. Many families expected female servants to take the virginity of the family sons or be the husband's concubine.

The tight all-male structure of medieval towns barred

women from administrative jobs in towns and from most guilds. Wives often worked at their husbands' trade, where they became experts themselves but were denied full guild membership until they were widowed, and then lost it if they married a nonguild man. Widows' inheritance of masterships thus functioned as dowries for men. The few female guilds were in the lowest-paid trades—spinning and ale-making—and had male heads. They existed mainly to prevent women who did piece work at home from stealing materials and to protect urban women from competition by rural cottage industries.[7] Craftswomen's wages were set by law at half what men were paid for the same work. These regulations made women almost incapable of independent self-support.

Widows could sell real estate, a potentially lucrative business, or run alehouses or inns. In many French or English towns, married women did business as *femmes soles*, independent women. A *femme sole* could buy or sell land, make contracts, and do business without a man's aegis. English *femmes soles* were shipwrights and supplied horses, wheels, armor, and jousting equipment for kings. Some men feared that women might incur debts their husbands would not honor, since they adhered only to her as a *femme sole*.

In this period, a pattern was established that still characterizes women's employment: it was marginal, periodic, and low paid. A marginal worker is hired last, fired first, and let go with impunity because of bias. Male employers, who tend to assume that men support women, offer women periodic work to accommodate what they consider is women's primary (unpaid) work—reproduction. Before marriage, girls were domestics or worked in shops or mills, often earning their dowries. They were expected to stop work at marriage until childrearing was over, then were rehired to spin thread or brew ale. Older women worked as midwives and alewives. This pattern remained in place well into the twentieth century, into my own young womanhood. Women worked as healers, apothecaries, and surgeons, but, after universities began, healers had to be licensed. A university degree was necessary for a license, but women were barred from universities, so women healers were illegal. Female barbers and barber-surgeons in England joined male surgeons to found the Royal College of Surgeons, which they were later barred from. Women were more and more frowned on even as midwives and barbers.

Yet they worked, everywhere: in fields outside town, for half the rate paid men, or doing laundry, which paid more. In Germany and Czechoslovakia they worked in mines, panning, hauling, and sorting ore; they did heavy labor on construction projects, carrying stones and water to mortar mixers, collecting moss and bracken to cushion the roof tiles of houses, and bunching thatch for roofs. For a pittance, Italian women carried sand to build cathedrals, and French women carried stones and bricks to build colleges, cleaned out latrines, and dug ditches. Women were tailors, bakers, grocers, drapers, mercers, spur-makers, and water-bearers. They sold poultry and fish in markets, but were not accepted in long-distance trade. When they were barred from markets, they cooked and sold food in the streets, or they walked miles out of town seeking used clothing, wheat, tallow, beer, and fish—whatever they could sell in town—and selling town-made goods in the country. Sometimes they were fined for this activity.

Some women turned to crime. Most woman criminals in England committed petty theft or received stolen goods.[8] Women stole things like thread or food for the family; they fenced what male family members had pilfered or helped men break, enter, or steal. Women probably committed most of the infanticide but were rarely prosecuted, because many husbands ordered it and wives were required by law to obey their husbands. The sexes were punished alike, housed in the same cells, and hanged together, except for murder of a spouse—husband-murder was treason, for which women were burned at the stake. Crimes against women were occasionally reported but rarely tried, which may have been just as well, since men were punished for rape by being forced to marry the victim.

Most of the women who went on the first crusade were killed or enslaved by the Muslims. Almost everyone on Peter the Hermit's later crusade of poor people and children died or was enslaved. Yet when the crusades became professional military expeditions, women went as pilgrims: the armies contained almost as many women as men. The women were needed to set up campsites, collect fuel, cook and serve food, launder, and clean latrines. They dug trenches before battle and, after it, nursed the injured and washed and prepared dead bodies for burial. They were prostitutes, a major business for townswomen as well. Prostitution was the only occupation in which women earned more than men.

Prostitution was illegal in most places, but the fines levied on prostitutes provided a steady income for towns (as they still do). Many approved of brothels to curb male rampages. Between 1436 and 1486, for example, gangs of young men, mostly the sons or servants of residents, preyed on Dijon women. They broke into the houses of spinsters, widows, or wives whose husbands were away to rape them, sometimes dragging the women through the streets to an empty house where they kept them for days, repeatedly raping them. City officials solved this problem by setting up municipal brothels. They filled them with the women who had been assaulted in the gang rape.

At Worship

Multitudes of late twelfth- and thirteenth-century women could not find husbands, but were prevented by law from earning enough to support themselves. Many wanted to enter convents, but the church made this difficult. Church authorities required convents to take only the women they could support and opposed founding new female orders. High-ranking men of the church or state filled the few available places with female relatives. Established convents with space accepted women with dowries but barred poor women. Women with wealth or power could no longer found and maintain convents because of church restrictions. Women were barred from so many activities—legal, economic, and religious—that all female groups required the presence of men. Almost all male monasteries were in orders that excluded women; the few orders willing to accept women made them live strictly cloistered. Poor, single, pious women usually became the lowest class of nun in a convent or servants to an anchoress.

Jo Ann McNamara says that, theoretically, a woman could survive as a recluse by spinning or tatting, so long as she had a servant to spin with, they fasted often, and they took no worldly pleasure.[9] This scenario is hypothetical, however, because ecclesiastics denied women permission for a reclusive life if they could not show they had the means to support themselves and the minimal two servants required to guarantee their chastity. At the same time, clergymen distressed by rampant prostitution in the towns urged single men to marry prostitutes as a charitable act, and the church established convents for penitent women. McNamara concludes that it may have been easier to enter a monastery as a former prostitute than as a virgin.

In the enthusiasm following the Gregorian reforms of the

late eleventh century, some Christians dreamed of a wholly spiritual church whose members lived like Jesus' apostles in poverty. In the twelfth century, Cathars in the Languedoc district of southern France founded such a church. Manichean in doctrine (seeing good and evil as utterly separate), the Cathars believed that the spiritual world only was subject to god; the material world and the body were Satan's. As ascetics, they had no churches, but met in houses where the "perfect" preached. The perfect, the most ascetic Cathars, swore publicly not to lie, take oaths, or renounce their faith; rather, they renounced the world—property, sex, and food generated by animal intercourse (meat, cheese, eggs, and milk).

Each region was governed by a bishop, and each community by a deacon. Women were drawn to Catharism, probably because they could become perfect and lead ceremonies, although they could not be bishops or deacons and could lead prayers only if no male perfect were present. Only upper-class women preached or debated, but they were dismissed scornfully if they spoke in men's presence. Still, in this sect, women could achieve status and participate in services. Rich women perfect sometimes made their houses centers for Cathar women and formed communities, supporting them with inheritances or by engaging in trade or cottage industries. Some boarded and educated girls.

The church disapproved of Catharism and, in 1208, Pope Innocent III launched a crusade against it. Called the Albigensian crusade after Albi, where the Cathars lived, the crusade was ostensibly religious, but politically driven, intended to expand the power of the French king. The church held an inquisition of Catharism in 1233, then went to war. It emptied women perfects' houses, wrecked Languedoc cultural and political life, and exterminated the Cathars.

Pious women sought ways to live a religious life in an increasingly hostile climate. In the Lowlands, northern France, and southern Germany, women invented beguinages—self-supporting female communities. Individuals built cells near abbeys, hospitals, or leper-houses, to pray and serve the needy. In time, they joined together to pool resources. They swore chastity, but took no solemn vows and could leave the group if they wished. Hardworking, organized, and frugal, they lived simply, wore nunlike clothes, and supported themselves by nursing, weaving, lace-making, embroidery, manual labor, or teaching children.

Beguines managed their own spiritual lives. They were assigned confessors, but they heard each others' confessions, led prayers and rituals, wrote their own psalters, and listened to women preachers. Some were mystics with private visions of god or belief in a god of love who removed the taint of sin from sexual passion; some directly challenged the church. Most acknowledged the authority of bishops, but bishops lacked real control over them. This independence made the church, especially Pope John XXII, uneasy. The church, fearing female autonomy, had tried since the Council of Mainz in 1223 to impose male control even on women who took private vows of chastity without entering a convent.

Beguines challenged the church in another way: despite avowed principles of charity, the church gave mainly lip service to the poor and sick; it was threatened and shamed by movements, like the early Franciscans, that were devoted to the poor. The beguines lived in actual poverty, sharing and doing community service; some beguinages opened hospitals for the poor or commercial corporations, which were profitable partly because the women were frugal.[10] Medieval beguinages negotiated with towns for the right to follow an occupation and for tax relief as charitable organizations; they used whatever they won to serve the community.

This activity earned them the enmity of the guilds. Threatened by being undersold by women who worked for mere subsistence, using their surplus to help the poor and sick, the guilds lobbied the state to act against the beguines. The state seized beguine property. The church pressured the women to put themselves under its control by joining convents—even though there were no places for them in convents. It accused them of sorcery and claimed their nursing was a cover for seduction. A few of the women who insisted on their own version of Christianity were called in by the Inquisition and burned at the stake. Some were later canonized. By the fifteenth century, persecution by church and state succeeded in suppressing most beguine orders. Beguinages remained as non-religious havens run by women for poor women and children. (Some still exist in Amsterdam and Brussels.) Whenever they tried to sustain themselves, set up an industry, or gain immunity from taxes, they were persecuted anew. Female autonomy was not allowed in Europe.

In Arts and Sciences

Women made technical innovations in home workshops, contributing to inventions for the mechanical fulling of cloth, for the polishing and crushing of things from olives to ore, for reducing pigment to paint or pulp to paper, and for tanning mills. Some created works of art in glass or lace, or the "fine" arts.

Julian of Norwich, a mystic, wrote in the tradition of the artist-abbesses Hroswitha of Gandersheim, Hildegard of Bingen, the learned Heloise, and Herrad of Hohenbourg. Her *Revelations* is one of the most famous and masterful mystic works in English. Nuns copied and illuminated manuscripts, leaving precious examples of this form. Women worked on some of the great Books of Hours: Bourgot, daughter of Jean LeNoir, illuminated such books with her father; Anastasia painted illuminations and miniatures for Christine de Pisan; and Marcia, a pagan virgin named by Boccaccio, left an extraordinary miniature self-portrait. Margaretha Van Eyck, who created masterpieces with her brothers, is never mentioned. The Bayeux Tapestry is only the best-known example of medieval needlework to cross the line from handicraft to art.

Despite the increasingly masculinized society, women were major patrons of the arts. Eleanor of Aquitaine and her granddaughter Blanche of Castile held "courts of love," probably salons where literature was read and wittily discussed. Male and female troubadours traveled about the countryside, singing for their suppers in verse usually dedicated to an unattainable lady. The thirteenth century is known for the poetry of courtly love, a new "feminized" poetry or chivalric literature that eroticizes feudal conventions. The main convention of courtly love was a knight in love swearing fealty to a lady, offering her homage and service. If she accepts, she promises him succour when he needs it, rescue if he is captured. The hallmarks of courtly love—free choice and mutuality—sharply distinguish it from marriage, a mode of property exchange giving men power over women and foreclosing mutuality. Courtly love subsumes mutual love in adulterous relationships. Chivalric literature may or may not have reflected reality, but it was popular in medieval courts where women rulers determined the character of social life. "Feminine," it valued eroticism, mutuality, politeness, and respect.

Some female troubadour poetry survives; it differs from men's, using a conversational tone, not idealizing love or the lover, and avoiding the game element of poetry—set forms, allegory, and word play.[11] The Countess of Dia composed lyrics like this one:

> I have been in great distress
> for a knight for whom I longed;
> I want all future times to know
> how I loved him to excess.
>
> Now I see I am betrayed—
> he claims I did not give him love—
> such was the mistake I made,
> naked in bed, and dressed.

Marie de France was recognized as a great writer in her life-time. We know little about her but assume she was of high birth, since she spoke and read Latin, French, and English and was familiar with ancient and contemporary literature. She lived at the twelfth-century court of Henry II of England and Eleanor of Aquitaine, where she sang her work accompanied by a harp. Her graceful, elegant lays resemble those of her male contemporary Chrétien de Troyes, though he is far better known than she. Both wrote "romance," a narrative centered on knights and ladies and featuring chivalric adventure, erotic love, and supernatural beings, events, and objects like magic rings or capes. Marie's lays, shorter and more compressed than Chrétien's, have tighter structure because they focus on one central action. She is more interested in character and emotion than in plot or moralizing. Her eagerness to legitimate women's writing is poignant.

Joan Kelly-Gadol wrote that courtly love literature was intended to permit the expression of female sexual desire.[12] The romance eroticized European literature, and female rulers fostered it; Eleanor of Aquitaine patronized Marie de France and

Bernard de Ventadour; Marie de Champagne patronized Chrétien de Troyes and Andreas Capellanus, author of the famous *Art of Courtly Love*. This supposedly sexy treatise is actually sexist: it describes the long ritual service knights must offer to win a lady but tells them not to bother to seduce lower-class women, just rape them. Andreas is generally so crude that critics now think that Marie de Champagne dictated his fine passages on courtly love.

The *Romaunt de la Rose*, the narrative poem still read in colleges, was begun by Guillaume de Lorris around 1240 as an allegorical description of courtly love. A lover tries to reach a rose—the lady's love; the brambles and thorns he encounters represent difficult aspects of the lady's character. Guillaume died, and Jean de Meung completed the poem in 1399. But his was a different poem, in a different tone—cynical, rationalistic, and woman-hating. It was enormously popular throughout Europe.

Christine de Pisan, a gentlewoman educated by her father, married young. Widowed early and left impoverished with three children and a widowed mother, she may have earned money copying manuscripts. In 1393 she began to publish her own work. She had a vast scope, writing poems, romances, allegories, and treatises on French politics, military strategy, international law, and the idea of historical destiny, a life of Charles V of France, and the only contemporary biography of Joan of Arc. She was a great writer, but is important today mainly for her feminism, and especially her retort to Jean de Meung's scathing denunciation of women. In *Le livre de la cité des dames* (The Book of the City of Ladies), using convention-al male defences of women as her model, she lists "extraordin-ary" women—those who transcended their female nature—and recounts famous women's virtuous lives. But she also does something never done before when she describes men's abuse of women—cruelty, battery, and starvation of their families. She incurred the wrath of her male contemporaries, but she offers no solution to women's dilemma beyond patience, dissimulation, and endurance. However, in presenting life problems from a woman's point of view, she was unique.

Jean de Meung's conclusion to the Romaunt and Christine de Pisan's response ended the age of courtly love. The fourteenth century ushered in a different morality.

The Fourteenth Century

Thirteenth-century Europe had prospered: the new land opened up was productive even if the soil was poor. Optimistic people had many children, and the population grew. But in the fourteenth century, this attitude changed. The temperature of Europe fell: farmers had to abandon their now nonviable farms in Scandinavia and Greenland. Greater rainfall brought flooding throughout northwestern Europe, ruining crops. Overworked farms in fertile regions produced less. Famine was rife; peasants were so desperate they ate the seed grain for the next year's crop, along with cats, dogs, and rats. Still they died. Then the plague hit, finding people at their weakest.

In 1347 a merchant ship anchored at Messina, Sicily, bearing rats infected with bubonic plague. The rats ran for land, carrying fleas that had bitten them and which then bit people. The disease swept Europe with incredible speed: people fell ill from just inhaling the germs. Bubonic plague attacks the lymphatic system, swelling the groin or armpits: black spots on the limbs presage diarrhea and death, providing the name "Black Death." The even deadlier pneumonic form killed in one to three days. The disease devastated China from 1331 on; swept the western

Mediterranean in 1347; raced through Italy, Spain, and France in 1348; infected northern Europe and England in 1349; reached the Crimea in 1346; and spread to Scandinavia and Poland in 1350. So widespread it is called a "pandemic," it recurred in the fifteenth century and, slightly weakened, again in the sixteenth and seventeenth centuries. Ships with no living passengers floated the seas; crops rotted in fields no one was left to harvest; textile mills and other small enterprises were abandoned. People fled to the country to escape contagion; the pope retired inside his palace and barred all visitors. A rumor that Jews had caused the plague by poisoning drinking water in Christian communities provoked a pogrom: thousands of European Jews were murdered—16,000 at Strasbourg alone in 1349.

By 1450, half to two-thirds of the people of Europe had died from famine, flood, or plague. Half the English succumbed, half of all the European urban populations. In 1335 Toulouse had about 30,000 residents; in 1430 it had 8000. In the mid-thirteenth century the Tuscan countryside near Pistoia had about 31,000 people; in 1401 it numbered less than 9000. It killed young adults: when it was over, the population resembled an hourglass, with very old and very young surviving. For some reason, during later waves of plague, women began to live longer than men. For centuries women had experienced shorter lifespans than men because of poorer diet, early childbirth, arduous work, continual pregnancy, and parturition. For the first time they were outliving men, perhaps because women as a caste developed resistance to the plague.

During this period, despite the plague, Europe was torn by war. German princes fought for dominance, and France and England fought intermittently for over a century. After the Norman invasion of England in 1066, the French ruled England from France, where Norman kings preferred to live.

Only gradually did the seat of power shift to England and, after the reign of John (son of Eleanor of Aquitaine and Henry II), English kings claimed sovereignty over French lands. Indigenous French kings challenged the Norman title in the Hundred Years' War, fought from 1337 to 1453. The English won at Crécy, Poitiers, and Agincourt (1415), but when the dukes of Burgundy sided with England, France was at risk of losing not just a war but its independence.

Then Joan of Arc appeared. Born in 1412 to a French peasant family in the village of Domrémy, Jeanne d'Arc drove the plow and spun. She was not especially religious, but, at thirteen, she met Saint Michael and some angels in her garden and suddenly became willful, challenging society's class and gender rules, and utterly sure of her vision and mission. Over time, other holy figures appeared to her, ordering her to relieve the siege at Orléans, have the dauphin (crown prince) crowned at Rheims, free the duc d'Orléans, and restore Paris to the French crown.

She kept her visions to herself until she was sixteen, then lied to get her parents to take her to the local lord, who could introduce her to the dauphin. The lord said she needed a good slapping, but she would not desist. Tense and anxious, she insisted she had only a year to fulfill her mission. Finally, the lord took her to the dauphin at Chinon. In men's clothes, she burst into the court, seized the dauphin (whom she had never seen), and convinced him and his courtiers that she was sent by god. Subjected to a test, she wielded a lance and ran at a tilt in a tourney, things she could never have done before. She so impressed the duc d'Alençon that he gave her a horse. She struck the priests and nobles who interrogated her as direct, honest, and simple. A gold crown and buried sword appeared as she predicted they would.

She brushed aside the dauphin's advisers, who disagreed about strategy, for she had her own. In time, the dauphin, the army, and the local citizens placed trust in her. Word traveled to the English soldiers, who also believed the young woman was an emissary of god. She led troops into battle on horseback, in armor. She attacked a stronghold, set a ladder on the bastion of a bridge, picked up a fallen standard, and rushed to the top of a trench, calling to her men. She fought one battle almost singlehandedly: a blow on the head cracked her helmet and she was hit by crossbolts in the neck and thigh, but she would not leave. Somehow, Joan understood the new methods of warfare and knew how to place artillery. Seasoned warriors praised her strategy. Once she broke the siege of Orléans, other towns surrendered simply at the sight of her. After the dauphin was crowned king, he wanted to quit, but Joan insisted on completing her mission. Fighting on her own authority, she and her men were stranded in battle. She was captured and held for ransom, and neither the king nor the council tried to redeem her.

The English believed that a woman who broke gender rules was a witch, so they kept her fettered day and night, guarded by men who threatened rape. She was interrogated twice a day without counsel. The English clergy intimidated, confused, tricked, and threatened her with torture, demanding that she eschew male clothes and admit herself an agent of the devil. Joan held fast and twice tried to escape. Granting she might say what they wanted if they tortured her, she warned them that she would recant afterwards. She spoke to these men as an equal. Finding her attitude and her clothes unbearable, they condemned her to death. When she heard her sentence, she faltered, said she had lied about her visions, and begged to be admitted to the church forever. The English shaved her head, put her in a dress, and sent her back to her cell. Three days later she again donned male clothes, saying her voices had disapproved of her behavior and her fear of the fire. They put her back in a dress and burned her, disposing of her ashes so that no relic remained of her martyrdom. The seventeen-year-old girl took half an hour to die.

Much is known about Joan, who was considered extraordinary in her lifetime: people spoke about her and recorded her inquisition. But the information was kept hidden. She embarrassed the church, which retried and rehabilitated her in 1456, but did not sanctify her until 1929, and then not for her faith or heroism but as a "simple, honest girl," "a good Christian." Still, she is a potent iconographic image in France, a girl with a sword in one hand and a red oriflamme (the ancient royal standard of France) in the other.[13]

War provoked class struggle throughout Europe. After the plague, the demand for labor generated high wages, causing inflation and great suffering for peasants. When Britain won Poitiers in the Hundred Years' War, it captured the king and nobles, who had to be ransomed. The French aristocracy expected the peasants to pay the ransoms, but they rebelled, burning castles, murdering nobles, and raping noblewomen. The nobles took a month to unify, then massacred the peasants and reasserted control.

The English king, needing money for war, imposed a head tax on adult men. Here, too, the peasants rebelled: Wat Tyler led 100,000 of them in the Peasants' Revolt of 1381, the most serious lower-class rebellion in English history. Demanding higher wages and fewer manorial obligations, they burned local tax data, looted wealthy houses, marched on London, and executed the lord chancellor and treasurer of England. Richard II, at fifteen, proved his courage and guile: he went out to meet the mob and promised to abolish serfdom and maintain low rents. The peasants went home flushed with victory. Then Richard sent men to hunt down and execute their leaders; Tyler was killed during the negotiations. Richard crushed the uprising cruelly and kept none of his promises.

Peasants also rose up in Florence, Germany (in Lübeck, Brunswick, and elsewhere), and in Spain (in Seville and Barcelona), where they viciously attacked Jewish communities. At such times the aristocracy dropped their rivalry and united, deploying their advantages—money for troops and experience in war and leadership—against the lower classes. By the time the Hundred Years' War ended, French kings controlled all of France except Calais.

When the plague abated, Europe's economy restabilized. So many had died that extraordinary opportunities existed for the survivors, and younger brothers, runaway serfs, journeymen, and women emigrated to towns searching for better-paid work. Towns and trade burgeoned. Credit, large-scale banking, double-entry bookkeeping, insurance, and capital investment had developed. Feudalism was changing to capitalism.

The first capitalists appeared around 1000, merchants derisively called *pieds poudreux* ("dusty feet") who acquired a stake (capital), bought goods, then traveled on foot or horseback to sell them at a profit. Earning profit was dishonorable in feudal society, which bartered or traded goods. Merchants were looked down on but prospered, despite feudal law. Nobles were not too scornful of them to borrow money from them, and, eventually, merchants persuaded indebted nobles to modify feudal law with law favorable to commerce. Feudal law, which regulated fiefs, knightly service, and contracts between lords and vassals, affected merchants only when a commune acted as a corporate vassal. By the thirteenth century, merchants had connections to kings (who always needed money); "law merchants" and lawyers, who understood market relationships, began to deal with contracts, property, and trade. By 1600 the main principles of capitalist law had replaced feudal law. The two systems coexisted until the revolutions of the seventeenth and eighteenth centuries abolished feudal privileges.

The Narrowing of Experience

From the twelfth through the fourteenth centuries, Europe was gripped by a new drive to intellectual and institutional uniformity. Elites tried to impose uniform thought and behavior; educators defined knowledge not as understanding or awareness but as a specific curriculum, and measured accomplishment by examinations. Education had been informal and personal: teachers were chosen for their reputations, people studied with them as long as they wished and stopped when they wanted to. The schools of Plato and Pythagoras did not define the parameters of knowledge (curricula), organize faculties, or award degrees. The new universities (or corporations, discrete groups with a charter to act as individuals) dictated what must be learned in what period and who should teach it. For the first time, learning was measured: a quantitative standard was imposed on a qualitative experience. Men were "done" when they received a degree.

A bachelor of arts (men in holy orders could not marry, women could not attend) spent about four years learning the *trivium*—Latin grammar, rhetoric, and logic; a master of arts spent another three or four years mastering the *quadrivium*—mathematics, natural science, philosophy, and music. Advanced degrees in theology or medicine could take many years more. The form of education taught students what was and what was not important in their society. Omitted from the curriculum were emotional and spiritual forms of knowing.

Logic was fundamental, but logic concerns language only; as the twentieth-century philosopher Ludwig Wittgenstein showed, logic has nothing to do with life or even thought. Indeed, every area of study involved learning a particular language to deal abstractly with subjects themselves narrowly conceived and defined. Knowledge itself was defined as abstract and linguistic with an instrumental purpose—to understand and control the natural and social world. Socrates taught that knowledge was good because it led to truth: now knowledge was valued because it was a form of power.

Late medieval education, which laid the foundation for all later Western education, fostered instrumental thinking. It sees people and things as means to ends rather than as ends themselves. With the language of mathematics or logic, men could manipulate "reality," disconnected from physical and emotional reality. Use of such languages is called *reason*. But to ignore physical and emotional experience is to imply that they are inconsequential. Medieval education sanctified this division as if it arose from nature, not from a human definition of knowledge.

Western thought still separates knowledge from its root in life and experience. Because of this division, exalted fields of study like philosophy, theology, and science can be used to support inhumane political and social doctrines and policies. Within the narrow confines of "legitimate knowledge," nature and its creatures, including women, are mere matter to be penetrated and controlled by mind. Instrumental thought first affected women healers, but soon pervaded all disciplines. The new learning accompanied and supported rising capitalism; the new science generated industrialization. Both eased life, but led to the dehumanization of people and to brutalism towards people and nature.

So great was men's faith in reason that a scholar, Thomas

Aquinas, tried to anatomize theology; his *Summas* established definitions of humanity that stood for centuries. Refining Aristotle's split between women, "mechanics" (manual laborers), and slaves, who were bound to the necessary, and elite men, who had volition, Aquinas described the universe as a hierarchical triangle: at the apex was god, below him the angels, then man. Woman was beneath and opposite man. At the bottom were beasts. Using the neo-Pythagorean division of moral qualities (like yin and yang), Aquinas declared man made in the image of god—active, formative, and tending towards perfection. Woman, man's opposite, was passive, material, and incapable of perfection. Man was associated with the limited, odd (singular), light, and good; woman with the unlimited, even (undistinguished), plural, dark, and evil. This polarity introduced gender as a concept into mainstream intellectual life.[14] The sexes were defined, seemingly forever—and, indeed, these definitions are still part of popular thinking.

The emphasis on education increased literacy extraordinarily. By the mid-thirteenth century the University of Paris had about 7000 students, Oxford about 2000. Intelligent, energetic, assertive low- and middle-class men could now rise in society. In the mid-eleventh century, less than 1 percent of Western Europe was literate; by the fourteenth, 40 percent of Florentines were literate; by the end of the fifteenth, 40 percent of Britons were literate. A few mainly upper-class women were taught to read and write to keep account books, deal with litigation, and consult medical manuals, but most women were illiterate. Noblewomen, however, often commissioned books.

Only in Italian universities could women study. They became professors and physicians, like the scholar Veronica Gambara and the great poet Vittoria Colonna. In 1330 the daughter of a Bolognese jurisconsult took her father's place in the lecture room, but taught from behind a curtain. Such women were rare. Anna Comnena founded a medical school in Constantinople in 1083, where she taught, practiced medicine, and wrote history. A thirteenth-century Persian princess built a medical school and hospital; a woman was court astronomer for the Seljuks; and Hildegard of Bingen wrote treatises on medicine far ahead of her time. Trotula's treatises on gynecology and obstetrics remained major medical resources for centuries afterward, yet she is remembered as Dame Trot, the author of children's stories. Renaissance editors attributed her medical works to a male name, Trotus. Paracelsus, the "father" of modern medicine, was taught by women. During the witch hunts, he burned his text on pharmacy, explaining he had "learned from the Sorceress all he knew." Tycho Brahe's sister did astronomy jointly with him, but only he is remembered.

The church too strove for uniformity. Pope Innocent III, eager to ferret out and punish deviations in belief, set up courts of inquiry into religious behavior and belief, accusing people of heresy. In an innovation in human moral life, these courts scrutinized belief and declared any failure to uphold dogma a sin. A later pope sanctioned the torture of accused heretics, but the church did not burn them. Heresy was a crime against both canon and state law, and secular authorities also held inquisitional courts and used torture as a mode of inquiry. An accused heretic was burned when the church withdrew its protection from him or her.

Yet deviations were rife in reformist sects. A fourteenth-century English cleric and independent thinker, John Wycliffe, criticized the wealth, worldly power, and hierarchical structure of the church. He denied that priests had the authority to confer absolution and attacked a sometimes venal system of confession, penance, and indulgences. He and his followers translated the Bible into English (in language adumbrating the great King James version), though translating the Bible into the vernacular was forbidden. The church deplored laymen, and especially women, reading the Bible directly. Clerics said women should sit and spin and cackle, not try to read material far above their intelligence. But Wycliffe's followers, the Lollards, believed in learning about religion from scripture, rather than from a clergy they did not trust. Women thronged to them, as they do to any movement offering them greater autonomy, and agitated for the right to preach. When Wycliffe denied the doctrine of transubstantiation (the mystical transformation of wafers into Christ's body and blood), the church condemned Lollardism and arrested his followers. England did not permit church inquisition or torture, so the Lollards were tried in royal courts. They were obliged to recant, fast, or be publicly beaten. One poor old Lollard, Isabella Chapleyn, was excommunicated and sentenced to twelve beatings.[15]

State religions had often required people to make ritual obeisance to gods symbolizing the state; they demanded not faith, but deference to the state. They might punish a refusal to offer ritual as blasphemy. Rome persecuted Christians not for their creed, but for refusing to bow to its emperor and official deities. Judaism had an orthodox position and required adherence to a law, but religious scholars were free to argue religious points and their discussions had an honored place in the religion. Until Catholicism, no religion imposed a dogma everyone had to accept, condemning other views as "heresy" and punishing them by an extremely painful death. Thereafter, absolute ideologies, both political and religious, became commonplace.

Oppression creates backlash. As the church excluded women and rejected faith in favor of dogma, people (especially women) moved towards mysticism and an emotional experience of the godhead, creating the cult of Mary. Jesus' mother did not attract much attention before the twelfth century, but, later, she was everywhere. Orders took her as patron, and new cathedrals were named for her (the Notre Dame in Paris, Chartres, Rheims, Amiens, and others). Mary was like the old Mother Goddess—tender, merciful, compassionate, open, as the rest of religion was not. Although not god, she could intercede with god, providing a route to forgiveness that the mysterious trinity did not. Marianism became a powerful movement within Catholicism, remaining so to this day.

Marianism did not affect the status of women, who were shut out of public life and forbidden independence. Institutions "professionalized" many disciplines, meaning only those with university training were licensed to practice law, ethics, or medicine. Since only men could attend universities, only men were licensed. Today we define professionalization as high standards and wide dissemination of knowledge, but the medicine taught in medieval universities was no better than traditional lore. Based on a theory of humors and astrological readings, it could be downright lethal. Physicians killed as many patients as they helped. Most important, universities trained all educated men to see women through Aquinian/Aristotelian lenses, as deformed men, passive, matter without aspiration, a different species from males.[16] Their training gave lawyers a sacrosanct basis for judging women incapacitated and denying them legal rights; theologians backed this view with religious sanction; and physicians offered the sexes different cures for the same disease.

Men passed more and more laws limiting women. In Siena, where capitalism and a mercantile and manufacturing economy had developed in the thirteenth century, women had capital and invested cash dowries in business ventures. They became money changers, signed contracts, lent money, sued and were sued. With dowries protected against their husbands, widows had considerable autonomy. But in the late thirteenth century, Sienese men passed laws barring women from law courts and from controlling money and set up a special court to hear women's suits against men. Property laws were changed to stop women from bequeathing their dowries. Women often broke social codes by leaving their property to other women, mainly poor older widows. But the men's code required property to remain in the family in male hands: failure to abide by it was seen as betrayal. By the sixteenth century most Italian cities had decreed that women whose fathers died intestate could inherit nothing, despite the relationship.

In most Italian cities, middle- and upper-class women were kept in the home until their majority (at twelve before the fifteenth century, fourteen after), remaining legal minors all their lives, barred from doing business or traveling. In contrast, all classes of men traveled, gaining a rough education. Some Italian states barred women from courts; their depositions were taken at home or in church. A widow needed her family's consent to remarry, and a father could confine his daughters to a cloister for life by a provision in his will. Women had some protections—they were rarely held responsible for their fathers' debts. Widows could use their husbands' property if they were chaste and single. Lower-class Italian women were wretchedly poor and allowed only the worst-paid work as domestic servants, charwomen, launderers, and water carriers; they made shoes, dresses, and hats, wove and embroidered, cooked, barbered, and kept inns. In Venice they rowed. Everywhere, they ran brothels and hustled.

The disasters of fourteenth-century Europe inflated the

economy; dowries also inflated, to the point that even affluent Italian families were able to marry only one daughter. Unable to pay dowries, poor families sent daughters into domestic service to earn their own. In 1523 a quarter of the adult women in Coventry were domestic servants.[17] The word "maid," unmarried woman, became synonymous with domestic servant. Maids usually married late, in their twenties, after they had accrued a small dowry, for women's wages were extremely low. Some had sexual lives before marriage and, when they wed, they chose men their own age or younger. Many women did not marry at all.

In strong guilds, men began to expel women. A provost of Paris refused to let a glass cutter's widow take apprentices, even though she knew the craft, because the skill was too delicate for a woman to teach: men, he knew, were "right" and dextrous, women "left" and clumsy, despite the fact that women were expert at lace-making.[18] Everywhere in this period, women were pushed out of guilds and increasingly limited to dressmaking, brewing, domestic service, and street vending of food. Englishwomen had an ancient monopoly on making bread and ale, both highly perishable products; when these industries specialized, men were able to push women out because baking bread suddenly required capital for wheat threshers, flour makers, brick ovens, and distribution systems. Women had no capital, so men took over the baking industry and organized powerful guilds. Women had probably invented brewing, which required only household tools and labor. They followed their ancient occupation until hops and beer were introduced, making ale less perishable, and brewing became a factory operation, a technology requiring capital. Women were thrust out of the work.

A 1356 German law barred women from inheriting and

from jobs they used to hold—levying troops, holding courts of justice, coining money, and participating in legal assemblies. In the late fourteenth century women were barred from making contracts, managing goods—even their own—and succeeding to the French throne. Still, the constriction of Europe's women was not over.[19]

CHAPTER 2

FEUDALISM IN JAPAN

FEUDALISM AROSE IN JAPAN at about the same time as in Europe. In both places it emerged from the constant war among petty rivals, men's difficulty in delegating authority, and the cult of machismo. Militaristic societies disdain women, who nevertheless often achieve autonomy and power in such cultures by default. Militaristic Spartan and Aztec men, though not feudal, set themselves above women and ceded the domestic and commercial realms to the "inferior" sex. Soldiers in feudal Europe also set themselves above women, the domestic, and the commercial, and there, too, women often wielded power and acted independently despite lacking legal personhood. Women kept society going while men were absent—they grew food, raised money for war, and made clothing and weapons. When men returned, they centralized power, created relatively stable borders, and took measures to shackle women again in every area.

Japanese women had high status before feudalism, whereas the status of European women varied from one region to another. Japanese men, unlike the Crusaders, did not go abroad to fight; they fought locally. Fighting almost continually, they lacked the energy to dominate women. War abated when one man won and evolved a system of delegating control. Japan is smaller than California, and near-totalitarian control was possible. When women were degraded, they were subjected nearly absolutely.

Before Feudalism

There are signs in Japan of a Paleolithic culture from c. 8000 BCE; two Neolithic cultures endured into the Common Era. Only one aboriginal people remains, the Ainu, a dispossessed group in the far north. Over the centuries, the Japanese islands were invaded by Mongols, Caucasoid Siberians, and people from Southeast Asia and the Western Pacific. But the main early influence on Japan was Korea.

An early Japanese creation myth describes how she- and he-who-invite (Izanami-no-mikoto and Izanagi-no-mikoto) made land and sky, discovered sex, and gave birth to fourteen islands and thirty-five deities. Wanting a "lord of the universe," they created the Sun Goddess Amaterasu no Ookami (Heavenly Shining Great Deity) and sent her to heaven to rule. The creation myths of most early cultures emphasize interrelatedness, and in Japan, interrelatedness remained paramount in religion (as it did in business, too). Everything was intrinsically connected: female and male, heaven and earth, people, land, and gods. These myths, which delight in "female" elements—sex and fertility, warmth, light, and energy—went unrecorded until (as usual) a ruling clan co-opted them to support its claims in the eighth century. Veneration of the Sun Goddess dates at least to the second millennium BCE, however, as shown by archaeological remains—ancient sundials and family shrines replete with phallic menhirs and female figurines.

In the third century BCE, migrants from the continent brought metallurgy and wet-rice culture to Japan. Migration continued, mainly from China during political upheavals. In the first century CE, the center of Japanese culture was Honshu, near the Yamato Peninsula. At this time there was no system of writing, trade was done by exchange, and clothes were of hemp or bark, but the people made exquisite pottery, wooden bowls and cups, mats, baskets, and lacquer ware. They lived in matrilineal clans often led by women, each with its own deity, supposedly its ancestor. The clan leader was both war chief and head priest(ess). From 2500 to 250 BCE (the late Jomon era), women divers *(ama)* were important enough economically to be mentioned in records. They lived in matrilineal, matrilocal, matristic communities, and still live this way in Japan and Korea.[1]

In 57 CE a Chinese history called Japan the "Queen Country" for its many female rulers. Japan's ancient tradition of the *miko*, a woman who could hear and transmit the voices of gods, may have grown into a political role, the priestess-queen. After decades of war under a male king, the people chose Himiko, a priestess-queen, as ruler. Japanese society was already stratified and slave holding, and in 238, when Himiko opened diplomatic relations with China, she gave its court thirty male and female slaves. A man acceded to the throne when Himiko died, but people would not obey him. After some contention, order was restored when Iyo, a thirteen-year-old girl, perhaps Himiko's daughter, was made queen.

Legend reports that Empress Jingu, wife of Emperor Chuai,

was chief priestess, warrior, and perhaps a *miko*.[2] The gods told her that Japan should conquer a land to the west. Her husband, who took part in this divination ceremony, said he saw no land to the west; enraged, the gods took his life. Jingu became regent and led a seaborne expedition to what proved to be Korea. The Korean kingdoms submitted without a battle. There may be truth in the legend: Japan did invade Korea in 364.

A third-century Chinese chronicle describes Japanese society as egalitarian: "Father and mother, elder and younger brothers and sisters live separately, but at meetings there is no distinction on account of sex." But Chinese émigrés had male-dominant customs, which influenced the Japanese. Elite Japanese men may have adopted polygyny in the third century CE. In the fifth and sixth centuries, clans competed for dominance, trying to control territory. In the process, Japan grew militaristic, hierarchical, and more male-dominant. Slaves, perhaps war captives, became common. By this time, clans were occupational groups, or guilds, with hereditary membership of diviners, weavers, clerks, washerwomen, or wet-nurses for the imperial family. People could enter and leave guilds by marriage, adoption, or widowhood. Some guilds were independent, like the one responsible for religious rites. Agricultural workers' and artisans' guilds unionized low-status people, who were almost serfs, to refuse corvée and military conscription.

Chinese culture became the standard in Japan. Adapting Chinese ideographs to their different phonetic structure, Japanese wrote with them. After the fifth century, official documents were written in Chinese, mainly by Chinese and Korean immigrants and their descendants. Indeed, Chinese became the prestige language—Japanese literature, thought, history, and philosophy were composed according to Chinese models, and in the Chinese language.

In 552 the king of Paekche (western Korea) sent Japan a gift of Buddhist texts and images, asking for military aid in return. A powerful noble, Soga Umako, found Buddhism both a symbol and a rationalization of centralized power, and he adopted it. Japan's national religion, Shinto, was structured like the political system, in a loose confederation of clans that granted each one local autonomy. Soga wanted to make his clan dominant and to centralize control, and he tried to impose Buddhism as a state religion. The hereditary Shinto priests/priestesses and one military clan opposed this move; they allowed Soga to build a temple for the Buddhist image, but not to train priests. In 577 a Korean priest brought some ascetics to Japan. Soga appropriated the priest and ordered him to ordain three young women of Soga's choice. Buddhism did not accept women as priests, but the Japanese tradition of priestesses was strong: Soga thought them the best liaisons to the gods of the new religion. He waged a contest of gods for forty years, until 592, when he triumphed and enthroned Empress Suiko, the first ruling empress in historical time. Then Soga imported and propagated Chinese culture.

In the late sixth century, nobles read classical Confucian texts. Confucianism emphasizes the secular, as well as male dominance, obedience to authority, and ethical and orderly social organization. The Japanese absorbed what they could use—the theory of yin-yang and the monarch as the Son of Heaven—and ignored the rest. Chinese ideas did not change attitudes towards women immediately: in the seventh and eighth centuries, half of Japan's rulers were women; six empresses ruled between 592 and 770.

In this period, however, the Japanese absorbed Confucian and Buddhist ideas and centralized the government into a bureaucracy. To abolish matrilineality and matrilocality and establish patrilineality, they passed the Taiho Code in 702 and the Yoro Code in 718, both of which discriminated against women in property, marriage, and divorce. Chinese Buddhism was more woman-hating than the Indian form, which, unlike Hinduism, did not deny women salvation. Later Buddhist sects not only denied women salvation but taught that they suffered from original sin and five obstructions, which prevented them from reaching the five states of spiritual awareness open to men. Later Buddhist doctrine taught that woman's only avenue to salvation lay in being reborn as a man.

But women's status in Japan was so high that the laws had little effect. Families still traced descent through females, and women named royal children in the seventh century. The Chinese belief in a male sun did not eradicate the Sun Goddess Amaterasu, who remained the highest deity. Female physiological processes—menstruation, loss of virginity, childbirth— were still holy because they produced blood and were believed to be the root of female magical powers. Holiness made them taboo. In an Ainu tradition, a man who saw menstrual blood on the floor of a hut rubbed it over his chest as a means of empowerment; an old saying attributed purifying powers to menstruating women, "wives of the *kami*." Shrine virgins were merely unmarried women.

Gradually, holiness was debased into pollution. In early Shintoism, fertility was the primary value, and purity the primary ritual value.[3] Women's purity had the power to remove pollution. The extremely solemn ritual for the purification of all Japan, held twice every year, invokes four female *kami*. Purity, not avoidance of sex, was a spiritual or psychological state to which virginity was irrelevant. The sacred and the sexual were integrated; Japanese legends describe women who are "possessed" by the *kami* both sexually and spiritually. Shinto authority and priesthood were inherited by the clan's children, not transmitted from male to male in a Buddhist hierarchy. Two elements of Buddhism were alien to Japanese thinking: priestly celibacy and the exclusion of women from religious ceremonies.[4] Since women were barred from being Buddhist priests, Buddhist ceremonies in Japan were often celebrated by a Buddhist priest and a Shinto priestess. Buddhist temples near Nara admitted women worshippers.

In time, the Fujiwara clan usurped Soga power. There were still some powerful women. Empress Gemmei (707–15) built the first permanent Japanese capital at Nara. She saw to completion the *Kojiki*, the oldest extant Japanese book and the earliest chronicle, which Emperor Temmu commissioned in 682 to record ancient oral material. Written—dictated—by Hieda no Are, a shrine-keeping scholar, *Kojiki* was for centuries attributed to a man.

From 710 to 784 the era was called Nara after Empress Gemmei's capital. Princess Abe became Empress Koken when her father abdicated in 749. In 758 she abdicated in favor of a very young prince. A few years later a powerful priest, Dokyo, persuaded her to banish the young emperor and to rule again as Empress Shotoku. All emperors had been influenced by advisers, but in an increasingly anti-woman climate, the elite claimed that Shotoku's association with Dokyo portended theocracy and demanded that women be excluded from the throne. They moved the capital from Nara, where Buddhist influence was strong, to the site of today's Kyoto. The new Capital of Peace and Tranquility, Heian-kyo, gave its name to the era 794–1185 (Heian). The elite, who were also influenced by the Chinese, modelled the city on Chang-an, the capital of Tang China. The Fujiwara clan would remain in power for three centuries. Wars and struggles for succession abated during this period. The government abolished clan structure and tried to centralize power, but was not strong enough. The emperor deferred to tradition and appointed male clan heads as lords in their own territories, thereby creating a male bureaucracy as in China.

Regional households, with administrative and military organizations of their own, grew strong. Large landowners evaded taxes and added to the burden of peasants, who sometimes ran away in desperation. Clans in frontier regions expanded their holdings by seizing land from aboriginal groups or clearing unused land and treating the new acquisition as their own, not the crown's. Emperors also gave land to courtiers or religious groups, diminishing their private resources. Before long, prestige more than power kept the Heian rulers dominant.

In the early eighth century the government transformed Shintoism from a hereditary occupational clan to a bureaucratic male-dominated institution. It assigned Shinto priests both rank and duties as government officials and forbade priestesses to exorcise, perform healing rituals, receive oracles, or communicate with the gods. Male priests educated in Chinese divination now performed these roles. Women lost centrality in religion, and religion lost centrality in the state, becoming just one more bureau.

The qualities that had made women holy became signs of pollution. Suddenly, sexuality was sin: purity was opposed to it, and only virgins were pure. New laws prohibited a man from staying in the same house with a woman the night before going to a shrine, and also forbade a menstruating woman from going to a shrine until ten days after her period, three of which had to be spent in purification. New mothers could not visit shrines until ninety days after their flow stopped and, for a hundred days, could not use the same cooking fire as men. Women were barred from climbing Mount Fuji, which was too holy to suffer their pollution. Buddhist temples built in the ninth century now barred women. Holy women now traveled the country in bands, divining or prophesying; in the north, bands of blind women were mediums for utterances from the dead.

Increased woman hatred led to changes in customs: now, upper-class wives were virtually imprisoned in the *kicho*, a curtained room at the center of Japanese houses. The most exposure they were permitted was letting their sleeves protrude from the curtains. Only husbands and fathers could see their faces; one great lady of the time would not show herself even to her parents, saying "Ghosts and women had best remain invisible," as the chronicler who quoted her wrote approvingly. A woman in a *kicho* could barely tell day from night. She could converse only with husband, parents, and female servants; otherwise, she communicated by letter or intermediary. These women did no productive work in the household or with their children, but sat for hours on end staring at curtains. They enjoyed sedentary occupations, like calligraphy, writing poetry, and composing music, and they often mention "suffering from leisure." Allowed to go out to some festivals and temples if they were encased in walled carriages, noblewomen were taught to read and write, but not in Chinese.

Yet despite this isolation and limited education, it was eleventh-century Japanese women who wrote the masterpieces of Japanese literature. There was a long literary tradition of women authors; they had always incanted, recited, and composed poetry. Men showed off their Chinese learning in stilted, mediocre prose and formally correct Chinese-style poetry. The problem was that Chinese did not suit Japanese attitudes. Some men wrote lyric poetry in Japanese, but the women had the genius. Women, two in particular, became the Dante and the Shakespeare of Japan. Writing in Japanese, they described the realities of their world and their feelings in sophisticated, allusive literary styles. These two women are Murasaki Shikibu and Sei Shonagon.

Murasaki Shikibu wrote poetry, a diary, and *The Tale of Genji*, the monumental classic of Japanese literature. She was learned in Chinese and history, but tried all her life to hide it, fearing mockery or disapproval. Serving in the court of a remarkable empress, Shoshi, she wrote of court life in *The Tale of Genji*. Genji is a prince surrounded by women. The heroine, Murasaki (Shikibu was nicknamed "Murasaki" after her heroine), is first in Genji's affections but not in rank. Unlike conventional authors of the period, Shikibu did not describe the luxuries of court life or exalt family pride, but focused on women's suffering and sacrifice under the pressures of society and politics.

Like Shikibu, Sei Shonagon was the educated daughter of a middle-ranking noble and served in an empress' court in the early eleventh century. *The Pillow Book*, sketches and vignettes containing thoughts and impressions, is witty and familiar to all Japanese students. The heroines of these works do not rebel or let themselves show any emotion that will displease men. But woman writers emphasized women's silent suffering and quiet competence, not the passivity, obedience, submissiveness, or cheerfulness stressed by male authors. Shikibu's heroine, a superb poet and calligrapher, also manages a household, taking loving responsibility for those in her care. The Japanese court fostered an elegant culture in this period and formed an exquisite taste in art and style that still endures. This culture was largely created by women.

Japanese women retained some rights until the Middle Ages. Laws specifically forbade men from beating wives (although this assault was penalized less severely than others), but most husbands had concubines or second wives. Women inherited property, including land, and often managed it. Inadequately educated to read or write theoretical work, however, they were barred from public office. Japanese women no longer had a voice in their society.

Courtship customs of this period are charming: parents made the initial overtures, usually through a liaison. When agreement was reached and the couple had consented, the boy sent a thirty-one syllable poem to the girl. She (or a family member or a female servant) would reply. If the letters sustained their interest and gave them good impressions of each other, the boy visited the girl. Going to her bedroom at night, he stayed until dawn for three nights running and sent a letter after each visit. On the third night, the pair was served rice cakes, symbolizing the coupling of gods: they were married. The next day the bride's family gave a feast, constituting a public announcement of the marriage. Most marriages were matrilocal, called *muko-iri kon*, "taking a husband." The groom resided with the bride's family or just visited her, or the couple lived in a dwelling attached to the bride's parents' home. This arrangement, as we have seen, puts a wife in a strong position: she can turn to her family for advice, help, and protection against abuse. In divorce, a man simply left, taking whatever household goods he had brought with him: the house belonged to the woman.

In this period, a fad developed among noblewomen for blackening their teeth with oxidized iron filings. Later, married women did it; in the next century, so did men.

The Kamakura Period, 1185–1333

When the Heian government collapsed, two powerful clans tried to take over. The Taira and the Minamoto fought for dominance for thirty years, ravaging the country. When the Minamoto won, they set up headquarters near modern Tokyo in Kamakura, giving the period its name. Minamoto Yoritomo, not wishing to appear a usurper, took a military title, shogun, "chief general," and masqueraded as the emperor's servant. Ferocious wars had so devastated the land that most small farmers had surrendered their farms to warlords in return for protection, becoming essentially serfs in a manorial system that complemented the feudal structure of the upper classes. Warriors called *samurai*, like European barons, adopted a set of standards to legitimate their claims of superiority: valor, loyalty, and death rather than dishonor, either in battle or through *seppuku*, suicide by disembowelment.

Men who practice self-discipline and austerity usually place extreme restraints on women. Although the samurai followed this pattern, the tradition of powerful women was still alive. Men were occupied with war and developing a system of government, so women were allowed to take public roles in this period. In 1232 the *Joei Shikimoku*, or "Formulary of the Joei Era," became the legal code of the samurai; it gave daughters equal rights of inheritance with sons, the right to bequeath property by will, and the right to revoke a will after it was approved by the shogunate. Women could fulfill feudal military obligations by proxy. Rich women who became independent had considerable local authority; they could manage their own estates, sometimes by proxies, and sue at law over land, winning even against men. *Joei* laws echoed Confucian condemnation of widow remarriage and punished conviction of a grave crime—rebellion, murder, or piracy—by confiscating the property of both husband and wife.

In Japan, as in Europe, the most powerful women were widows. One of these was the remarkable Hojo Masako.[5]

Daughter of a military magnate, Hojo was drawn to her father's ward, Minamoto Yoritomo. When her father tried to marry her to a high court official, she refused, revealing her feelings for Yoritomo. Her father locked her up, but she escaped and eloped with Yoritomo (an unthinkable act a few hundred years later).

Yoritomo became shogun; when he died, Hojo's elder son succeeded him, but Hojo ruled. Her love for Yoritomo had soured and she had no love for their sons. She limited her son's absolute power by empowering her natal family, setting up a council of retainers made up of her father and other relatives. When the son protested, she had him killed. Hojo's father and his favorite concubine then tried to take the reins of government from her, but she exiled him. She negotiated with an astute court lady, the emperor's favorite, and the two calmed and mediated relations between the court and the shogunate. When Hojo's second son was assassinated, she instantly summoned from Kyoto a court noble's two-year-old son, the great-grandson of Yoritomo's sister, as titular shogun. She made her brother regent and continued to rule through him. Because she had become a nun at her husband's death, she was called Ama Shogun, "the Nun-Shogun." As the real ruler of Japan after the shogun died, she began the regent system and is considered the founder of Japanese feudalism.

Women who accepted samurai values could hold power, but all women suffered from samurai marriage practices. Japanese folk tales of the period describe considerable sexual freedom (as do medieval European folk tales and Chaucer). Adultery was common in Japanese fiction, especially among nobles and farmers: the important thing was discretion, protecting husbands from loss of face. But in law, female adultery was a crime. We do not know the facts of behavior. Early in the samurai era, female adultery (and male adultery with a married

woman) were punished by confiscation of estates and banish-
ment. Most men had concubines, servants whose children
might rise. Samurai usually took only one official wife, but as
many concubines as they wished: Hojo Makaso's bitterness
against Yoritomo and their sons may have arisen from her rage
at the number of his concubines.

During the Kamakura, men restored an old tradition that
let them cast off wives at will, expelling them from their beds
when they reached thirty and replacing them by a younger
woman, though not divorcing them. Men could also divorce
rampantly: high-ranking courtiers made a career of marriage,
exchanging each wife for a richer or more powerful one as often
as they changed their clothes.[6] Women who were divorced for
cause lost any property their husbands had given them, even if
by contract. Blameless wives were supposed to be able to keep
such gifts, but if husbands refused to give them up, women
needed legal and financial resources to regain them.

Women were virtually barred from divorcing. A woman's
only escape from an intolerable marriage was flight to a temple
that gave women sanctuary. Because there were few such sanc-
turies, not all women could reach one. Moreover, escape to an
asylum meant abandoning one's children. Escape had to be well
planned, for the woman was dragged back if the husband's servants caught her before she reached safety. In time, common
law decreed that a woman who managed to throw her shoe
through the temple gate could not be forced to return home.
Once in the temple, she had to serve for three years before she
could submit a petition to be restored to her parents' home.
Fugitive wives had to show good cause before the temple would
initiate proceedings for them. A petition from a later period
came from a woman who was married at fourteen and whose
husband had for eight years consorted with prostitutes, stayed

away from home for days at a time, refused her support, assaulted her brutally, and ordered her to become a prostitute for him. She promised to commit suicide if she did not obtain her freedom.

When the Kamakura ended, women still had the rights to inherit property, income from lands, and some offices on an estate (mainly steward or economic administrator). Their rights within marriage had been curtailed, but most marriages were "monogamous"—men had one principal wife and subordinate concubines.

In the twelfth century, Zen Buddhism spread to Japan from China. In Zen, a person reaches enlightenment not through study or intellect but by insight, reached when harmony exists between the self and nature. As a "shortcut" to enlightenment, emphasizing physical discipline, self-control, and meditation, Zen attracted the samurai, who valued the first two qualities. Dogen, who brought Zen to Japan, recommended the worldly and spiritual equality of women, who thronged to his community outside Kyoto. Later, when he moved his temple to a remote mountain, it became a male monastic community. Buddhism, which had slowly been domesticated to female deities and family relationships, never had female leaders.

The Muromachi Period, 1333-1490

By the fourteenth century, feudalism was firmly entrenched in Japan. The Kamakura regime fell and the new shoguns could not control the country. In the upheaval of the next 150 years, people believed that only military strength and shrewdness would save them. In this atmosphere, women lost any semblance of rights or equality.

Provincial noblemen, *daimyo* (great names), ruled their

fiefs like petty autocrats, invading citizens' private lives. For two hundred years, until Japan was unified around 1600, no central authority enforced laws or protected people even from bandits. Men were reluctant to leave land to women, fearing they could not defend it in the face of continual warfare. Yet civil war had long pervaded Japan and such fears did not crop up earlier; moreover, men too had trouble defending their land. Blood ties had declined in importance, and, as always in these conditions, women lost power. Japanese women had held power partly because of the Japanese respect for kinship—birth outweighed gender in ritual, inheritance, and status.

Early in the Muromachi period, women could will property to their children; later, they had only use rights to property. Almost no widows inherited property in this period; land was entailed to a male heir after a widow's death. Families with no sons adopted their daughters' husbands. Before the Muromachi, the son deemed most capable (not necessarily the eldest) became chief heir and got the major share of the property. Siblings were given enough to support themselves and were expected to obey the chief heir, who was responsible for the clan's feudal obligations. Now entire estates went to one son: younger sons were disinherited and daughters' inheritances, always less than sons', shrank to *kesshoryo*, "toilet money." A thousandth of an estate—enough for combs, powder, and perfume—was all the eldest daughter needed during her lifetime.

Younger sons lived by leaving the clan to form other alliances. Penniless, daughters had to offer their loyalty to whoever supported them. Basic relationships changed: contractual feudal bonds of financial dependency became more important than blood bonds. Marriage gradually became totally patrilocal—called *yome-iri kon*, "taking a wife"—and remained so until about 1950. A bride lived with her husband's family, who had total control of her. In divorce, she was ejected from the house and lost the children. And, since women no longer inherited property, men were quicker to divorce them. Customs were determined by class, however, and different classes adopted different marriage forms. The move from matrilocal to patrilocal marriage occurred most swiftly among military classes, whose main bond was father-son. In strict samurai families, the sexes were educated apart and were segregated even in the family after the age of seven.

Buddhist temples sponsored a new theater, Noh (skill). Noh focused on restless spirits desiring release from the earth. Women would not be banished from the stage until the Tokugawa period in the seventeenth century, but were already frowned on: like Renaissance English drama, Noh was performed only by men, but had stereotypical female characters who tended to be emotional and centered on their love of men or children. Male characters were usually soldiers caught in political conflict, recalling their battles, or reciting lyric poetry; a few of these poems celebrate longevity and marital love. Symbolic and restrained, Noh provided an emotional release that was increasingly denied in behavior. A comic form, *kyogen*, "mad words," was often performed alternately with Noh. *Kyogen* plays reversed social distinctions: clever servants outwit pompous lords; a man observing his wife mimics her, appearing to dread her awesome, formidable figure.

Some women worked. In the fourteenth and fifteenth centuries, hereditary teaching clans of female teachers—spinsters, nuns, and widows—taught merchants' daughters mathematics and bookkeeping. Women were no longer a significant voice in Japanese literature (and would not be again until the late nineteenth century). They had traditionally worked as quasi-religious reciters and singers, and now they created a new literature as *jongleurs*. Addressing all classes, they sang about male and female heroes in pain or suffering transients in an immutable social order. *Jongleurs* of both sexes sang of twelfth-century battles, miracles associated with shrines, and conflicts of good and evil; they also gave new versions of classical tales.

Towards the end of the fifteenth century, in the Sengoku period, civil war broke out. Japan verged on complete political chaos and, from 1490 to 1600, the country as a whole was almost never at peace. Yet commerce and the arts flourished. In 1542 Portuguese merchants landed in Japan, followed soon after by Europeans of many nations bearing trade goods, firearms, tobacco, and Christian missionaries of the Catholic faith. Overseas trade brought prosperity to the hard-to-control countryside, while firearms and gunpowder changed the nature of war. Defence now required walled castles, and lords had to be rich enough to build them.

After the sixteenth century, the samurai strictly enforced laws denying women inheritance or divorce and executing them for adultery. Urban men too became stricter, and pretentious ones among them imitated the samurai degradation of women. But village customs remained relatively unchanged: grooms still lived with the brides' families, and adultery was not a serious matter. No one was executed for any act that did not affect the samurai class.

The Tokugawa Shogunate, 1603-1867

By 1590 Hideyoshi had unified most of Japan. The only man in Japanese history to rise from peasant to national ruler, he proved to be a brilliant military commander: he is still a national hero. He died in 1598, and Tokugawa Ieyasu made himself shogun, imposing strong central government over the state's feudal structure. His system, "centralized feudalism," assured his clan, the Tokugawa, of perpetual control of the office, and the era is called the Tokugawa or the Edo, after his capital at Edo (now Tokyo).

Long regarded as a symbol of national and religious unity, the emperor had no political influence whatever and maintained his court at Kyoto in useless splendor. The actual ruler, the shogun (a hereditary office), claimed about a quarter of Japan's farmland as his personal property, including mines and key strategic and commercial centers. Ieyasu divided the rest of the country into provinces called *han*, each controlled by a *daimyo*, whom he forbade to make alliances or wars with each other or the outside world. He did not tax them or interfere with their internal government, but obliged them to build roads, contribute to the construction of castles, and attend him in the capital every other year. By forcing the *daimyo* to maintain expensive residences in both the capital and their own domains, he kept them from amassing enough wealth to threaten him. And a corps of secret police stationed throughout the country maintained close surveillance on them. Each *daimyo* was required to leave his wives and children hostage in the capital when he returned to his estate. During this period, women were important mainly as hostages and victims.

The shogun, the *daimyo*, and the samurai who worked for them constituted an elite ruling class distinguished by dress and manners. A merchant class also grew stronger throughout the Tokugawa. Like other elites, however, the military class scorned the merchants, whose prestige and legal standing placed them near the bottom of society. But, as always, the merchants grew rich and many aristocrats fell into their debt. The real bottom layer of society, the peasants, whose taxes contributed the state's main revenue, were relieved of military service and forced to surrender their weapons. Hereditary local elites ran village affairs, except for tax-collecting and administering justice.

Ieyasu was interested in foreign trade and technology, but his successors feared foreign dominance, closed Japan to outsiders in 1640, and forbade Japanese to travel abroad. In 1597 Hideyoshi had begun to persecute Christians; Ieyasu halted that terror, but later shoguns restored it, fearing Christian domination like that in other parts of Asia. When a 1637 peasants' revolt against oppressive taxes escalated into a Christian revolt, the authorities extirpated Christianity, at a great cost in lives. The shogunate promoted a new version of Confucianism, reviving the yin-yang duality and stressing loyalty to the lord and duty to parents. Henceforth, every man had his place in a hierarchy of subordination, and his very survival depended on it. Even the proud samurai now depended on a lord for rice rations; sustenance required absolute obedience. As a samurai stood to his lord, so his family stood to him—to eat, one had to obey.

After placing every noble, class, and piece of land under regulated surveillance, Ieyasu tightened control over women. Governments pacify men resentful of supervision with stricter controls over women, and it is interesting that the drive towards regulation and uniformity occurred almost simultaneously in Japan and in Europe. The new rigid Japan energetically propagandized the Confucian rule of three obediences: a woman was subject to her father in youth, her husband in marriage, and her son in widowhood. But that was the theory; in practice she was subject to her parents in youth, her bullying mother-in-law in marriage, and, in widowhood, she in turn bullied her daughter-in-law. A woman of the military classes could never become head of the house, inherit rice rations, and pass on that right.

She was forever precluded from economic power: her husband was her feudal lord. Like Chinese women, she had no place in her natal family and was considered extraneous to it. Morals books of this period emphasize that women do not belong to the blood line: wives are merely instruments to ensure continuation of the male line. A saying of the time, *Hara wa karimono*, means "the womb is on loan": wives or concubines are human incubators who transmit what is important—male genes.[7]

The Chinese marriage model became almost universal in Japan: in all but the most rural areas, a bride entered her husband's house and remained there for life. The new wifely ideals taught her to rise early, before the rest of the family, go to bed late, and work diligently all day everyday; to devote herself utterly to her husband's welfare, obey him unquestioningly and cheerfully, and tend his parents and children. Wives could be divorced for being remiss in any of these duties. A wife was protected against divorce in only three situations: if she had no home to return to, if she had served her in-laws faithfully until they died, or if she had married a poor man who had since become rich. Yet a man could divorce a woman with a three-line letter. For example:

> To Fuyu Dono,
> It is my pleasure to divorce you hereby. Therefore hereafter there is no objection to your marrying anyone whomsoever.
> Witness my hand, the eleventh of the seventh month.
> Tama Saburo

> To Yokoyama Shosaburo,
> I received your daughter to wife, but since she does not please me, I now divorce her. Hereafter, there is

no objection to her marrying anyone else. For this
reason I make this declaration.
Witness my hand, sixth month Kansei 10,
Iwase Tomojiro Keishin

Women could not initiate divorce and were terribly dis-
graced by it. A woman married into the military classes could
not divorce on any grounds unless her husband consented.
Unhappily married women were expected to commit suicide; if
a woman dared to go back to her family, her father was supposed to force her to kill herself. Her only alternative was sanctuary in a divorce temple.

In Confucian style, widows were forbidden to remarry, and
laws governing adultery were tightened. Earlier, laws forbade
men from murdering a wife or her lover for adultery, but as
men gradually defied the law, courts proved tolerant. By the
Tokugawa, law required men to kill adulterous wives. The
slightest compromise of a samurai wife was punished by death.
Men could not by definition commit adultery unless they had
sex with another man's wife. They were urged to keep concubines to improve their chances of begetting a male heir. Wives,
not allowed to display jealousy of concubines, were exhorted to
tend them kindly.

Japanese culture propagated male and female ideals.
Puppet theater, wildly popular in the late seventeenth and early
eighteenth centuries, showed women acting kindly to wayward
husbands and their concubines. In plays and in novels, women
yearned for love or pleasure and were willing to die for it—and
did. Moral works reinforced the strictures on women's nature
and place. Phrases containing the word *woman* became pejora-
tive; in Chinese classics, the word for *woman* meant "base"; in
Chinese and Japanese, phrases like *woman's words, woman's*

benevolence, or *the loyalty of women* all connoted small-minded ignobility. The traditional belief that even delicate women were competent managers faded; they were characterized as utterly incompetent, irresponsible, unreliable. A manual on fire prevention taught readers that "women are such feckless creatures [and] are very careless in leaving household possessions and clothes lying about."

Strict Buddhist sects held women incapable of salvation because they suffer from the five obstructions. Tendai or Shingon Buddhist texts condemned woman as "originally an agent of the six devils . . . born as woman to prevent man from following the way of Buddha." If you are a woman, "you must regard yourself as the agent of the devils sent to destroy the teaching of Buddhism"; your husband, "even if he seems more lowly than you . . . is the personification of the Buddha and has the sense of reward and punishment as well as that of mercy . . . You have married a Buddhist saint."[8] "Woman is the emissary of hell; she destroys the seed of Buddha. Her face resembles that of a saint; her heart is like that of a demon . . . Every woman, noble or humble, is a sinful being . . . A woman has no home in the three worlds"(she does not exist in the past, present, or future). Confucianists agreed: "There is nothing as disgusting as a woman."

The most widely read Confucianist, said to be the most important influence on Tokugawa moral standards, was Kaibara Ekken (1630–1714), author of *The Great Learning for Women* (which is sometimes attributed to his wife, Token). Here are some passages:

> Woman is by her inborn nature of the quality of yin,
> or softness. She lacks wisdom, is noisy, evil, and finds
> it difficult to follow the path of righteousness.

It is a girl's destiny, on reaching womanhood, to go to a new home and live in submission to her father-in-law and mother-in-law. . . . Should her parents, through excess of tenderness, allow her to grow up self-willed, she will infallibly show herself capricious in her husband's house, and thus alienate his affection, while, if her father-in-law be a man of correct principles, the girl will find the yoke of these principles intolerable.

The sage of old [Confucius] taught that, once married, she must never leave her husband's house. Should she forsake the *way*, and be divorced, shame shall cover her till her latest hour.

[There are Seven Reasons for divorce]:

1. Disobedience to her father-in-law or mother-in-law.
2. If she fail to bear children . . .
3. Lewdness.
4. Jealousy.
5. Leprosy or any like foul disease.
6. A woman shall be divorced who, by talking overmuch and prattling disrespectfully, disturbs the harmony of kinsmen and brings trouble on her household.
7. A woman shall be divorced who is addicted to stealing.

The great lifelong duty of a woman is obedience . . .

Let her never even dream of jealousy. If her husband be dissolute, she must expostulate with him, but never either nurse or vent her anger.

The five worst maladies that afflict the female mind

are: indocility, discontent, slander, jealousy, and silliness. Without any doubt, these five maladies infest seven or eight out of every ten women, and it is from these that arises the inferiority of women to men. . . . Such is the stupidity of her character that it is incumbent upon her, in every particular, to distrust herself and to obey her husband.

Fictional heroines of this period lack the main characteristic of heroes—selfhood. Since most women were illiterate, they did not create a literary image of themselves. Moral guidebooks taught that "a woman does not need to bother with learning; she has nothing to do but be obedient." If she could write to instruct the dyer who tinted the cloth from which she sewed clothing, that level sufficed. Women were raised to be servants.

Some fathers educated daughters; some women (mainly childless women with educated samurai husbands) painted or did scholarly work. One dutiful wife, Hanaoka Kae, daughter of a wealthy farmer, married a physician; competing with her mother-in-law to be his guinea pig in experiments with anaesthetics, she earned honor by enabling him to develop painless surgery—at the cost of her eyesight. Women of the merchant class had more interesting lives, helping to run family businesses, work that gave them a voice. Some merchants left monopoly rights in a trade to daughters. Since merchant wealth lay in capital, divisible in ways land is not, fathers often gave daughters dowries their husbands could not touch. Until 1550, merchant women could own land under certain conditions. Shuho managed her husband's pawnbrokerage and sake business and founded a very rich family. With money and leisure to cultivate their talents and enjoy pleasures, merchant women went sightseeing and to theaters. Fictions portray them as strong-minded and pleasure loving.

In seventeenth-century Japan, women were required to kill themselves if they were sexually assaulted. Women who survived rape or failed to die before it was consummated were judged to have consented. At marriage, samurai women were given daggers to use on themselves in such cases, and those who killed themselves during an attack were honored. To this day, women in Japan are held responsible, and blamed, for male violence and sexuality.

Tokugawa rulers organized prostitution, establishing licensed pleasure-quarters. *Yugo*, women of pleasure, were confined to such districts in Kyoto, Osaka, and Edo. By 1679, Japan had over a hundred such quarters. When farming suffered in the seventeenth century, peasants sold their daughters and sisters into prostitution. An influx of male officials and bureaucrats in cities created a huge demand for whores, ranging from skilled courtesans who chose their customers to ordinary prostitutes obliged to have sex with any man who paid them. Girls were indentured until a certain age (usually twenty-seven), when they could leave and set up in business for themselves, marry, or become a man's lover. Some were only children when they were sold by destitute fathers to owners who raised and educated them. Little is known about the many male prostitutes.

Like fifth-century BCE Athenian men, seventeenth- and eighteenth-century Japanese men used sex with their wives for procreation and sex with *yugo* for recreation. It was unseemly to show affection to a wife, and disastrous to fall in love with a prostitute: Japanese men were urged to form no bond to a woman that might influence them. Wealthy men played elaborate ritual games—poetry contests, mock weddings—in tea houses, where ranked courtesans took professional names from characters in *The Tale of Genji*. Tea houses in pleasure quarters not only showcased new styles in music, fashion, art, and literature but nourished cabals and political intrigue. Later, a new male elite married tea-house women.

A separate class of performers and waitresses was allowed to work in areas designated for entertainment but not to have sex with customers. Such a ban was impossible to enforce. Geishas ("persons of skill") were at first male jesters and drum-bearers who sang and did comic turns at parties. Female drum-bearers appeared later and, by the end of the eighteenth century, they outnumbered male entertainers and were regulated as a distinct profession. Professional prostitution was alternately tolerated and abolished, the latter, finally, in 1957. Geishas were allowed to continue.

As usual, peasant women had both more freedom and more material misery than higher classes. Raising wet rice is very time-consuming and, until recently, was done entirely by human labor (as it still is in China). Both sexes grow rice, but women do most of the labor. They seed beds, then flood them; when the seeds sprout, they transplant seedlings from wet beds to wet fields. Traditionally, it was young women who transplanted, to transmit their fertility symbolically to the plants. They form a single line, bend, and push the plant roots into the soft mud at regular intervals. They must do so quickly, constantly bent over. They often sing, along with others singing and dancing along the embankments, and some rice-planting songs are very old. The Japanese are acutely aware of the quality of rice and revere rice-cultivators' way of life. They pay high prices for rice, rather than lower tariffs and admit cheaper imported rice. Rice is precious in Japan: in the Tokugawa, farmers could not afford to eat it.

Peasant women raised silk worms (sericulture) and other

crops. Women made silk, worked in textiles, wove, dyed, gathered seaweed, or dove for pearl oysters or abalone. A Victorian scholar wrote that poor women were never subjugated to the same degree as middle- and upper-class women: they had more liberty and higher status because they shared men's work and worries: "If she happen to have the better head of the two, she it is who will keep the purse and govern the family."[9] Most poor men were not harsh to their wives, especially in rice-cultivating or fishing families, because these occupations require cooperation.[10] Folk literature of this period is pervaded by nagging wives, and early twentieth-century sociological studies of remote villages show little male domination. But men bought peasant girls as prostitutes or slaves from impoverished fathers and brothers—a formerly forbidden negotiation.

Rebellion was difficult in the Tokugawa era, for armed uprisings were quickly squelched. Women too were denied escape: only a few managed to become nuns, do scholarly or literary work, or remain unmarried and carry on their family's craft or trade.

Near the end of the Tokugawa era, Nakagawa Miki, a hardworking, tenderhearted wife of a prosperous farmer, went into a trance that revealed her mission—to found a temple that would save the world. She founded a new religion, Tenrikyo, "church of heavenly reason," which the government and the police tried vainly to suppress. When her husband died, she gave away their possessions and roamed Japan in great poverty, preaching charity and cheerfulness. She helped so many women in childbirth (perhaps with psychological or herbal easements) that she became known as the goddess of safe childbirth. She was arrested or imprisoned twenty times between the ages of seventy-eight and eighty-nine; her ill-treatment earned her enormous attention and she even converted the police to her cause. One of her primary concerns was raising women's status: repudiating the idea of female pollution, she renamed menstruation "flowering." Tenrikyo, a form of Shintoism, now claims three million adherents in Japan, North and South America, Africa, and Southeast Asia. Priestesses head a third of its 15,500 churches, but men dominate its theoretical aspect, writing all the articles in official Tenri texts.

Other religions founded in Japan after the Tokugawa period—half of them founded or managed by women—have more than twenty million members today: Japanese women have reclaimed their ancient religious role. The Tokugawa shogunate, and feudalism, ended in 1868. By then, Japanese women were fixed in the subordination we associate with them, against which they still struggle today.[11]

PART TWO

EXPANSION AND
APPROPRIATION,
1500-1800

DURING THIS EXTRAORDINARY PERIOD in human history, people seemed to explode with restless energy. Patriarchy had
triumphed over most of the Western and Eastern worlds, but
much of the globe remained unknown and mysterious. As if
some mental shackle had burst, men suddenly rose up in curios-
ity and greed to explore and appropriate Africa, Southeast Asia
and the Pacific, and South, Central, and North America. Except
for North America, this territory is now called the Third World
or the South. In all of it, Europeans slaughtered indigenous
peoples and seized their land, their natural resources, and, sometimes, their bodies, in a frenzy of religious fanaticism and
capitalist greed. In a brief span the peoples of these territories
were subdued—enslaved or domesticated into servants—much
as women had been over a much longer period.

CHAPTER 3

CONTROL TIGHTENS
IN EUROPE

THE MODERN WORLD was formed in the sixteenth century.
Historians often call the years from the sixteenth through
the eighteenth centuries "the early modern world" because,
during that period, institutions like the family, the economy,
and the state took on the form that characterized them until,
approximately, the end of the Second World War. (The postwar
twentieth century is therefore often called the postmodern
world.) The changes that occurred in Europe in this period
affected the lives and thought of people across the globe, in a
preview of the present "global politics."

Politically, primarily feudal systems were gradually abandoned, as European states adopted centralized monarchies. An
insurgent bourgeoisie clamored for rights, which it sometimes
won. An economic system based on production for use—a
combination of self-sufficiency and barter—gave way to

production for profit, a largely capitalist money system. Large landowners turned self-sufficient manors into farms worked for profit and their serfs into wage laborers. Many serfs were cast off the land. At the same time, a new drive sent men exploring the globe. While most were motivated by profit and the search for riches, sometimes concealed by religious fervor, others were driven by a joy in expansion, an opening of the mind to the unknown.

Medieval Europeans, even the rich, lived in considerable discomfort—barons lived much like the poor. By the sixteenth century, more people owned more things, some even luxury goods. People had always suffered and died from war, disease, and famine, but now a new economic force intruded on them. Men transformed the old system of markets and created vast new ones, building huge personal fortunes at a terrible human cost. For the first time, a seething mass of destitute homeless people, most of them women, appeared in Europe, and economic, political, and social differences between the sexes widened. The traditional system of family production in Europe persisted into the twentieth century, but where the new system took hold, only men could earn a living wage. Women were increasingly restricted to unpaid production at home, domestic maintenance, and reproduction. Only poor women worked for pay, receiving wages too small to sustain them.

Perhaps most important was the psychological explosion, the bursting of some psychic restraint or bond to family, community, deity, church, or even to the earth itself. In a liberated mood, men sought knowledge for the power it provided. They challenged old beliefs and generated new philosophical positions, scientific research, political revolutions, and exploration of the globe. They set out on expeditions to probe and acquire the world. Humans had long had ships that could sail the widest oceans, but until the sixteenth century they lacked the impulse to use them in this way.[1] Now they sailed to places they had not known of, places that had for millennia followed their own traditions, and they brought their linear, aggressive Western thinking with them. Their arrival changed the host countries irrevocably.

This explosion, at once material, intellectual, and moral, was an expression of what I call the "masculine mystique," as a parallel to Betty Friedan's "feminine mystique." Friedan's term refers to the discrepancy between the reality of women's lives and their image of a proper woman's life. The masculine mystique is precisely the same: the false image of men as motivated by a drive for power more important to them than life itself. To live by a mystique is to live in bad faith, to live a false life. For both sexes, trying to live out an image makes life miserable.

Reality is inconsequential to gender rules, which is why they are so rigid. The male myth promises men transcendence of human vulnerabilities through domination (so, for instance, when a Chaka man is initiated, he claims he no longer defecates). If a man has enough power, he is freed from the vulnerabilities and fears that haunt lesser men. From Coriolanus, who did not feel his wounds in battle, to Stalin at the height of his power, locked in the Kremlin, friendless, loveless, and with a taster for his food lest it be poisoned, this myth is a delusion. It makes the fateful assumption that power is a good, ignoring the isolation, fear, and paranoia that follow in its wake. The masculine mystique transforms ends into means: people, relationships, pursuits, and abilities become mere objects to control. Even worthy enterprises are infected by the use to which they are put. Without other ends, satisfaction is impossible.

The masculine mystique did not arise in the sixteenth century; it is as old as patriarchy. But whereas it guided a few men in earlier periods, in the sixteenth century it became wide-spread, affecting lowly men and high; men advanced scientific rationality with messianic zeal, suggesting that the mechanical world view was "a crusade against the irrational, the mystical, and the feminine."[2] By our period, power has become the most desirable goal on earth, one women, too, adopt as the dominant value. Regardless of women's collusion with or opposition to men, men identify women with the elements that the myth insists men repudiate: weakness, vulnerability, and the transiency associated with the body, emotions, and nature.

European women were affected, in turn, by the Reformation, the witch hunts in Europe and beyond, changes in the nature of work, and their near-total imprisonment within the family. But even as their rights were being increasingly nullified, women were laying the foundations for revolt. At the end of this period, women participated in revolutions in America and France, and, for the first time in history, protested their status as women, as a caste.

Early Modern Europe

After the plague receded, the population of Europe grew wildly, mainly in cities: by the sixteenth century Lyon had 60,000 inhabitants and Paris, 100,000. No one knows why, but more women than men lived in cities—about 110–20 women to every 100 men. For millennia, society had been supported almost entirely by agriculture, by the lowly, scorned peasant. As manufacturing and commerce became a new source of wealth, a new class developed, the middle class. Growing larger and stronger, it squirmed under the rule of the princes of the church and state and began to protest.

The Reformation

Religious groups had challenged the church since the twelfth century, complaining of clerical abuses. They urged the church to live like Jesus, as an entirely spiritual body. Some thought Christians should live in poverty; others, like the Cathars, thought they should eschew sex. Many urged dissolving the church hierarchy, saying that priests were ignorant, corrupt, and negligent and that religious authority was intolerable. Others were outraged that the church taxed (and thus profited from) priests who kept concubines or used prostitutes. A quarter of all Dutch priests had concubines or wives; Strasbourg and Geneva clergy were noted for their free sexual behavior. Few people attended mass, and when cities grew and parishes doubled or tripled in size, the church did not assign more priests or insure that those in place knew their parishioners' dialect. Women especially were inactive in religion: the heart of lay religious activity was male confraternities.[3] In fellowships organized by craft or ritual, laymen held masses, banquets, and processions. To heighten the sense of belonging, most confraternities excluded women, even their wives and daughters. Of thirty-seven confraternities in Rouen between 1500 and 1550, only six had any female members.

In 1517 Martin Luther (1483–1546), a German priest intent on reforming the church, nailed a document containing ninety-five "theses," or points of argument, to the church door at Wittenberg. He denied the pope's right to forgive sins and the Catholic doctrine of salvation by works, for he believed that salvation came from grace alone; he also condemned the sale of indulgences as a way to obtain forgiveness for sins. Luther's dramatic act launched a series of religious protests and revolutions that swept Europe. Church and state were one, despite frequent conflicts between them, so any reform of religion meant reforming the state as well. The Swiss Huldreich Zwingli, the French John Calvin, and the Scots John Knox joined the protesters, or protestants.

A sect of Anabaptists emerged in the Low Countries, Germany, and Switzerland. Believing that religion was a matter of free choice and that only adults were capable of choosing a faith, they opposed baptizing children. They believed in religious tolerance, communal sharing, and community autonomy. Since a community owed no loyalty to any state but itself, its members should refuse to do military service or hold public office. But Anabaptists had contradictory views about women: they accepted them as priests, but some groups practiced polygyny; they sanctioned the laws of an Anabaptist community in Münster, Germany, which allowed men to execute their wives for insubordination and decreed that all women between certain ages must marry or be expelled or executed.

Protestant sects proliferated: Baptists and Congregationalists, for instance, separated from the mainstream. Quakerism and Methodism, founded in the seventeenth and eighteenth centuries, each had a distinct character but believed that salvation came from divine grace, generated by faith, not good works, and that Scripture, not church law and priestly interpretation, should guide Christian life. Such a premise implies equality, and Protestants stressed "the priesthood of all believers." They opposed the privileges and powers of the church hierarchy, insisting that a church is a community of believers with an unmediated relation to god. Protestants also altered the traditional Christian view of sex.

It was taken for granted in medieval thought that women were more sexual than men and had little control over their lasciviousness; men could control their erotic drives, remaining abstinent, if women were not present to tempt them. This presumed difference in libido was the basis for rules constricting and excluding women. Many Protestants, though puritanical about sex, body, and pleasure, did not accept the Catholic teaching that renouncing sex was "higher" and purer than practicing it. And priests' sexual behavior had demonstrated that men were no better than women at renunciation. So Protestants believed that the clergy should marry: indeed, they insisted that everyone should marry.

Great numbers of priests left Catholicism to join the reformers, but most nuns refused to leave their convents. Given the economic constrictions on women, they had little to go to. In regions they controlled, Protestants abolished convents and expelled nuns against their will. They scoffed at convents as dumping grounds for unwanted daughters and dismissed nuns' reluctance to leave, charging that they wanted to stay for frenzied sexual promiscuity. Genevan authorities simply transported nuns to the nearest Catholic region, while English nuns were given pensions and sent back to their families.[4] When Protestants tried to close Swedish convents, there was such an outcry that the government was forced to maintain them on the condition they accept no new novices. Many nuns suffered greatly from no place to go, for no communities of single women replaced the convents.

To join a Protestant sect in the early years was to make a marked political choice. Most women who did were of middle-level urban society: some joined with their husbands, but others joined on their own. Many female French converts were independent—small entrepreneurs, widows, and eccentric market women drawn by the same lure that always draws women to religion: the promise of more freedom and autonomy, and a chance to use their talents.[5] If grace alone brought salvation, if anyone might receive it, and if the Scripture taught and refined faith, then each person had to read the Bible and women had the right to think and speak for themselves. Licensing clerical marriage also somehow redeemed women.

Protestant sects advanced an ideal of sexual equality, as the priesthood of all believers superseded the church hierarchy. Protestants integrated some activities, letting the sexes worship and sing together in church choirs and abolishing confraternities. Believing that girls should be able to read, so that as mothers they could teach their children religion, Protestants set up reading classes for poor girls and women in the cities.

Both Protestant and Catholic churches wanted women members, but at the same time they despised the female sex and used women as a target in their struggle for power. Catholic men called Protestantism a "woman's religion," appealing to people with weak wills, feeble intellects, and a tendency towards heresy. Protestant men saw Catholicism as appealing to ignorant, superstitious, sexually unbridled women. For men on both sides, the worst fact about the other religion was its appeal to women.

To combat the Protestant Reformation, the Catholic Church reformed its practices and set up inquisitional courts to sniff out heresy, thereby initiating the Counterreformation. Religion flavored sixteenth-century wars: Catholic and Protestant states battled each other with ferocity and a conviction of their own rightness. As riots ripped cities, Catholics attacked Protestants or their churches, and Protestants defaced Catholic churches. The persecutions were extraordinarily cruel, creating martyrs on both sides.

In England the state religion fluctuated with the monarch in power. Henry VIII split from Rome early in the sixteenth century when he wanted to divorce Katharine of Aragon; his son, Edward VII, only ten years old when he acceded, tended towards Protestantism under an uncle's influence. When he died at sixteen, Henry's daughter Mary Tudor acceded. Although she had been forced to disavow her religion, Mary was Catholic, like her mother Katharine. She married a prince of Spain (an ardently Catholic country) under whose influence she re-established papal authority in England and began to persecute Protestants. By the time of her death five years later, she was known as "Bloody Mary." The great Elizabeth I then acceded and tried, over her long, wise rule, to end persecution, mediating warily between Catholics and reformist Puritans, who wished to extirpate all Catholic elements from the English Church. Elizabeth executed Mary, Queen of Scots, in an attempt to eliminate a center for Catholic agitation.

A Protestant revolt against Spain in the years 1568–78 led to civil war in the Netherlands. In France, to reconcile the Catholics and the Calvinist Huguenots, Margaret of Valois, the sister of the French king Charles IX, was affianced to the Huguenot Henry of Navarre. The wedding drew hundreds of Huguenots to Paris, including their leader, Gaspard de Coligny. On the eve of the wedding, St. Bartholemew's Day, August 24, 1572, Catherine de Medicis ordered Henry of Guise, the leader of the Catholic aristocrats, to murder Coligny. In the ensuing riots, the Huguenot gentry were nearly wiped out and, in the provinces, 12,000 French Huguenots were killed.

Women took part in this turmoil. To declare herself a Protestant, a woman needed only to avoid church on Catholic feast days, replace her hoop skirt with a plain black dress, and join a reading group for Bible study with Protestant friends.[6] Bolder women printed and distributed Protestant pamphlets, held illegal Protestant assemblies in their homes, joined street marches, sang prohibited marching songs, and dug foundations for Protestant churches. Hundreds of Protestant women cornered priests in the streets to harangue them; crowds smashed religious statues and baptismal fonts. Some Huguenots fled to England or Geneva, the Protestant strongholds; others went to war, bearing arms for their god; and many died at the stake, claiming the joys of martyrdom.

Catholic Frenchwomen formed all-female groups to throw stones at Protestant women, clumps of mud at Protestant pastors, and, once, in Aix-en-Provence, to beat and hang the wife of a Protestant bookseller. They joined the Ursulines, the Sisters of Charity, and the Christian Institutes of Mary Ward to do good works. Across the English Channel, Catholic women hid priests in their houses, held secret and illegal masses in their homes, and joined the "underground railroad" to help priests move through the country to celebrate mass—and were executed.

Religious men often did not appreciate the behavior of religious women. Catholic clergymen were most outraged by the act most often cited in the Protestant literature of the period—a pure, simple Protestant woman refuting a priest by quoting Scripture. But when Protestant women argued with their own pastors, the Protestants had a turn at outrage. Marie Dentière, an abbess in Tournai expelled from her convent for heresy, married a Protestant pastor and emigrated to Geneva, which was in an upheaval over religion. When she visited the Poor Clares there to exhort them to abandon their convent, they spat at her. Undaunted, Marie continued to preach and publish religious works, including a defence of women against attacks by both Catholic and Protestant clergy. The pastors were horrified. Marie always claimed she was preaching to women only, but women prisoners preached to both sexes in jails, women got up in pulpits and read from the Bible, and one woman argued publicly with her pastor. A movement began in Paris to permit lay preachers (women and unlearned men) to prophesy.

At root, Protestant leaders were not really concerned with women except as a force to be used. John Calvin, the mildest of the major leaders, said woman had been created subject to man and should accept her inferiority "to the more distinguished sex." Luther considered sex pleasing to god, but said of women: "Let them bear children until they are dead of it; that is what they are for." John Knox, furious at Mary Tudor, wrote a tract, *First Blast against the Monstrous Regiment of Women*, which described female rulers as "visitations of God's anger." Shortly after he published it in 1558, Mary died; Elizabeth I, who succeeded to the British throne, never forgave Knox his attack, even though it was not directed at her.

The Effects on Women of Religious and Social Changes

When the conflicts were over, England, Scotland, the Netherlands, the Scandinavian countries, and northern Germany were Protestant, and Spain, Italy, France, Belgium, and southern Germany were Catholic. For women, both the Protestant Reformation and the Catholic Counterreformation had mixed consequences. Protestants permitted no female communities, convents, or religious orders, no place for women who wanted to live without men. The Protestants denied power to the saints and the Virgin Mary, eliminating the few female figures that Christians could beg for intervention. Calvin advised women in childbed, used to calling on Mary and Saint Margaret for help, to groan and sigh to the Lord. Men too lost male saints, but they retained a male god. Protestant women were forbidden to organize orders devoted to social welfare.

For a brief period, the Catholic states allowed women to found new orders again. In 1535 Angela Merici founded the

Ursulines to teach girls, but the church eventually forced them to adopt a rule, wear special clothing, and live cloistered. Still the order spread and survived. Englishwoman Mary Ward founded the Institute of the Blessed Virgin Mary in Belgium for the same purpose. Hounded by the Jesuits and the papacy (see volume 1, chapter 10), it disbanded officially in 1629 but went underground, resurfacing in 1840 with church approval. In 1634 Vincent de Paul and Louise de Marillac founded the Daughters of Charity. Their careful strategy allowed this group to escape papal suppression and to grow into the first female order devoted to nursing and social work.

In the private sphere, women benefited from Protestantism mainly in principle. Since everyone had to marry, Protestants tried to make marriage a more companionable, mutual relationship. In Geneva, however, Protestants took over the government and established consistories, councils of middle-class men who took on the job of policing society for violations of marriage and sumptuary laws. Here, as in many other Protestant states, laws limited consumption, forbade dancing, card playing, and excessive drinking, required austere living, public fasting, and avoidance of fashionable clothes, and penalized "overdressed" men and, later, women. For the first time in history, men who beat their wives were called before a governing body. Irked at this infringement on their prerogative, men grumbled that they would beat their wives if they chose. However, the Geneva Consistory was effective enough that, by the end of the century, the city was often called a "women's Paradise." Yet it threatened men guilty of wife beating only with loss of communion, while punishing women who scolded their husbands with three days in prison on bread and water.

The Protestants made an important innovation in sexual rules, asserting the right of wives to divorce. Catholic canon law accepted that both partners could initiate separation or annulment in principle, but, in practice, it considered only male claims legitimate. Unhappily married women were further trapped by their inability to support themselves and their children. At first, consistories were gender-blind in judging cases of sexual offence—Calvin urged "differentiated equality," an avoidance of "male tyranny" and "female autonomy." Between 1564 and 1569, of 320 inhabitants of Geneva banished for marital problems, 56 percent were men. But by the early seventeenth century the status quo was back: men who had sex outside marriage were given reduced sentences, while "unchaste" women were whipped through the streets and banished. Eighteenth-century Geneva averaged one divorce a year; and England, from 1670 to 1799, granted only 131 divorces, mostly to nobles wanting second wives to bear sons.

The establishment of schools for girls did not immediately help. In the 1560s–70s, only 28 percent of elite Frenchwomen could sign their names, and lower-class women were illiterate. French municipal colleges taught only boys, as did most Parisian schoolmasters. Elite men and artisans—printers, goldsmiths, surgeons—could read and write, and male leather and textile workers were fairly literate. Only unskilled male workers and women were illiterate. On the eve of the French Revolution in 1789, 65 percent of men and 35 percent of women in France were literate. More women in England than in France were literate at the end of the eighteenth century. After Marie Dentière's tracts in 1538, no book by a woman was published in Geneva for the rest of the century. After the Reformation, women published under pseudonyms, for the first time in history.

As centralized control and male dominance increased in late medieval Europe, a compulsion to uniformity emerged. In many places, the state or the church persecuted "heretics," Jews, Muslims, homosexuals, lepers, single women, and other "deviants." The church so disliked poverty that it suppressed "poor" orders, came close to declaring the Franciscan order heretical, and wiped out the Knights Templar, a military religious order, burning their leaders. It eradicated the Albigensians and suppressed beguines. Under its banner, soldiers in the first crusade slaughtered thousands of Jews in the Rhineland before going on to Jerusalem; later, many states expelled Jews or forced them either to convert or to wear yellow badges. Jewish ghettos, like the first one in Venice, were set up to protect Jews from mobs. Some cities banished lepers and persecuted homosexuals: Edward II of England, the last openly gay king, was deposed and killed by a red-hot poker thrust up his anus; his lover was castrated and killed.

After the Reformation/Counterreformation, pastors no less than priests expanded the repressions: consistories exercised surveillance over private life as the Inquisition did over religious belief. Historians hypothesize that the period was anxious because of the plague, climatic changes, and dislocations attendant on a shift from an agricultural to a manufacturing base. Increased controls only heightened this anxiety.

Churches extended control over marriage. Before the Reformation, most weddings were informal; sometimes a couple simply agreed that they were married. The betrothal of John and Marjory in 1371 has no promise to "obey" or any mention of god.[7] Standing with friends, John Beke, a saddler,

> Called . . . Marjory to him and said to her, "Marjory, do you wish to be my wife?" And she replied, "I will if you wish." And taking at once the said Marjory's right hand, John said, "Marjory, here I take you as my wife,

for better or worse, to have and to hold until the end of my life; and of this I give you my faith." The said Marjory replied to him, "Here I take you John as my husband, to have and to hold until the end of my life, and of this I give you my faith." And then the said John kissed the said Marjory through a wreath of flowers.

Protestant theologians transformed marriage into a complex public ceremony. They decreed that betrothal was not valid unless witnessed by two adults, and a marriage not legal without a church ceremony. Catholics followed suit. Until the 1750s, however, there was no standard wedding ceremony. Church law recognized the marriage of very young people if both consented. Under pressure from propertied men, states overruled the church to give fathers more control. This change affected mainly the children of the well-to-do: poorer children had much voice in their mates.[8] Even among the rich, though, many young people were fatherless—since most people died by thirty.

The Pastons, British fifteenth-century landed gentry, are famous for their letters, written by a husband who was usually away from home and a wife who ran the estate. They show great affection between the couple, but less for their daughter, who wanted to marry their bailiff. They cruelly pressured her, haranguing, threatening, and even beating her. In the end, she won. In the eighteenth century, Lady Mary Wortley Montagu wrote that she had been hectored, locked up, and threatened with forced marriage to her parents' choice. Anne Wortley, another eighteenth-century heiress, wrote: "People in my way are sold like slaves; and I cannot tell what price my master will put on me."[9] In 1753 Britain decreed that marriages of people under twenty-one, without consent, were illegal. For centuries,

England had permitted divorce in cases of adultery, desertion, long absence, or extreme incompatibility; by the end of the Reformation, remarriage after divorce required a special parliamentary act for each case.

Marriage patterns differed in northern and southern Europe. In the north, most newlyweds set up their own households, so needed property—a piece of land, a house, and agricultural and domestic tools. Both partners were expected to contribute to the household. Young women had to wait until their parents died to inherit enough to marry or, if the parents were poor, to earn the money to set up a household. Girls entered domestic service at eight and worked to twenty-four or -five to earn enough to buy a bed, some linens, and a few pots and pans. Boys worked and saved to buy a piece of land with a house. Most had to work until twenty-seven or older before they could marry. Such couples did not have large families because of the late marriage age, birth control (many couples practiced *coitus interruptus*), infanticide, and early death. There was either little sexual intercourse outside of marriage or use of some form of abortion, for illegitimacy rates were very low.

In the south, especially in Italy, families lived in clans, and sons were married in their mid-twenties to girls of seventeen or eighteen chosen by their parents. Women were traded between families to cement alliances. Even peasants' daughters were pawns in a complex traffic in women. Never having had independence, women did not lose it in marriage, but they did lose identity in the transfer from one family to another. Conflicts between families tore their loyalties, and men blamed women for being unreliable, unfaithful, wavering, unstable, and fickle—*la donna mobile*.

As trade and commerce grew, fathers tended to give daughters cash dowries, not land; when they died, daughters got no inheritance and their husbands' families controlled their dowries. The families, not wanting widowed daughters-in-law to remarry and remove these dowries, exerted great pressure on them to stay within the marital family. Many widows were very young because they had been married as girls to older men. In the sixteenth century, most widows in England soon remarried, often to widowers; by the late eighteenth century, many were left without means and never remarried. In the intervening years, for the first time, two-thirds of the poorest group in society were widows.

In the mid-eighteenth century, 30 percent of the daughters of Scottish nobles never married. Aristocratic fathers wanted to increase the "family" wealth and married their sons to the daughters of wealthy commoners rather than those of their own class. But noblewomen could not marry "down." Single women of the propertied classes had no way to support themselves and had to live as dependents in their brothers' houses: the only way women could gain economic security and adult status was to marry. Huge numbers of women lacked both during this period: 14 percent of Frenchwomen born between 1784 and 1789 remained spinsters (women who died after fifty without having married), as did 40 percent of the female population of eighteenth-century Lyon. Celibacy was commoner in cities, where women outnumbered men, than in the countryside.

The Effects on Women of Economic Change

Women were essential in trade as their husbands' indispensable partners, as they had been in the Middle Ages. A guildmaster's wife ran the shop when her husband was away and usually took it over if he died. Widows ran iron-mongering and roofing shops and lighter crafts—10 to 15 percent of the shops in any craft. But the work a woman did depended not on her training or skill but on her relationship to a man. In the mid-1400s, wherever they faced competition, guilds began to limit widows' rights. First, they restricted a widow to finishing only work already begun and allowed her to take over the business only if she had a son to inherit it. By the mid-1500s, most guilds forbade widows from hiring new apprentices or journeymen and sometimes from keeping those they had. Widows' workshops became too poor to support a woman, much less her family. Widows begged for relief, but men indulged only those who pleaded weakness, thereby reinforcing men's conviction of women's incapacity.

The craft guilds grew meaner because they were suffering. Merchants had invented a new system: they bought raw materials, transported them to the country, and hired rural workers to finish the product on a piece-work basis. This "putting-out" system circumvented guild regulations and drew work from the guilds.

Women turned to manufactures that were not regulated by guilds. These were the cheapest products: soap, candles, thimbles, brooms, brushes, needles, pins, combs, and wooden bowls and spoons. They made such items in their "spare time" (after doing field work or laundry all day or working as porters), because any work that women were allowed to do paid too little to support them. Except in cities where the guilds controlled cloth production, women everywhere worked in it. Guilds gradually eliminated women from weaving, draping, tailoring, and cloth cutting. Widows and single women were allowed to produce only the cheap cloth used by women, like veiling. Male authorities were determined to keep women from living independently; more and more, carding wool and spinning, which paid a pittance, became women's work. It fit into the discontinuous rhythms of women's lives—it could be picked up or put down while she rocked her baby's cradle with her foot or waited for the soup to boil.

City councils expected jailed women to spin and prostitutes to spin between customers. A young woman of extraordinary education was presented to James I of England: she wrote and spoke fluently Latin, Greek, and Hebrew. He asked, "But can she spin?" Merry Wiesner writes of an eighty-year-old widow with only one hand who still spun, and a suicidal woman in Memmingen who was chained to her hospital bed in such a way that she could still spin.

Famines and shortages provoked riots over the price of bread. In times of starvation, men abandoned their families or sent their children to seek work as servants or apprentices or to become vagrants. Desperate families exposed new infants, and during food shortages in 1693–94 and 1709–10 parents abandoned children as old as seven. In Aix-en-Provence they regularly placed children in orphanages when they couldn't feed them, sometimes only temporarily.

Working as hard as they did, women had little time for children. A woman spent roughly two-thirds of her married life pregnant or nursing a new baby. Among the upper classes, babies were sent to wet-nurses at their husbands' command. City women who worked for wages in ateliers or in food businesses also sent their babies to wet-nurses in the country. Wet-nursing gave poor rural women a way to earn some money and kept city women working. But the practice ended when city businesses enlarged and putting-out spread in the countryside. Children not sent to a wet-nurse to be raised might be put into service or apprenticed at the age of seven or eight; expected to work hard and not always fed well, they were sometimes punished extremely harshly by their masters and mistresses. Some went into the lace industry, which employed mostly girls from five to fifteen, many of whom ended up blind.

Infant mortality was very high: about a quarter of the children in French villages died in their first year, and another quarter before they reached twenty. The average age at death was thirty, though more women than men died during childbearing years. Undernourished women became infertile or had trouble conceiving, and they were more likely to miscarry, have a stillbirth or a weak baby, or die during childbirth. Many marriages ended early because of death.

Some historians have minimized the effect of children's deaths on parents, arguing that they protected themselves by not loving their children fully. The records of a seventeenth-century British healer suggest otherwise. The Reverend Richard Napier, a theologian, astrologer, alchemist, and conjurer, was mainly a healer and, like most ancient healers, he treated ills of the mind and body without distinguishing between them. His fees were so low that the poor could consult him. His casebooks show that about 3000 of his 60,000 consultations involved ills we would call psychological, over 2000 of them in women.[10] Equal numbers of women and men were upset at economic problems and unhappy courtships, but about half the women despaired at oppression and beatings by cruel or drunken husbands and fathers or "searing grief" at losing a child.

Until the late fifteenth century, women physicians appeared on community citizens' lists. Increasingly, however, only men who had studied medicine at a university were called "physician." Barber-surgeons and apothecaries who had completed formal apprenticeship had always been considered professionals, but in this period female barber-surgeons disappeared from official records. Authorities allowed some women to handle minor problems like eye infections, skin diseases, or boils, so long as they charged low fees and didn't advertise. But even this level of activity distressed male physicians, who claimed that female practitioners damaged the status of their profession. Some men argued that god had not given women such talents, so women who practiced medicine must have learned it from the devil.

In England, the sixteenth-century enclosure movement shrank the number of farms. "Enclosure"—fencing open land for sheep pasture—was intended to produce more wool for the textile industry, which employed many people. But it dislocated and dispossessed families that had lived on a manor for centuries and needed land to survive. Landowning aristocrats controlling Parliament passed hundreds of "enclosure acts" abolishing village commons—common green spaces where poor people like widows could graze their one cow. By 1700, half of England's farmland was closed in, despite farmers' protests and struggles: there were about two landless farm workers for every landed farmer. Thousands of independent, self-sufficient families were reduced to day labor; marginal, vulnerable to any crisis, they worked for wages on large farms, in the putting-out system, or as domestic servants.

The wives of landless men worked as hired hands, domestic textile workers, or both. The survival of a farm laborer's family depended on the wife's ability to earn wages. Most women did needlework—spun, made lace, sewed, knitted stockings, plaited straw, made gloves—raised vegetables, or tended animals at home. In seventeenth-century England, 100,000 women and children made lace; altogether, the clothing trades employed a million women and children. Spinning paid as little as 5 sous a day in Picardy in the late seventeenth century. Male weavers earned twice that.

Small farmers increasingly left their holdings to the oldest son, forcing younger sons and daughters to go to cities to find work. There, lacking a family network to protect them, they were open to exploitation. The overwhelming majority of girls entered domestic service, doing the dirtiest and most onerous chores in return for room, board, and a pittance at year's end—at death, many owned nothing but the clothes they were buried in.

Female servants, who were often required to fill male employers' sexual demands or take their sons' virginity, were severely penalized if they became pregnant. In parts of Germany, mother and child were integrated into a family and given inheritance rights, but in most of Europe, pregnant servants were generally cast out, with no place to live, no job, and no way to survive. George Crabbe's poems in *The Borough* powerfully render the plight of such mothers—often children themselves—in rural England. Some were forced to give birth in religious or charitable hospitals, extremely unhealthy places dreaded as symbols of poverty and death, which pressured women in labor to reveal the fathers' names. But if women gave birth without a witness and had stillbirths, they were accused of infanticide.

Once a woman bore an "illegitimate" child, she had few options but prostitution. In the Middle Ages, most large urban centers had municipal brothels that regulated prostitutes, protecting them from violence and severe exploitation. But during the Reformation, religious authorities closed the brothels and forcibly ejected the prostitutes. Prostitution continued, but now women were prosecuted for it, not protected.

Women had to be married, and men grew increasingly concerned with girls' virginity and wives' chastity. To force women to marry, authorities made their independence almost impossible: women were allowed only the most menial and lowest-paid work; they were "proletarianized." But not all women could marry: there were more women than men, and women tended to outlive men. Single women living alone in cities made up a quarter to a third of all households. We know of their existence because they were listed as too poor to pay taxes. Living in rented rooms, cellars, or attics, they made simple objects the government let them manufacture and sell or did laundry, earning barely enough to survive. These facts were ignored in the drive to uniformity and control. Extending state power over women, men forbade them to appear in court, as they had earlier; in many cities, city councils appointed guardians to appear in court for women. Guardians also decided if remarried widows could keep their children.

Increasingly, authorities passed laws aimed at unemployed people—"masterless" journeymen, vagrants, day laborers, mercenary soldiers, camp followers, beggars, itinerant actors, and musicians. Officials feared these people intensely and built institutions to confine them. Simply ignoring what the enclosure movement did to people, a 1630 British royal commission declared: "These people live like savages, and are neither married, buried, or baptized; and it is this licentious freedom that has caused so many to find pleasure in vagabondage." At first the new institutions were called "houses of correction"; later, "workhouses." Germany built its first *Zuchthaus* in 1620. By the seventeenth century, confinement was common.[11] Of a Paris population of 100,000, 10 percent were interned and over 30 percent were beggars.

Asylums for housing the insane confined mainly single, jobless people. Authorities claimed that the interned were unwilling to work and lived in wild, unattached vagabondage by choice; their wildness threatened public order and decency. In truth, such people could not find work, and officials feared they would rebel, especially in times of economic crisis. The married were rarely confined: authorities saw marriage as tantamount to an oath to uphold the state's order, to work, and to eschew the vice of idleness: the male-headed married household was the primary institution for social control. But independent women aroused anxiety: in late fifteenth-century Metz, an ordinance decreed that "all married women living apart from their husbands, and girls of evil life, shall go to the brothels."[12] Insisting that marriage was women's only "natural vocation," Protestants called women without men "masterless." New German and French laws forbade single women from moving to cities, required widows to move in with a son, and obliged single women to live with male relatives or employers.

The Witch Trials

It was in this climate that the witch hunts began. It is natural for people to hate and fear their oppressors, yet many also identify with and even love their oppressors and become complicit with them. But oppressors, probably from a mixture of guilt and fear of reprisal, also hate and fear those they oppress and impute their negative emotions to their victims. Over history, women have generally been more complicit than rebellious towards men and have shown more love than hate as they took care of children and men and contributed to the institutions of their society. No data suggest that women have grown more rebellious. It is likely that, as men gradually strangled women, women's guilt and fear increased.

Educational institutions recognized only orthodox knowledge and considered the kinds of knowledge women possessed to be sinister and subversive. Mothers taught daughters about herbs and healing, or methods of easing labor pain and causing abortion. Women knowledgeable in these areas were called "cunning women" or "blessing witches." Sixteenth-century Scots used the terms *wise woman* and *witch* interchangeably.

Male physicians, who were university trained, tried to drive women from all areas of expertise; they targeted wise women, accusing them of witchcraft. The hunt to track down deviance had extended to "masterless women," or women alone—widows, poor women, old women, especially poor old women with a bit of land. But the witch hunts had to make all women anxious: even in regions where no witches had been burned, women feared gathering in groups lest they arouse suspicion of witchcraft.[13]

Just as male authorities were declaring witchcraft "the single greatest threat to Christian European civilization," the *Malleus Maleficarum* (The Witches' Hammer) appeared. Published in 1486 by two Dominican inquisitors, it asserted that witchcraft existed, especially among women. The Dominicans had tried fifty people as witches, all but two of them women. That witches exist is doctrine, they said; not to believe in them, heresy. That they are female is self-evident: "Where there are many women there are many witches. . . . When a woman thinks alone, she thinks evil. . . . There are three things in nature, the Tongue, an Ecclesiastic, and a Woman, which know no moderation in goodness or vice. . . . I have found a woman more bitter than death and a good woman subject to carnal lust." Women are witches because, like Eve, they are "feebler both in mind and body" than men, more impressionable, credulous, and carnal. Formed from a bent rib, they are defective; their slippery tongues cannot keep silent. The Inquisitors gave a false derivation for the word *woman* from the Latin *femina* as *fe-minus*, "of lesser faith." Without even a glimmer of insight, they linked women's subversiveness to their economic and political dispossession: because women hate being weak and not able to rule, they asserted, women become a "wheedling and secret enemy" who always deceives and is vengeful, bitter, and open to "an easy and secret manner of vindicating themselves." In other words, witchcraft.[14]

The printing press that put the Bible in the hands of lay people also gave them the *Malleus*, which was swallowed whole by the most advanced thinkers in Europe. In 1487 the Theological Faculty of the University of Cologne endorsed it. Sixteen editions were published in the next thirty-odd years, and sixteen more by 1660, with translations into French and German. In 1490 French authorities passed laws condemning witches to prison or to death. Scotland, Russia, Denmark, and England soon followed.

Even before the appearance of the *Malleus*, Christian male physicians had moved to eliminate women from the profession, insinuating that even trained female physicians were witches and urging that they be fined and imprisoned. Informally trained healers were even more vulnerable: male doctors accused them of giving women contraceptives, abortions, and ergot to ease labor pain in violation of church law. Doctors wanted medicine to gain the prestige that law and theology possessed, so they excluded women to further that goal. In their campaign to label women and Jews professors of magic and allies of the devil, they took a high moral and intellectual line, allying themselves with God and the Law.

Members of "heretical" sects like the Albigensians or private prayer circles were also accused of witchcraft. Most of those killed were women who were old, poor, and alone—without men—women who did not fit the mold, and marginal or outcast women like priests' former concubines, prostitutes, diviners, and herdswomen.[15] Men were pushing single women into starvation, and old poor women were in trouble. An old woman might go to a neighbor's door begging for food or help and be turned away with scorn, curses, and a blow. She might retort by cursing; if, later, the milk soured or the baby fell ill, the guilt-ridden neighbors believed she had caused the ill.[16] Witches were accused of making men impotent, devouring newborn babies, turning neighbors' milk sour, keeping their butter from setting, making cattle die, and causing children to fall ill. A male relative who coveted a woman's bit of land might accuse her. At the same time, both Protestants and Catholics crusaded against single mothers charged with infanticide. A husband's right to order a newborn killed was accepted, and laws forbidding infanticide were directed only at women, women alone, "masterless"—the majority of those accused of witchcraft.[17]

The church set up inquisitional courts to sniff out heresy. They always offered victims a choice between the stake and submission to the Catholic Church; since many people submitted, the Inquisition, infamous though it was, executed far fewer people than secular courts. Italy and Spain, where the Inquisition dominated, persecuted and burned Jews and Muslims but few witches. Spain tried many women, but burned only eleven "witches"; tolerant Holland burned almost no witches; and England, which did not permit torture, also killed comparatively few women.

The tortures were terrible: stretching on the rack, the *strapado* (being hung by the arms above the ground, so the shoulders dislocated), or a chair with a spiked metal seat that could be heated. Tortured women confessed to rendezvous with the Devil, flying on sticks to black masses, killing babies by spells and potions, fornications with imaginary animals, and other macabre inventions. Little girls were charged and burned. Men were accused, but they were in the minority: 85 percent of those killed were female.

Estimates of how many were killed by Protestant authorities start at 100,000, but many regions have not been studied. The witch trials began in Austria—Austria and southern Germany, Bavaria, and Switzerland burned more women than anywhere else. Germany and Bavaria were each responsible for at least 3500 deaths. Some German cities killed six hundred a year; the Wurzburg region, nine hundred in a year; in Como, a thousand. In Toulouse, four hundred women were killed in a day; in the bishopric of Trier in 1585, two villages were left with only one female inhabitant each. The craze spread along the trade routes to England, Scotland, Scandinavia, Spain, Russia, and Italy: thousands of women were tried, tortured, and cruelly killed. In London, a Scotsman confessed to causing the deaths of over 220 women; people paid him 21 shillings to accuse a woman.

As it waned in Western Europe, the craze hit Poland, which burned the second greatest number of witches. In the late sixteenth century the mania escalated out of control, as women began accusing their judges of witchcraft! The chief prosecutor of witches in Rottenburg confessed and was executed. When male officials were named, the learned men who had begun the craze, and under whose aegis it had continued, decided to end it. Refusing to hear new cases or use torture or execute, they declared eccentricity an illness rather than the devil's work. But the frenzy crossed the Atlantic to New England, and trials continued in Spain into the seventeenth century, in Poland into the mid-eighteenth century, and Russia into the nineteenth century.

Unvanquished Women

Some women could not accept the place patriarchy assigned them; others managed to fulfill themselves within it. Near the end of the period, a few challenged the premises of their oppression. Many women in the Early Modern Period achieved success in business.[18] A Genevan entrepreneur with good connections and business acumen made a small fortune. Genevan widows could go on producing in their husbands' name if they obeyed guild rules and used male labor in their shops. The resourceful Glückel of Hameln bore thirteen children, raised twelve (an amazing survival rate), worked with her husband in a jewelry and brokerage business (and alone after he died), and arranged her children's marriages. She also wrote her *Memoirs*.[19]

Unlike Frenchwomen, elite Englishwomen retained traditional class rights to govern state, manors, manorial courts, and hold local elective office; some could even vote. Emerging radical religions in the seventeenth century accepted women as full members, able to debate, preach, vote, and prophesy. One sect, the Levellers, wanted to abolish rank and establish a democratic state—but one in which women could not vote. Women thronged to new sects against their husbands' wills or left the husbands and took new ones. During the English Civil War, women preached publicly, despite Anglican pamphleteers' hysterical claims that women demanding sexual equality were destroying the family: one woman regularly preached at London's General Baptist Church.

The Quakers (Society of Friends), founded in 1648, allowed women to speak and act publicly, encouraged their speaking at services, and accepted them as almost equal with men. Women gave the first Quaker sermons in London, Ireland, and North America and founded the first Quaker mission in the Ottoman Empire. The Society gradually slid into patriarchism, but it may have generated feminism: many American feminists, like the Grimké sisters, Susan Anthony, and Lucretia Mott, were Quakers.[20]

Democratic religious movements sprang up outside

England; the most famous woman preacher of the period was Anne Hutchinson, leader of the Antinomians in Massachusetts in 1636 (see below, chapter 6). In 1637, in Calvinist Edinburgh, women rioted when Charles I imposed the Anglican Book of Common Prayer on religious services; their shouts drowned out the dean's reading, and they threw stools at the Bishop of Edinburgh. When they were expelled, they stoned the doors and windows of the church.

Women, who were responsible for feeding the family, often rioted over food. Riot was their response to millers who adulterated flour (for more profit), distributors who hoarded wheat or bread, or prices that were too high. The new laissez-faire capitalism led authorities to lift price controls on bread and grain: prices soared and people went hungry. Those who led and participated in the riots were not the hungry, but the lower-middle classes demanding that prices be low enough that the poor could eat. In 1642, during the English Civil War (1642–48), over four hundred working women thronged Parliament petitioning for changes in trade policies. A mob of women went to market "with knives stuck in their girdles" to force down the price of corn in Northampton, England, in 1693; "a Lady with a stick and a horn" mustered a mob in Durham (Stockton) in 1740. Authorities were terrified at Haverfordwest (Pembroke) in 1795, not by angry miners but by the wives who incited them. A Birmingham newspaper described riots at Snow Hill as the work of "a rabble urged on by furious women." In 1800 a law required millers to make only whole-wheat flour. In response, in Sussex,

> a number of women . . . proceeded to Gosden windmill, where, abusing the miller for serving them with brown flour, they seized on the cloth which he was

then dressing . . . and cut it into a thousand pieces, threatening at the same time to serve all similar utensils he might in future attempt to use in the same manner. The Amazonian leader of this petticoated cavalcade afterwards regaled her associates with a guinea's worth of liquor at the Crab-Tree public house.

Even Frenchwomen, who were strongly socialized to obey, rioted. Led by a woman called *la Branlaïre*, they protested the taxes at Monpellier in 1645, shouting death to the collectors who were starving their children. One benefit of not being taken seriously was that rioting women were legally exempt from punishment. Consequently, rioting men often wore female dress; in 1629 in Essex, England, women and men dressed as women followed "Captain" Alice Clark in a grain riot. Although women were not supposed to act with violence or anger, people tolerated their behavior in these cases. The authorities were outraged, but people felt women had a moral right to fight on behalf of their families. Market women regularly broke or ignored the stringent restrictions placed on them, raising prices, withholding produce from market, and forcing customers to buy less desirable merchandise. They sold house to house, a practice authorities disliked because they could not control it, and it could be used to resell stolen merchandise.

Some women escaped repression by masquerading as men. Dutch women disguised themselves, enlisted as sailors, and worked their passage to Dutch-controlled Batavia, where many single Dutchmen worked. A Spanish nun, Cataline de Drusa, fled her convent in men's clothing and enlisted on a ship leaving Seville in 1603. Acquaintances saw her as a short-haired young man with a light step, shorter and less arrogant than most men but too tall to be a woman—only her hands seemed female. She worked on ships and as a mule-hauler in Vera Cruz and remained in service for twenty years, rising to second lieutenant. In 1624 she was tried for murdering a man, but she declared that the court could not hang her because she was a woman and a nun. She became a popular hero, and the king of Spain gave her 500 ducats. She was formally invested in the Cathedral of Seville as "La Monja Alférez" (nun second lieutenant).

Learned Women

Between 1200 and 1400, Italian scholars rediscovered and translated Greek classics, an event called the Renaissance (revival or rebirth). These translations were translated in turn by European scholars, generating an intellectual movement called *humanism*—Greek thought centered on humans, not god. Classical learning (the study of Latin and Greek languages and texts) became fashionable: noblemen compiled libraries, did their own translations, and oversaw their daughters' education. Many noblewomen became accomplished scholars.[21]

Louise Labé, who was born c. 1520 to a newly rich rope-maker in Lyon, was educated in languages, music, and riding, and was said to have fought as Capitaine Loys during the siege of Perpignan in 1542. She married a rope-maker thirty years older than she, whose age may have freed her to hold mixed-sex literary salons in her house, read what she pleased, and write openly about her beliefs and feelings. In 1555 she published her poems, and her fresh spontaneous sonnets showed great artistry and an extraordinary sensuality, shocking for a woman. In 1972 they were finally translated into English. Either because of her poetry or her Catholic religion, Calvin called her *plebeia meretrix*, "common whore," fueling other Protestant attacks on her for scandalous behavior. She left one volume of vivid, brilliant poems.[22]

Educated women were stifled by marriage. Cassandra Fedele (1465–1558), a writer considered a youthful wonder by Florentine poet-humanist Angelo Poliziano, fell ill after marrying and did not write for seventeen years. Madeleine des Roches (b. Poitiers c. 1520) struggled for education and the right to write. In one poem she laments being "locked up at home" with a spindle instead of a pen, driven witless, bitter that "Men have all the authority/ Against reason and against equity." She did not publish until she was almost sixty (1578), but she made sure her daughter Catherine (b. 1542) was given the resources to pursue an intellectual life. Mother and daughter wrote and published together a substantial body of work— poems, philosophical and pedagogical tracts, a tragicomedy, translations and letters.[23] Catherine stayed with her mother, never marrying; they died the same year.

Marie de Gournay (1565–1645) came from a large, aristocratic French family impoverished by the father's death in 1577. Her mother was unsympathetic to learning for women, and she struggled to teach herself Latin without a grammar or dictionary by comparing Latin passages with French translations. Adopting Montaigne as her mentor, de Gournay risked her life to meet him and edited his works after his death. She devoted her life to study and travel through a France torn by civil and religious conflict, where marauding troops menaced roads. Montaigne and others admired her, but most men ridiculed her vast learning and lack of a husband. She wrote a feminist tract asserting sexual equality and attributing women's inferiority to their lack of education.

In England, too, feminist ideas appeared in print. Mary Astell (1666–1731) grew up with her mother and aunt in a community of women in Newcastle, moved to London, and published political and religious tracts. A staunch Royalist throughout her life, she defended the prerogatives of crown and church—deference to authority pervades her feminist work. She protested male dominance, yet accepted that wives should show "nonrebelliousness in the face of intolerable commands" by their husbands. But she wryly commented on the argument that men deserved dominance on grounds of greater strength of mind and body: "'Tis only for some odd accidents, which philosophers have not yet thought worth while to inquire into, that the sturdiest porter is not the wisest man." She urged educating women in a kind of Protestant convent where upper-class women could live single and protected and develop their minds. She herself never married.

Astell was forgotten until the late twentieth century, a fate that may be rationalized by her regressive attitudes towards religion and politics. But what about Aphra Behn (c. 1640–89)? Extremely popular in her own time, Behn was purged to the point that some men claimed she never existed. An orphan, in her early twenties she went to Surinam, met a black prince who had been enslaved (whom she later wrote about), and took a spy as her lover. She worked as a spy herself, married, and settled down writing plays. Restoration theater was witty and bawdy and Behn wrote to suit it, but bawdiness was forbidden for women and she was scurrilously attacked. Still, her plays were produced, and her poems and novels were published. Behn was the first Englishwoman to earn her living by her pen. Her plays are often revived in England.

This intellectual revolution, humanism, was first discussed by the sixteenth-century thinkers Erasmus and Thomas More. In the next century, Francis Bacon asserted that human reason was a tool for understanding and for conquering nature, and he urged empiricism, or experiment. John Locke believed that knowledge was not innate but acquired by observation of the external world. Such intellectual priorities fostered the eighteenth-century Enlightenment. French *philosophes*, like Bacon, attacked medieval modes of thought rooted in received authority and tradition, deriding them as superstitious. As Protestants rebelled against religious authority, asserting the individual's right to read and interpret Scripture, so the *philosophes* rebelled against intellectual authority, asserting the individual's right to acquire knowledge. Their revolutionary doctrines of the individual rights of men and citizens became the foundation of modern democracies. Believing that the base of knowledge was individual consciousness, they argued that man, through reason, could discover the laws of nature and social organization. Reason was innate, but developed through education, which shaped intellect and personality.

Bacon's work became the base of modern science; the *philosophes'* work became the base of social and political science. The ideas of Enlightenment thinkers like Voltaire, Diderot, Montesquieu, and Rousseau spread across Europe, inspiring the Scots David Hume and Adam Smith. Rousseau's maxim "Man was born free, and everywhere he is in chains" is a famous example of the challenge hurled by these men at tyranny and the power of fathers. But their challenge was limited. They claimed that individuals were born with rights and powers, including the ability to reason for themselves and to have equal rights to choose their religion, education, work, and form of social organization. Yet the *philosophes* as a group were not egalitarian: despite their principles, they were committed to monarchy and to a class system that held some people (like servants) inferior and others (like women) a different species. Diderot and Rousseau feared and mistrusted women and were as woman-hating as medieval monks; Montesquieu and Voltaire assumed that women were formed for domestic subordination not by an old-fashioned god, but by nature.

The Enlightenment defined women as a distinct species cursed with an uncontrollable sexual appetite and a deformed intellect. The *philosophes* brilliantly analyzed social conditions and condemned injustice and abuse of power, without ever recognizing women as victims of either. They probably never read Mary Astell: "If absolute sovereignty be not necessary in a state, how comes it to be so in a family? Or if in a family, why not in a state? . . . Is it not then partial in men to the last degree to contend for and practice that arbitrary dominion in their families which they abhor and exclaim against in the state? *If all Men are born Free*, how is it that all Women are born slaves?" Those *philosophes* who supported female education were considered wildly radical.

Despite the pervasive misogyny, women made a place for themselves in the Enlightenment. They used an accepted mode of social life and hosted gatherings, or salons, in their homes. Brilliant, wealthy women invited the most famous people of the age for conversation and refreshment. They nourished the men intellectually and socially, created connections among the thinkers, and engaged in debate with them. There were three sorts of salon—literary, philosophical, and political—and in these arenas for exchanging ideas, one could learn in pleasure.

The talented or famous were invited to many salons, and everyone in society knew that Pascal and La Rochefoucauld would be found at Mme de Sable's, Montesquieu at Mme de Tencin's, Voltaire at Mme de Deffand's, and d'Alembert at Mlle de Lespinasse's. Salons enabled women to engage in intellectual discourse despite their exclusion from universities and their ignorance of Latin, for the salons used the vernacular. They provided learned men with an admiring audience and an opportunity for argument, and educated new-rich men trying to rise in society in table manners and social behavior towards women—the finishing details of cultivated gentlemen.

Even though they had no feminist agenda, salons became the seat of a debate about Woman's Nature. The *philosophes* wrote endlessly on the subject, especially on women's education. Perhaps the salons exposed contemptuous men to intelligent, articulate women for the first time and shook their notions of Woman. Or perhaps women lobbied in the salons for further education. Choderlos de Laclos (1741–1803, author of *Les liaisons dangereuses*) wrote a much-read *Discours* arguing that education, unlike society, could encourage women to recognize their potential. There was even a vociferous quarrel waged among men about whether women should run salons. The *querelle des femmes* was based in the question of whether women were human beings.[24] Some men argued that women did not have souls, were not created in the image of a male god, and were merely a link between Man and the Animals. But the subtext of their claims, though never explicit, was political. The salon women were educating newly rich and promising men who were trying to rise in the social hierarchy. Nobles, wanting to remain a small, exclusive body, opposed salons for this reason. But the women fervently believed in their work, since it implied that anyone could be educated to rise, that even common people (even women?) had the potential for education and accomplishment. Both sides agreed on one premise: if women were included in the social and political structure, their influence would change society's value system. Feminists still use this argument and are still opposed by those who do not want society changed.

From 1751 to 1765, Denis Diderot and Jean d'Alembert issued their *Encyclopedia*. Composed of essays by many authors, it tries to sum up all contemporary knowledge of science, art, and crafts in an egalitarian form, alphabetically ordered. Only two pieces are by women—an anonymous article and an engraving by Mme Delusse. Nevertheless, the *Encyclopedia* does not hesitate to define women as a caste.[25] One essay asserts that women were born with a natural equality to men in marriage which had been undercut by law and tradition; another describes women as weak, timid, false, shrewd, and poorer at concentration than men, while granting that societal corruption and poor education contributed to their faults; a third alternates in seeing women as failed men and men's equals, blaming part of their failure on education.

Some dedicated people tried to educate girls, but Enlightenment arguments for women's education shared Enlightenment biases. If women were no longer defined as evil and subversive, they were not yet men's equals, but filled a special role in a different social sphere from men. The intelligent, supportive Françoise d'Aubigné Scarron, governess to the children at the French court and confidante of Louis XIV, became the Marquise de Maintenon, the king's secret wife, and founded St. Cyr, a school for girls, with his help. She and her adviser, Abbé Fénelon, argued that, as mothers, women had to educate, so they needed education themselves. Even a strong feminist like Mary Wollstonecraft, writing during the French Revolutionary period, could urge the education of women only on grounds that it would make them better mothers.

The Early Modern Period left women a mixed legacy. Economically, it constricted them severely. Since the first states, women as a caste had been denied a political voice, but most states let elite women hold power. In this era, many states rescinded the right of women of noble or rich families to inherit or bequeath property and increasingly kept ordinary women, even widows and single women, from supporting themselves.

Men wanted to foreclose not just power but independence for women. Yet the most devastating blow to women's economic well-being was unintentional: a shift in the way people conceived of work. In traditional societies, which continued to exist long after some regions had industrialized, almost everyone worked—together. The household, which was also a factory and/or a farm, held women and men of all ages, working together: husband, wife, servants, children. The division of labor overlapped and no one was paid. People produced food and goods for use and trade. Cash was rare.

Capitalism changed this system: men with capital (which women could not obtain) founded large establishments for brewing or baking, or enclosed land that had been worked by tenant farmers, evicting thousands of families from their ancestral homes. Large-scale enterprises swallowed up small ones. These innovations were not aimed at subjugating anyone but at profit. By the late eighteenth century many people worked for cash wages. Most women were constricted within the home; working as hard as they ever had, they were unpaid and dependent on their husbands in a way they had not been before. Their work was essential, but it was devalued because it was not paid. In the next century, women's domestic work would be redefined as nonwork.

Under the guise of complete objectivity and scientific precision, Enlightenment men injected sex differences into every discipline. A major late seventeenth-century French thinker, Poulain de la Barre, offered a rationalist argument for sexual equality, but most Enlightenment men felt that it was "unbecoming" for women to write and publish on equal terms with men. Like their woman-hating predecessors, they felt female sexuality threatened male individuality. Baldly, women controlling their own bodies would undermine men's sense of control. Forced into almost total economic dependency and confined in the home, women were helpless to stop men from bridling their sexuality.

As men in the Early Modern Period shut women up in men's houses and denied them political and economic power, more women asserted the power of the pen. Both Enlightenment and Protestant men insisted that women be confined within the home: but Protestantism granted them the right to basic literacy, and the Enlightenment granted them the power to benefit their children. Women did the rest. Women, not men, extended Enlightenment individualism and human rights to women. But they had to deal with an intellectual world polarized by gender, in which only men were productive, reasonable individuals with rights; despite the extraordinary busyness of women in all areas, only men were deemed capable of accomplishment. Women now had to struggle against not just economic constriction and prejudice but an intellectual structure defining them as an alien species.[26]

CHAPTER 4

EUROPEAN APPROPRIATION
OF AFRICA

I T IS INEVITABLE that societies that worship power either defeat or convert societies that value peace, felicity, and harmony. Europeans, greedy for adventure and the wealth of the Indies, explored and invaded Africa, the Orient, the Pacific islands, Southeast Asia, and North, South, and Central America. Everywhere they went, they took a craving to loot and plunder, a lust to acquire and dominate. They also introduced their weapons and diseases. Everywhere they went, they traded cloth, guns, and ammunition for luxuries (gold, silver, copper, spices, ivory, tea, coffee, cocoa) or even humans (slaves). Everywhere they went, their guns, their greed, and their diseases left behind devastation and converts to power-worship. They swallowed territories, created empires, and colonized them.

Africa, larger than the United States and Australia combined, has hugely diverse environments. Its brilliant skies and clear air cover the driest deserts and the hottest, wettest places on earth. It is pierced by glaciers on its highest mountains and steamed by rain forests. Africa has mangrove coasts, savannah grasslands, enormous lakes, and three of world's major rivers— the Nile, Niger, and Congo. It is home to many peoples and cultures and to five main language groups encompassing hundreds of languages, almost all of them oral during most of their history.

Although many cultures flourished in Africa over the millennium, little, if anything, was written down. This suggests that if or when states arose in Africa, they were not like the states we have examined, which were dedicated to exalting the power of the chief (emperor, priest, king, *lugash*) in some permanent form. Africans had their own myths, as the northern nations did, but because most of the continent was wrenched willy-nilly into the world of violence, many myths are lost. So, most of what we know about early Africa comes from outsiders—traders, merchants, explorers—all of them male and so steeped in patriarchy that they could not comprehend matrilocal marriage. Their contempt for non-Western cultures and for women deformed their picture of the societies they visited. Unlike Islamic or European women, African women farmed, so outsiders saw African (and Native American) women as powerless drudges. In fact, work gave African women a voice in their communities: they marketed what they grew and kept the proceeds, so had an independence that Western women lacked.

Historians have only recently begun to try to explore the African past untrammelled by blinders. Study of women's experience is even more recent. The account offered here, focusing on some regions and periods about which we have information, is divided into sections treating the time before 1450, 1450 to 1600, and 1600 to1800. Post-1800 events will be discussed in volume 3, chapter 1. In this text, *Africa* means sub-Saharan Africa; *North Africa*, the territory north of the Sahara.

Human life began in Africa, which has been settled since hominids first emerged. For millennia, Africans lived by gathering and hunting, limiting their population to the number they could feed; thus, the continent was sparsely settled. Eventually, women in some groups began to grow grain. In dry seasons, pastoralists moved annually from semidesert to grasslands, passing through harvested fields; the leftover grain fed their animals. All three types—gatherer-hunters, horticulturalists, and pastoralists—were egalitarian, sharing resources and living without authorities or military associations. Their only leaders were priestesses/priests who enacted religious rituals. Africans worshipped the forces of nature, which included their ancestors.

Before 1450

Scholars now know that the Sahara Desert was once a green plain cooled by rivers: in its midst, in a barren rocky area called the Tassili, waves of migrants created an exquisite set of rock paintings about 6000 years ago, depicting people and animals peacefully coexisting. One rock painting shows women gathering grain, either wild or cultivated. A sexual division of labor appears: women are shown gathering, farming, and making baskets, pots, jewelry, and tools; men are shown tending animals, hunting, and working with stone. But both sexes danced together in rituals, and women were depicted with evident respect.

Early African cultures were as diverse as the terrain. Some were states—hierarchical lineage systems or empires dominating several societies—but most people lived in small bands or villages as gatherer-hunters. When outsiders encountered them, the !Kung San lived in the Kalahari Desert in groups of about thirty-five, without clear hierarchical structures or male dominance. Both sexes gathered. Marriage was not binding and could be broken at will. Children belonged to their mothers, although the !Kung did not conceive of possessing children, who were free. Today, these peoples, the only gatherer-hunters left, are changing their customs: !Kung women's rights started to diminish when they began to live in villages.

In northeast Africa, Kushites herded cattle, grew cereal, and in the second millennium BCE built cities in Napata and Kerma; these cities developed into a wealthy Nubian state, Kush. Before 1000 BCE, Kush sold ivory, ebony, ostrich plumes, and slaves to Egypt and other states across the Red Sea. Nubians settled in Egypt, and Kush ruled that country for about a century c. 800 BCE. Several dynasties of black Pharaohs may have been Nubian. Kush had script, sculptured reliefs, and monumental architecture—tombs, palaces, and temples. Herodotus mentions the ruins at Meroë, north of Khartoum. Nubian society was stratified; it had a small elite, a large laboring class, and it practiced human sacrifice. Women often ruled in Meroë: a mound at Wad-ben-Naqa was identified as the palace of a famous *candace* (ruler), Amani-Shakhete, whose portrait still exists. Her rule, from 41 to 12 BCE, was followed by that of other queens. The biblical Acts of the Apostles records the Christian Philip preaching to a high official of the queen of Kush.

Horticulturalists speaking a Bantu language lived in present-day Nigeria at least from 3000 BCE; they produced bountiful harvests of sorghum and rice. Plenty usually generates population growth, and, indeed, around 500 BCE, Bantu-speakers began to migrate. They spread to the Congo basin, Angola,

Zambia, East Africa, Kenya, and through Zimbabwe into South Africa, crossing the Limpopo River around 300 CE. Settling in inhabited regions, they assimilated with the residents; in the process they spread their language, which was spoken throughout Africa: by 1300, when most African languages had acquired their modern form, there were over 400 language clusters and thousands of dialects in Bantu.[1] They either spread horticulture or merged their methods with local methods that terraced, irrigated, and selected plants appropriate for the local terrain. They also probably spread iron technology.

Africans smelted iron earlier than any other people: smelting sites existed in Ghana, Nigeria, Tanzania, and Ethiopia by the sixth century BCE. By 500 CE, ancestors of the Haya of modern Tanzania had invented a sophisticated technique for producing carbon steel in forced-draft furnaces, another process not known in Europe until much later. Long before Europeans, Africans hunted with iron spears and replaced digging sticks with iron hoes, which allowed them to plant more deeply in the earth for greater yields. About 1000 they learned to make stronger, heavier iron tools, which also spread across the continent.

Boers claim they reached South Africa at the same time as Africans, but archaeological evidence places Africans in the Cape by the fourth century. Huge stone walls called Great Zimbabwe ("stone houses," neither fortifications nor parts of buildings), built between 1250 and 1450, marked a city of almost 18,000 people, stratified socially and economically. A Zimbabwean mining empire traded with Europe, mainly Portugal, long before the Boers arrived.

Myths usually attribute the decay of a golden age to the discovery of mining. These stories suggest that mining altered life in many societies. Elsewhere, people settled in villages, permanent holdings practicing horticulture. Using iron hoes in the fertile land of that era, women produced enough food to feed everyone, so some villagers could follow other occupations—trading, art and manufacture, politics, and religion. As the population grew, territories became crowded and groups of people moved from the river valleys up to higher, drier lands or along the coast. Some groups entered territories that others felt they "owned," causing conflict. War began.

We do not know why stratification arose in Africa. A society that produced a surplus could permit occupations other than farming, but all members would still work, trading what they produced for what they needed. Stratification ranks groups hierarchically, so that an elite can live parasitically without working. In most of the world, one group would force others to support it; in Africa, this behavior would violate traditions millennia old. In most of the world, a priesthood seems to have exalted itself and its activities and demanded payment and control over the population for its services; when militarism evolved, soldiers took over the priesthood, making similar demands. The creation of stratification in most African communities occurred otherwise. What triggered the idea of superiority in this egalitarian world?

The idea of superiority may have arisen in secret societies and hunting cults, probably always all-male groups. Aggressive gangs may have invaded small communities; one lineage branch may have grown large enough to dominate its kin. Men wanting children to bear their names and enrich them rebelled against matriliny. By kidnapping and enslaving women, they cut their natal bond of rights and obligations. Guarding the women's sexuality, they started patrilinies. This may be the way patriliny itself began. However it began, economic and social stratification always entails male superiority. Four concepts are linked: moral superiority (the idea that some people are better or worthier than others); economic superiority (the idea that some have the right to live parasitically on others' labor); male superiority; and a religion positing a transcendent, omnipotent god who legitimates claims of superiority by divine kings. Despite the existence of women chiefs, there was no divine female kingship.

When Europeans penetrated Africa, its kingdoms were tight at the center and loose at the fringes, as we imagine early Mesopotamian city-states to have been. Most people lived in egalitarian communities (some of which survived into the twentieth century). Vanquished clans probably paid tribute just to be left alone. Some states were held together only by a set of bureaucrats loyal to a king. In some groups, chiefs claimed the authority formerly held by a consensus of kin-group elders or priests and priestesses. East African women often became priestesses to gain political power. Women were also chiefs, prophets, and diviners.

Aspiring elites establish domination by force, but force is never enough. "Winning" is never done: people rebel against what they perceive as oppression—they resist, refuse to work, flee. So conquest has two phases: military suppression and propaganda. To consolidate victory, the winner must present his domination as justified, right. The main model for domination is parental control of a child. The metaphor of ruler/parent and populace/children is common, but a populace is not helpless and does not need to be protected and guided like a child. The metaphor is used not because it resembles governance but because it presents domination as sanctioned by nature. The parent/child relation is the only human relation in which domination is needed, but in nature, caretaking parents are influenced by children.

Like rulers in other early states, African elites used religion for sanction. To legitimate claims of supremacy, to persuade the vanquished to accept their subordination as "right," the winners concocted myths that explained or vindicated their control. Here, too, conquerors tended to retain myths and religious figures familiar to the conquered, inserting small changes to justify their new supremacy. The superiority of the new elite is celebrated as a victory in the new myth.

Sexual stratification arose quickly in Africa, compared with Mesopotamia or Egypt, especially in regions exposed to Islam. Even before social stratification, positions of authority had become hereditary and men in many villages had succeeded in asserting polygyny and patrilocal (virilocal) marriage. Polygyny allowed a patrilineal clan to grow swiftly: a strong clan could commandeer women and land, assigning each man many wives, who would produce both crops and children.

Many West Africans and other groups remained matrilineal. The indefatigable Ibn Battuta, who visited West Africa in 1352, wrote that Africans were named for their maternal uncles, not their fathers, and men left their property to their nephews, not their sons. Other early sources report matrilineal descent among the Asante and other Akan peoples of Ghana and Mali. Cape Xhosa-speaking women retain their clan name throughout life, and the capital of the Swazi is always the village of the queen mother, who rules with the king. The first to break with matrilineality were the Bambara: *Ban-ba-ra* or *Ban-ma-na* means "separation from mother." Marcia Wright explains that early elites stressed their difference from the common people: if most of the clans they ruled were matrilineal, the elite would adopt patrilineal succession; if the clans were patrilineal, the rulers adopted matrilineal succession. That in later periods most elites were patrilineal supports the assumption that most people had been matrilineal.[2]

Whatever form of descent-tracing is used, men dominated society, controlling land, marriage, and dependents. When a man died, his position passed to his eldest son; his possessions, including wives and unmarried daughters, passed to his sons and brothers. A widow had to accept a brother-in-law as husband or leave the village and jeopardize her sons' rights to the land she had farmed. If her children were over seven, she could not take them with her—they belonged to the patrilineage.

Most patrilineages sold women in marriage for bride-wealth. (Africans see bride-price marriage not as a sale but an alliance of families.) Bride-price is payment of goods or cash made by a groom's family to a family for a bride. Bride-price marriage treats women as commodities with the potential to produce children, food, and service. The subtext of dowry marriage is that women are dependents needing support from men, even though women reproduce and work in societies with dowry. In dowry, a bride's family pays a groom's in return for a promise of support. Dowry marriage could be seen as the purchase of a groom who will father children and provide support, but no one refers to dowry as groom-price. Whatever form marriage takes, the language used to describe it makes the woman, not the man, the one exchanged. Bride-price is commonest in matrilocal groups (where grooms live with the brides' people); both dowry and bride-price occur in patrilocal groups (where brides reside with the grooms' people).

Most African women farmed, following one of two systems.[3] In regions with few people and much open land, women practiced "shifting hoe culture": men cleared one or two acres of land in the forest or bush a couple of times a year, and women raised two to three crops, then abandoned these fields to lie idle for decades, moving to new ones. In such cultures, men did little except clear land and, sometimes, acquire it by force. Where population was dense, groups might move to remote mountainous areas safer from aggression and practice "intensive hoe culture," which required men to work harder, building terraces or irrigation systems. Women then rotated crops and used organic fertilizers to restore fertility to the land. In both systems, women worked the fields with a hoe for four to eight hours every day. After fieldwork, they did their second "job," fetching water and firewood, caring for children, and processing food—drying, shelling, storing, grinding, and cooking it.

In precolonial Africa, few men farmed. They did so only in certain groups like the Senufo or Yoruba, plow societies, or among Islamic converts who kept women confined. Plows were rare in the precolonial era; when they came in, men often (but not always) took over agriculture. But men who farmed were young and dependent; household heads did nothing. In herding societies, too, young or dependent men tended animals and women farmed; senior men did little or nothing. But male heads of household ran the political structures that united communities. Male dominance and parasitism were even stronger in slave states like Burundi, in which we can see the origins of problems still wracking the area today. The Tutsi conquered the Hutu; the Tutsi king gave land and cattle to his male kin, called nobles, who had the right to labor service and tribute from Tutsi commoners and all Hutu. Tutsi commoners tended the royal cattle, and Hutu men worked royal farms as serfs. This hierarchy was echoed among the women: noble Tutsi wives supervised the agricultural labor of male Hutu serfs, while commoner Tutsi wives cleaned cattle kraals, churned butter, and farmed. A Hutu wife had to maintain her family alone—her husband worked for the Tutsi—and had to kneel before him when she brought him his gourd of beer.

Most pastoral societies were patrilineal and patrilocal. Five to six independent households lived together in a village; they moved twice a year between pastures chosen for the season— wet or dry. Household heads were equal; male elders controlled property, directed herd movements, negotiated water rights, and arranged marriages. Men were polygynous, and each wife built her own one-room house inside the village compound. Men built a thorn fence around the village to serve as a cattle kraal at night. Young men herded and served as soldiers. Women brought cattle into marriage and worked harder and longer hours than men, but were seen as social and economic dependents with no rights over the cattle, which were used to feed the family. The milk and butter a woman produced had to be shared among kin; her cattle was her sons' bride-wealth. Some women had a say about where they lived and chose their own sexual partners; Igbo women united to ridicule or publicly punish men who, for instance, hit their wives.

Most Africans belonged to three kin-groups: a lineage, an extended family living with others, and a nuclear family. Within lineages, both sexes had rights and obligations towards kin. They could own some land and some cattle, but they were expected to help siblings materially at naming ceremonies, marriages, and funerals. Women could not hold formal leadership positions in patrilineages but they did discuss lineage affairs, and the older they were, the more influence they held. In matrilineal societies, women held leadership positions and authority equal to men's. In both, rank accrued to age: older sisters had higher rank than younger brothers, and in societies where men prostrated themselves before their elders, they did so for women as well as men.

A lineage was a set of extended families claiming descent from a common ancestor. These families usually lived together in a compound, with their houses built around an open space.

When monarchs were elevated above and lived apart from their kin-groups, they still honored their obligations to the lineage. The lineage allocated land and titles; the compound was the seat of the local court and the base for mobilizing people for public works and service. The hierarchy within compounds was based on age or seniority in marriage into the group, so older women had power even in patrilineages.

Status within families was determined by blood, marriage, and other criteria. Women were defined as wives, sisters, mothers, grandmothers, sisters-in-law, aunts, and cousins. In many African societies, the terms *husband* and *wife* referred to status as well as the sexual relation they denote in the West. *Wife* was a woman bound to serve another as well as a woman married into a compound or lineage. *Husband* was a term of authority; a female husband had rights over the procreative capacity of a wife. A woman with status and, usually, wealth bought a wife, mated her, and kept any children born from the union. A wife owed service to a husband, female or male. Within a conjugal family, husbands always had authority and status, although patrilineages required greater deference from wives than matrilineages.

The most independent African women were probably in West Africa. In West African societies free of Islamic influence—Ibo, Tallensi, Yoruba, Asante, and Nupe—Niara Sudarkasa writes, women occupied high positions in formal structures of government, some with parallel male and female chiefs.[4] Throughout this region, women belonged to trade and craft guilds and spoke publicly on matters of local importance like taxes, maintenance of markets, roads, wells, and streams. They testified on their own behalf in courts or hearings. (Women in Europe at this time had no such rights.) Men controlled external affairs, but women supplied the rations for men's expeditions, so had a voice in them and sometimes led armies or financed campaigns.

As far as we know, there was always a division of labor by sex in Africa. If both sexes farmed (like the Ibo), they raised different crops. If both sexes wove (like the Yoruba), they produced different kinds of cloth on different types of looms. If both sexes traded, they exchanged different commodities. Men did long-distance trading, while women dominated local markets. Most often, men hunted, fished, or herded animals. Women farmed, did most of the childcare, prepared the food, and usually manufactured cloth. Sudarkasa emphasizes that no indigenous African society attached different value to the labor of women and men working at the same tasks, or paid women and men differently for the same work.

Each sex controlled its own resources: what a woman produced was her own (in contrast to Europe, where women's earnings belonged to their husbands). Each partner had obligations to her or his lineage apart from the conjugal unit, and neither could veto the other's decisions. Many West African societies had parallel structures of control, where each sex handled its own affairs: male political and religious leaders guided men, female leaders guided women. Women sometimes led both sexes, but could not join the male secret societies, which were the foundations of the political process in states and were sometimes excluded from councils of chiefs. They were usually represented on leadership bodies by the heads of the women's hierarchies. Societies with parallelism were ruled by queen-mother and king-son combinations.

We do not know when slavery began in Africa. Before the European invasion, everyone was in some sense bound: no one could survive without a lineage, which granted each person land and/or animals, a spouse, and a place in the community.

When men asserted power as a higher claim than blood ties, they forced lineages into a relation with an external power—a state or maybe just a petty king—but their sense of being bound remained the same. Indeed, people may not have been able to imagine any other way of life than one binding them to each other and to the land. But lineage bondage was primarily empowering; bondage to a king or state was primarily enslaving. The old system involved reciprocal responsibilities: it gave people rights to resources (a home, land, animals, help in obtaining a mate) and imposed certain obligations (gift-giving on ceremonial occasions, participation in councils, and occasional labor service). The new system at first retained the old, but required people to produce a surplus to maintain a head, as well as his servants and lineage, while offering them dubious "protection" in return.

In Africa, labor had various forms. In "free" labor, people worked lineage land and shared equally in resources. But there were also pawns, serfs, slaves, and clients. Pawns were collateral for debt, like indentured laborers; they could be redeemed or become permanent slaves. Clients, mainly men, attached themselves to a more powerful person in return for maintenance and rewards—a wife, perhaps, or a slave. Serfs were peasants bound to land and to a lord. Slaves, owned outright, had the right to marry, procreate, work in their own time, and keep their earnings. The earliest African slaves were almost certainly women captured in raids or battles. African men wanted slave women for several reasons, but primarily because removing a woman from her lineage broke her obligations to it; thus, her children belonged to her owner's lineage and the woman had no escape from abuse. Indeed, the only way men in matrilineal societies could increase their patriline was through slave wives. Also, since African women did most of the farming, their work increased a lineage's wealth. And to possess many wives, slave or free, was a sign of status and wealth. So men wanted female slaves. Most slaves in Africa before and after the European conquest were female. In groups like the Hausa of the West African Sahel, all slaves farmed.

Slaves and free in Africa lived alike, doing the same work. Slaves were integrated into the household: females were often made wives and heads of families claimed all children as their own. Female slaves were used to pay debts or for sacrifice at the funeral of an important owner, as were male slaves and free wives. Most African households owned a few slaves. Before the European intrusion, only wealthy families in the Muslim sultanates of the West African Sahel owned large slave-forces to work in their farming villages or their households. The Atlantic slave trade of the sixteenth to nineteenth centuries, however, fostered the growth of highly centralized military African states with huge slave labor forces.

What was unique and definitive in the African experience was that Africans resisted organization into social-political structures like states or empires. States formed in Africa much later than in the Middle East or Europe, and then often to counteract Middle Eastern or European pressure. This reluctance is often taken as an indication of African "backwardness," but, as we have seen, state formation is always oppressive, involving the domination by one group of all others and depriving everyone, dominator and dominated, of autonomy. The greater the central control in a state, the greater its oppressiveness. In this light, African resistance to state formation was positive and self-protective. In response to European intrusion, however, more states arose in Africa. (The process of state formation still continues in Africa, explaining the wars that convulse almost the entire continent today.) There is contagion in power-worship: power-seekers either annihilate or convert those in their path. The only African societies able to resist European invasion were those that converted, forming strong states; the rest perished.

States arose in Africa mainly as a result of external forces—trade and exposure to Islam and Christianity. In the early centuries of the Common Era, Romans and Carthaginians traveled in horse-drawn chariots to central Saharan oases to trade dates, cloth, and glass beads for gold, ivory, pepper, and slaves. This trade built Awkar (Ghana) around the fourth century CE. In the sixth century, Nubian states emerged along the upper Nile. Nubians exposed to Christianity by contact with Byzantine Greece created a sophisticated Christian civilization, making fine pottery and building beautiful cities, brick monasteries, and cathedrals adorned with paintings. Despite Muslim attacks, Nubian kingdoms endured into the fourteenth century.

After the seventh century, Indian and Arab traders began to land at Indian Ocean ports in East Africa, from present-day Somalia to Kenya and Tanzania. They settled along the coast, buying iron, gold, palm oil, and products of the hunt like ivory, rhinoceros horn, and leopard skins. The Bantu-speaking inhabitants welcomed and married them and gradually converted to Islam. By the tenth century, East African society was based on trade in rhinoceros horn, turtle shells, ivory, gold, rock crystal, slaves, and copper transported to the coast from central African copper mines.

By now, most Africans had iron implements. Towns specialized in crafts like woodcarving, weaving, music-making, jewelry-making, storytelling, metallurgy, or salt mining. In some, men only mined salt; in others, women only. A craft was often passed on in a family. Until the nineteenth century, most villages were isolated, trading internally or within a small radius. But the lure of profit changed the way of life of interior and coastal East Africans: production methods altered to fill new demands. Those with money mustered young men for aggressive hunting and recruited both sexes for intensive farm work to feed merchants, soldiers, traders, artisans, and slaveowners. These workers were often slaves, and soon traders bought slaves too.

By the tenth century, African trading networks reached Persia and Arabia and extended south to Bantu fishing communities and the Shona empire in Zimbabwe. Bantu-speakers from the interior, refugees from Islam, Arab merchants from Shiraz on the Persian Gulf, and merchants from Northwest India migrated to East Africa. They competed to control the trade of gold mined by male and female Shona-held slaves and began to export rice, beeswax, ambergris, honey, timber, and grain. As demand grew, merchants increased production by intensifying the work of slaves on the plantations.

Gradually, from the eleventh to the fifteenth centuries, as Arabs and Indians intermarried with local Bantus, a new culture and Bantu-rooted language emerged, both called Swahili from the Arab word *swahila*, "people of the coast." The culture, syncretizing Bantu, Arab, and Indian roots, was Muslim and ruled by Arabs or Swahilis. By the twelfth century, Shirazi Arabs writing Arabic had erected Muslim city-states with unique mosques along the coast south to Mozambique. They founded dynastic families, which became the ruling class. By the mid-thirteenth century, thirty to forty city-states dotted the coast and its islands—wealthy, cosmopolitan, homogenous, independent, and highly stratified. Those who started with money kept it: the rich ruled. Merchants never had to stir themselves to travel inland; goods were brought to them, balanced on the heads of slaves who were marched in columns for

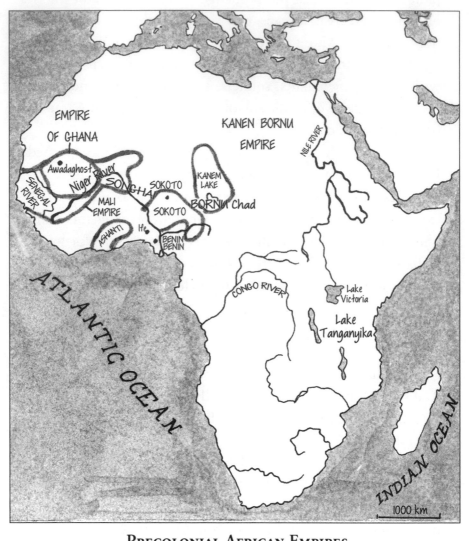

PRECOLONIAL AFRICAN EMPIRES

hundreds of miles along primitive bush tracks to the port cities of Kilwa, Mombasa, and Malindi. On arrival, the people and the goods they carried were sold and shipped to Arabia, Persia, or India.

Each city was ruled by a dynastic family. In the early sixteenth century Duarte Barbosa visited Mombasa, which was ruled by the Mazrui, a Swahili dynasty, and described it as

> a very fair place, with lofty stone and mortar houses, well aligned in streets. . . .The wood is very well fitted with excellent joiner's work. It has its own king, himself a Moor. The men are in color either tawny, black or white and also their women go very bravely attired with many fine garments of silk and gold in abundance. This is a place of great traffic, and has a good harbor, in which are always moored craft of many Sofala and those which go thither and others which come from the great kingdom of Cambay and from Malindi; others which sail to the isles of Zanzibar.

The finely attired women were of the ruling class, wives or concubines of merchants, plantation owners, and administrators. Decorative objects intended to reflect the prestige of men, they were cultivated, reading Arabic and reciting Swahili poetry. Men's wealth was measured by the number of concubines they owned and the lavishness of their women's dress. Concubines fetched the highest prices of all female slaves and were served by female slaves, but remained slaves themselves, as did their children.

By the time Europeans arrived in Africa, the continent was home to about a hundred million people, highly skilled in farming, who had adapted root crops and bananas brought to

Africa from Asia. Land being plentiful, it was not a measure of wealth. What was needed was labor, and family heads collected dependents—wives, slaves, and clients. The larger a person's following, the richer and more powerful he or she was considered. Africans were expert in making and using iron tools, gold mining, and smithing. Their weaving, ceramics, and sculpture were of such quality that, today, they are exhibited in museums. African priestesses and priests developed complicated theories of origin based on precise knowledge of the workings of the stars and planets. In some regions, the Africans built political entities with divine kings ruling over loosely organized clans with considerable autonomy. Muslims believed in centralized power and their own holy book and system of law, and they opposed the African political structure. And, at this time, Christian influence was mainly limited to the northeast, to what is now Ethiopia.

1450 to 1600

The Portuguese reached the Cape Verde islands in 1445 and the southern coast of West Africa, the "Slave Coast," in the 1470s. Vegetation and African diseases to which Europeans were not immune made it treacherous: death was so common that the region was called the "White Man's Grave." But Europeans were willing to risk death to get rich. They brought Africa the essentials of Western culture: cloth, arms, gunpowder, ideas of private property, institutionalized male dominance (patriarchy), and Christianity. They also brought smallpox and cholera, which spread wildly when Europeans penetrated the interior. Epidemics probably killed more people and disrupted social patterns more than the slave trade that formally began after 1553.

In the first century and a half, Europeans established trading networks on the Atlantic; trade also intensified on the Indian Ocean. Europeans propagated Christianity wherever they had influence; Muslims spread Islam in the Sudanic states and the east coast. The continent was trapped between two militant religions serving as advance guard for ideologies foreign to Africa. We will examine the effects of this conflict on some regions of Africa.

Atlantic Coast: Kongo

In 1482 the Portuguese built a fortress on the coast of what is now Ghana, then worked their way through West and Central Africa. The experience of one region, Kongo, illuminates the European impact in this period. Traditionally, the Bakongo traced descent and succession matrilineally. Women headed families: kin-groups or lineages owned land collectively, but property, houses, and lands were inherited through women. As was usual in Africa, the marital unit was fundamental; married women were expected to produce and prepare food for their children, husband, and sometimes his kin. The division of labor remained the same over the centuries and was described by an eighteenth-century European visitor:

> The manner in which the man and his wife regulate the house-hold is this: the man is obliged to build a house, to clothe his wife according to her status, to care for the trees, to help pull up roots in the fields when needed, and to bring the wine which he gets every day from the palm trees; and if any of this lacks, he will not live in peace in his home. The woman is supposed to provide food for her husband and children.

The writer scants the labors of women, who went together to work in the fields at sunrise and returned at noon, when the sun was hottest, to pound grain for the evening meal, eaten two hours before sunset. (During the day they ate only light food—manioc snacks, peanuts, and palm wine.) After the long tedious pounding, they boiled the flour into cereal served with a sauce, raw vegetables, fruit, and wine. They grew three types of millet, maize, cassava, sorghum, garden vegetables, and legumes, raised chickens, and caught fish, providing a varied diet with good nutrition: infant mortality and life expectancy rates were equal to or better than those in contemporary Europe. Every September, women slashed and burned the fields, removed roots, raised the soil into small mounds with a hoe, and planted. They planned crops for harvesting throughout the year (harvests were exceedingly abundant), leaving plots fallow after two or three crops. They gauged potential yields, put aside seed for the next year, and followed drainage patterns to get the most from the land. Only occasionally in the dry season did they have to resort to gathering wild foods. They also made pots and baskets.

The men provided tree products—fruit, bananas, palm oil, palm wine, building materials, buildings, and the wine and oil for the sauce for the evening meal. They also built and repaired homes and made cloth of tree bark or leaves. They made their wives' hoes, hunted, and traded for salt, meat, fish, and imported goods. Both parents tended children. Seventeenth-century Bakongo lived in villages of thirty to fifty compounds with 150 to 300 people.[5] Wild animals roamed by night in sparsely settled areas, so villages were hedged or sturdily palisaded.

The two sexes lived in separate worlds but were interdependent: life was impossible outside a household. Marriage was the glue binding households, groups of households, and the entire village. It required an exchange of bride-wealth, a large amount in the seventeenth century (before European intrusion it could be a token—a hoe or a chicken).[6] A young man could not by himself amass the amount needed to buy a wife. His kin helped, but did not try to control the supply of women (as elders do among the Aborigines). Marriage was negotiated by the hopeful groom and a member of the household of the woman he wanted to marry; the couple then had a trial marriage to test sexual compatibility while the elders negotiated the price. Because marriage was so costly, most men were monogamous; those who could afford more than one wife had them to display status. Widows probably remarried: in rural districts few men had more than six wives, and some were the aged widows of kinsmen.

Villages were made up of groups of intermarried households of a couple of dominant lineages, regulated by a "republic" of kin. These units existed before Kongo was a state, and they exist still. Some villages specialized, mining iron or salt. In 1700 Dutch traders visited a village in which a hundred women extracted salt, and another that traded fish; in a third, the entire male population made palm cloth. The living arrangements of Kongo people fostered equality and changed little over the centuries, but a major change in the seventeenth century altered their lives—the rise of an elite class and the introduction of slavery.

Most of the elite lived in two towns, Mbanza Nsoyo and São Salvador. Towns were only large villages, except that villages held mainly free people and, after European contact, towns held mainly slaves and their descendants. Villages owned the land around them; the food grown there was shared according to need. Town-dwellers had to pay rent on fields in the form of labor. The state of Kongo centered in the monarch (*mani Kongo*) in São Salvador, a wealthy, luxurious town of over 60,000 people. The king and nobles were Mwissikongo, who were culturally distinct from Bakongo commoners. The king ruled with a royal council of usually twelve titled dependents, who managed a bureaucracy responsible for collecting taxes, the military, the judiciary (which controlled rural courts, overseeing uniform law enforcement), and personal servants with great influence on policy and administration: a *mani Lumbo* (major-domo) held great power in the royal council.

When the Portuguese arrived in Kongo in 1482, they were amazed by its opulence and sophistication and eager to ally with the *mani Kongo*. He, too, was eager for diplomatic and economic relations: his son Affonso even converted and tried to convert the kingdom to Christianity and European ways. The Portuguese settled in the port of Luanda and began to seek slaves for their Brazilian plantations. Kongo had no slaves (nor did its neighbors), but it had serfs, most of them doing temporary labor to requite debt or punish crime. The Portuguese pressured Affonso to sell them his serfs, but he refused to enslave his people. However, Catholic missionaries with great influence on Affonso persuaded him to raid neighboring lands, especially Ndongo to the south, for slaves. (Christian missionaries in Africa were often slave dealers.) Affonso's son continued these wars after his father's death, but without his success. Expensive, fruitless wars led to Kongo's decline.

Portuguese religion, slave trading, and a new concept of property altered the kingdom. The ruling class became Christian, many able to read and write Portuguese. Nobles lived parasitically, supported by an extensive tribute system and large slave-worked plantation villages. Women managed farms and farmed; men, too, farmed, growing millet under the direction of nobles. Intensive supervised plantation work produced enough food to support 15–20 percent of the population, assisted by slaves and nobles' household servants. Slaves also served in the army. Owners arranged marriages for their slaves, whose children became subordinate branches of the owners' noble lineages. Marcia Wright points out that for Africans, slavery was essentially a means of transferring power from one lineage or domain to another: as I mentioned before, getting a child by a slave woman was the only way a man could increase his father's lineage in a matrilineal society. Female slaves were totally owned: their labor, their childbearing capacity, and their sex lives belonged to their owners. Male slaves owed only labor to owners. Although some were subjected to the humiliation of performing female farming tasks, they were treated like sons and given the same freedom as clients and non-lineage subordinates.

As usual, peasants maintained the elite. Nobles were posted in rural areas to collect and forward taxes to the capital; since concessions of provincial land reverted to the king at death, nobles could not accrue land for their lineages, so they did not marry locally, preferring São Salvador women with connections. Lacking ties to the folk they oversaw and judged by their efficiency, they were often so zealous that they provoked peasants to rebel and despoiled provinces. Wealth consisted mainly of slaves—even frugal missionaries had twenty or thirty. Nobles arrived in villages with large entourages of slaves and commandeered provisions for them. If the peasants resisted, they were rounded up and enslaved by the noble, who then burned the village. In villages most frequented by nobles, people refused to sow abundantly or raise cattle, preferring to live in penury than feed their oppressors, and they built villages off main roads to avoid casual plunder.

Noble households really controlled the state; political

conflict occurred between households, not individuals. Rulers were male, but women were active politically, especially retired widowed queens who retained authority. Women held high office: in some districts in Nsoyo, only women ruled; other provinces were governed by women who took male consorts. Many women ruled at the marquis level. In the 1650s four of Garcia II's twelve-member royal council were women. Remarried widows influenced Kongo politics as heads of house-hold. During the civil war, women ruled de facto even if men ruled by law. Noblemen had many wives: a missionary wrote that having ten or twenty wives elevated a man to the status of "great man." Even slaves had more than one wife—so many men had been transported that there were surplus women.

The slave trade expanded. Caravans of chained captives threaded the countryside, and slaves were sold at public mar-kets. Most slaves sold locally were women. To escape slave-traders, people fled to the countryside, attaching themselves to households, for the unattached were fair game. A new elite emerged—men in commerce and trade. By 1701 people were selling each other wildly; raiders captured ever greater numbers from the interior beyond Kongo. Constant war drove the Kongo elite to rural areas. Luxurious São Salvador, with its plenitude of resources, magnificent court, religious establish-ment, army, bureaucracy, and multitudes of slave laborers, was destroyed and the Portuguese set up puppet kings. Women farmers kept the country going.

After 1715 Europeans restricted the foreign sale of locally born and "Christian" (Catholic) slaves to "heretics" (Protest-ants). War abated, but slavery did not end: many Bakongo slaves remained in the kingdom, dependent on local lords who, to maintain status, had to head a domain. Mwissikongo men competed with each other in setting up paltry royal centers where nobles and peasants lived in similar circumstances. Noblemen made their former adornments, wives, do farm labor. During the centralized monarchy, nobles could carve out careers in the bureaucracy, church, and commerce; by the eighteenth century, no opportunities remained but commerce, and even those who boasted royal blood wore rags.

Many people felt religion would revitalize the country, so joined revival movements. Male and female prophets announced visions of political and religious reorganization. Kimpa Vita, a priestess of Marinda, was a Mukongo noble knowledgeable about elite intrigues and channels of power.[7] At twenty-two, when she fell ill and seemed to be dying, St. Anthony, who was especially revered by the Portuguese in Kongo and Ndongo, appeared in the guise of one of her brothers—that is, black. Recovering, she renounced material things, took the name Doña Beatrice, and announced her vision: Kongo must be reborn and São Salvador rebuilt. She created an origin myth based on traditional Bible stories: Kongo was the holy land, Jesus was born in São Salvador, and Africans had founded Christianity. People said she died on a Friday, pleaded her cause in heaven, was resurrected on Sunday, and became a saint. By 1704 she was a recognized religious/political leader in São Salvador.

Instead of imitating whites, as Affonso did, Beatrice asserted black identity. Blacks differed from whites because they were formed from a different substance: whites were made of a soft stone; blacks, of a tree like a fig tree. She stressed black consciousness, emphasizing the value of black experience and proclaiming power to the people. Her followers rejected European dress for traditional bark-cloth. Claiming that the golden age would begin when São Salvador was fully rebuilt, Beatrice offered strict laws to unify the many peoples of Kongo. These laws were not Christian; among other things, they permitted polygamy.

Appalled by Beatrice, the Portuguese urged the puppet *mani Kongo* Pedro IV to suppress her. He did not dare to until Beatrice, who claimed to be a virgin, bore a son. Once people began to doubt her, Pedro dared to arrest her. He intended to send her to the Bishop of Angola for trial, perhaps hoping she would escape along the way, but Capuchin missionaries forced him to have her tried by a royal council.[8] After she was sentenced to die at the stake, Beatrice recanted, but the council still burned her with her baby in her arms. Believing her a saint, her followers rose against Pedro, but he won. Although Beatrice had revitalized society, Portuguese Kongo was not ready for black pride.

1600 to 1800

The Atlantic slave trade greatly intensified in the early seventeenth century. The Dutch, British, and French were building huge plantations in South America and the Caribbean, often in unhealthful, swampy regions. Few people willingly lived in such atrocious conditions or worked hard enough to make the plantations succeed. Colonists decided that slaves were the solution to their labor problem and, after the mid-seventeenth century, slaves replaced gold as West Africa's main export. The Portuguese controlled slave trading until about 1650, when the Dutch took over, to be supplanted in 1672 by the British Royal African Company, a joint-stock company chartered by Charles II. With hundreds of ships and a monopoly on English–African trade, the Royal African Company built eight forts in West Africa, to which it sent manufactured goods and took back slaves for England's Caribbean colonies. Many men went to

Africa seeking their fortunes in slave export; by the early eighteenth century, they, not companies, dominated the slave trade. In the late eighteenth century, young men bought for £26 on the West Coast were resold in the New World for £40—a good profit if a man lived to reap it.

Transportation of slaves outside Africa was not new: two million Africans, mainly women, were exported from the continent after 800 and sold in Arabian and Indian markets, writes Rosalyn Terborg-Penn.[9] The trade increased after 1100 to become a major business in Ethiopia, the coast of East Africa, and the West African savanna; slaves were the major export from the Nile Valley and Ethiopia. Egyptians, Arabs, and Indians wanted slaves mainly as status symbols—some North Africans bragged of owning over 5000 people. From 800 to 1500, Muslims trooped almost four million Africans across the Sahara to be harem women and servants in North Africa. When the Atlantic trade began, women, for the most part, were still being transported across the Sahara and the Indian Ocean. Women were already enslaved within Africa; the first African slaves were captive wives, and there was little difference in status between a wife and a slave.[10] Most African miners were slave women.

What was new about the Atlantic trade were its numbers and the male sex of most of the slaves exported. The Atlantic trade peaked in the mid-eighteenth century, declined in the early nineteenth century, when many states barred slave trading, and officially ended in the late nineteenth century. But trade in women continued well into the twentieth century, for they were still given as pawns in the 1930s.[11]

Slaves captured inland were marched on rugged paths to the coast, often in shackles. The journey was long and arduous and some died on the way. Those who reached the coast were locked in warehouses to await shipping in lots of about 250; some died there. The next leg, called the Middle Passage, was the most feared by both captives and captors. On shipboard, captive men were usually shackled in pairs on a lower deck, where they could barely breathe; women and children were chained until the ship was well at sea, then freed and permitted to go out on deck for air. A trader could count on losing 10–20 percent of his captives during a voyage—more if it took a long time or an epidemic broke out. But 20–25 percent of the sailors conveying the slaves also died, and only 10 percent of the men who ran the Royal African Company's forts in Lower Guinea lived to return to England. Revolts were common during the voyages: more than 150 uprisings of captives were recorded in the 300-year history of the Middle Passage.

From West and Central Africa to the coast, people were seized and sent to Brazil, the West Indies, and, later, North America. After depleting whole populations, the traders moved on, searching for more capives. Most ravaged were Guinea, the Akan States, Togo, and Benin (not Benin City but present-day Nigeria), which together came to be known as the Slave Coast. Guinea's tropical forest and small farms had been inhabited for at least 10,000 years before European intrusion in the fifteenth century. Muslim slave traders had earlier invaded Upper Guinea; most of those exported to the Americas from Upper Guinea were war captives (sometimes high-ranking men), criminals sentenced to slavery, or people seized to pay debts. In southern Guinea and the West African coast, less touched by Islam, people lived in villages bound by lineage, some of which had consolidated into small kingdoms. The Gold Coast (named for its gold mines) referred to thirty small kingdoms called the Akan States—later, the Asante kingdom. By the 1700s slave traders had raided Lower Guinea (now Togo and

Benin). The Adja kings of this region became middlemen in the trade for their own profit.

Most enslaved females remained in Africa, cut off from their kin-groups; women, who had been enslaved for 1300 years, cost more than men in Africa. Most male Africans were sent abroad, because plantation owners in the New World preferred men, thinking they worked harder than women. But male slaves rebelled without women, so New World owners began to bring women, who, they found, worked equally hard.

Some transported women had been free; others, enslaved. All slave women worked double time, first for their owners in the fields or the household and then for their own families, continuing through pregnancy and childbirth. Abortion violated African mores, but women aborted themselves rather than bear slaves—in Zaire and western Sudan, for instance, slave women bore fewer children than free women. In Africa, female slaves were supervised by free women, who tried to assimilate them into their society. If there were enough slave women on a plantation or in a household, they supported each other. Questions remain about female owners' treatment of women slaves, though, when Wright studied autobiographies by central African female ex-slaves, she found that female chiefs acted as women slaves' protectors, and not, as male chiefs did, just as brokers. Still, there is evidence of female resistance: abortion, escape, refusal to conceive, and revolts.

The extremely fertile, densely settled West African coast was not totally devastated by the removal of huge numbers of people, but Angola, further south, the main source of slaves for Portuguese Brazil, was severely depopulated. The slave trade ruined or destroyed millions of lives and altered, forever, African political, social, and economic arrangements. Europeans built trading posts in Lower Guinea, and local chiefs supplied them with African raffia-cloth, shells, and enough slaves to fill their ships. Ambitious Africans gathered followers to raid inland territories with imported guns. By controlling inlanders' access to European cloth, beads, alcohol, tobacco, and arms, they obtained humans to sell to the Europeans. Those who wanted to defend themselves needed imported arms; those who rejected the madness and tried to go on living in their traditional way— like the Igbo—were annihilated by slave raids. Newly warlike groups produced kings who founded states that became the kingdoms of Asante, Dahomey, and others. In 1724 King Agaja of Dahomey and, in 1789, the *almami* of Futa Toro tried to stop the slave trade, but it was too profitable. African rulers were unwilling to support them and they gave up.

Nzinga of Angola

Some African women actively resisted European predation. Nzinga of Angola was one such leader, better documented than others. Born in 1581, she was the daughter of the *ngola kilu-anji*, ruler of Ndongo in what is now Angola, home to the Mbundu people. The *ngola*, a great soldier and tyrant, was killed around 1618. His eldest son, Mbandi, became *ngola*. By that time, Nzinga (who was also called Anna Zingha) was married and had a son.

Mbandi's first act was to murder all those who might challenge his status, including Nzinga's son; then he started killing the chiefs who had backed his claim to the throne. With her husband and sisters, Nzinga fled the capital, Mbamba, and settled in Matamba. Mbandi, who was ruthless towards his own people but craven towards the Portuguese, yielded them central Ndongo. He begged Nzinga's help in negotiating a peace treaty. With no inclination to help her son's killer but wanting to protect her people from enslavement, Nzinga went to Luanda. She had little to bargain with: Mbandi had ceded everything and the Portuguese had named a puppet *ngola*. Her meeting with the Portuguese governor became a legend in Africa, for she was a great diplomat.

Preceded by musicians and serving women, Nzinga made a grand entrance into the meeting room, only to find it empty except for the governor's throne. This arrogant discourtesy did not faze Nzinga, who had one of her women bend over on hands and knees. She was seated on her when the governor entered. He demanded that the Mbundu return all Portuguese prisoners; smiling, Nzinga agreed, on condition that all captured Mbundu—most of whom were being worked to death on Brazilian plantations—also be returned. After discussion, they agreed that Portugal would recognize the *ngola* as ruler of an independent Ndongo and withdraw its army if the Mbundu would return Portuguese prisoners and ally themselves with the Portuguese in the slave trade and in a war against the Jaga. The Jaga were homeless wanderers—escapees, ex-slaves, and criminals—and some Europeans claimed that they were cannibals who kidnapped children to increase their band.

Nzinga believed that Portuguese treatment of her people might improve if she accepted their faith, so she remained in Luanda to be instructed in Christianity, and even took the governor's name as her Christian surname. But when the Portuguese armies did not leave Ndongo, she refused to return any of the escaped slaves. Mbandi, meanwhile, had gone to Luanda and prostrated himself before the Portuguese, begging for protection against his own people. The Mbundu now turned to Nzinga to lead them. In a brilliant and dangerous decision she allied with the Jaga and killed Mbandi on his return from Luanda. Wary, he had sent his son to safety, but she persuaded the Jaga leader to capture the boy and kill him too. In 1624 she abolished slavery and offered sanctuary to all escaped slaves.

Nzinga knew she could not defeat the larger, better-armed Portuguese armies by ordinary means, so she invented a different kind of war—guerrilla warfare—for this purpose. She was a great commander, moving her army constantly, swiftly, attacking and immediately withdrawing. She blocked the Luanda trade route, inserting herself so the Portuguese had to buy slaves from the remote interior, not Mbundu, from her. In 1630 she invaded Matamba, defeated the ruling queen, and settled her people there, offering haven to the Jaga or any escaped slave: her Mbundu assimilated newcomers. She used various strategies to unite Africans against Portugal; she had her men infiltrate the Portuguese armies, for instance, to persuade black soldiers they were fighting on the wrong side. Her soldiers raided settlements held by the Portuguese puppet *ngola*. She broke with the Jaga chief when he looted Matamba, just as the Dutch were horning in on the Portuguese slave trade.

Nzinga's success against the Portuguese inspired the *mani Kongo* to attack them, and while Portugal was mustering an army to deal with the allied Africans, the Dutch landed at Luanda and forced the Portuguese into the interior. Nzinga knew that the Portuguese would get reinforcements from Brazil and that she could not beat their cannon, but she did everything she could to weaken them. She surrounded them in a settlement at Massangano and held them under siege. After some months they broke out, killed 2000 of her army, and captured her two sisters. She retaliated, winning some battles with Dutch and Kongo aid. Then the Jaga, wanting to regain their slave trade income, went over to the Portuguese.

Nzinga persisted and had almost defeated the Portuguese when reinforcements arrived from Rio de Janeiro. She carried on with Dutch help, but the Dutch were defeated and Kongo submitted to the Portuguese. Nzinga, who was now over sixty, had to retreat to her refuge, the Matamba highlands, yet she fought on guerrilla style. The Portuguese had strangled one of her sisters, but the other remained captive. To free her and to protect Matamba and her people, Nzinga accepted Portuguese overtures in 1656, was rebaptized, and sent 130 slaves to redeem her sister Barbara. It had taken the Portuguese forty years to defeat her.

General Nzinga dressed like a man and kept a harem of young men dressed as women—her wives—and a council of elders to advise her. At seventy-five Nzinga disbanded her harem and married one of her youngest wives. She married her sister, Doña Barbara, to the general of her armies, naming her as successor. When she was over eighty, she sent an embassy to the pope and arranged a festival to celebrate his reply, dressing as an Amazon and doing mock battle with her women. She died in 1663 at eighty-two. Doña Barbara ruled Matamba after her death. Two centuries later, Europeans took over all of Africa, and Angola lost its independence. The African resistance used methods similar to Nzinga's. A rich literature about Nzinga exists in Angola and elsewhere in Africa. The people call a prehistoric imprint on a rock near the Cuanza River "Queen Jinga's footprint," as if her feet could mark stone.

Amina of the Hausa

Many West African Hausa city-states had women rulers. The Hausa origin myth tells of a woman who leads her people to a land near water, where she settles to establish her people's traditions; and Hausaland was ruled by a dynasty of seventeen queens.[12] Clans broke away to found separate villages sharing language and culture, and, by the twelfth century, Hausaland was made up of seven walled centralized city-states—Kano, Daura, Rano, Biram or Gaun Gabas, Katsina, Gobir, and Zazzau—ruled by dynasties claiming semidivinity. These sibling city-states constantly competed and refused to consolidate, so, despite wealth and strength, most of them were dominated by an outside power. Muslim merchants filtered in over the fourteenth century; in the fifteenth century, Fulani herdsmen invaded. The Muslim Fulani had been wandering for centuries but settled down to live by trading. They established centers of Islamic learning with the Muslim books they carried. Most later Hausa rulers were Muslim, but rural people retained their old religion.

Only two leaders ever unified the Hausa states. The first was Amina of Zazzau. Although Muslim historians omit women, one mentions Amina. Near the turn of the sixteenth century, the eighteenth ruler of Zazzau converted to Islam, in which only men can rule. When the twentieth king, Nohir, died sonless in 1535, his brother inherited the throne, then died. The city designated Nohir's daughter, Bakwa Turunku, as ruler. Bakwa Turunku fought the Nupe while her slaves built a new capital, Turunku. As the town grew, she saw it would not have a sufficient water supply, so built a fort further north overlooking the Galma River, naming it Zaria for her daughter. Later, Zazzau was called Zaria.

Bakwa Turunku's older daughter, Amina, was sixteen when her mother was named to the throne. Men courted the princess with gifts of slaves and expensive clothing, but she refused to marry. Accounts of her life conflict: either Amina succeeded her mother on the throne in 1536, reigning until 1573, or Karama, a male, acceded, and Amina's military exploits led her to succeed him on his death in 1576. In any case, for thirty-four years she was a powerful military commander who tried to unite the

Hausa states by force. The Sultan of Sokoto, Muhammadu Bello, wrote: "She made war upon these countries and overcame them entirely so that the people of Katsina paid tribute to her and the men of Kano. She also made war on the cities of Bauchi till her kingdom reached to the sea in the south and the west." The ruler of Nupe sent her forty eunuchs and ten thousand kola nuts. She unified the Hausa.

Amina became a legend, said to have built many fortifications and encampments. One story claims that she took a new lover in each town she conquered, ordering him to be beheaded when she left the next morning. She created the only Hausa empire by leading an army of fierce horsemen into battle. Modern Hausa still sing her story, and a Nigerian stamp bears her image. Historians think Amina may have been responsible for a huge expansion of trade in fifteenth- and sixteenth-century Hausaland, when the work of Hausa weavers, smiths, tanners, dyers, and leather workers was in great demand.

In 1734 Bornu conquered the Hausa, who remained independent artisans whose work enjoyed wide demand. They also remained Muslim, but widespread corruption in the late eighteenth century generated a revolutionary movement aimed at reforming religious practices. From this upheaval, Usman dan Fodio formed a new state, the Sokoto Caliphate. Proclaiming a purified Islam, he forced people to convert to Islam. His descendants, including his educated daughters, founded educational and religious institutions that kept Islam alive in later centuries. Islam tends to keep tightening control over women, especially in prosperous regions. The Hausa increasingly segregated women and excluded them from public life. As women were placed in purdah, Amina became a mere memory. However powerful women were in early periods, the tendency is always towards greater male domination.

East Africa: The Shambala

A group called the Washambala settled in an inland region of the Shambala Mountains in Tanga (in present-day northeast Tanzania). It sprawled over three different agricultural zones, so people traded crops and manufactures with each other. Settlers from diverse areas of East Africa migrated there, bringing different languages and cultures, but, in time, they adapted to the language and culture of the Washambala, who themselves had derived from many different ethnic origins.[13]

Before colonialism, the Shambala lived in neighborhoods encompassing several villages: each held several lineages. The head of the strongest lineage in the dominant village directed production, defence, and war for the entire people. The strongest lineages tended to hold the oldest residents: they created rituals, established village history, and allocated land to new settlers. They justified their domination by an origin myth. In one version, Sheuta usurps rule from the previous chief, Bangwe, a "murderous" woman, by using his expandable penis to penetrate and skewer her to death during coitus. In another, he triumphs by satisfying Bangwe sexually; when her women followers also want sex with him, Bangwe refuses to share him, so the others reject her and name him chief. The first myth suggests that male dominance among the Shambala was accomplished by male violence against women.

Lineages traded with each other, exchanging tobacco, livestock, and women; people could marry within their neighborhood but not within their lineage. Neighborhood heads, led by the strongest leader, governed the clan. The clan controlled surpluses, trading food for livestock, and mobilized young men to build and maintain the irrigation system, to terrace mountain slopes for cultivation, and to raid nonclan villages for women, children, and loot—cattle and stored grain. But this rule from above chafed lineages and sublineages, who seceded from the clan and sometimes forcibly seized other groups' land. In the late sixteenth and early seventeenth centuries, war was near constant.

The system exalted strong men; those who controlled the most land drew clients who served them in return for livestock, women, and protection. Men with land also controlled the labor of clients or pawns. During famines, people were pawned by their lineage heads or pawned themselves for food. A lineage, the primary unit of production and reproduction, consisted of an elder male, his wife or wives and children, married sons with wives and children, sometimes in-laws, and slaves, clients, and pawns. Each had its own homestead. Lineage members who were unrelated by blood or background were assimilated by myths asserting ideologies of kinship and lineage. Blood bonds were not sacrosanct: elders sometimes gave kin, usually young women or girls, to other clans to pay a fine, compensate for a crime, repay a debt, or cement a new alliance. Elders did not work but wielded great power—it was essential to keep their favor. Insubordinate sons or clients could be denied wealth for brides or fines, And, without bride-wealth, men could not marry. If fines were not paid, the offended lineage could enslave a man who had impregnated an unmarried girl or had sexual intercourse with another man's wife and also enslave his kin.

Bride-wealth was paid to a woman's lineage in installments: the first payment, made before she left her father's house, covered rights to her labor, sex, and her future offspring; the second payment was made at the birth of her first and sometimes second child. It reimbursed the woman's lineage for relinquishing its claim and letting the new offspring become a member of the husband's lineage. The bride received limited rights in what was called the "cow of affinity," given as part of the second payment. This cow's calves, held in trust for the woman's sons, were part of their bride-wealth fund. She could not exchange the cow or lend it to a client, as the patriarch could with other stock.

The patriarch held all property in trust for his lineage, but he controlled it absolutely. When an elder died, the property was divided equally among his wives for their sons; the sons of his senior wife acceded to leadership. There were arguments over succession, but new heads were usually conciliatory; they tried to keep all lineage members as emblems of power. Wives did not inherit in their own right; they were property to be inherited. A wife's only rights were to a house of her own and different kinds of land sufficient to produce enough food to keep her and her children. A patriarch could at any time alter her holding. Wives were obliged to feed and maintain themselves and all others residing in their homestead, and to process and store food. Women also tended the aged, the sick, and the children, who, especially girls, were expected to plant, weed, irrigate, guard crops against birds and monkeys, harvest, and collect wood and water. Men cleared land, did heavy hoeing, helped harvest, guarded crops from larger predators like wild pigs, and undertook the major hunting, long-distance herding, and raiding; boys helped herd.

Like male elders, female elders did not labor in the fields, but they supervised the work of sons, unmarried daughters, junior cowives, female slaves, and female pawns. Women were not expected to produce a surplus: they did subsistence farming. They were responsible for the necessary, for keeping the lineage alive. Men were responsible for generating wealth, by augmenting the number of livestock through raids or natural increase and by marrying or selling daughters, pawns, and slaves. They also gained wealth by working as blacksmiths, hunters, or soldiers, making medicine, or by raising and selling tobacco—a man's crop, grown on land allocated to men, grown by them but also by their wives and male and female slaves. Tobacco was sold throughout Tanzania and Kenya.

In the seventeenth and eighteenth centuries more immigrants entered Shambala, causing conflict. Some groups conquered and absorbed others; some expanded and vied for dominance. Finally one clan, the Kilindi, conquered all the others and founded a state. They introduced a kind of feudalism and an origin myth to justify their rule. Mbegha, a god representing the Kilindi elite, conquers Shambaa (representing the Shambala) by "making them all women": he is strong, they are weak; he is a hunter, they are cultivators; he provides meat, they produce starch. The myth justifies Kilindi rule but also reflects the devaluation of women's work in an economy increasingly based on money; it shows gender roles becoming power relations. To the Kilindi, the title "king" meant "owner of the land." Shambala history illustrates what is probably a universal economic progression: at first, land is communally held; then a patriarch holds it in trust for his lineage (members of which had claims to it); then, in early states, a head man literally owns all the land, allocating it at will. Revolutions win other men the right to own land—but no revolution until the feminist movement ever won women the right to own land.

Dahomey

Dahomey, originally Fon, lay in the hinterlands of Allada in West Africa. Founded either by a prince who fled Allada after a conflict over succession or by a gang of bandits, Robin Law writes, it probably became a state in the 1620s (it is mentioned as Fon in the 1680s).[14] A significant entity in the early eighteenth century, it repudiated an alliance with Allada in 1715, defeated Allada in 1724, and conquered the coastal area, Whydah, in 1727. Its decline seems to have occurred simultaneously with its expansion, since from 1720 to 1823 it paid tribute to the Oyo Empire. But it remained influential until the 1890s, and the Fon people still exist. Dahomey offers a striking example of European hypocrisy about slavery. Supporters of the slave trade called Dahomey militaristic, despotic, and brutal. They said that it practiced human sacrifice, that its small, highly disciplined army decapitated and sacrificed captives, and that its king was a cruel despot who oppressed a servile population. Slave traders argued the humanity of selling captives rather than killing them: slavery saved lives!

It is true that Dahomey was militaristic, killed many captives, and accepted that its king owned everything and everyone in the kingdom. However, as always in Africa, centralization was looser than Europeans imagined: tradition and the power wielded by chiefs restrained the king. The slave trade itself generated militarism in Africa. Robin Law believes that Dahomey was a new kind of African state, one that emerged to maintain order and integrity in the face of the slave trade.

Some facts support this view: Dahomean kings disavowed kinship—the usual base of legitimacy—in favor of military force, rule by might. They presented the state as a larger family, writes I.A. Akinjgobkin, superseding the traditional African political system of decentralized kin-groups, which no longer protected people from the disruption and incessant warfare caused by the slave trade.[15] Karl Polanyi points out that Dahomey's controlled economy at least ensured subsistence for all. The country seems to have been managed efficiently, taxes were recirculated, and people were protected from export and from the impact of slave labor on royal estates and corvée labor in Whydah.[16] Dahomey did not sell its natives, even slaves, out of the country unless they had broken a law. The king held a monopoly on the long-distance slave trade until the mid-eighteenth century, when private merchants brought slaves from the interior to the port. Using slave labor supplied by the king, private merchants also controlled the palm oil trade that succeeded the slave trade. Law thinks that Dahomey was organized to protect Dahomeans by enslaving others.

The state emerged in the usual progression: one lineage asserted its royalty (superiority), backed its claim with military force, claimed all land in the name of the king, and required all communities to pay tribute to use traditional lands. The royal lineage used women as a means to transform kinship relations into class relations: by controlling women, the rulers achieved indirect control of men. They deprived all women of freedom, and, though a few gained status, their power was severely circumscribed.[17] Nevertheless, elements of the political structure suggest that Dahomean rulers valued and feared women more than men.

The new elite used several strategies to transform the political organization from a collective of lineages into a state. They humbled the lineages by forcing them to pay tribute of food, crafts, animals, and labor; if they refused, the royal clan used hoodlum tactics, sending goons to attack women going to market and demanding fees for "protection" from them, or forcing people to buy "insurance" against natural disasters. Rural women still marketed their goods and controlled their own resources, but a male official in charge of the marketplace collected fees for stalls and tolls for roads, infringing on women's prerogatives. Still, market women had more freedom and authority in their sphere than elite women in theirs. In later periods, village women refused to marry state officials because their wives were secluded and could not market. When France colonized Dahomey in 1892, market women still had more autonomy than elite women.

The elite lived parasitically on slaves—people from neighboring groups who had been captured in raids, or those convicted of crimes or pawned for debt. Slaves produced food and goods on royal plantations, maintained the royal compounds, served the elite, or were sold for export in Whydah. To recruit soldiers for state-organized slave raids, officials took a prominent older man hostage: if half the healthy men of his lineage did not show up to serve on the raid, he was killed; if a particular man did not show up, his wife, mother, or sister was taken. Women designated "wives of the king" and women convicted of crime were sent to villages to entice young men into sex, then charge them with rape; rapists were sentenced to military service. Women forced to act as prostitutes became prostitutes, heavily taxed by the government. Most soldiers were temporary draftees.

But the standing army was a regiment of about 4000 women, called "wives of the king." These soldiers lived in the king's compound but, unlike other "wives," did no productive work. They left the royal compound in troops with an advance guard of slaves who struck down anyone who did not give way. Given military training, they were famous for their ferocity.

After the 1720s, agents of the king visited every village in the kingdom every three years, rounding up all girls around the age of thirteen. Families were required to give a daughter as tribute; the king sent them gifts in return. Taken to the capital, Abomey, the girls were divided in groups. Selection was supposed to be an honor, but some of the chosen girls killed themselves. The unchosen were sent back to their villages. Some of the girls were designated to be servants to the king, or symbolic "wives," trained as domestic workers or soldiers. The king had other wives too, who had been sent as gifts by prominent men to cement political alliances. The king might use these women sexually, but their sons could not become king—succession was determined by struggle among the sons of the king's concubines. The winner usually slaughtered the losers.

Another means of controlling women, and men through women, was to require every male bureaucrat and state agent to send a woman, who stood to him as a mother, to live in the king's compound and to be executed if her "son" proved disloyal. These women managed the king's pawns and lived on what the pawns and slaves produced. If they refused this role, they could not stay in the royal compound; but if they left, their "sons" lost their position—or their lives. Men's affection and respect for mothers or other female relatives was manipulated to create loyal bureaucrats, obedient villagers—a compliant society. State-controlled women had high status and certain rights—they lived in leisure and produced nothing, which may have seemed a luxury when others were working in the fields. But they did not control their own lives, especially their sexual and reproductive lives: they were forcibly removed from kin and made subject to state authority. The king's daughters, who had more freedom than other women, were often placed in the harems of bureaucrats as spies for their father. If they were not married to bureaucrats, however, their husbands lived with them in the royal compound at Abomey and their children inherited from them. Royal princesses were free to take lovers, but their sons could not inherit the kingship.

The idea of controlling men through women may have flowed from Fon tradition, in which women were very powerful. Dahomean religion also stressed sexual complementarity:

both sexes headed the cults and secret societies that guided the spiritual life of villages, just as all offices in the Dahomean political structure had male and female counterparts. Elsewhere in Africa, the highest rank a female slave could reach was favored wife, while male slaves could rise as ministers of state, advisers, soldiers, commanders, governors of provinces, and trading agents. But in Dahomey, female slaves were ministers of state, counsellors, soldiers, commanders, provincial governors, trading agents, *and* favored wives.[18] Both sexes needed a powerful male to rise, but females had to be part of the royal household.

The palace was the kingdom's administrative center. All its activities were aimed at enhancing the material welfare of the king and his lineage, and were managed by palace servants who were expected to uphold and extend the king's power. These servants, who were at the very core of state power, absorbed and redistributed most of the female slaves who were brought to Dahomey from outside for labor and service and who reproduced, thereby enlarging the royal family and the staff of permanent slaves. In the late nineteenth century, palace women had varied legal and social standing, but their status was so unlike that of any other women in Dahomey that their contemporaries simply called all of them *slaves*. Though all were legally the king's wives, only some were his sexual partners; some could visit their families, others could not; none could ever leave or divorce their "husband"—in this they were slaves, for commoner wives could leave their husbands at will and survive.

Dahomey had three social classes: royal *(ahovi)*, commoner *(anato)*, and slave *(kannounnon)*. Status was unchangeable from birth: *ahovi* were born into the royal lineage; *anato* were born in Dahomey; and *kannounnon* entered the state by captivity or purchase. Commoners took their parents' status, slave or free, and some were bound to perpetual servitude. Those with two slave parents had the lowest status. The state annually went to war for slaves; at the end of each campaign, the king ceremonially purchased all the captives and distributed them, giving some as rewards to loyal subjects (like the female and male soldiers who captured them) and assigning others as soldiers, royal household servants, or workers on royal plantations. A few were ritually sacrificed to the ancestors. Until about 1850, some were sold abroad.

Rank could change: it was determined by one's position within the elite, the army, and among the servants. Slaves could occupy any category: the second highest job in the kingdom, queen mother, one open only to a woman, was usually filled by a slave. The queen mother, who was never the real mother of the king or born of any branch of the royal family, complemented the king, "mirroring" his functions. Every level of social organization among the Fon rulers of Dahomey was mirrored. Two sets of male ministers of state (one sat on the right hand of the king, the other on the left) were paralleled by two sets of female ministers; the army had two male and two female commanders, one for the right wing, one for the left. The king was mirrored by several figures—the queen mother, earlier kings, and symbolic figures. All offices were dual: a male (usually) held office outside the royal household, and a female within. Women on the state council made national policy decisions.

Visitors to Dahomey in this period testify to the power of women within and outside the palace. Foreign men commented that the king was surrounded by women and could not be seen or spoken to without their intercession. Female ministers took part in council deliberations and heard judicial appeals from the districts; one Westerner claimed that their influence was decisive, "it being a leading feature of Dahomean polity that in the counsels of the King the female sex have the ascendent."[19]

Another wrote, "The king's women play a considerable part in the politics of the country; they attend council meetings, their opinions have great weight with the king. They are the ones who refresh his memory on certain facts and prompt him on his addresses or speeches to the chiefs and to the people."[20] Women sat on the grand council, which met each year to discuss issues important to the nation as a whole. A Western observer wrote that the women in the council not only had the first vote but fined those who disagreed with them. Women participated in public debates held at court.

Also in the elite were the sacred *kposi* and *dadasi*, religieuses required to be celibate. Priestesses performed rituals to gods and the ancestors; high-ranking priestesses were responsible for maintaining the link between ancestral spirits and the kingdom. It was taboo to speak to the *kposi*, whose function is unknown. The elite also included potential sex partners of the king—about a thousand women, most of them slaves. Some had been married before: kings valued youth and beauty, but not virginity.

The next rank of women was the military. Dahomey had a women's army from at least 1720, but it was not made permanent until the reign of Gezo (1818–58). About a fourth of the palace women were soldiers, mostly captives trained from childhood in loyalty and fighting skills. Others had been sent to the palace as punishment for stealing or for "crimes" like adultery, bad temper, strong will, or being scolds, or had been condemned to slavery because their husbands or their fathers had been accused of disloyalty. These soldiers were an elite corps. The French who attacked Dahomey in the late 1880s were shocked at their ferocity, soldiers trained to die rather than retreat. The women were required to be celibate, yet they were sometimes given to men as gifts.

Occasionally even the king took a military woman as a lover, like Tata Ajache, a slave woman who had been captured as a child and trained as a soldier. She distinguished herself in battle by killing a man and was rewarded with gifts of cloth, cowries—and a fetus from King Glele, who swore her to silence. When her pregnancy was discovered, she was interrogated and beaten to force her to reveal the father, but she kept her vow. Glele transferred her to the elite and presented her with a house, two female slaves, cloth, and baskets of cowries and beads. To kings, loyalty was the highest virtue. Tata Ajache could have been killed—pregnant soldiers were occasionally executed as an example. Most, however, were punished by being sent to the front lines; still, many had children by the king and other men.

Ahosi were "wives" or dependents of the king. They could be female, male, or eunuch, for the word *wife* denoted status, not sex. The largest group of *ahosi* were servants; as always, the lower their status, the freer the women. *Ahosi* could leave and enter the palace at will. They processed and transported palm oil to Whydah, manufactured pots and other clay products, sewed uniforms for over two thousand women soldiers, and prepared food for daily consumption and for war parties and ceremonies, sometimes for many thousands at a time. They were responsible for maintaining the huge royal treasury of gifts and imported goods. Some of them trained soldiers or did reconnaissance spying, or were sent as prostitutes to seduce and denounce men for having intercourse with other *ahosi*, an act that was punishable by induction into the army. *Ahosi* were often given as rewards or offered to male or female visitors; all soldiers had at least one *ahosi*, though some had as many as fifty. Elite women had even more. King Gezo put an *ahosi* in a brothel in Whydah with 333 slaves; he took the brothel earnings, but let her keep the children who were born there.

The least free people were *gandoba* and *hwemesi*. *Gandoba* were probably descendants of slaves, held in perpetual servitude at the king's disposal. They were sent to serve an officeholder; the person might change, but the *gandoba* remained attached to the office. If a palace wife displeased the king, he could take back her *gandoba*. The status of *gandobas'* children depended on their sex: sons joined the lineage of the *gandoba's* master, but daughters became *gandobas* in turn. *Hwemesi*, women incarcerated in the palace for crimes committed by their lineage heads, were given as slaves; their children were part of the lineage of their owners, no matter who their natural father. Sons of bound women could sometimes escape bondage, but daughters could not.

Within the palace hierarchy, female slaves and commoners could get rich and reach the highest offices. High officials received royal titles, land, palm trees, and slaves. They could trade at Whydah, selling slaves through subordinates (probably lineage kin) who negotiated and managed their property. Although they were bound for life, they could own and bequeath property to female kin in their patriliny or rise to become queen mother; most, however, were slaves. Complex rules guarded succession, and power-struggles always followed a king's death. The key to victory was possession of the palace at Abomey.

In principle, free Dahomean women were full members of their patrilinies; in practice they were less important than men. Women headed compounds, but men put men at the center of the lineage. Slave *ahosi*, without lineage ties to Fon society, were even more marginal. One can understand why their contemporaries considered all palace women slaves. Whatever power, influence, or wealth they held inside or outside the palace, their bodies belonged to the king, not themselves. The king, or his rules, decreed whom they could see and whether they could go out, have coitus, or have children. Their sons were taken away from them.

Dahomean political structure is fascinating because it reveals openly the basic assumptions of patriarchy. The king wanted children to enlarge his lineage, but also total control over women's reproduction. To bear children, palace women needed permission, which devolved on their rank and function. Kings, and powerful men in general, preferred slaves and commoners as sexual partners, finding them more trustworthy and faithful than elite women. Slaves and commoners, with no power base of their own, could get things only by pleasing a superior male, so were probably more compliant than women with resources. Even women with enormous powers, with perhaps more influence than the king's male advisers, were utterly bound, slave or "free."

The fates of free women and slaves differed only slightly. Free women were forced to leave their kin at marriage, live in an alien compound with a strange man not of their choosing, and have sex with him. Slave women were forcibly taken to alien lands, to live among strangers not of their choosing, and often have sex with them. Free women could fulfill their obligations to their lineages, keeping alive the option of return if they were abused; slave women could not and had little hope for escape. In the late 1700s five slave women who managed to escape to their own country were hunted down, recaptured, and publicly executed. Captives and *ahosi* were often sacrificed. Intractability or recalcitrance was punished by sacrifice, sale at Whydah, or drowning in the sea.

Free women's and slaves' lives and work were about the same: both endured their culture's ambivalence about women.

In Dahomey as elsewhere, women sought as wives and honored as mothers were indispensible because they produced most of the food and all of the babies. They held high positions and great responsibilities, but, at the same time, were viewed as weak, deceitful, and treacherous. Women soldiers denied their femaleness, claiming, "We are men, not women." Slaves were thought more dependable than princesses, whose sexual freedom made them threatening. Slaves could achieve high rank and positions of trustworthiness, yet were also despised as inferior. Dahomean society was brilliantly designed to extract the most from women while keeping them under men's hand. Kings attended more to female advisers than to male, yet controlled men by their ties to women. Nowhere does men's esteem for and fear of women appear more clearly.

Like the Oyo Empire, of which it was a tributary, Dahomey seems to have been intentionally structured like a prison; controls held it together, enabling it to resist the overwhelming pressure of European aggression. It closed in on itself to protect itself, as the Western socialist bloc did in the twentieth century. I will discuss the Oyo Empire and other African strategies for dealing with European aggression in volume 3, chapter 1.[21]

CHAPTER 5

EUROPEAN APPROPRIATION
OF LATIN AMERICA

EUROPEANS SET OUT not just to explore the globe but to acquire it. Explorers sought a sea route to Asia, where they hoped to find new sources of gold and Eastern spices. Sailing in the service of Isabella of Castile, the Genoese captain Christopher Columbus stumbled on a "New World" when he landed in the Bahamas in 1492. At that time, many culturally distinct peoples occupied the Western Hemisphere. A million Nahuatl-speakers lived in clans in Anahuac, Mexico's central valley, and Caribs, Ciboneys, and Arawaks were sparsely settled on the Caribbean islands. In the southern continent, Inca dominated the Andes; Guaraní and Tupian inhabited Brazil, Paraguay, and the Guianas; and Bari, among others, lived in Colombia and Venezuela. These people had experienced war before the Europeans arrived; some, like the Bari, had retreated to inaccessible regions to escape it. Several of these groups were sedentary (horticulturalists, both sexes farmed), while others were semisedentary (women farmed, and men hunted, fished, and fought). Andeans worked massive state-run plantations, with terracing and irrigation projects. In Anahuac, people did complex farming, making swamp land arable; Guaraní, Tupian, and Bari did slash-and-burn farming, so they moved often.

Women were subordinate in most of South and Central America. Some groups lived in theocratic kingdoms ruled by chiefs *(caciques)*; Caribs settled in small villages. The women farmed, while the men fished, fought, and traveled great distances in dugout canoes. They brutally subjugated their wives, many of whom were Arawak, taken in raids, who spoke a different language from the men. Europeans claimed that the Tupians were cannibals, but this charge was later disproved. Other groups like the Taino were peaceful.

Waves of explorers hit the shores of this world in the fifteenth and sixteenth centuries. Columbus died thinking he had landed off the coast of Asia, but Florentine Amerigo Vespucci, in journeys from 1499 to 1502, knew he had reached a land mass between Europe and Asia. In 1500 the Portuguese Pedro Alvares Cabral found Brazil; in 1513 the Spanish Vasco Núñez de Balboa crossed the Isthmus of Panama to stand amazed at the Pacific. Iberians explored North America: in 1513 Juan Ponce de León reached paradisal Florida, Juan Rodriguez Cabrillo sailed along the coast of California, Hernando de Soto stumbled on the Mississippi River, and Francisco Vásquez de Coronado explored southwest North America. In the explorers' wake came *conquistadores* like Hernán Cortés, who treacherously conquered the Aztec Empire, and Francisco Pizarro, who conquered the Inca and won the richest silver mines in the world. Conquistadores subdued Bolivia, Colombia, and Chile, in cruel conquests.[1] Spain and Portugal dominated the New World.

Most Indians lacked writing, so what we know about them comes mainly from their conquerors, who invariably justified their own brutality by portraying their victims as subhuman. A few compassionate Catholic priests who accompanied the adventurers recorded the predation with shudders. All the invaders, however, were male and were uninterested in indigenous women or their culture. We know little about these women until the years after the conquest.

Conquest

Columbus had promised a pension of 10,000 *maravedis* a year for life to the first man on his ship to sight land, so Rodrigo was excited early on October 12, 1492, when he saw moonlight gleaming on sand. But Columbus claimed he had spied a light the night before, so took the pension himself. Yet he was a zealot who wrote to Pope Alexander VI, "I hope in Our Lord to be able to propagate His holy name and His Gospel throughout the universe."[2] Dedicating his journeys "to the glory of the Holy Trinity and . . . the holy Christian religion" and believing himself on a holy mission, Columbus saw divine intervention everywhere and never set sail on Sundays. He sought gold above all, but only, he said, to finance an expedition to recapture Jerusalem from Islam. All the Iberians claimed they were serving church and crown: Bernál Díaz del Castillo, who accompanied Cortés, wrote more truthfully, "We came here to serve God and the king, and also to get rich."[3]

Columbus landed in the Bahamas, where, he wrote in his journal, the Arawak, a handsome, well-built people, swam out to greet the strangers "naked as their mothers bore them, women as well as men." The most beautiful people he had seen, they were "so naive and free with their possessions that no one who has not witnessed them would believe it. When you ask for something they have, they never say no. . . . They offer to share with anyone" their corn, cotton, spears, yams, and cassava. Struck by the gold ornaments he observed in their ears and in a woman's nose, Columbus demanded that they lead him to the source of the gold. They could not, so he abducted some of them, sailed to Cuba and Hispaniola (Haiti and the Dominican Republic), and built a fort—Spain's first gift to the New World. When he left for Spain, he stationed sailors at the fort, killed two gentle Arawak for trading fewer bows and arrows than his crew had demanded, and took several hostages (who died of cold on the journey). The seamen left behind soon ravaged the island, seeking the illusory gold, and used women and children for sex and for labor. The indigenous men then turned on the visitors and killed them.

In Spain, Columbus' extravagant claims of gold and slaves won him seventeen ships and 1200 men for a return to the Caribbean. Sailing from island to island looking for gold, he found only Indians, whom he took as slaves. He wrote: "My desire was to pass by no single island without taking possession of it . . . I built here a village and gave many presents to the *quibian*—for so they call the lord of this land—I took possession of lands belonging to this *quibian*. As soon as he saw the houses we had built and a lively trade going on, he determined to burn everything and to kill us all." He seized the *quibian*'s family, but "they hanged themselves from bridge-poles with some ropes they managed to find, bending their knees to do so, for otherwise there was not enough room for them to hang themselves properly."[4]

Persistent search revealed no gold to fulfill Columbus'

promise to the Spanish crown, so he took slaves instead, sending his men on a slave raid in 1495. Michele de Cuneo, a nobleman of Savona and a member of the expedition, reported on it:

> When our caravels . . . were to leave for Spain, we gathered in our settlement 1,600 male and female persons of these Indians, and of these we embarked in our caravels on Feb 17, 1495, 550 souls among the healthiest males and females—anyone who wanted to take some of them could do so—each man was thus provided with slaves, there still remained about 400 to whom permission was granted to go where they wished. Among them were many women with children still at suck. When we reached the waters off Spain, around 200 Indians died, I believe because of unaccustomed air, which is colder than theirs. We cast them into the sea. . . . We disembarked all the slaves, half of whom were sick.

> While I was in the boat, I captured a very beautiful Carib woman whom the Lord Admiral gave me; brought her into my cabin, and she being naked as is their custom, I conceived desire to take my pleasure. I wanted to put my desire to execution, but she was unwilling for me to do so, and treated me with her nails in such wise that I would have preferred never to have begun. But seeing this . . . I took a rope-end and thrashed her well, following which she produced such screaming and wailing as would cause you not to believe your ears. Finally we reached an agreement such that, I can tell you, she seemed to have been raised in a veritable school of harlots.[5]

Desperate, Columbus tried to force the Indians to produce gold: those who brought the required amount were given copper tokens to hang around their necks; Arawak found without tokens had their hands cut off and bled to death. But except for dust in the streams, there *was* no gold. When the Indians fled, the Spanish hunted them with dogs and killed them. The Indians mustered an army, but the Spanish, with muskets, horses, and armor, prevailed and hanged or burned the prisoners. Finally, Arawak began to kill themselves and their babies with cassava poison. Within two years of Columbus' landing on Hispaniola, half of Haiti's 250,000 Arawak were dead. Fifty years later, 500 remained alive, and, by 1650, there were none. Thus did Spain "civilize" the New World.

In 1493 the Spanish ordered Columbus on his second voyage—to take 1200 Spanish settlers to Hispaniola to appropriate Taino land. Until the Spaniards arrived, the Taino lived by fishing, gathering, and horticulture, but the Spanish enslaved them, forcing them to work plantations and mines and savagely punishing resistance. A priest accompanying the Spanish, Fray Bartolomé de Las Casas, chronicled Spanish treatment of the Indians who had welcomed them or surrendered to them. Las Casas wanted to influence the court's Indian policy and increase priestly power in the New World, so he wrote vividly sensational accounts, presenting Indians as docile victims. But the atrocities he described were real: the Spanish "spared neither children nor the aged nor pregnant women nor women in childbed, who were disemboweled and dismembered as if sheep in a slaughter house."[6] Taino who survived the conquest did not survive the occupation: most were dead in a few years and all were extinct within decades, killed by the Spaniards or by disease.

As chaplain to Pánfilo de Narváez' troops in Cuba, Las Casas accompanied Spanish soldiers one morning who stopped to eat in a dry riverbed full of stones. They sharpened their swords on the stones, then, marching to a village, decided to test their weapons. "A Spaniard . . . suddenly drew his sword—then the whole hundred drew theirs and began to rip open the bellies . . . cut and kill those lambs—men, women, children and old folk, all of whom were seated, off guard and frightened, watching the mares and the Spaniards." Having killed everyone in sight and in a nearby house (flooding it with blood), they bet on who could slice the bodies in half, decapitate them, or gut them with a single stroke or pike thrust.

Indians not killed by arms or forced labor died of disease. Smallpox had ravaged preindustrial Europe more lethally even than the plague, infecting 95 percent of its population and killing one out of seven people in sixteenth-century Spain. The Europeans who survived were immune but carried the germ; Hispaniolans, without immunity, were destroyed by it in 1518; Las Casas wrote that only 1000 Tainos survived—a mortality rate near 90 percent in a people already wasted by measles and influenza.

In 1519 Hernán Cortés sailed to the New World with a few hundred men. Landing in the Yucatan, he was greeted by Aguilar, an expatriate Spaniard, and by Maya men who gave him women, including the young Malintzin. Her Nahuatl-speaking mother had enslaved her as a child to a Maya-speaking Tabascan chief. She also spoke Nahuatl, the Aztec language. Spaniards call her La Malinche or Doña Marina.

Learning that the Aztec had gold, Cortés sailed north to Veracruz. The landing of a bearded white man had been prophesied as a sign that the deity and ruler Quetzalcoatl had returned, so the Aztec king, Moctezuma (Montezuma), was terrified by Cortés' arrival. He sent a hundred runners with rich gifts and a plea to leave, but the gold and silver only whetted

Cortés' lust. Moctezuma thereupon forbade Aztec subjects to feed the strangers, who starved until the Totonac, defying the order, invited the Spaniards to their villages and fed them—but not out of mercy. The Totonac wanted Spanish help in overthrowing the Aztec, who, each year, took their children for sacrifice and as slaves.

Cortés agreed to assist the Totonac and marched towards Anahuac with about 400 Spaniards, 200 Totonac bearers, and 40 chiefs as guides. Just as the Aztec had forced vassal tribes to worship Huitzilopochtli, so Cortés now forced his Indian followers to accept Christianity. In Anahuac the Spanish saw beautiful cities and found the food—bread, game, vegetables, fowl, freshwater fish—more plentiful and varied than in Spain. They also saw bloodied altars and the mutilated bodies of Aztec subjects. Wherever Cortés went, defecting soldiers joined him, and he ended with 20,000 Indian troops. At Cholulu, where four hundred towered temples stood, more beautiful than any churches in Spain, Cortés invited the headmen of these people to meet him. They came unarmed to the main square with thousands of retainers; Cortés' men, posted around it with cannon and crossbows, immediately mowed them down, looted the city, and left.

At first Cortés had a chain of interpreters, but the linguistically gifted Malintzin quickly learned Spanish, so Cortés needed only her. She always sided with the Spaniards. In Tenochtitlan, the Aztec capital, she translated gestures as well as words and took the initiative when necessary, addressing Moctezuma directly in ways she knew he would understand. Cortés found her indispensable, for everyone recognized her importance. At first he gave her to one of his men, but after leaving the coast he made her his lover. She bore his child, but following the conquest he married her to Juan de Jaramillo, a conquistador. She had another baby and lived thirty years more.[7]

Indians regarded Malintzin as more than an interpreter—she is mentioned in every account and present in every image they made. A drawing of Cortés' and Montezuma's first meeting shows the two men on the margins and Malintzin in the center, as the dominant figure. The Indians obeyed her without question, wrote Bernál Díaz del Castillo; the Aztec dubbed Cortés "Malinche." After they gained independence, however, Mexicans condemned Malintzin for betraying native values and submitting to foreign power. She became the "most hated woman of the Americas."

Díaz del Castillo described the enchanting approach to Tenochtitlan: villages rose out of water, a broad causeway led to a city of towers, temples, and houses white against green mountains. Inside the clean and orderly city, trees bordered a web of canals and cobbled streets, the rooftops laden with flowers. The palaces and villas were more magnificent than the homes of Spanish nobles, and the Tlatelolco marketplace was twice the size of Salamanca's—each day, 60,000 people exchanged a wide variety of goods.

Moctezuma received Cortés graciously, offering him whatever he wanted. Cortés demanded that the king convert to Christianity, but just then he was called back to Veracruz. After he had imprisoned Moctezuma, he heard that Cuba's Spanish governor had sent an expedition to Veracruz under Narváez to seize Mexico from him. Cortés went to meet it, leaving a contingent of soldiers behind. The captain left in charge attacked unarmed Aztec nobles, an assault that spurred them to unify under the leadership of Cuauhtémoc. Meantime, Cortés bribed Narváez's men by claiming he had only Christian intent, but then he crushed them. On his return to Tenochtitlan, Cortés was ambushed by Cuauhtémoc's Aztecs, who killed half his men. Cortés retreated but left behind the seeds of destruction. When he returned in three months, the people of Tenochtitlan were dying of smallpox.

Moctezuma was killed, probably by a Spaniard. Despite the epidemic, the Aztec repelled the Spanish siege for three months, until August 1521. Cortés drew Indians from the surrounding local tribes to bolster his force, exploiting vassal groups' hatred of the Aztec to muster a large army. But the Indians who supported Cortés as their liberator from Aztec control found that Spanish control was even worse. Soon, Indians complained that the Spaniards were taking their women just as the Aztec had.

In Peru, Francisco Pizarro, like Cortés, used treachery, terrorism, and negotiation to conquer the Inca Empire within three years. In a frenzy for gold and power, the invaders killed each other: Diego de Almagro conquered Bolivia, then was killed by Pizarro, who was killed in turn by Almagro's followers. Spaniards conquered Colombia and explored Chile and Brazil. Fighting in Chile and Argentina was extremely fierce because the indigenous peoples had never been subjugated.

The territory now called Brazil came to European attention when Portuguese explorer Pedro Alvares Cabral landed there in 1500. In the next decades, Portuguese wood traders set up posts on the coast. Portuguese castaways, deserters, and criminals settled there, taking Indian lovers and Indian names. Portugal did not fully control Brazil until the 1540s.

Spaniards settled North America too, founding St. Augustine, Florida, and New Mexico (Santa Fe in 1610). By the late eighteenth century Spain had colonized North America from California to the Texas coast. Indians in their path were ravaged by European smallpox. Anahuac suffered nineteen major epidemics of measles and typhus in 1531–32 and waves of smallpox in 1538 and 1559. Epidemics of pleurisy, measles, mumps, and *cocoliztli* swept Mexico, killing a large proportion of the population.

In 1500, eighty million people lived in the Americas; fifty years later, there were only ten million. From archaeological remains, tribute rolls, and eyewitness accounts by early Spanish settlers, demographers estimate that twelve to twenty-five million Indians inhabited Mexico before the conquest. A century later, about 1.2 million were left: 90 percent had been annihilated by war, murder, and disease. Spanish colonists demanded tribute and corvée; these obligations ruined Indian agriculture and caused famines that weakened the people, who then succumbed to disease. Apart from the great epidemics, the Mexican population died from malnutrition, common illness, and destruction of their traditions. A Spanish commentator noted that Indians were vulnerable to disease because of exhaustion from hard labor. They had lost the will to live.[8]

Missionaries declared that god had sent the epidemics to demonstrate his power and to persuade the Indians to submit to Spain and its church. Todorov cites *Historia* by Motolinía, a Franciscan who arrived in Mexico in 1524 and who opened his account with a description of ten plagues "sent by God to chastise this land."[9] But Europeans also caught an American disease: syphilis. Carried to Spain in 1493 by sailors on Columbus' first expedition, it spread swiftly, ravaging sixteenth-century European popes, kings, burghers, and peasants. References to "cures" and eroded noses pervade Shakespeare—Henry VIII died of it, Cesar Borgia was disfigured by it, and Pope Julius II supposedly withheld his foot from the kisses of the pious because it was covered with syphilitic sores. And the greed that inspired the Spanish conquest backfired. At first the influx of gold and silver enriched Spain, but sudden wealth created soaring inflation that raised the price of Spanish goods abroad and lowered the price of imports. Spanish industry collapsed even as Spanish kings, elated by the seemingly infinite New World wealth, waged extravagant wars on Holland and England. In the end, the conquest wrecked Spain's status as a major power.

Colonization

Spain was the epitome of the Counterreformation state.[10] As Reformation ideas of individualism, education, and male equality spread through northern Europe, Spain immured itself in tradition. Its church and nobles grew more absolutist; its bureaucrats vetoed free enterprise, encouraged state capitalism, and tried to increase income by exploiting mines and plantations rather than by fostering scientific experiment and industrial development. The mercantile theory current in this period held that colonies, like slaves, existed solely for the benefit of their owners. Home countries absorbed colonial exports at set prices and forbade the colonies to manufacture, so they had to purchase goods from their conquerors. Barred from developing their own industry for centuries, colonized countries became impoverished.

The conquistadores in the Americas fought each other, trying to carve out kingdoms for themselves. After crushing them, with difficulty, the Spanish king sent viceroys, governors, bishops, and *audiencias* (courts of law) to run the Spanish colonies: North America, Mexico, Peru, Cuba, and Chile. In their wake came clerics, lawyers, merchants, notaries, artisans, farmers, and women. Most of these women were single and arrived in official retinues or as servants in large households. They were seeking opportunities not available to them in Spain in the seventeenth century, but many returned after a period abroad. The Spanish built Mexico City and Cusco on top of conquered cities, but also established remote cities like Lima, Montevideo, Santiago, and Buenos Aires.

These towns were laid out in a similar plan: a central plaza was bordered by a cathedral, the governor's house, and other public buildings, part of a grid in which artisans and merchants set up shop. These structures were surrounded by Indian, *mestizo*, mulatto, and freed black *barrios*. Cities were Spanish enclaves; the country, Indian. Conquistadores, rich miners, and, later, landowners built palaces in the viceregal capitals. Spanish-owned plantations expanded along the coast, worked mainly by mulattoes and blacks. Urban and rural areas had quite different lifestyles.

In 1494 Portugal acceded to Spain all the Americas but Brazil, which it began to colonize in 1535, dividing the land into "captaincies." Duarte Coelho took possession of Pernambuco with his wife, Doña Brites de Albuquerque, the sole European woman in the colony, who ran the captaincy during his frequent absences. They tried to enslave the Tupinambá who lived near Pernambuco to grow sugar, cotton, and tobacco, but bellicose Tupinambá men disdained farming as "women's work" and resisted. Many died.

The captain of southern São Vincente induced sugar growers to build six mills in a decade. His and Coelho's captaincies succeeded but most failed, so Portugal ended the system, placing Brazil under a governor. The first governor arrived at the capital, Bahia, in 1549, with farmers, artisans, women, and six Jesuits. Brazil was relatively autonomous then, with few priests and lax crown control. Most Portuguese ran plantations and, by the seventeenth century, Bahia monopolized the European sugar market. Brazilian-born men, kin to each other, became a rich and powerful agrarian aristocracy, *senhores de engenho* (sugar growers), despite their undistinguished origins. Many *mamelucos* (the offspring of Portuguese men and Indian women) lived like noblemen on large estates.

In 1515 Spain made some effort to encourage family colonization and ordered Spanish officials going to America to take their wives along; if a wife chose not to go, her husband needed her consent to leave. Spaniards whose wives went with them usually returned home after their terms—few Spanish women chose to live permanently in New Spain.

Both Spain and Portugal used similar systems of colonization in the New World, ruling through viceroys and advisory councils appointed by the king. Councils heard appeals of viceroys' decisions and acted as watchdogs, reporting directly to the king. Kings controlled the American church, appointing church officials, approving all new churches and convents, and sharing their income. The church served the crown. Both states established *encomienda* (trusteeship) and *ripartimiento* (corvée). When Spain finally recognized that colonial wealth lay mainly in land, it adopted a trusteeship system in which land remained in Indian hands but Indians were required to pay tribute to Spain. This system professed to protect Indians from exploitation and to be educational: as Indians worked land under an *encomendero* (trustee), they would learn skills and Christianity. In fact, it made them serfs or slaves. *Repartimiento* was forced Indian labor on Spanish agricultural and construction projects. Christians called *encomienda* and *repartimiento* god's reward to Iberians for placing heathens under Christian rule, guaranteeing their spiritual and material well-being.

God's intentions were opaque, however. Muslims had conquered much of the Iberian Peninsula in the eighth century. Portugal ousted the Moors in the 1200s, but it took the

Spanish seven hundred years to do so. When the Ottoman Turks took Constantinople from Christians in 1453, the pope responded to hysteria about a resurgent Islam by fomenting a Christian crusade against European Muslims, and the Castilian court mounted unsuccessful military campaigns against the Moors in Granada. After Isabella of Castile married Ferdinand of Aragon in 1469, they faced rebellious nobles in their kingdom; it took twelve years to bring them under control. The royal couple could not give full attention to Granada until 1482, when they regained it in the *Reconquista*. In 1492 Spain cast out all Muslims—and began expelling Jews.

The Moors left a legacy behind. Whether the Moorish occupation influenced Iberian attitudes or reinforced existing traditions, the area was highly repressive towards women. In Spanish law, "only in exceptional situations does the woman enjoy full civil rights. . . . The single woman is always submissive to paternal authority . . . the married . . . inside the orbit of a new power as *acusado* as the first. Only the state of widowhood permits the woman to earn her full civil rights." And no married woman could inherit without her husband's permission.

As men define themselves as the opposite of their image of women, Spaniards defined themselves in opposition to Muslims and Jews. (Later, they defined their women in opposition to African slave women.) Muslims were excellent farmers, using irrigation and intensive labor to coax bountiful harvests from arid Spanish soil. They were also expert craftspeople whose textiles, handicrafts, and metalwork were finer than that of the Christians. Nobles and gentry, puffed up with medieval aristocratic values, exalted war and warriors and scorned manual laborers, artisans, peasants, tradespeople, and bankers. The Spanish left farming and crafts to "infidel" Muslims, and finance and banking to "infidel" Jews, whom they treated as beneath them. Spain never regained the knowledge and skills lost when its Muslims and three-fourths of its 200,000 Jews left the country.

The Iberians carried these attitudes to the New World. Disdaining manual work, they forced Indians to till the land while they raised cattle, a "gentlemen's" occupation. In Mexico, Spanish laws forbade Indians to own or kill cattle and permitted cattle-grazing on Indian land *before* the harvest. Instead of eating meat, Indians were "eaten" by it.[11] With cattle eating the crops, Indians lacked food, especially maize: prices rose eight-fold in 1545–55. In the 1550s, beef cost an eighth as much in Mexico City as in Spain, while Indian communities suffered widespread malnutrition and famine. Men for whom meat was a luxury in Spain ate it daily in Mexico. Without a profession or trade, white men in New Spain were comfortable and well fed.

The Spanish treated the Indians appallingly. Jonathan Kandell cites the bishop of Yucatán, Diego de Landa (who was himself a torturer), describing a Spanish captain who hanged Indian women on trees, then hanged their infants on their mothers' feet. They cut off hands, arms, legs, women's breasts; they threw Indians into deep lakes and marched them chained together by the neck. If they fell ill or slowed their pace, the Spanish cut off their heads, rather than pause to release them, and stabbed children who could not walk as fast as their mothers. Las Casas says that Spaniards grew "more conceited every day"; they refused to walk any distance, so "rode the backs of Indians if they were in a hurry" or were transported on hammocks by Indians, who ran in relays to "carry large leaves to shade them from the sun and others to fan them with goose wings." He also spoke of "so-called Christians" who met two Indian boys carrying parrots, took the parrots, "and for fun beheaded the boys."

Conquistador colonists impatient to become rich drove workers as they would not drive animals, especially in the mines, where they obliged people to work unpaid. Mines were the richest source of Mexican revenue to the Spanish crown by the 1540s, but miners, on average, died at twenty-five. Indians were forced to work in mines for months at a time as *tamemes*, or bearers, as part of the tribute they owed. Underfed, they collapsed under unbearable loads. Las Casas wrote that "they suffered and died in the mines and other labors in desperate silence, knowing not a soul in the world to whom they could turn for help."[12] In mining, workers strip mountains from top to bottom and bottom to top a thousand times; they dig, split rocks, move stones, and carry dirt on their backs to wash it in the rivers, while those who wash gold stay in the water all the time with their backs bent so constantly that they break; and when water invades the mines, the most arduous task of all is to dry the mines by scooping up pansful of water and throwing it outside.

Foremen used women miners sexually: "Each [foreman] . . . made it a practice to sleep with the Indian women . . . in his workforce, if they pleased him, whether they were married women or maidens. While the foreman remained in the hut or the cabin with the Indian woman, he sent the husband to dig gold out of the mines; and in the evening when the wretch returned, not only was he beaten or whipped because he had not brought up enough gold, but further, most often, he was bound hand and foot and flung under the bed like a dog, before the foreman lay down, directly over him, with his wife." After six to eight months, sufficient time to dig enough gold for melting, up to a third of the miners died. Some miners' wives stayed at home miles away, farming alone. The Spanish demanded tribute and taxes from cripples, the blind, or the maimed who could not work or who lacked food. Taxes were so high that Indians could not live. Floating corpses clogged the canals of Mexico City and the lake around it, and corpses of workers who had simply dropped at their work dotted the fields. Some clergymen spoke against this treatment, but they also coerced Indians to build the churches, hospitals, and monasteries that appeared everywhere.

The punishment for rebellion was enslavement. Ravaged by epidemics, war, and forced labor, few people rebelled but many were enslaved. Some fled to the hills; pursued, they were killed or enslaved. Nuño de Guzmán, the governor of Mexico City, sold 10,000 of its 25,000 subjugated Indians into slavery; the rest fled with their lives, though, without land, they had no livelihood. In a 1535 letter a crown agent, Vasco de Quiroga, asked what crime a consignment of "rebellious" slaves (men, women, and children, some under a year old) had committed and was told they had fled from Spaniards and hidden in caves.[13] The Spanish branded slaves on the face with their owner's initials each time they were sold, and some bore three or four sets. "A man's face, created in the image of God, has become a piece of paper in this country," Quiroga wrote. In the 1540s Spain abolished Indian slavery in Mexico and other New World colonies, but it continued under the guise of punishment for crime.

The clergy justified the murder of Indians by claiming that the Indians were cannibals, sodomists, naked, stupid, dishonest, mentally unstable, and full of vice.[14] Yet Las Casas wrote that Indians were veritable Christians, indifferent to material goods: with no desire for riches, they were not eager to work hard and content with what they need.[15] Even sympathetic men saw Indians merely as instruments: the Franciscan missionary Jerónimo de Mendieta wrote that God was killing Indian workers by disease and "filling the thrones of heaven with Indians" to punish the Spaniards for their cruel labor practices. In the end, ninety-five of every hundred Mexicans died.

Official Catholicism in Mexico is epitomized by the Dominican Diego Durán, whose *Historia de las Indias de Nueva España y Islas de la Tierra Firme* is a monument to zeal. Urging churchmen not to rest until idolatry was eliminated, he insisted on total conversion: no individual or part of an individual, no practice, however trivial, could be overlooked. Outraged that Mexican Indians assimilated their religion with Christianity, Durán sniffed idolatry even in dreams: "[The natives] should be examined [in confession] regarding what they dream . . . there may be reminiscences of pagan times." Indians used religion to resist and maintain their cultural cohesion, so priests pressured youngsters to reveal where idols were hidden and to inform on any who did not attend mass or marry in the church—all of which were crimes punished by whipping. Inquisitional officials forced children to testify against parents tried for idolatry or other sins.

The Mexican church did not limit persecution of the Indians to ideology. Priests forbidden to charge fees for sacraments charged Indians for weddings, burials, baptisms, masses for the dead, even confession, and made alms compulsory in many parishes. Priests colluded with local Indian *caciques* to steal community funds.[16] In time the church became the largest corporate landowner in Mexico. Christian missionaries taught Indians only the basics of religion, believing that Indians, incapable of understanding Christian doctrine in depth, would spread heresies; the church barred Indians from ordination as priests. The College of Santiago Tlatelolco in Mexico City, which successfully taught Indian boys Latin, philosophy, and theology, lasted only a few decades because the Spanish disapproved of "overeducating" the Indians.

Lay Spaniards debated whether Indians were a human or a subhuman species. One chronicler asserted they were naturally lazy, vicious, melancholic, cowardly, deceitful, and shiftless, and that marriage among them was not a Christian sacrament but idolatrous libidinous coupling—they even committed sodomy. In the mid-sixteenth century it became fashionable to consider Indians as children. Claiming they were not yet *gente de razon* like whites, Spaniards forbade them from starting enterprises that might compete with their own. For decades after the conquest, they barred Indians from owning cattle, sheep, and horses; Spanish guilds in Mexico City barred Indian craftsmen, declaring that their skills and products were inferior. When guilds let Indians join after 1550, they set quotas and made them permanent apprentices.

Soon after he arrived, Cortés wrote to the Spanish king that Mexico was so densely inhabited that not a palm's length separated cultivated plots. Forty years later, Díaz del Castillo wrote: "I . . . never tired of looking at the diversity of the trees, and noting the scent which each one had, and the paths full of roses and flowers, and the many fruit groves—of all these wonders that I then beheld, today all is overthrown and lost, nothing left standing." A century after the conquest, Mexico was uncultivated, a stark arid home to a few dying tribes. Spaniards deforested the Valley of Mexico, cutting down 25,000 trees each year for building, and burning large tracts to create meadows for grazing. Rain washed the treeless soil into valley lakes. By the early seventeenth century the lake system had shrunk by a third; wastelands grew between Lake Texcoco and Mexico City and the smaller lakes around them. The Spanish filled in the canals that wove through Mexico City until only a few were left.

The countryside belonged to ranchers with huge estates *(haciendas)* for cattle-grazing. The cattle drove away any

Indians who remained. Their abandoned farms merged with arid fallow land, which in time was good only for grazing. Only Spanish cattle barons could live on it. Ranching, though less labor-intensive than horticulture, still requires workers. To escape the burdensome tribute demanded from their communities or the arduous, dangerous construction work in the capital, Indians came to work on the haciendas. Once there, they could never leave—they became peons, bound by a debt system that precluded them from ever repaying what they owed. (Some historians, stressing the extreme measures owners took to keep peons bound, suggest that many did escape.)

While the Spaniards cursed them, calling them idlers and lazy vagabonds, the Indians did most of the work in colonial Mexico, building churches, palaces, irrigation works, and villas, transforming Anahuac in eighty years. By 1600, Spaniards held more than half its farmland. To wipe out the Indian religion, the church burned Mexican books; to erase evidence of earlier power and autonomy (which could fuel revolt), the Spanish destroyed monuments and razed cities, erecting cathedrals and monasteries on the sites of Aztec, Inca, and Maya temples. It was not enough to destroy the civilization; they had to destroy the memory too.

The harder the Spanish impressed Indians, the faster they died. Desperate for labor, the colonists began to import Africans. Slaves had to be conveyed, clothed, fed, and housed, but the sharp decline in Indians made this effort worthwhile. By the late sixteenth century, over 60,000 African slaves lived in Mexico—more Africans than Spaniards. Among the major supporters of black slavery were the priests, who opposed forced Indian labor but who bought, sold, and exploited black slaves. The church partially defrayed the cost of building the Cathedral of Mexico City by selling African slaves in the provinces. Jesuits used black slave labor to run their ranches, plantations, and mills. In the seventeenth century the College of St. Peter and Paul purchased more than five hundred slaves, listing them in account books as "items."

Slavery in Latin America

The Indian nobility died out or sank into destitution, leaving only a few wealthy, politically powerful *caciques* of lineage in the early nineteenth century.[17] Indian commoners' wills listed windowless adobe huts, pottery, clothes, a hoe, ax, sleeping mats, stool, table, or chest, and sometimes a few acres of land. Late sixteenth-century Indian farmers grew maize for all of Mexico City; fifty years later, wealthy Spaniards made Indians work as sharecroppers or peons to grow their maize, and only 2.5 million Indians remained of Mesoamerica's 25 million (and 1.3 million of Peru's 9 million). Caribbean Indians were almost exterminated.

When rich silver deposits were discovered in Mexico and Peru in the 1540s, more labor was needed to mine it. Las Casas, the "protector of the Indians," urged Charles V of Spain to allow 4000 African slaves to be imported to work the Antillean mines. A slave-worked sugar mill was built in Hispaniola in 1530 and, before long, on other islands. In 1559 the first epidemic (probably smallpox) hit Brazil, killing thousands of Indians, and the Portuguese began importing Africans as slaves to plant sugar.

In 1550 virtually no Africans lived in northeastern Brazil; by 1585, 2000 Africans worked in Pernambuco's sixty-six sugar mills alone; by 1600, Brazil had 50,000 African slaves. In 1700 there were 560,000; by 1800, 1,891,400; and by 1900 there were over 3.5 million African slaves in Brazil. Spanish America had about 1.5 million. In the 1600s, England, Holland, and France seized Spanish islands to build their own sugar plantations. They all trafficked in slaves. By the seventeenth century, blacks outnumbered whites in the islands—ten of the twelve British West Indian islands were nearly 90 percent black; in Jamaica, 30,000 whites ruled 250,000 blacks and 10,000 free. Only in Bermuda were whites 52 percent of the population.[18]

Costly, skilled black slaves had slightly higher status than Indians in Mexico (though not elsewhere), and the Spaniards feared them. In the early 1600s, runaway slaves preyed on travelers on the Mexico City-Veracruz road; in 1611, after a white owner beat a female slave to death, blacks stoned the viceroy's palace and inquisition offices. Such events so unnerved the Spanish that, in 1612, they mistook a stampede of escaped hogs for a fugitive slave attack and accused twenty-nine men and seven women of conspiring to overthrow Spain and found an African kingdom in Mexico. Claiming they had confessed, under torture, to foment the murder of all white colonists, authorities hanged them before a huge cheering crowd. After exhibiting their severed heads on pikes, they placed blacks under a sunset-to-dawn curfew, barring them from owning or bearing arms, buying liquor, or assembling.

Throughout Latin America, but especially in the Caribbean, slaves were treated with a cruelty unknown elsewhere. The "brave new world" was not an idyllic experiment but a hell on earth for most inhabitants. Africans were seized by force, conveyed across a huge ocean to alien lands controlled by people whose language they did not speak, who worked them under excruciating conditions, fed them badly, and beat them savagely and often. African slaves in the Caribbean lived an average of seven years.

Barbados was the first island to become a major sugar

producer. The earliest colonists used both slaves and indentured servants. Most slaves were the only Africans in a household. Through the 1620s there were more indentured servants than slaves and the two were treated the same; the only difference was the term of servitude—servants' terms were finite, and slaves', permanent. Servants were white, very young, and mainly men: of emigrants leaving England for Barbados in 1635, 94 percent were male, and 91 percent were between ten and twenty-nine years old. There were no couples and no children under ten; the few females were probably from London or Edinburgh brothels or prisons.

Indentured servants were cheap and cheaply held. On arrival, they were lined up to be viewed by planters, who, subsequently, often resold them to each other. When Richard Ligon visited Barbados in 1657, he found that slaves were treated better than servants: they did the same hard labor, were poorly housed, and fed mainly loblolly, a thick gruel of boiled maize which slaves would not eat. Servants had meat only when an ox died.[19] They were subjected to a host of penalties for misdemeanours—pregnancy doubled a woman's term; marriage without an owner's consent meant two years' extra service. They were fined and whipped, but could not be whipped naked.

Planters and servants ate mainly loblolly, potatoes, and bonavist (a kidney bean), with "bone meat" twice a week. Slaves were fed mainly toasted maize, bonavist, and a bunch of plantains a week ("when they had plantains, they didn't complain"), "no bread nor drink but water," and slept on boards with no cover or sheet. "The Negres" being "more than double the numbers of the Christians," fearful owners forbade them to touch weapons, even though "they are fetch'd from severall parts of *Africa* . . . speake severall languages . . . and one of them understands not another."

Africans fascinated Ligon, who found them "timerous and fearfull, and [therefore] bloody, when they finde advantages . . . if one commit a fault, give him present punishment but do not threaten him; for if you do, it is an even lay, he will go and hang himselfe to avoid the punishment." Planters bought slaves right from the ship, naked, so they "cannot be deceived in any out-ward infirmity. They choose them as they do horses in a mar-ket; the strongest, youthfullest, most beautifull yield the great-est prices." The best males cost £30; females, £25–27; children, less. Owners bought mainly males. When male slaves com-plained, owners promised to buy women the next time. Purchased women were up for grabs: "the bravest fellow" picked first and "so in order, as they are in place; and everyone of them knowes his better and gives him the precedence." So a woman was doubly enslaved—to an owner and to a mate not of her choice. Yet their situation was more tolerable at that time than later.[20]

At first, white servants did the mechanical jobs and super-vised the slaves; male slaves did the heavier manual agricultural tasks, and females, the easier agricultural and domestic tasks. When the islands shifted to monocrop sugar production in the eighteenth century, women were pressed into highly regimented labor in a rigid work cycle. Sugar cane is planted continuously, so it may be harvested all year. Even when men outnumbered women on a plantation, more women than men worked in the hot fields, constantly weeding, digging, and cutting cane—a highly arduous task lasting four to six months. Male slaves worked the "Ingenio . . . the Primum Mobile of the whole work: the Boyling house with the Coppers and Furnaces, the Filling room, the Still-house, and Cureing-house; and in all these, there are great casualties . . . if any thing in the Rollers, as the Goudges, Sockets, Sweeps, Cogs, or Braytrees, be at fault." But Ligon was less appalled by injuries to slaves than by cattle dying.

In Jamaica, owners took children away from their mothers as soon as they were weaned, placing them with a "driveress" in the grass gang (slaves worked in gangs under a driver). At four, children were put to work weeding; at twelve, to other tasks. Between twelve and nineteen, most girls tended livestock and worked in the house; after that, until they grew old or died, they worked in the fields. Slave elites were exclusively male, except for a midwife, doctoress (traditional healer), or head housekeeper (often a privileged mulatto lover). Women did not get prestigious skilled jobs involving boilers, carpentry, or masonry. Male slaves had a wider range of jobs; females were confined to field, laundry, and domestic work. In 1756, on a large estate in British Jamaica, seventy of the ninety-two women were field hands, while only twenty-eight of the eighty-four men did field work; nineteen were tradesmen. Women not in field work served in the house: there were two cooks, two "house wenches," and one washerwoman. Old women carried water, were drivers, or oversaw the work of small children. Two were doctoresses. Similar patterns existed on other British plantations.

In the fields, the sexes were roughly equal: both did backbreaking work; both suffered the same pain and punishment. In British colonies, slaves were turned out of their quarters at 6 a.m. and worked until sunset or later.[21] Field work was arduous, monotonous, and degrading. Field workers were treated as part of the capital of the plantation, like animals, and were maintained at subsistence level. They worked hardest of all and their living conditions were worse than those of craftsmen and house slaves; their health and death rate were worse, and they were most often punished by whippings or confinement in the stocks. Women cut cane even in the ninth month of pregnancy.

Yet women field workers lived up to five years longer than men. The workday in the grinding season could last twenty hours, for owners considered four or five hours sleep enough for a slave. A Cuban account of the end of the grinding season notes that the oxen were skeletons dying from overwork. One coffee planter in nineteenth-century Brazil expected a year's work out of his slaves: he could get enough out of them in that time to repay his initial investment and reap a good profit. Few of his slaves lived longer.

Sexual life began early, especially for girls, who were sexually free. Women disliked marriage because it confined them to one man who expected to be served, which was extra work.[22] Traditionally, African women nursed babies for several years, avoiding sexual intercourse. They maintained this custom in the Caribbean, but many babies died. Historians attribute the high infant mortality rate to the physical and psychological effects of dislocation, stress, and overcrowding as severe as that in Nazi concentration camps, but the women were also underfed, overworked, and physically abused. Some aborted themselves rather than bear children into slavery, and over half never gave birth at all. Rhoda Reddock writes that all the available data indicate that slave women resisted having children. At first only Creole slaves (those born in the New World) refused to procreate, but, as the number of Creoles increased, such resistance became general. Abortion and even infanticide, a crime for Africans, became common.

White planters always used African women sexually; white female servants and African men could be lovers until the 1640s, when laws barred "miscegenation." Penalties for interracial sex depended on color and status: Africans ("heathen") were branded or whipped, indentured servants were given extended terms, and free people (though probably not white men) were fined. Freed servants began to live together and start families. By the early 1700s there were as many white women as men because women lived more healthfully and longer than men. A new economic system made slaves cheaper and more efficient, leading to fewer white servants and more slaves. Whites were overseers, artisans, and bookkeepers and always superior to slaves. By the 1740s, cohabitation of a white woman and a black man was too heinous to acknowledge.[23]

White men saw black women as "hot constitution'd ladies" with an "inclination to white men." Of course, the inclination belonged to the men. In excuse, some cite the dearth of white women in the Caribbean, where there were nine whites to every hundred blacks in the 1750s. But all classes of white men throughout Latin America, married and single, sexually exploited African women. They were also exploited by white men in the United States who had white women living with them in stable families.

Owners valued slaves as units of labor, not childbearers, and made few concessions to pregnancy or childcare. Women given too little food and sleep, frequently whipped, doing heavy labor for long hours, and living in poor sanitary conditions naturally suffer gynecological disorders. Amenorrhea from severe malnutrition was common (anorectic girls often stop menstruating); harsh beatings injured ovaries and endocrine systems, causing menorrhagia (heavy bleeding). Plantation slave women had a higher sterility rate, more miscarriages, fewer children, and earlier menopause than free women in comparable societies.

Whites justified forcing women to work until parturition and to return soon after by avowing that African women bore children as easily as orangutans. British law required pregnant women to be given lighter tasks six weeks before delivery and for three weeks afterward, but owners ignored this rule: women who complained were flogged. Jamaican planters were known for their callousness about pregnancy. One pregnant woman confined to the stocks for misconduct was released only a few days before her delivery and died of puerperal fever. White overseers and bookkeepers bragged of kicking "black women in the belly from one end of Jamaica to another."

For white men, African women embodied earthiness, sexuality, and physical strength. White girls in Jamaica married very young, often giving birth at twelve, yet whites regarded blacks as sexually precocious. Before 1790, slaves defined as nonhuman had no legal protection: owners had complete control over their chattels. In theory, a slave could register a plea with an attorney or a magistrate, but could not testify against a white person.

In the course of the seventeenth century, tobacco prices fell, impoverishing small farmers. Large farmers quickly swallowed up their land. A group of Dutch planters left Brazil for Barbados with new sugar technology and enough credit to buy African slaves for large-scale sugar production. Soon, all available acreage was put into sugar and food had to be imported. Prices rose. Slaves grew sugar more efficiently than servants did, so planters leased fewer servants. Most freed servants left Barbados because, without land, they were destitute. Poor free whites left too: the 37,000 whites in Barbados in 1629 fell to 17,000 by 1680, while the 50 slave inhabitants in 1629 grew to 37,000 in 1660. Large planters united to pressure the state to codify master/slave status. By 1700, both law and practice identified Africans with chattel slavery and plantation work.

Around 1780 the slave trade hit a snag—for many reasons. British sugar growers in India and the East Indies, who did not use slave labor, demanded "equal rights" with Caribbean sugar-growers. At the same time, slave revolts disrupted the plantation system. Meanwhile, the capital amassed through the trade was being spent on industrializing in the home countries, but industry did not use slave labor; rather, it needed cheap raw materials and markets for its products. West Africa, a source of raw materials and cash crops, could not provide them because it had been severely depopulated. Industrial owners began to support the abolition of slavery.

Foreseeing abolition, governments tried to "reform" slavery and make slave forces self-replenishing before the source was cut off. A series of acts—the British Amelioration Acts of 1787, the French Ordonnances de Louis XVI, the Spanish Código Negro Carolino of 1785 and Código Negro Español of 1789— made similar "reforms," encouraging slave marriage and nuclear families, discouraging "illicit" relations as tending to reduce fertility, and restricting the number of work days and improving the diets of pregnant or nursing women. Officials urged planters to set up infirmaries for slaves' infants and to give slaves a yearly clothing allowance and "provision grounds" for growing their own food. Spanish colonists resisted these reforms, and owners in the Caribbean never adopted the 1789 Código Negro Español. Schemes for boosting slave reproduction failed: slave women of childbearing age were now mainly Creoles, and adamant about not giving birth to slaves. Some planters (mostly in the United States) began to breed slaves by force. A breeding-farm in Trinidad produced thirty babies a year: a healthy infant fetched 500 pesos.

Britain abolished the slave trade (but not slavery) in its colonies in 1807, France in 1818, and other colonial powers in 1819–20. But the trade—and slavery—continued. To forestall the rising demand for abolition, in 1823 the British tried to reform their slave colonies, succeeding in Trinidad and British Guiana but not in Jamaica, Tobago, or Barbados. West Indian planters, resentful at having to feed their slaves, created a black-controlled economy by giving each adult slave a plot of marginal estate lands on which to grow their own food. The reform acts required them to allot enough land to feed a slave and time to cultivate it, so planters freed Caribbean slaves from plantation work Saturday afternoon and Sunday. Able to trade or sell any surplus at the Sunday market, slaves were devoted to their own plots and cottages. If owners took them away, curtailed these rights, or tried to sell the slaves themselves, Africans resorted to a traditional form of resistance—willful carelessness and indolence. In this period, many owners sold their slaves, disregarding family bonds and community attachments.

In Brazil, slavery was the major form of labor. It penetrated every aspect of life: people were classed as owners or owned, and even poor people owned slaves, for they were cheap, abundant, and available. An overwhelming number of female slaves were used as concubines. White men continued to prefer African mates, and their offspring increased so much faster than whites' that some towns were run by mulattoes. The Portuguese crown was still trying to reverse this situation in the eighteenth century: in 1726 Dom Joao V barred mulattoes or white men not married to (or widowed by) white women from public office. Slaves were restricted in marriage: there were more male than female slaves, and a woman could marry only a man who worked on the same plantation. They were not forbidden to marry, as they were in the United States, but slave marriage was discouraged. Owners who allowed it did not always permit slaves free choice.

By 1800, Africans dominated the internal marketing trade in the West Indies. By 1819, thousands of them did business in the streets. Like West African women, female slaves became prominent marketers and higglers (middlewomen), selling prepared foods, manufactures like baskets, and surplus crops. Keeping the profits gave them some economic independence of their owners—who feared them as clever, cunning, and untrustworthy. Indeed, planters seemed to fear women generally—the reform they most resisted was abolishing the flogging of female slaves. They insisted it was necessary, pointing out that men flogged even free women.

By the early 1800s, productivity slackened on British Caribbean slave-worked plantations, partly because of slave resistance. From 1815 to 1838, planters tried to squeeze profit from increasingly unproductive estates by driving slaves harder and trying to control by fear. But physical punishment only increased slaves' resentment, alienation, and rebelliousness. One man wrote, "The whip . . . does not correct but multiplies faults." When mechanized tools were introduced, men were trained to use them, but women still did manual work. Despite "reform," plantation conditions deteriorated in the last years of slavery.

A male historian claimed that black women, able to rise as concubines, identified with white society, adopted white values, and acquiesced in slavery more than men. Yet planters found women less compliant and more troublesome than men; they complained regularly in contemporary writings of "female demons" who verbally abused white male overseers and of "bothersome" domestic servants who shirked and feigned illness. More than men, women were accused of lying, stealing, inciting unrest, insolence, extreme laziness, disobedience, quarrelling, and disorderly conduct. Planters protested an 1823 law forbidding them to flog slave women in Trinidad, saying that female slaves, "notoriously insolent," deserved punishment more often than males. They continued to punish men with fifteen to twenty stripes (on average), and recorded punishing women with the stocks or solitary confinement.

Some women were repeatedly punished for defiance. Records from plantations in British Guiana for part of 1827 show that women were reprimanded more often than men. Among 171 slaves, the 34 punished included 21 women. Punishment (mainly whipping) not only pained but humiliated, as it was administered publicly by slaves and witnessed by whites "before the House" or some other public space. Many black women, who seem to have been utterly intransigent, tried to foment revolt in work gangs, ran away, or poisoned their owners. Visitors found domestic servants (who adopted European manners and dress) discontent, idle, unmanageable, and a constant source of irritation. They stole small things; washerwomen managed to use more than twice as much soap, blue, and starch as washerwomen in England, and they had a deplorable tendency to lose articles of clothing. Their harassment sometimes caused owners to sell their estates.[24]

Whether women were less tractable than men we cannot tell, but records suggest that owners were harsher with women. The Reverend Henry Coor, when he was visiting an estate in Jamaica, saw the owner nail the ear of a "house wench" to a tree for breaking a plate. White mistresses were notoriously cruel to female slaves, their unwilling rivals for white male attention. Owners regarded healthy female behavior as intransigence: Jamaican owners, begrudging the time slave mothers spent suckling their babies, opened weaning houses to cut down on female "malingering." Women fought separation from their babies, even mutilating themselves to stay with them.

Sullen as slaves, Africans worked eagerly in the informal economy, cultivating their plots, higgling, and marketing with energy and enterprise. A completely intractable and clever Carmichael slave who was demoted from the house to the fields caused such disruption there that she was put in the stocks. Yet she kept her own grounds beautifully, ran a complete huckster's shop on the estate, and held very profitable dances at her house. Unmanageable as a slave, she was dynamic and enterprising in her own community. Her activities gave her some economic independence and self-reliance, in sharp contrast with the total dependence on husbands of owners like Mrs. Carmichael. In an instructive overstatement, a white man wrote that women domestics were so indolent, refractory, and vicious that the white women who had to manage them were more enslaved than they! Whites eager to emphasize their differences from blacks to prove their superiority let field slaves retain their African customs. Women fieldhands fluent in the rich Creole language used song and language-play to subvert white mastery, mocking whites in subtle and satiric *double entendres*. Women were the primary agents of slave emancipation: their obstructions bred a spirit of resistance that decreased productivity, and judging by estimates, late eighteenth-century Jamaican slaves produced only a fifth as much harvest as equivalent workers today.[25] But women were not only the backbone of resistance to slavery; they also created a family and community life that enabled Africans to endure.

Adapting tactics to conditions, they subverted or verbally abused whites, physically challenged officials, escaped to Maroon communities in Jamaica and Suriname, made liaison with escapees, and organized slave uprisings. To recognize their courage, we must realize how difficult resistance was. Early slaves were isolated in separate households, each alone, bewildered by an alien language and customs, and surrounded by white men with whips and guns. Later slave forces were ethnically and linguistically isolated because they came from various parts of Africa. Their one common characteristic—nonwhite skin—sufficed to enslave but not unify them. Community had to be created, forged from common suffering. It was women who built community and connection, inspiring revolt by their strength and daring.

By the 1820s, owners corrupted by their lifestyle were mismanaging their property and were in debt, so absentee Britishers bought their plantations. Most slaves now were Creoles, sharing language, culture, and group consciousness, and they mounted several serious revolts. In Jamaica the 1831 "Baptist revolt"—incited, allegedly, by radical Baptist preachers—drove families from their plantations.[26] England abolished slavery in 1833, but its colonies did not conform until 1838, when planters decided they could run their estates more cheaply with workers they paid but did not maintain.

After emancipation, African women remained in their slave positions: the sexual discrimination that had fixed them in menial work did not vanish. Nor did emancipation end exploitation, for some owners still forced children to work free despite protests by their mothers. Women in St. Kitts in 1834 mounted what a British official called "turbulent and rebellious" resistance to protest work conditions. Most owners, determining wages by sex and seniority, paid female workers half as much as men for equivalent tasks. At abolition, almost two-thirds of the slaves on Jamaican estates were women: they still made up 70 percent of cane-cutting gangs, where they earned 1s 6d a day (compared with 2 shillings for the head fieldmen), while men had moved up to more skilled, better-paid jobs. Inequity increased as planters hired fewer women, even for menial, low-paid jobs. When slavery ended in 1838, men made up 40 percent of the workforce; in 1842 they were over 60 percent. Women were marginal irregular workers until

1841, when the plow came to Jamaica.

Once slavery ended, however, more women married and had children and marriages lasted longer. The population grew 50 percent faster than it had before. In the Caribbean, material circumstances and male irresponsibility defeated white efforts to force blacks into nuclear families. In Argentina and Uruguay, Africans lived in black and mulatto communities in the early 1800s (some still exist on the Pacific coast in Colombia, Ecuador, and Peru). Even there, color determined class and women tried to marry "up"; men were fascinated by black women and mulattas promenading along city streets in gorgeous clothes and jewelry, the gifts of white lovers.

Women in Racist Societies

During the period of colonization, Iberian custom and law faltered in a chaotic frontier environment. Until about 1700, people often married without contracts: men gave women their word, but they did not always keep it. They tended to move back and forth between Iberia and the colonies. The mother of Sor Juana Inés de la Cruz had three children by a Spanish captain and three by another man, though she was legally married to neither. Marriage was formal when property was involved; then parents forced their children to marry. After 1700, royal decree and social pressure regulated marriage and made children subject to paternal authority until they were twenty-five. A royal decree of 1776 let fathers disinherit children who married without their consent after that age. These rules supposedly "protected" women, who were considered weaker than men in the face of worldly temptation.

At first the Spanish crown tried to keep Spaniards and Indians separate. The Indian realm was mediated through

Indian nobles *(caciques)*, who were exempt from the personal taxes levied on other Indians and mixed-bloods. But intermarriage made the policy unworkable. In unions of Indian women and conquistadores, marriages that were often intended to bind the two groups, elite Indian women maintained their status and distanced themselves from *indios del común*, or commoner Indians. Most conquistadors also had Indian concubines. Alonso de Mesa of Cusco lived with seven women and six "illegitimate" children. Pizarro's two Indian lovers produced four babies; Hernando de Soto, childless with his Spanish wife, fathered "illegitimate" girls in Nicaragua and Peru. The children of conquistadores and Indians were called *mestizo/mestiza*, from a new concept, *mestizaje*, meaning mingling of races. Fathers often legitimated such children, especially if the mother was an aristocrat, and they were accepted at first by both worlds. The crown urged Spaniards to marry these mothers, but it also encouraged Spanish women to emigrate, and limited the tours of men who had wives in Spain.

More Portuguese men emigrated to Brazil after 1550. Few women followed, so the crown chose poor young women of good family, called "Orphans of the King," to go to Brazil as wives. But few went: sexual imbalance persisted in the colony throughout the colonial period. Intermarriage was accepted until the Portuguese crown decided to increase the white population by sponsoring couples or families to emigrate from the Azores or Madeira and urging crown employees to take their families to Brazil. Giving government posts, grants, and offices only to men with white wives, it pressured white men to abandon Indian concubines and marry whites. But the white population remained small and men went on taking Indian or African concubines. Although domestic arrangements determined men's futures, they preferred women of color.

After the early years of colonization, interracial marriage became rare and interracial concubinage, common. To marry someone of caste, a white needed a viceroy's permission; the government consistently discouraged white marriage to blacks or Indians. Marriage to one of doubtful racial or religious origin threatened a family's social status. In time, Spaniards distinguished among people of mixed blood (*castas*): white/Indian children were *mestizo*; white/black, *mulatto*; Indian/black, *zambo*; white/mulatto, *morisco*; and *mestizo*/white, *castizo*. Castes were usually barred from public offices and ordination, but had higher status than Indians if they had white blood. Whiteness, tops in the racial hierarchy, brought economic and political prerogatives, but even it was ranked: Spanish newcomers were "whiter" than Creoles.

Once slavery began, it dominated Caribbean culture and distorted life for everyone. Spanish colonies had fewer slaves than the Portuguese, but the mere existence of slavery created racism. The Spanish valorized whiteness, placing fanatic value on "racial purity" maintained by tight controls over women. Studies of relations between white women of varied classes, upwardly mobile black women, and blacks who chose not to join white society show that all were negatively affected by slavery.[27]

Racism probably touched Indian communities the least. Rural women kept their old customs alive, resisting or modifying Spanish beliefs and creating a *mestiza* culture that spread across the continent. Peruvian women cooked the same foods as in Inca times—maize, quinoa, potatoes, and llama meat—and made chicha (corn beer), although it was no longer used in religious ceremonies. Sixteenth-century Inca chronicler Guaman Poma de Ayala complained: "Women do not confess . . . do not attend catechism classes teaching Christian doctrine; nor do they go to mass. They do not even know who are their parish priests . . . they do not obey their mayors or their *curacas*. . . . And returning to their ancient customs and idolatry, they do not want to serve God or the crown."[28] Defying Spain, women performed ancient ceremonies. The military adviser for the great eighteenth-century Peruvian Indian rebellion led by Tupac Amaru was his wife, Micaela Bastidas.

Rural Indian women were fieldworkers and servants. In cities, most were servants, paid so little that every Spanish household could afford one. "In Lima, the wife of one far from prosperous artisan was waited upon by a Negro woman slave, a freed Indian woman from Nicaragua, and a Peruvian Indian servant, aside from two slaves who aided her husband in his work."[29] Women were cooks, nursemaids, and midwives; they sold bread, chicha, fruit, and cheese in the streets or squatting in the plazas. In towns, they sold prepared food in plazas and markets, wove cloth, made candles and cigars, and worked in factories. Mencia Pérez, an illiterate *mestiza* from Tlaxcala, owned a small farm. She married a Basque innkeeper in 1570 and moved to Huemantla, where she bought land and a mill. After her husband died in 1578, she ran a carting business, becoming one of the richest people in the province.[30]

When indentured servants finished their terms, they entered society. Most came from lower-class backgrounds, but, because of the black slave class, whites had built-in social standing they could not have attained in England. In the West Indies, even a workman's wife could go out "in the best flowered silk and richest silver and gold lace . . . with a couple of Negroes at her tail, her complexion kept as white as possible to emphasize her superiority not only to black slaves but also to rednecked servants."[31] But superiority has a price, and, as we have seen, it is always higher for women than for men. White men had sexual license and customarily kept black concubines, but white women, raised "above" blacks, were expected to exhibit modest respectability and to act with pretentious arrogance.

African slave women had a voice that was denied to white women in their own society. They chose or rejected their black mates and fostered Afro American culture in regions with high black populations—Cuba, Colombia, Haiti, Venezuela, and Brazil. As in Africa, they ran the markets; as *Maesdos-santos* (priestesses), they dominated Afro Brazilian, Afro Cubano, and Haitian religions. Obliquely, black women created the standards for white women, because whites created their image of themselves in opposition to that of people they disdained (as men form their self-image in opposition to their image of women). Since black women did manual labor, white women did not. White girls—sedentary, educated poorly if at all, idle, waited on—tended to slovenliness. Heat and sickness made life risky and uncomfortable, especially during childbirth, and white women on the islands suffered acutely from isolation. Like slaves, they found stratagems to avoid work, claiming a host of female complaints.

Most early Spanish emigrants to Latin America came from Castile and Anadalusia, where women in upper-class urban families were confined. Because women were forbidden to be seen at windows, they were given cushions, not chairs, to sit on and were semiveiled in all of Spain except Catalonia. Spanish laws making women men's property held in New Spain, where daughters were subject to fathers, and wives to husbands. Some Mexican girls attended school or convents, or had tutors; few had secondary education and none, higher education: they were not supposed to be educated. Convents taught girls reading, writing, and the "womanly arts"—sewing, cooking, and embroidery. But the strict confinement of European Latin women was intensified by racism, making the lives of white women in the Americas virtually imprisonment.

White women, Creole or European-born, had high status solely by virtue of their color, which conveyed social and moral status: white women were "pure." But Iberian women were equal to Iberian men only in race; they had no voice in society and were burdened with responsibility for a legal concept of purity of blood, *limpieza de sangre*, devised to maintain white social supremacy. They were viewed as virtual walking incubators. To preserve women's "purity" (which protected the "family" and the "race," however men behaved), men guarded women's sexuality with dowries, convents, and *beaterios* (communal houses). An elite girl needed a dowry when she "took state" (married or professed as a nun). All girls were expected to take state—spinsterhood was shameful and rarely allowed. A daughter could be freed from *patriapotestas* (control) by her father or by a court order if he was incapacitated or had committed incest.[32] *Emancipada* (emancipated), she could buy, sell, lend, borrow, bequeath, or inherit property, litigate, and bear witness. But this freedom was rare.

Maria Nugent, the wife of a governor of Jamaica, kept a journal—a rarity for a woman in this period. Touring Jamaican plantations, she scorned the few "stupid and ill-bred" white women she saw, who "simpered and giggled" and could discuss only three topics: debt, disease, and death. But such women were married to "gross bores who ate like cormorants and drank like porpoises with resulting ill-health."[33] Planters driven by acquisitiveness lacked other interests. Most marriages were bound by property, not affection; wives who were unsatisfied emotionally or sexually were chagrined by the constant presence of concubines who, unlike their counterparts in the American South, appropriated their sexual role *and* managed the plantations. White men married for respectability and for property (and maybe for legitimate issue), but reserved any affection they were capable of for their lovers. As Bush puts it, white women were veneer, while black women were the solid underpinning of the emotional and familial lives of white men. White women's only point of pride was racial superiority, which provided an outlet for their self-contempt. Many found amusement in whipping black slaves, treating them harshly, and seeing them stripped naked and punished in disgusting ways. Their cruel behavior towards slaves expressed intense envy and jealousy.

Marriage among whites required a dowry. The lowest dowry a white man would accept was 3000 pesos, given to orphans or poor girls. Daughters of rich merchants or the nobility often had over 10,000 pesos; those of government employees or professionals had sums between those amounts. Seventeenth-century families bought their sons-in-law government posts costing 70,000 pesos. Outside the capital, a woman's dowry might be goods—metal bars, slaves, furniture, and clothes—and under 3000 pesos in cash. In the late sixteenth century, rich patrons set up foundations to give conquistadors' orphaned daughters (poor, legitimate, and with *limpieza de sangre*) the minimum dowry needed for passable husbands.

Dowry belonged to a wife: her husband managed it, but he could not alienate any of it without her consent; if he mishandled it, she could go to court and request the right to handle it herself. If a marriage ended through death or annulment, the dowry and its income had to be repaid before the husband's estate was divided; if a wife died first, her children or her parents received it. Some women received part of their husbands' assets at marriage; some managed their own property. Once a marriage was consummated, divorce or separation was difficult even if extreme cruelty was involved, but some women still initiated the long, expensive proceedings. Elite women accused of adultery were locked up—in private or institutional houses or in *recogimientos* (retirement houses).

Women could not hold public office, go to law, or make contracts, and they held economic rights only as widows. Some mature women, often widows, owned property and wielded considerable power. Most widows did not remarry but managed their households independently. Women who owned farms hired overseers to manage them but retained control. In 1800 Maria Josefa de Velasco y Ovando wrote to her bailiff: "About the current drop in the price of grain, it is to be expected at this time, as the small farmers sell quickly to take care of their pressing needs; but as we have no such needs, we will not sell now. Better, we shall buy as much maize as we can and sell it for profit in the future." The Countess of Miravalle, who was married at eighteen, had eight children. Forty-two when her husband died, she discovered massive debts. A brilliant administrator, she managed her property so well that she paid off the debts, provided for her children, and became one of the most influential women in eighteenth-century Mexico.

Well-to-do women owned sugar mills and businesses like printing shops, wax and cigar factories, or wine stores. Poorer women taught in or ran schools, owned card and wine factories, and sold hogs. Female artisans made and sold products and ran businesses with their husbands, often behind the scenes. In Mexico City in 1753, single or widowed women headed a significant number of households, working as bakers, washerwomen, cobblers, shopkeepers, leather tanners, wine merchants, vendors, tailors, and a porter. Lower-class women did the worst-paid jobs, selling clothes or food on the streets or toiling as domestics in cities, and working in the fields or as domestics in the countryside. Menial tasks were left to Indians and mixed-bloods. Poor white women could not easily make a living and maintain their superior status: to keep their "dignity," they had to work at home, so could only sew or teach girls, neither of which paid much.

Some girls entered *beaterios,* voluntary affiliations of women *(beatas)* who did not profess but, like the European beguines, took simple vows of enclosure, virginity, and poverty. *Beatas* did not need dowries: often poor, they sold clothes or homemade sweets and asked for alms. Religious or civil authorities insisted on controlling *beaterios* (as they had the beguinages), assigning priest-directors to confess the *beatas* and perform mass. *Beaterios* offered shelter to devout single women without dowries or to widows who did not wish to remarry. Founded by women, priests, bishops, or laymen, they dotted colonial Mexico. If a wealthy patron provided a building and maintenance, they could become convents.

Some Spanish colonial women became powerful abbesses in charge of convents. At the end of the seventeenth century, Mexico City had seventeen convents, Lima thirteen: every town of any size had one. Such huge numbers of women entered convents that historians have deduced that many preferred not to marry. Lima's largest convents were enormous; they had beautiful gardens, a chapel, common rooms, *seglarado* (student dormitories), a novitiate, an infirmary, a jail, quarters for retired women, and *celdas* (nuns' cells).[34] Nuns lived comfortably, waited on by slaves and servants, in sanctuary from a wildly acquisitive, misogynist, and brutal society. In convents, women used their intellectual, creative, and administrative talents: they managed their communities well as they made music, wrote histories, and carried on business.

Convents were socially and spiritually superior to *beaterios.*

In the late sixteenth century the usual dowry for a professing nun was 2000 pesos; a century later it was 3000 pesos, and after 1730, 4000. Besides the dowry, novices had to pay their living expenses before professing; profession itself could cost thousands more. Most nuns bought their cells for hundreds or thousands of pesos. Rich parents also endowed a *reserva*, or fund, which the convent lent out at 5 percent to bring a nun income for amenities. Thus, most nuns came from rich families. They had to provide birth certificates certifying race and statements notarized by several witnesses proving they had perfect and legitimate Spanish ancestry.

Some Mexican convents were founded specifically for single poor women. At least seventeen convents set up between the late sixteenth and late eighteenth centuries were explicitly purposed as havens for orphans, single women, or poor white girls without dowries. Sixteen were founded or promoted by widows or single women, and two others by very rich young orphans who had professed.

Indians were barred from most convents, even those they founded. The first convent to accept Indian women was established in Mexico City in 1724. A few white nuns were imported to organize it and they tried to rule the community, claiming that Indians were incapable of self-rule or of leading a proper religious life. The Indian nuns and their protectors protested, so the white nuns were transferred to other convents and no white novices were admitted after that. Then the Indians imitated white racial-social exclusivity and refused aspirants who were not full-blooded Indians of the *cacique* class. Commoner Indians who did manual work or domestic service had little chance of placing their daughters in Indian convents, and *castas* had none at all. At most, such girls could become convent servants. Africans were denied profession, though free Africans were hired as servants. Convents as well as individual nuns had slaves as servants.

Convents offered the only female education in colonial Mexico. Nuns had to know music and Latin for mass; poor girls often studied instruments, hoping a convent would take them as musicians with only a low dowry or none at all. Scholarly studies were not encouraged, and no convent had a library. La Enseñanza, the Order of Mary, the only teaching order in New Spain, gave nuns formal teacher training. In 1753 it opened a school to teach all classes of girls reading, writing, arithmetic, natural science, and European history. To meet the tremendous demand, it branched out in the provinces late in the century. Democratic lay schools were not founded until the 1770s. But convents were prime financial institutions: nuns were skilled accountants, often managing convent finances better than their majordomos. They earned income by offering loans and mortgages at 5 percent interest, most often to men but also to wealthy widows, women with houses and land, or rich families. When liens were repaid, convents reinvested the money in new loans or bought real estate. Larger loans were granted to few people, so only an elite had access to credit.

It was said in Brazil that white women left their homes only to be baptized, married, and buried. Portuguese women were circumspect because their men murdered them for any hint of suspicion. But two French sea captains described women cleverly outwitting their male guardians to flirt.[35] One visitor found São Paulo women elegant, great dancers, witty conversationalists, but confined at home sewing, making lace, and embroidering. He noted their "almost universal debility" from scanty diets, lack of exercise, and too many warm baths. Another noted women's lack of education, coarse manners, boisterous conversation, poor carriage, and coquettish airs. They were attractive, happy, and frank at thirteen or fourteen, but corpulent and stooped by twenty, from seclusion and boredom. Maria Graham, moving in high society, met educated sophisticated women—one was learned in botany and widely read, a feminist and "a true blue stocking."[36]

Education was rare in Brazil, too. In rich families, priests or relatives tutored the children in reading, writing, arithmetic, and music. Girls learned basic religion, home management, embroidery, and submissiveness. Boys might go to Jesuit colleges or Portuguese universities, but many rich girls were illiterate, their intellect, talent, and initiative suffocated by the profusion of slaves and by their own narrow role. Elite women went out rarely and never without a *dueña*, or in an enclosed palanquin borne by slaves. Inventories of their possessions show that they owned few clothes: they needed little at home. The only thing expected of them was *tomar estado*, "to take state," to guard their sexuality by marrying or by entering a convent.

Brazilian boys were under the *patriapotestas* of father or guardian until they were twenty-five, and women for life, unless they were emancipated (only some widows were *emancipada*). Until they were twenty-five, both sexes needed permission to enter into contracts or litigation or to marry. Girls were expected to be married by that age, especially in the sixteenth century, when families married off girls of eight or ten to much older men to forge profitable alliances. But canon law allowed boys to marry at fourteen, and girls at twelve or earlier, without a father's consent; in 1776 the crown limited this right, giving fathers the right to use "offence to family honor" as an objection to a marriage or to disinherit offenders. Still, girls eloped with men their fathers disapproved of, usually reconciling with them once the "family honor" had been assuaged. Few poor people or blacks married.

White men preferred their full-blooded Portuguese daughters to enter convents than to marry "beneath" them. As in Spanish America, women entered convents in droves, willingly or not. But there was no convent in Brazil until Santa Clara do Desterro opened in 1677, and the crown did not authorize another for fifty years. Santa Clara took only fifty nuns, and women not in convents were compelled to marry, so many Brazilian women sailed to Portugal to enter convents. Alarmed by this exodus, in 1732 the crown forbade white women to leave Brazil without royal permission, except Spanish women who had come with their husbands—and even they could return only with their men. Portuguese convents took women with pure Portuguese blood of good family and with dowries; they accepted rich women of shaky ancestry or behavior only as temporary residents.

Again, nuns in many convents lived austerely, meditated, and prayed, following monastic discipline. But others treated the convent like a private home. The nuns of the Convent of the Poor Clares in eighteenth-century Bahia came from prominent families. With many personal servants and much fine jewelry, they sparked scandal. In Salvador in the early 1700s, men often tried to place all their daughters in convents. Men going on journeys often locked their wives up in retirement houses for middle-class orphan girls until their return. These houses permanently held women suspected of infidelity, divorcees, and widows. Men in Portuguese and Spanish colonies were obsessed with guarding female sexuality.

Iberian fathers usually favored the oldest son, but they did not disinherit the others and divided their property among all their sons. Parents, obliged to arrange lucrative marriages for their children, had to buy sons proper careers, and daughters, dowries or the entrance fee to nunneries. Marriage to relatives was common: a widower could marry his wife's sister, an uncle his dead wife's niece. In Brazil, cousin marriage was the rule, not an exception.[37] Marriage among the propertied was an instrument for raising a family's financial or social status: a dowry compensated a husband for the expense of supporting a wife and gave a wife some independence. The dowry was usually money, often with land, houses, slaves, livestock, farm equipment, bales of cotton, tobacco, sugar, or rights to hereditary offices or objects. It might include beds, tables, chairs, tableware, or linens. Here, too, parents bought grooms public offices or habits in a religious-military order. Girls who lost fathers or both their parents were in jeopardy: without a dowry in a society that did not pay women for their work, their only recourse was prostitution. Rich men paid to raise and marry off orphans, and rich women left bequests for their dowries.

In Brazil, too, husbands managed dowries, though they remained a wife's property. She had to consent to the alienation of any part of it and could petition for the right to administer it herself if he mishandled it. If a marriage was annulled or a husband died, the dowry had to be repaid with income before his estate could be divided. If she died first, it was divided among her children or returned to her parents. A remarried widow controlled her first dowry—her new husband managed only the second. A groom often gave a bride *arras*—10 percent of his assets to be added to her dowry.

The behavior expected of Brazilian wives was laid out in a moral tract by Nuño Marques Pereira.[38] Spouses should be of roughly the same age and of similar social and economic status. To avoid malicious gossip and potential sexual liaisons, wives should shun priests and women of questionable repute, dress modestly, not demand more than their husband's means or social station can provide, and never speak disparagingly of husbands. Wives "must be strong, discreet, prudent. Within the home, they should be diligent; outside they should be retiring." At all times their conduct and mien should be exemplary—better long-suffering than extravagant. Wives were subordinate to husbands by divine law; secular law decreed that a wife might not even cut a hair from her head without his permission. Aware that husbands were often inconsiderate of wives (or worse), Pereira wrote rules for men too, but insisted that men must protect the body (sexuality) of females and urged fathers to keep their daughters always in their sight.

Dissolving a marriage was a long, expensive proceeding: if persuaded of the grounds, the church granted separations or annulments, which allowed both spouses to remarry. Most annulments were granted for forced or barren marriages. A woman probably could not use a husband's adultery, but she could claim that a husband had threatened her, abused her in an extreme physical or spiritual way, or endangered her by heresy or paganism. Records of the ecclesiastical tribune of Lima show that women often initiated such suits. If she was found aggrieved, a woman would recover her dowry, half the communal property, and custody of her children.

Many white marriages were barren, but in most, young women married older men and had one or two children. There were some multiple pregnancies: Isabel Gomes bore ten children. When she died she left nine, between the ages of twenty-three and one (the tenth was not listed).[39] Matronly by twenty, worn out by pregnancies and lack of exercise, women were considered old at forty, whereas men were not considered old until sixty. White infant mortality was high, but lower than the numbers for blacks. An engineer in Minas Gerais noted that white women were more fertile than mulattoes; black women's fertility depended on their status—free or slave.

No woman (and few men) in Brazil could vote, but women

with money and the right color and parentage had some legal rights and redress: they acted as executors of wills, could inherit and own land and property, act as head of household, do business, and sue. Some even sued their fathers for refusing to release their dowries. Husbands apparently permitted these activities because many Brazilian women held urban properties and ran plantations. In the seventeenth century, women made up 17 percent of the sugarcane growers in Pernambuco and Alagoas; at the end of the colonial period, women owned 16 percent of *engenhos*; one had two sugar mills in Recôncavo and 108 slaves. Women acted independently or as their husbands' legal partners in buying and selling property, borrowing money, going to court, and founding chantries. One sued her husband after two years of marriage for failing to confirm her dowry.

Discrimination was most cruel in marital law. Courts were lenient towards men who beat or killed wives suspected of adultery; if adultery was proven, men could divorce them, but murder was easier (as is still true in many Latin American countries). Women could not divorce men for adultery without a "second cause"—cruelty, desertion, or forced prostitution. In such cases, courts put a lien on a man's property until he arranged support for his estranged wife and children. The wife was placed with a "respectable" citizen or relative for six months, after which she could file the vicar-general for divorce.

Unhealthy as white women were, they married so young that most outlived their husbands. Few remarried. Various arrangements were made to support families after a man died. If at marriage a man had stipulated "division of properties," his wife legally kept half. If he made no clear statement, his property was sold and his wife got half the proceeds; debts and other legacies came out of the other half. If the proceeds of his property were less than his debts, his widow and heirs had to sell their property to pay them. If a husband died intestate or with children under the age of twenty-five, legal complications could tie up his estate for twenty or thirty years, leaving his widow destitute. The few recorded divorces show that courts divided a couple's property, awarding the wife half its value and custody of the children (unusual in that period), with the father liable for their maintenance. Usually, though, men just left on expeditions and never returned.

Many widows executed their husbands' wills, usually with the help of a male friend or relative who became her children's guardian if she died. Men who were not legally married or who had no children often left their property to women. Propertied widows rented out their plantations, took over their husbands' businesses, or ran large enterprises alone or with partners: Ana Maria Barboza de Penha de França, a widow experienced in mining, ran a gold mine with seventy slaves in the 1760s. Many struggled to remain independent, working small plots or running shops or black market enterprises. Isabel de Sousa, a widow with children and modest resources, asked for and received a league of land for raising cattle in 1726. Some Brazilian women ran estates or labored in gold mines or on cattle ranches or sugar plantations. Unlike women in Spanish and British colonies, who usually raised their children themselves in their native languages, Portuguese women in the slave culture of Brazil handed children over to black nannies.

Racism, however, began to lead men with legitimate sons to bequeath their estates to women—they feared, often rightly, that the sons might give them to slave-born children. Jerónimo de Burgos and his wife, fearing that their son might "dishonor" the family, set up a charitable trust, granting him the fruits if he did not marry anyone "tainted by the blood of the prohibited races." Many men disinherited their daughters or annulled widows' right to child custody if they remarried. Yet men expected their wives to take responsibility for *their* illegitimate children. A man whose concubine died often brought her children home to his wife to rear and educate. Some simply deserted concubines and children, and foundlings seriously drained Brazilian town councils. Owners often freed their concubines in their wills—one left his illegitimate children their slave mothers, who then became their children's property! Women were manumitted twice as often as men, although male labor was more valued.

Sor Juana Inés de la Cruz

Despite women's exclusion from educational institutions, a nun became the most educated, brilliant poet of the age. Juana de Asbaje y Ramirez de Santillana (1649–95), one of several illegitimate children of a modest provincial mother, had no resources but brains, beauty, and a thirst for knowledge. As a child she taught herself Latin and musical instruments. She wanted to dress as a man to attend university in Mexico City, but her mother refused to help her. Brought to the viceregal court at thirteen as a provincial prodigy, she became maid-in-waiting to the Marquesa de Mancera, the viceroy's wife, and a close friend of the Countess of Paredes, the wife of the Marquis of Laguna (viceroy in 1680–81). The countess had Juana's plays performed at court and her poetry published in Spain. Juana's playful, courtly poetry praised her patrons; using a male persona, she expressed passionate admiration for the Countess of Paredes.

The viceroy arranged a public debate for her with forty University of Mexico professors on theology, philosophy, mathematics, history, and poetry: she impressed everyone. Wanting to study without constant interruption—which a woman could do only by professing—she entered a convent when she turned sixteen. She later joined the Jeronymites as Sor Juana Inés de la Cruz; there she worked amid her own excellent library and was visited in the parlour by the most eminent literary and scientific minds in Mexico. She continued to write profane poetry, using human love as a metaphor for love of god, but always portrayed mind as genderless.

The church commissioned songs for masses and feasts from Juana, but was uneasy about her. The anti-intellectual Mexican church was obsessed with women: some clergy suggested that women might study the Bible, but Juana's confessor, Antonio Nuñez de Miranda, said they needed only enough Latin to understand mass. Although she probably had the best mind of her age and place, Juana could not attend university or preach and was criticized for importing books banned in Spanish colonies. She dared to deal with theological issues (the first woman in New Spain to do so), arguing that knowledge of science could only strengthen faith. One historian believes that her poems became feminist during a church crusade to imprison "wayward" women in a shelter.[40]

The church could not allow such a woman to flourish. In a casual conversation in 1690, when she was forty, Sor Juana discussed a sermon given years before by a noted Jesuit, Father Vieira. In general she praised the sermon but rebutted Vieira's rejection of the ideas of John Chrysostom, Augustine, and Aquinas. Much taken with her refutations, her friend asked her to jot them down. But, somehow, her letter found its way to the Bishop of Puebla, who published it with the title *Carta atenagórica* (Letter by an Athena), with a preface written by "Sor Filotea" (a pseudonym), as an argument between two females. The bishop praised the clarity and extensiveness of Sor Juana's thought but admonished her for stooping to "lowly earthbound knowledge" and warned her against descending to "ponder what goes on in hell."

Her text dealt with religion, and the reproof was factitious. Juana understood the bishop's real objection: as a woman, she had overstepped her place. In response, she wrote *Respuesta a Sor Filotea de la Cruz*, explaining that she had always had an urgent need to learn. Politically she agreed that women should not lecture publicly or preach, but, she continued, "surely, studying, writing, and teaching privately are not only allowable but most edifying and useful"—not for everyone, but for the talented, male or female. But then she crossed the line, arguing not that men's privileges and prerogatives be extended to women, but that they not automatically be given to men. She delicately disparaged stupid pretentious clergymen who *estudian para ignorar* (study to become ignorant).

Father Miranda broke contact with her, refusing to hear her confession. Other priests accused her of heresy, the church hierarchy shunned her, and people stopped visiting her. The vicereine had returned to Spain, and Juana had no secular protector of her stature. Totally isolated, she broke down and begged Miranda to hear her confession, writing—once in her own blood—to reaffirm her vows. She sold her books and instruments and devoted herself to acts of penance, self-flagellation, and mortification of the flesh. During an epidemic in 1695, she chose to nurse nuns, caught the contagion, and died. Her *Complete Works*, published in 1714, contain courtly and love poems, lyrics for songs, sonnets, lay and religious plays, some devotional exercises, and the famous letter of response. Like so many woman writers, she was soon cast into oblivion: no new edition of her works appeared between 1725 and 1910, and no modern edition until 1940. Yet her literary achievement was not surpassed by any colonial writer and she remains, perhaps, the greatest Spanish American writer—Latin

Americans call her the Ninth Muse. She is one of the world's great poets; a new anthology of her work appeared in 1989.[41]

Misogyny

The Spanish clergy, especially Mexicans, were not only preoccupied with sex but intensely woman-hating. Jonathan Kandell calls them an army in search of a mission who found it in women, at whom they aimed "the same missionary zeal once directed at stamping out Indian paganism."[42] The sermons of Francisco Aguiar y Seixas, the Archbishop of Mexico (1682–98), were violent diatribes against the evils and defects of females; what he really wanted to do was imprison all women, as responsible for sin on earth. Under his influence, priests waged war against women. Father José Vidal, obsessed with chastity, disparaged marriage as repugnant; Father José Montano preached that beautiful women had ugly souls; Father Salvador Rodriguez de la Fuente lobbied for a mural behind his pulpit depicting a prostitute tortured in hell.

Priests in street clothes, alone or in groups, went on nightly sorties collaring women in taverns, gambling halls, theaters, and brothels, terrifying them with visions of hell. Promising food and shelter, they enticed them to Belén and locked them up. Once inside its walls, they subjected the captives to sermons and urged them to confess. Most of the women refused to listen; they insulted the priests, defiantly stripped themselves in their presence, spat at them, and sometimes even hit them. In return, the priests had them whipped and starved. Some of the prisoners went mad, and one slashed her throat. Few of these women ever came out again. Yet some priests solicited women sexually during confession and a few were known to frequent brothels.

The New World Inquisition focused on heresy, especially Judaism, in major cities. It used torture in its examinations and, before it was abolished in 1821, it had burned about fifty "heretics" and terrified the entire population. It accused more men (including some priests) than women for the "sins" of Jewishness, heresy, bigamy, or womanizing. The Inquisition had no jurisdiction over indigenous people (most *brujos,* or shamans, were indigenous), but summoned women for witchcraft (as *brujas*), delusion, or heresy. As in Europe, the women accused were usually poor and single or were prophets or preachers. A Lima woman, Angela de Carranza, who was widely revered as Saint Angela de Dios, had written over 7000 pages of theological interpretation as the "Doctor of the Immaculate Conception" while running a business distributing religious articles. In 1688 the Inquisitional court arrested her and, six years later, locked her in a secret Inquisitional prison, publicly burning her writings, rosaries, relics, and medals.

There were few priests in the countryside, where communities tolerated ancient Indian or syncretic (mixed) beliefs like the African Christian *santería* (voodoo). Beneath a Christian surface thrived charismatic women prophets and healers with a strong vein of unorthodox belief and practices. A cult, the Virgin of Guadalupe, grew after Juan Diego, an Indian boy in Tepeyec (a town sacred to the goddess Tonantzin) saw her. The image of the Virgin of Guadalupe, imprinted on his cloak, came to symbolize Mexican nationalism. The symbolic opposite of Cortés' translator Malinche, it adorned the rebel banner on the eve of Mexican independence during the 1910–17 revolution, and Zapata's men also carried it into battle. Juan Diego was sainted by Pope John Paul II in August 2002.

A cult grew around Isabel Flores, called "the little rose" for the color imprinted on her cheeks. A girl of modest family who was not a nun, she wore a Franciscan monk's brown robe— and, after 1606, a white Dominican robe. Once news spread of her "miracles," she built a cell that drew devotees, mainly aristocrats. In 1617 an image of Christ was said to sweat when she prayed at it. When she died, troops were called in to control the hysterical crowds. To this day, *brujas* remain popular; even middle-class residents of sophisticated Mexico City, Bogot, and Rio consult them.

Good Relations between Colors

Some blacks and whites forged loving bonds. In their wills, white men often manumitted or left estates to black or mixed-blood "wives" and children. In 1762 Jamaican white men left nonwhites £200,000–£300,000, four plantations, seven animal pens, thirteen houses, and considerable land, rousing the elite to pass laws decrying "inconveniences arising from exorbitant grants and devices made by white persons to negroes" and limiting them to £2000.

Free women of color were scorned, but they were freer than whites; those with property became a leisured, well-to-do class who bought slaves themselves and founded the black elite that dominates Caribbean society today. But however prosperous or respectable, they could never forget they were concubines, not wives, and in white men's power. Some of these women exploited their relations with whites. The Barbadan Rachel Pringle-Polgreen persuaded two white men, Pringle and Polgreen, to help her build a lucrative tavern business, and, when she died, she left whites most of her money.

At the end of the colonial period, white women owned 20 percent of the slaves in Recôncavo and Bahia; most owned fewer than five, but the largest single slave-holder in the region was a woman. Many discussions of Latin America focus on whether women or men—or Spaniards or Portuguese—were kinder to slaves. Such analyses seem self-serving and irrelevant.

Slavery is inherently evil, however kind the owner. That it is evil is apparent from its effects on both owners and owned: it makes everyone connected with it miserable. All slaves lived in fear of the master, and all slave owners lived in constant terror of slave revolt.[43]

CHAPTER 6

EUROPEAN APPROPRIATION
OF NORTH AMERICA

Conquest

ABOUT 1000 CE the Viking Leif Ericsson landed on the North American coast. He left no settlement, and Europeans were unaware of the landmass until the Florentine Giovanni Caboto (John Cabot), like Columbus seeking a sea route to India, stumbled on it in 1497. The Spaniards Juan Ponce de León (1513) and Pánfilo de Narváez (1528) explored Florida, Hernando de Soto and Vásquez de Coronado the southwest (1539–42), and others the west coast, leaving outposts at St. Augustine and Santa Fe. Finding no natural resources in the continent, Spain set out to conquer the native societies and to force them to find and extract some. Since Spain had no plans to colonize this territory, it sent no women until Francisca Hinestrosa arrived in 1539. She was probably the first European woman in North America when she landed at Tampa Bay with her husband, a soldier with de Soto. She died in a battle with Native Americans in 1541 in the Mississippi Valley.

Seeking a nonexistent "northwest passage" to Asia, Giovanni da Verrazano explored the east coast from Florida to Nova Scotia in 1524, followed a decade later by Jacques Cartier, who sailed the St. Lawrence River and built a settlement at Quebec. French Basque fishermen based in Montreal traded with Abenaki beaver-trappers in Maine who wanted European cloth and metal tools. In 1609 Henry Hudson sailed the river named for him and, after 1624, the Dutch settled the Hudson Valley. By 1638 Swedes had settled along the Delaware River.

The English who would defeat the Dutch and gain territorial control and cultural hegemony over eastern North America were the last to explore and settle it. Wanting a New World base from which to attack Spain, Queen Elizabeth I sent Sir Walter Raleigh and his half-brother Sir Humphrey Gilbert to establish one: Gilbert died in the attempt, but Raleigh landed at Roanoke Island and, in 1587, sent ninety-one men, seventeen women, and nine male children to colonize Virginia (which was named for Elizabeth, the "Virgin Queen").

The colonists tried to farm Indian land. Eleanor Dare was five months pregnant when she left England with her husband and father, John White.[1] After enduring three months on stormy seas and one in tropical wilderness, Eleanor gave birth on August 18, 1587, to the first English child born in the New World, Virginia Dare. Nine days after his granddaughter's birth, White returned to England to replenish supplies and get help. But war erupted between England and Spain and he could not leave England. After Spain's Armada was destroyed in the summer of 1588 and the sea lanes were opened, White was further detained by Raleigh's near bankruptcy. He finally went back to Roanoke in August 1590, but found not even a human bone.

England did not repeat its attempt until 1605, when some prosperous gentry and merchants, with visions of huge profits dancing before their eyes, set up a joint-stock company to colonize North America. King James I chartered the Virginia Company, which sent 144 men and boys to the New World. Forty died on the voyage; the rest tried and failed to settle in Maine. In May 1607 they sailed south, landing in a Virginia swamp they named Jamestown for the king. After eight months, thirty-eight remained alive. Accounts suggest that the men starved rather than accept the harsh discipline of the Virginia Company. They worked six to eight hours a day and spent their leisure hours "bowling in the streets," until Captain John Smith, one of the founders, imposed a quasi-military regimen that sustained them for a while. No women came with the first settlers, but in 1608 seventy new arrivals included Anne Forrest and her maid Anne Burras, who was all of fourteen. Soon afterwards the girl married a laborer, John Laydon, in the first English wedding in any English colony.

When Smith left, conditions quickly deteriorated, and some of the starving colonists resorted to cannibalism during the winter of 1609–10. The company solicited men and women for "the better strengthening of the colony," and four to five hundred people sailed in 1609. Most of them died: of 8000 English emigrants to Virginia, only 1300 were alive in 1624—and they survived only because Native Americans, whose land they had usurped, helped them. Yet they raided Indian settlements, burning the corn that had helped them survive.

Native Americans

Native American societies ranged from the vast, complex empires of horticulturalists in Central and South America to small seminomadic matrilineal or patrilineal gatherer-hunters in the far north. About four to six million people speaking a thousand languages lived in North America in the fifteenth century: "tribes" were linguistic groups—and groups that were geographically separate spoke related tongues and shared similar cultures.

In regions unsuitable for farming, the people gathered and hunted. Nomadic and seminomadic bands on the Great Plains and in what is now Canada for the most part ate the large game they hunted. The major gods of hunting tribes like the Siouan-speakers of the Great Plains were tied to animals, and their major festivals were connected with hunting. Paiute and Shoshoni of the Great Basin (Nevada and Utah) lived in kin-groups and sometimes banded together; women gathered seeds and berries, while men hunted small game. Some groups farmed. The Chinook of Washington and Oregon, and others who lived near the sea, ate fish and shellfish, grew vegetables, and gathered seeds and berries. Arikara of the Missouri River valley and Algonkians of eastern Canada and the northeastern United States hunted large game and cultivated corn, squash, and beans. The women in such groups taught Europeans to grow corn and potatoes, cook shellfish, and cultivate herbs and berries for preventive and curative medicinal use, and they introduced the newcomers to artichokes (for stew), peanuts, peppers, and pumpkins.

Before 1000 BCE, southwest Pueblo Indians like the New Mexican Zuñi and Hopi had built sprawling villages of terraced multistoried houses nestled in cliffs and mountains for easy defence. They grew squash and beans by dryland farming techniques, placing their gardens at stream mouths to catch the runoff from rains. Horticulture tends to foster increased population, and Pueblo villages held hundreds of rooms. Long before European intrusion, these people built irrigation canals and dams. Pueblo Indians considered horticulture "men's work," but Hopis, Zuñis, and Navajos believed that corn came from the Corn Mother, daughter of the Earth Mother and the Sky Father. Women owned the houses, furnishings, and crops, which were shared communally. They gardened, cooked, nursed the sick, and made pottery, baskets, and cotton cloth. Game was supplemental: it was hunted by men, then preserved and stored for the winter by the women.

Pueblo Indians lived in autonomous villages managed by a council of ten to thirty men. Their major gods were tied to cultivation, and the main festivals celebrated planting and harvest. People had to marry outside the clan. A wife initiated divorce by putting her husband's belongings outside the door, signalling him to return to his mother's home. A mother's brother, not the father, disciplined children and taught sons to stalk animals and catch fish.

By the Common Era, people in the Ohio River valley called Moundbuilders had made huge earth sculptures shaped like birds, humans, or serpents—one, more than 3 miles (5 kilometers) long, enclosed 40 hectares. Moundbuilders traded ornaments and weapons with western, Great Lakes, and Gulf of Mexico tribes. About 500 CE, as this culture waned, another emerged in the Mississippi Valley. Thousands of villages centered in what is now St. Louis did advanced horticulture and built huge earthen mounds for burial and ceremonies dedicated perhaps to the goddess. The largest Mississippian mound, approximately 98 feet, 5 inches (30 meters) high, with a rectangular base broader than Egypt's Great Pyramid, rose near Cahokia, a city of about 30,000 people who wove, dressed hides, engraved copper, and made tools, pottery, jewelry, and salt. This culture was egalitarian.

The largest linguistic groups east of the Mississippi were

the Algonkians and Iroquois in the north and the Muskogeans in the south. Among them, women did horticulture, gathered, prepared food to store or eat, and tended children. Men cleared land and hunted large game. Most eastern villages were built defensively, surrounded by wooden palisades and ditches. Northern Iroquois lived in large, rectangular, bark-covered longhouses; Muskogeans and southern Algonkians, in thatch longhouses, each holding an extended matrilineal family. Women had considerable power in these societies. In the 1650s a French Jesuit visitor wrote: "No poorhouses are needed among them, because they are neither mendicants nor paupers. . . . Their kindness, humanity and courtesy not only makes them liberal with what they have, but causes them to possess hardly anything except in common." They raised children gently, teaching them communal solidarity but also independence, equality, and sharing. They disliked obedience and were shocked at the way whites treated children, calling the English "the men who beat children."

The northeast, from the Adirondacks to the Great Lakes, was the territory of the Iroquois League, a powerful alliance of Mohawk (People of the Flint), Oneida (People of the Stone), Onondaga (People of the Mountain), Seneca (Great Hill People), and Cayuga (People at the Landing), who spoke the same Iroquois language, held land in common, worked together, and shared everything. The Iroquois League, a complex political hierarchy, linked villages to tribal units and tribes to a confederation. Southwestern and eastern horticultural tribes lived in villages of a thousand people or more. Like the Pueblos, the Muskogeans lived without government in autonomous villages headed by village councils. Women were leaders or chiefs among horticulturalists (especially if they were the cultivators), but not among nomadic hunters. Iroquois women were not chiefs, but they controlled the men who were; chiefs remained in the league only as long as women approved of them. Female chiefs were most common and strongest in the southeast: the Lady of Cofitachique governed a large network of villages in what is now South Carolina in the mid-sixteenth century.

Native Americans had no domesticated animals larger than llamas, but American vegetables—corn, beans, squash, manioc, potatoes—were more nutritious and produced higher yields than European rye and wheat. Europeans took home Native American foods and brought back domestic animals—an exchange so enriching to the diets of both continents that the world's population, static for centuries, doubled in the next three hundred years. Europeans took up American tobacco, believing it had medicinal effects. Spaniards imported horses and traded them among the tribes, until they became part of the life of western Indians and nomadic buffalo hunters. In the end, however, interaction with Europeans lost Native Americans their land, their culture, and their lives. Many died from disease, for they lacked immunity to smallpox, influenza, chicken pox, and measles. In some regions, their mortality rate was 90 percent.

In dealing with the intruders, Indians negotiated and manipulated events just as the whites did. Until about 1650, colonists had to adapt to Indian goals and purposes to advance their own, and Indian trade rules governed the fur trade. After they defeated the Narragansett in "King Philip's War" in 1676, however, colonists quickly conquered nearby tribes and took their land.

When the British arrived, six tribes of Virginia Algonkians allied in the Powhatan Confederation tried to draw other groups into the Confederacy. Powhatan did not attack the strangers who were usurping their land, but, during their first year, he sent a message to John Smith. Zinn quotes the English version, which is not verbally accurate, but conveys his meaning and spirit:

> I have seen two generations of my people die. . . . I know the difference between peace and war better than any man in my country. I am now grown old, and must die soon; my authority must descend to my brothers, Opitchapan, Opechancanough and Catatough—then to my two sisters, and then to my two daughters. I wish them to know as much as I do, and that your love to them may be like mine to you. Why will you take by force what you may have quietly by love? Why will you destroy us who supply you with food? What can you get by war? We can hide our provisions and run into the woods; then you will starve for wronging your friends. Why are you jealous of us? We are unarmed and willing to give you what you ask, if you come in a friendly manner, and not so simple as not to know that it is much better to eat good meat, sleep comfortably, live quietly with my wives and children, laugh and be merry with the English, and trade for their copper and hatchets, than to run away from them, and to lie cold in the woods, feed on acorns, roots and such trash, and be so hunted that I can neither eat nor sleep. In these wars, my men must sit up watching and, if a twig break, they all cry out "Here comes Captain Smith!" So I must end my miserable life. Take away your guns and swords, the cause of all our jealousy, or you may all die in the same manner.

But the Europeans could not hear. During the winter of

1609–10 (called "the starving time"), some colonists fled to the Indians, who fed them. When summer came, the colony head sent to ask Powhatan to return the runaways. Claiming that he offered "noe other than prowde and disdaynefull Answers," the English sent soldiers "to take Revendge": they raided an Indian village, killed many people, burned their houses, cut the corn growing around the village, seized the queen of the tribe and her children, tossed them into boats, rowed out, threw the children overboard "shoteinge owtt their Braynes in the water," then stabbed their mother to death.

But whites still joined Indian groups. "Going native" was so common in the Virginia colony that it was made a capital crime. This law did not end the defections, which subverted Englishmen's sense of superiority over the "savages."[2] In 1613 an English officer kidnapped Powhatan's daughter Pocahontas, who converted to Christianity and married the widower John Rolfe. This alliance ushered in a brief period of peace between the Powhatan Confederacy and the British at Jamestown. (In 1617 Rolfe took Pocahontas to England to present her to the king and queen, but she died soon after, no older than twenty-two.)

In 1617 the Virginia Company introduced the "headright" system as an incentive to Britain's poor, granting whoever paid the passage 20 hectares of land. Overpopulated England suffered high inflation, and the homeless dispossessed throng who trod the roads of a land torn by religious upheaval faced dwindling prospects. Many emigrated, and they seized Indian land for tobacco farms. The Indians protested and, in 1622, Powhatan's brother Opechancanough led an attack to expel them, killing 347 people—about a fourth of the colonists. The Indian uprising destroyed the Virginia Company, which had made no profit. But the colony endured. James I revoked the charter and made Virginia a royal colony ruled by his appointees.

Relations between Indians and settlers had utterly soured. Having tried and failed to enslave the Indians, the British found, as Powhatan had warned, that they did not enjoy constant war, and they decided on a policy of extermination. Reinforced with men and arms from England, the settlers prepared to attack Indian villages treacherously. The Indians knew the terrain better than the English and could not be tracked, so the English peaceably watched as the Native groups settled and planted their corn. When it was ready for harvest, they attacked by surprise, killing as many Indians as they could and burning their corn. Opechancanough began a new war against the settlers in 1644, but this time he failed and died in battle. In 1646 the remnant of the Confederacy submitted to English rule.

Like the Spanish, the English held an unshakable belief in the superiority of their civilization and did not comprehend Indian social structure. East-coast Algonkians did not inherit rank, leaders were not always born to their position, and status was not always inherited through males. Rather, decisions were made by consent of the tribe. Many tribes were matrilineal, and women had an important voice in tribal affairs. In England's full-blown patriarchy, men ruled women and other men, inherited the right to rule, and ruled autocratically. Britons expected Indian leaders to be men with absolute power, but none of them held such a position. Indians and Britons also had widely different ideas about property. Most eastern tribes held land communally and allowed others to hunt and fish on it; they could not conceive of buying or selling it. In England, property was an individual right. Bewildered by these traditional communal rights, Britons insisted that only intensively cultivated land was property, and they simply rode roughshod over Indian land rights.

French Settlements

Spain and France colonized other parts of North America. Holding Florida and New Mexico already, Spain settled Texas in the 1600s and California in the 1700s. Spaniards also tried and failed to enslave Native North Americans, who knew the land better than they did and easily escaped. Spaniards too feared retaliation—Indians might follow their example and enslave captured Spaniards. Moreover, the Catholic Church had banned Indian slavery in Spanish colonies.

The French colonized New France (present-day Quebec) in 1608 with poor people, for the most part—single peasants, married soldiers, and foundlings from asylums. Many of them later returned to France: Quebec barely grew until the young King Louis XIV and his minister Colbert bribed émigrés with a subsidy of 300 livres a year for families of ten, 400 for families of twelve or more, and 20 for girls and boys who married before the ages of sixteen or twenty, respectively. Between 1640 and 1700 the colony grew from 400 to 15,000. Seventeenth-century New France was a "golden age" for women, according to historian Jan Noel. Guilds and seigneuries had not yet arisen, so there was little distinction between domestic and wage labor. Women, being few and much in demand, enjoyed better legal, social, and economic standing than in France.[3] This view has been disputed, but it is true that women in New France were punished less harshly for witchcraft or adultery than those in New England or Brazil.

To block Spain and England in their advance, France founded colonies around the Gulf of Mexico: Mobile, Alabama, was founded in 1704 by seventy-five soldiers, a priest, and twenty-three girls as wives-breeders, with two nun chaperones.[4] New Orleans clamored for women and, in the 1720s,

France sent eighty female prisoners from Paris with three nuns. The settlers protested, so in 1728 it sent twenty-three *filles à la cassette* (casket girls), so-called for their trunks of clothes and linens. More arrived periodically until 1751: Louisianians later bragged of descent from casket girls.

French explorers mapped Canada, the Great Lakes, and the Mississippi valley and set up a network of settlements and forts from New Orleans to Canada to trade for furs. In the early 1600s, French Jesuits settled at these posts to convert the "heathen." Carol Devens studied their relations with "domiciled" Indians—those living near French missions for protection or recuperation.[5] Most of our information about these people comes from records kept by the priests. The Montagnais-Naskapi, Algonkian, and Ojibwa, who occupied Canada from Labrador to Lake Winnipeg, had similar cultures. For all, sexual division was fundamental, pervading every aspect of life—reproduction, production, food distribution, spatial arrangement, ritual, and authority. Men lived in camp but their lives focused on the bush, where they hunted large game and fur-bearing animals. Their value to the group resided in their role as hunters; their authority and status depended on their success in hunting. They believed that success in the chase required the cooperation of animal spirits and guidance by supernatural spirits who came to them in visions or dreams. Moving between bush and camp, men controlled neither: animal spirits "owned" the bush; women, the camp.

Women worked together fishing and hunting small game near the camp, providing most of the food. When men brought back game, women butchered, processed, apportioned, and distributed it. This job gave them power while reinforcing their sense of community and interdependence. They tanned hides, made clothes and tools for men in return for meat, assigned families living space, and chose campsites. "The women know what they are to do, the men also; one never meddles with the work of the other," a Jesuit wrote, explaining that men make canoe frames, women sew the bark with willow withes; men shape the wooden frames of raquettes (snowshoes), women thread them. Men hunt and kill animals, women follow to skin the animals and clean hides. He quoted an Indian: "To live among us without a wife is to live without help, without home, and to be always wandering." Native American women held their own rituals: the Jesuit Paul Le Jeune noted that they ate special food, held separate feasts, performed dances different from men's, and possessed special spiritual power during their menses and childbirth. Women's spiritual power was innate, whereas men had to acquire knowledge to communicate with their spirit guides.

Women's bodies were their own: in most tribes, they were sexually free before and after marriage. A French visitor, Baron Lahontan, wrote of young Ojibwa women: "Let her Conduct be what it will, neither Father nor Mother, Brother nor Sister can pretend to control her. A Young Woman, they say, is Master of her own Body and by her Natural Right of Liberty is free to do what she pleases." Women were highly valued for bearing and rearing children; after weaning babies at two or three, they tended them communally. "The father and mother draw the morsel from the mouth if the child asks for it—they love their children greatly," Le Jeune wrote. Women independently limited their fertility through abortion and long periods of nursing and abstinence. In contrast to European women, most of whom gave birth every other year in their fertile years (increasing their risk of death), Indian women bore an average four to six children. Indians never imagined rape until they saw Europeans perform it. Some tribes frowned on adultery: the Narragansett held men responsible.[6]

The Jesuits labored to alter these humane customs. Le Jeune tried to persuade a man to enrol his son in the mission school, but the man explained he had to defer to his wife's wish that the child stay home. Le Jeune lamented: "The women have great power here—a man may promise something and if he does not keep his promise, he thinks he is sufficiently excused when he tells you that his wife did not wish him to do it. I told him then that he was the master . . . in France women do not rule their husbands."

Priests were especially dismayed by easy divorce. An Algonkian man would return to his own clan, leaving the woman the land, the house, and the children. A French governor of the settlement at Trois-Rivières wrote, "Divorce is not an odious thing among them . . . when a woman wishes to put away her husband, she has only to tell him to leave the house and he goes out of it without another word." For Indians, divorce was a reasonable answer to marital conflict.

French society and religion were patriarchal, built on male dominance and privilege, and Frenchmen tried to impose these values on the Indians. French traders dealt only with Indian men; French merchants wanted furs trapped by men, not the small game, utensils, tools, and clothing women procured or made. The church was determined to change the morals of "Savages." Father Allouex of the Ottawa mission wrote: "The fountainhead of their religion is libertinism; and all these various sacrifices end ordinarily in debauches, indecent dances and shameful acts of concubinage." Europeans recognized "squaw chiefs" as queens, but their comprehension ended there. They saw Indian women farming and men hunting: in their world, peasant women worked in the fields and hunting was a sport, so they concluded that Indian men were lazy and women were slaves and drudges. Because they could not conceive of female sexual freedom, they saw Indian women as concubines. The Jesuits resolved to force Indians into monogamous, irrevocable marriage founded on male authority over women's activities and sexuality and to eradicate sexual freedom, divorce, and polygamy. To this end, they taught men to be brutal to women, knowing that the key to establishing patriarchy is male control of women.

As keepers of traditional rituals and customs, Indian women resisted the Jesuits from the beginning and were wary of the European fur trade, technology, and religious proselytizing. Father Dablon of the Ottawa mission complained, "Old women will not even lend an ear to our instructions." When his cabin burned down, Father André of Green Bay was sure women had set the fire; as he explained, an "old woman especially blamed me because I said that 'The evil spirit should be neither obeyed nor feared.'" Some bands fended off the Jesuits: "They even prevented us from entering their villages, threatening to kill and eat us," wrote a missionary. Lahontan recorded the Jesuits warning Indians of eternal damnation in another world where fire would torment heathens. The men would exclaim, "That's admirable!" but the women would cry derisively, "If their threats be well grounded, the mountains of the other world must consist of the ashes of souls."

Jesuits considered women the major obstacle to men's conversion, recording incidents of women's resistance over the years. Le Jeune recalled a convert's wife arguing: "Dost thou not see that we are all dying since they told us to pray to God? Where are thy relatives? where are mine? most of them are dead; it is no longer a time to believe." After a 1639–40 smallpox epidemic, a Jesuit persuaded some Montagnais to take refuge at the Sillery mission; after exposure to the priest for some time, the men exploded: "It is you women who are the cause of all our misfortunes. It is you who keep the demons among us. You do not urge to be baptized . . . you are lazy about going to prayers; when you pass before the cross you never salute it; you wish to be independent. Now know that you will obey your husbands." When they tried to force the women to submit, one fled into the woods: the men resolved to chain and starve her if they captured her.

The Jesuits supported the men's zeal in forcing Christian law on their women with increasing brutality. Converts at Sillery seized a woman who had left her husband and imprisoned her without food, fire, or cover in January. Missionaries urged women's husbands or brothers to beat them for defiance. Christian kin of a resistant girl flogged her publicly for accepting the attentions of a nonconvert and forced all the girls in the community to watch, tacitly threatening similar punishment. Yet the Jesuits did not teach women religion, expecting them to convert on men's orders. Le Jeune explained, "It is not becoming for us to receive [women] in our houses." Women had real objections to Christianity: a Montagnais convert argued that women "are more numerous than men, if a man can only marry one the others will have to suffer."

French hunger for furs also altered the Indian economy and their customs: wanting European tools and weapons, Indian men spent more time trapping or hunting and neglected their other work. They came to prefer the food Europeans traded to their own. While women fished, hunted, and gathered nuts and berries, the French traded Indians bread, tobacco, peas, beans, prunes, kettles, awls, iron arrowheads, hatchets, blankets, and cloaks in 1616; ten years later, they traded more sophisticated nightcaps, hats, shirts, bodkins, sheets, swords, ice picks, knives, raisins, and crackers. Europeans provided the manufactures from which women had gained some of their importance in Indian society. Women's processing of skins—scraping, stretching, and tanning—remained vital to fur production, but was now controlled by men. Indians had been seasonal nomads following game—"The choice of plans, of undertakings, of journeys, of winterings, lies in nearly every instance in the hands of the housewife"—but women lost control when the search for fur dictated the group's moves.

Before European intrusion, hunting had been religious as well as productive; it provided men's social, spiritual, and communal identity. But as Indian men took up European tools designed for trapping, the old religion no longer worked for them and they lamented that they could not contact their spirits and animal guardians. As their traditional source of self-definition faded, men found a replacement in Christianity. Women did not depend on the supernatural for identity and went on drawing it from communality. Christianity's emphasis on individualism attracted men and alienated women, so the Jesuits tried to isolate women from each other, limiting their collective and ritual activities. Men who no longer hunted grew more sedentary, and the priests broke them into independent nuclear families, ending the reciprocity and interdependence that had characterized communal and sexual relations.

Native American women saw the Jesuits as part of a package of change they disliked and resisted. But it was too powerful for them to stop. Indian communities were seriously weakened by epidemics, overhunting depleted animals with valuable fur, and shamans could not control either disaster. Women who chose conversion over imprisonment or flogging often continued to stress sexual division and female autonomy in terms of Catholic mysticism. Another Jesuit, Chrétien LeClerq, complained of Micmac converts who, "usurping the quality and the name of *religieuses*, say certain prayers in their own fashion." Some created a virtual cult of the Virgin, worshipping the one female symbol in Catholic ideology. They gathered at Ursuline convents and focused on female autonomy in a language that was acceptable to the missionaries. But Indian life would never be the same: the fur trade altered and degraded women's work and placed greater value on men and their work. Missionaries legitimated and fostered male dominance, just as male colonists bypassed influential Indian women to deal with men and appointed men when they named new rulers.

Colonization

The American origin myth is that the United States is a "meltingpot," a refuge where the persecuted and oppressed from across the world can find material well-being and freedom. North American society did begin with the interaction of diverse peoples from three continents—Native Americans, Africans, and Europeans. And, at some point, the elite did urge assimilation, but what it wanted was that newcomers relinquish their ethnic identity and adopt the mores of the dominant group. From the start, the Puritans intended to exterminate the Indians, and the immigrants interacted with violence and greed. America was never the "city on a hill" the Puritans described. The most we can say is that many Americans still harbor high ideals for their nation.

English culture was dominant in eastern North America partly because more English emigrated than any other group. Africans, the second largest, first arrived in 1625, when the Dutch imported four African men and Virginia imported twelve male and eleven female Africans.[7] Africans were usually slaves. By 1776 about 500,000 Africans, a third of them women, lived in the colonies.

Most English immigrants were indentured servants who contracted before boarding ship in Europe to work for five to seven years in return for passage to the New World and for food, clothing, and shelter during their term of service. On arrival, the ship's captain sold them for the price of their passage. They could not negotiate the length or kind of service. Planters wanted field workers; like the Spanish, they assumed that men were stronger than women and, in the seventeenth century, bought thousands of young Englishmen to work the tobacco fields of Chesapeake (Virginia and Maryland). About 75 percent of these indentured servants were men aged fifteen to twenty-four; until 1640, there were six men to every woman in Virginia, and few children.

Women in the South

English Catholics fleeing persecution colonized Maryland: 220 men, some with wives, settled near Chesapeake Bay in 1634. The number of women grew when Cecil Calvert, Lord Baltimore, offered grants of 100 acres to all immigrants, male or female, who paid their passage to Maryland; children were given 50 acres, and those bringing women servants under forty got 50 acres for each one. Elizabeth Beach, Mary Tranton, and Winifred Seaborne (single women or widows) brought female servants and set up estates.

Maryland treated women with unusual respect. The oath of allegiance officials swore to Calvert used the word *her* as well as *his*.[8] The person mainly responsible for this attitude was Margaret Brent (c. 1601–71), of prosperous English Catholic gentry, who emigrated to Maryland in 1638 with her sister Mary and four other women and five men, bought land, and set up a feudal manor. Remaining single, Brent controlled her property and acted as judge and attorney for herself and for others—from 1642 to 1650 she appeared 124 times in Maryland courts as an attorney.

Calvert, the proprietor, so respected Brent that, as he lay dying, he named her his executor with power of attorney. In 1648 Brent marched into the Maryland legislature chamber and demanded two votes—one as a landowner, and one as Calvert's executor. She had almost persuaded the representatives when Calvert's successor, Thomas Green, thundered "No!" ending the session. In 1650 Maryland tried to curry favor with the new Protestant Lord Protector of England, Oliver Cromwell, by denying Catholics privileges. The Catholic Brent and her sister moved to Virginia and built a plantation they named "Peace."

All other English colonies were Protestant—Virginia recognized only the Church of England. Jamestown began to thrive when Britain sent both men and women settlers, abandoning the Spanish model of colonization. Farmers without families were not motivated to produce a surplus. Over James I's objections, Virginia settlers founded an assembly to oversee local affairs; the Virginia House of Burgesses gave white male landowners some self-rule. In 1619 it begged the king to send women because "in a newe plantation it is not knowen whether man or woman be the most necessary."

To obtain women, the government decided to shanghai a hundred or so "young and uncorrupt" girls, force them aboard ship, and sell them as wives to Virginia men for the cost of their passage. Ninety girls were impressed in 1620, fifty in 1621–22; all were soon married, but men clamored for more, insisting they needed women to wash their clothes and nurse them. Through terrorism and rape, the sex ratio became three men to every woman.

A 1650 report to Parliament urged colonizing South

Virginia (North Carolina) and promoted silk production, in which "women or children are as proper as men." Fearing that Spain would encroach further north, in 1663 Charles II of England gave eight cronies a charter for Carolina. They fostered emigration by charging only small sums for 100 acres for each husband, wife, child, and manservant and 50 acres for each woman servant and slave. But the first Carolina settlers were migrant Virginians, not Britons. South Carolina, a separate colony in 1670, encouraged immigration by giving 50 acres to all family members and 50 acres rent-free for ten years to indentured servants after the expiry of their terms. The last colony settled, Georgia, bordered Spanish Florida, so London trustees set up a feudal system, granting land to male soldiers who would protect the border. In 1732, 114 poor English men, women, and children settled it with James Ogelthorpe.

Chesapeake, the first area settled, was humid and disease ridden, leading to a high death rate. Newcomers endured "seasoning," a bout of illness (usually malaria) during their first summer. Survivors could anticipate dysentery, influenza, typhoid fever, malarial recurrences, and other diseases. Among male servants, 40 percent did not live long enough to be freed; the rest died within twenty years. The uneven sex ratio left many people single; most women married, but marriages were brief. Servants had to wait until their term of service ended, so married late, and half of all marriages ended within seven years with the death of a spouse. Most people died in their late thirties or early forties.

Most servants came unwillingly. Agents for shipowners and merchants kidnapped or lured people with false promises. Some were ejected from overcrowded prisons or sold by their fathers. Terms of indenture lasted four to fourteen years, during which servants could not marry without a master's consent, earn extra money in their spare time, or vote. They were considered property, like slaves, and worked ten- to fourteen-hour days, six days a week, in a climate warmer than England's. Masters had to clothe, shelter, and feed them adequately, and they contracted to educate boys and some of the girls. They could sell or discipline their servants, but beatings were not to be "excessive." Owners often ignored these rules, and some servants fled to escape harsh treatment.[9] When servants' terms ended, they got money or land.[10] A quarter of a million indentured Britons came to America; 80,000 of them were women, who worked in fields or in houses, married, or took lovers. Mary Morrils, an indentured servant sold to Peter Folger for £20, married him and became Benjamin Franklin's maternal grandmother.

At first, masters gave servants who finished their terms "freedom dues"—tools, clothes, livestock, corn, tobacco, and land. But tobacco prices fell in the 1670s for fifty years. Good land grew scarcer and more costly, and Maryland dropped land from freedom dues. After 1681, freed men in Maryland had a choice of working for wages or tenant farming; women could do day labor or marry. Fearing that these women might become dependent on the state, colonial legislatures quickly passed laws impressing those with no visible means of support into bound labor. Women were thought especially prone to vice and immorality—Virginia and Massachusetts did not let female transients settle in their territory. At first, colonies granted land to woman settlers—Maryland and South Carolina gave male and female heads of families the same allotment. But men soon began to oppose the right of single women to own land. The Maryland Assembly decreed in 1634: "Unlesse [a single woman] marry within seven years after land shall fall to hir, she must either dispose away of hir land, or else she shall forfeit it to the next of kinne, and if she have but one Mannor, whereas she cannot alienate it, it is gonne unless she git a husband." The law was vetoed, but its import would triumph.[11]

With conditions so rough and loose, women freed from servitude were often completely free. Most free women married, many of them "up." Most colonists married traditionally, monogamously, joined established churches, and built one-family houses, assuming the right to own property. They grew their own food, found their fuel, and manufactured their clothes, soap, and candles. Settling Chesapeake was backbreaking work: land had to be cleared before the tobacco could be planted, tended, and harvested by hand. People lived in virtual shacks, possessed only farm tools, beds, and basic kitchen utensils, and ate badly—mainly pork and corn. With few towns and no schools, southerners spent lonely lives on isolated farms.

Most women bore only two or three children, compared with five or more for Englishwomen at the time, reflecting the poor conditions. The majority of whites lived in extended families. Bereft by frequent death and remarriage, they lived with half-brothers and -sisters, stepsisters or -brothers, stepfather or -mother, aunt, uncle, orphans, and wards. As in England, divorce was virtually nonexistent, and legal separation, rare. Over a third of people lost both parents before reaching maturity. County courts named guardians for propertied youngsters and bound poor ones into service. There were few clergy, sexual life was relatively free, and many brides were pregnant. Men died too young to control their children through money; they tended to give them great freedom in their wills, allowing them to inherit at sixteen or seventeen, perhaps to protect them against greedy kin or guardians. Chesapeake husbands left their wives larger portions of their estates than those in other colonies and often named them executors. The Maryland legislature gave widows more legal autonomy than other colonies; Chesapeake colonies let them challenge husbands' wills if they inherited less than a given minimum of their property, and many widows remarried and retained control of their husbands' estates.

Most people were immigrants until about 1675, when a lower birth rate and better economic conditions in England ended emigration. Most colonial women married, often older men, had one or two more children than their mothers, and were widowed with young children. Southern women married younger than their contemporaries in Old or New England— at sixteen to nineteen. As settlers become acclimatized and moved out of unhealthy saltwater lowlands, birth rates and life expectancy grew, and native-born whites began to outnumber immigrants. Marriages lasted longer, fathers reasserted control over children, and men over women.

As indentured servants grew scarce in the late seventeenth century, Chesapeake tobacco planters desperately needed labor and decided to import slaves. Virginia had imported Africans in 1626, but had only 1500–2000 in 1670. In the most tragic event of American history, between 1650 and 1750, Virginia imported over 200,000 Africans—Yoruba, Ibo, Ashanti, and others. South Carolinians had begun to cultivate rice, at which many Africans were expert, and their knowledge enabled English planters to raise it profitably. The transition to black slave labor was gradual but conclusive—all things conspired to make slavery seem a solution to planters.

Slavery is lethal to any society. It devastated the Africans who suffered it and advanced patriarchy in the south. If it eased the workload and improved the material well-being of whites who lived on others' labor, it also burdened them cruelly. Slavery wrecked democracy among farmers: those who could afford large slave forces stopped renting uncultivated fields to tenant farmers—mainly former indentured servants. Without land, they had to do day labor for wages. Large landowners grew rich and became an untitled aristocracy; those with one or two slaves slid into a lower class, and the gap between the two groups became impassable. Slavery confined white women even as it gave them that old sop—status. Slavery not only caused Africans unbearable suffering but injured owners, harming all of society.

Africans arrived heartbroken in a strange land, unable to communicate in the foreign language. Initially, many were indentured like whites and later freed, but only twenty years after the first Africans were sold at Jamestown in 1619, colonies were binding people of color and their children for life. Soon, darker skin was equated with enslavement: African Americans were fixed in slave status by the late 1600s. The color difference justified whites in seeing blacks as nonhuman. Almost immediately, legislatures became obsessed about interracial sex, but really, about sex between white women and black men (white men always used black women slaves sexually). In 1660 the Virginia legislature forbade interracial marriage and placed heavy penalties on interracial fornication, yet tacitly accepted white male behavior by decreeing that children born of interracial unions take their mothers'—slave—status.

At first, like indentured servants, most slaves were male. The proportion of male to female Africans was as unbalanced as that of southern settlers, remaining so until the mid-eighteenth century, when planters found it cheaper to breed slaves than buy new ones. Nevertheless, they did not let slaves marry legally. In North America, as in the Caribbean, slave women bore few children because of exhausting labor, harsh treatment, and poor diet and medical care. African women retained their tradition of nursing children until they were nearly four, another factor that may have lowered the birth rate. About a third of colonial slaves were female; they did fieldwork, planting, plowing, digging, and harvesting along with men. Some cleaned, nursed, laundered, and cooked in the big house, and at the end of the day they went back to their own quarters and did the same things for their families. One slave explained that they worked "from can to can't from the time they could see until the time they couldn't." White men rampantly exploited African women sexually. Some owners sent slaves to work for others, pocketing their wages. "Binding out" was supposedly reciprocal; in return, owners promised better conditions or amenities or lessons in reading, writing, or math. But few honored their promises.

Women in the Middle Colonies

The Dutch founded New Netherland in 1623 when its West India Company sent thirty colonist families to New Amsterdam, where 270 people lived by 1626. Its 1636 building program—church, brick kiln, bakehouse, lime kiln, minister's and midwife's houses—shows consideration for women, suggesting they had influence in the colony. Under Dutch law, single women had the same property rights as men and could marry under a Dutch-Roman version of "usus" law that let them control their property after marriage. Women kept their own names, bought and sold property, and did business without their husbands' permission. New Netherland women had more authority in the family than Englishwomen. As soon as they settled, the Dutch hired a teacher and used his house as a school for reading, writing, and sometimes arithmetic and contemporary history. Children too poor to pay could attend school "for God's sake." Many women must have been literate—Albany Dutch mothers taught their children, especially religion. But

Dutch religion was rooted in a belief in pervasive human depravity. Seeing children as their only hope for ending it, teachers stressed both knowing and fearing the Lord.

In 1655 the colony absorbed Swedish settlements on the Delaware River, but the Dutch government had less interest in New Netherland than in Africa, Brazil, or what is now Indonesia. Holland's economy was healthy, and few people accepted incentives proffered by the Dutch West India Company. So the colony imported African slaves. In 1664 Charles II of England, simply disregarding the Dutch, gave his younger brother the Duke of York the land between the Connecticut and Delaware rivers, including the Hudson Valley and Long Island. York assembled a fleet, sailed to America, anchored his ships off Manhattan Island, and demanded that New Netherland surrender. It did, and its 5000 inhabitants passed into English control. Most colonists were Dutch; others were English Puritans, French-speaking Walloons, Germans, Scandinavians, and other Europeans, with about 1500 African slaves—20 percent of the population—speaking eighteen languages and worshipping variously. York renamed the settlement New York, guaranteed religious toleration, and passed laws requiring parents to educate their children or lose them. For a time he allowed Dutch colonists to follow Dutch law, but curtailed the rights of married women. New York courts accepted Dutch wills written jointly by married couples until the 1690s, even though by English law women could not bequeath. The Dutch remained ethnically distinct in the Hudson Valley and controlled New Netherland for a half-century, until the American Revolution.

As soon as he took possession, York gave two titled friends the rich farmland between the Hudson and Delaware rivers (New Jersey). Luring settlers with generous land grants, the lords promised freedom of religion and a representative assembly (which they had no right to promise without the king's approval). When New England Puritan, Barbadian, and Dutch New York families moved to New Jersey, the lords quickly sold out to investors (thereby muddying land titles for years). Most shares were bought by Quakers who were fleeing English persecution, who acquired New Jersey in 1677.

By encouraging family colonization, Quakers also settled Delaware, when England took it from Holland in 1644, and Pennsylvania, after Charles II gave William Penn land between Maryland and New York. With a spiritual vision of a New World, Penn offered land on liberal terms, promising civil rights like trial by jury, bail, and religious tolerance—though only Christian men could vote. Welsh, Irish, Dutch, and Germans swarmed to Pennsylvania: by the 1680s it had 12,000 white settlers. A pacifist and relative egalitarian, Penn tried to treat Indians fairly, learning their languages, barring alcohol sales, regulating trade, and buying land from the Delaware (Lenni Lenape). His decency drew Indians from Maryland and Virginia, as well as the North Carolina Tuscarora, Ohio Shawnee, and Miami who were fleeing war with white settlers. But it also drew Scotch-Irish, Swiss, and Palatine Germans who had no respect for Indian claims to land and who continually brawled with them.

Women in New England

In 1603 James VI of Scotland acceded to the British throne as James I. An absolutist, he decided to retain episcopal church rule to increase his own power. Radical Calvinist Protestants, or Puritans, disliked this Catholic system: Congregationalists wanted to reform the English Church; Separatists saw it as too corrupt to be saved and migrated to Holland, which had religious freedom. But Separatists did not really want religious freedom: finding Holland too permissive, they decided to emigrate to the New World and build a society on their own principles. With permission from the Virginia Company to colonize its northern holdings, about a hundred people (thirty of them Separatists) sailed from Plymouth, England, on the *Mayflower* in September 1620. Two months later they made landfall farther north than intended, in Cape Cod, where, a few years earlier, about 90 percent of the Indians had died in an epidemic, probably chicken pox. The English settled without opposition.

Because they landed outside the territory chartered to the Virginia Company, non-Puritans challenged the authority of the Puritans who had obtained the permit. Puritans were suspicious of all "strangers" (non-Puritans) and, while still aboard ship, had worked out an agreement, the Mayflower Compact, establishing a "Civil Body Politic" and a basic system. Male leaders chose a governor and, at town meetings, made all decisions for the colony. (Later, Plymouth too created an assembly of landowning male settlers.) By spring 1621, half the settlers remained alive, mainly because Native Americans had assisted them.

In 1628 Congregationalist merchants obtained a royal charter for a Massachusetts Bay Company and sent a band of colonists to Cape Ann, north of Cape Cod. They made New England their headquarters and elected John Winthrop as governor, a post he held until he died in 1649. While still on shipboard, Winthrop had preached a sermon, "A Modell of Christian Charity," laying out his vision of the colony. He portrayed it in strong spiritual terms as "a city upon a hill," founded on principles of charity, sharing, and cooperation. Despite differences in wealth and status, which were ordained by God, they all needed each other, so were "knit more nearly together in the bond of brotherly affection."

In their own terms, the Pilgrims tried to realize this vision, founding a legislature and granting suffrage to all adult male church members in Massachusetts. Many colonists disapproved of private property in the brave new world, but they decided to give groups of families land grants for town sites and to allow each family a plot. Elite men got large grants, and some men got rocky or swampy land. Excluding nonwhites and women, the founders of churches and towns communally drafted the principles that would guide them. Soon Boston and Salem were busy seaports, towns grew among farms, and towns in the Connecticut River valley became commercial centers. But once the Connecticut valley was settled, the idyll ended.

Connecticut was the home of the Pequot Indians, who resisted English usurpation of their land and vainly tried to unite other tribes to fight it. After the English raided their villages, they attacked Wethersfield, a new town, killing nine colonists and kidnapping two. Englishmen led by Captain John Mason retaliated with Narragansett help in 1637. Fearing that the Pequots would overwhelm "his unseasoned, unreliable troops," writes Francis Jennings, Mason chose massacre over battle, setting fire to village wigwams and killing Indians who tried to escape.[12]

Like Spanish and French Catholics, English Protestants used their faith in male supremacy to justify white supremacy over "savages." The English were relatively peaceable in the early decades because they were few in number and not interested in converting Indians to Christianity. But they increased enough in the great migration of 1620–42 that they felt safe in unleashing terror.

In time, the Narragansett leader, Miantonomi, realized that the Pequot had been right about the English and, in 1642, tried to form a pan-Indian alliance. He failed and the English had other Indians kill him. In 1675 the settlers began to harass the Wampanoags on the south shore of Massachusetts Bay for their land. Puritan leaders who wanted war had trouble getting men to fight and, foolishly, they attacked the now neutral Narragansett—the largest and strongest tribe. Despite their pact with the former Narragansett chief, Massasoit, and the help he had given them, they killed his son Wamsutta, and his son Metacom (known as King Philip by the English) in turn became chief. The English attack unified the Indians: Metacom and his allies destroyed villages in Plymouth and Providence, killing or capturing a tenth of the able-bodied white men in Massachusetts. "Praying" (converted) Indian guides and scouts helped the English win in 1676, but "King Philip's War" proved to be, proportionately, the most costly and murderous in American history—9000 people died, two-thirds of them Indians, about fifty settlements were destroyed or damaged, and, for years afterward, New Englanders suffered starvation, oppressive taxation, homelessness, and America's first veteran problem.[13] The Puritans sold Indian survivors as slaves in the West Indies.

Afterward, subdued coastal tribes lived in small bands, trying to accommodate whites, trading with them or working for them. They did not want to join English society and tried to maintain their traditional way of life, though that goal became more and more impossible: the land was fenced, they could no longer move seasonally. Many died of European diseases or were kidnapped by colonists. Most kidnapped Native American men died, resisted, or escaped; women tended to remain with their white captors. Having children, they adapted, and many formed stable and enduring unions with white traders, giving them the pleasure of a bedmate, knowledge of Native American languages, and introductions to Indian trappers.[14] What women gained from these unions is questionable, but Indian women from Pocahontas on were diplomats between the two peoples. Mohawk Mary Brant kept her tribe loyal to the British during the American Revolution.

Shortly before the revolution, with her husband away on military duty, a woman known as Mrs. Hendee of Royalton, Vermont, was working alone in a field when Indians raided her house and took her children across White River. A historian described how

> with pallid face, flashing eyes, and lips compressed, maternal love dominating every fear, she strode into the Indian camp, regardless of the tomahawks menacingly flourished round her head, boldly demanded the release of her little ones, and persevered in her alternate upbraidings and supplications, till her request was granted.

> She rescued her own children then returned across the river and demanded the release of fifteen captured children of other settlers. She succeeded and so impressed the Indians with her bravery they offered the services of a strong young Indian to carry her on his back across the river—the fifteen children were apparently allowed to wade or swim.[15]

Given the chance to return home, many kidnapped white women chose to stay with the Indians, marrying them and raising their children as Indians, perhaps preferring Indian sexual politics. Some liaised with whites: Elizabeth Hammon, captured by Abenakis, wrote and delivered a letter offering a basis for a treaty during Metacom's War. When the English redeemed captives in King William's War (1689–97), the

Abenaki said they were "very loth" to part with Mistress Hull, who had written documents for them.

But some women like Hannah Duston, the most famous woman in New England in 1698, attacked the Indians. A week after giving birth to her twelfth child, she, another woman, and a boy were kidnapped by a band of Indians who killed her baby and marched the remaining three a hundred miles (161 kilometers) north. One night as the Indians slept, the captives attacked them with hatchets and killed all but a woman and a child, taking ten scalps (six children's) to prove their deed. Boston celebrated Duston as an "American Amazon . . . an archetypal heroine of New World frontier."[16] Lucy Terry, a sixteen-year-old slave who witnessed a 1746 attack on Deerfield, a frontier hamlet in northwest Massachusetts, wrote a twenty-eight-line poem vividly describing the massacre.

White women also committed one of New England's bloodiest killings in 1677, near the end of King Philip's (Metacom's) War. Some white men, escaping from the Abenaki with two Indian prisoners, walked into Marblehead, Massachusetts, hoping for rewards for the captives. Instead, a crowd asked why the Indians still lived; women picked up stones and bits of wood, killed the Indians, tore off their heads, and flayed them. No one identified or prosecuted them.

New York and Pennsylvania colonists continued to rely on Indian trade for profitable exports, like furs, to Europe; similarly, Indians continued to try to manipulate events to their benefit, using diplomacy and strategically playing one European power against another. Still, European instrumentalism not only defeated all other philosophies but destroyed human values whose lack we now lament. In the end, an Indian population of about ten million was reduced to about one million. In 1972 twenty-one Pequots remained in Connecticut.

Women's Work in the Colonies

Until about 1750, settlers traded only at Indian markets; colonists were fairly self-sustaining, producing little beyond their own needs. If they had surpluses, they traded them for salt, potatoes, sugar, rum, tea, or coffee. Itinerant shoemakers existed, but some settlers even made their own boots. They did rudimentary carpentry, made candles and soap, spun, sewed, knitted, and wove. Women plowed in spring and harvested in fall. In the middle colonies (New York to Chesapeake), women dug roots and potatoes, gathered flax, spread cut hay to dry in the sun, and picked fruit. Wheat-raising families toiled arduously from sunrise to sunset during harvest: grain must be cut when it is ripe or it spoils. Towns built grist mills to grind grain, cooperating on large projects like house-building, quilt-making, and boiling sugar cane to molasses.

North and south, most of the first houses were one low-ceilinged room with a fireplace and a window or two covered with oiled paper. The whole family slept, cooked, ate, and worked in this gloomy room, without any privacy. As they prospered, settlers built two-room additions on the other side of the chimney and later added lean-tos on the rear. They kept their best furniture—a table and chairs usually—in the main sitting room with their most precious item of furniture, a bed. Keeping a fire going was a round-the-clock job—some logs were so huge that dragging them in required a horse and chain. Every night the housewife carefully sifted ashes on the embers to keep them alive till morning; she watched the fire all day to make sure it was live enough to last the night. If it died, she sent a child to a neighbor with a fire pan or shovel for burning coals. Isolated families used tinderboxes to relight fires. Tinder, bits of scorched worn-out linen, ignited when sparks struck by flint were rubbed on steel. The chimneys, made of logs plastered with clay, were highly flammable, and fires often went out of control, setting the thatched roof and sometimes the whole house on fire.

Colonial women learned from Indian women how to vary their diet, making sugar bars (not granules) from maple tree sap and baking beans in earthen vessels buried in hot ashes.[17] Indian women pounded corn for hoecakes in a hollow stone, mixed the meal with water, and baked it on a fire; settlers ground grain with a mortar and pestle, and baked the dough on a shovel blade. Dessert was Indian pudding, a batter of beaten cornmeal, scalded milk, molasses, and cinnamon or ginger poured into a stone dish and baked all night in a brick oven. Colonists ate baked or stewed beans several times a week, with boiled meat or fish, vegetables, cornmeal, water, milk, and beer. Tea was prohibitively expensive, and coffee barely known. Women did all the cooking—heavy labor in an age of cast-iron pots and kettles. They lifted salt barrels, pounded grain, and churned butter. Cooking equipment was expensive—kettles often cost £3—but sturdy enough to last several generations. Families ate twice a day, an early breakfast and a mid-afternoon dinner from a single wooden trencher, using fingers, tin or pewter spoons, and one drinking cup. Only the rich owned a fork.

Every day farm women milked, fed cows, chickens, and hogs, gathered eggs, tended the fire and vegetable garden, and swept and sanded floors. Even meals made in one pot and served without ceremony took hours to prepare. Several times a week they baked bread, made butter and cheese, and cleaned the wood and iron utensils. Once a month they washed clothes in huge tubs. Daughters helped: by twelve, girls were proficient in domestic tasks. Couples rich enough to own a loom wove together at dusk, while children spun or wove. Women dyed cloth and yarn, sewed clothes, and braided rushes. Seasonally, they gathered herbs and distilled them for medicines, dipped candles, wove linen, and made soap.

Life was a little easier in the South than the North; a longer growing season let women spend more time outdoors raising abundant crops of potatoes and vegetables. Pigs left to forage or eat slops provided meat year round. The tasks of southern white women were like northern women's, except for less spinning and sewing. But northerners lived in communities, while many southern farms were on isolated frontiers where women had to handle and shoot rifles, hunt, trap, and repel predators. Plantation wives had few chores but immense responsibility trying to provide all the necessities of a large household. Their main daily job was teaching and supervising slaves, but every day they made delicacies (mince pies, cheesecakes, tarts, biscuits), drew up household menus, entertained frequent visitors, ran dairies, supervised gardens, ordered supplies, and doctored the family as well as servants and slaves. Even if husbands were at home, many women directed the planting, harvesting, storing, and marketing of crops and were astute traders or barterers.

On sheep farms, women had to card, or comb, wool—a time-consuming, arduous job. After shearing, they picked burrs and twigs from the fleece and carded it for spinning. They welcomed the appearance of professional carders who combed, cleaned, and dyed wool for a percentage of the end product. In time, people who hoped to trade product for service began to produce surpluses, and factors (merchants who resold goods to distant shops) sought country women to spin yarn in return for yards of woven cloth. When the English Civil War cut off shipments to the colonies in 1640, colonial governments urged women to spin and weave raw wool, hemp, and flax and to teach their children to spin. Massachusetts offered weavers a bonus of 25 percent over the cloth's value.

Later, governments made spinning mandatory for women and children—"all hands not necessarily employed on other occasions, as woemen, girles, and boyes, shall, and hereby are, enjoyned to spin according to their skill and abilitie." Every household with a spinner had to produce three pounds of linen, cotton, or wool a week, thirty weeks a year. In these years, women produced all the cloth and clothing and most of the shoes for the colonies.

Women had a protected monopoly on midwifery—mid-seventeenth-century male midwives were fined fifty shillings. Most colonies licensed and registered midwives who had been examined by a board: some were well trained in European midwivery schools. Colonial America had no medical schools or journals, few hospitals, and few laws governing healers. Many people practiced medicine; the occasional "doctoress" was as accepted and well paid as the semitrained "physic" (surgeon or healer). All colonies record female physicians; Mrs. Allyn was an army surgeon during Metacom's war. Plantation owners gave privileges to slave midwives and "doctoresses." Women were lawyers, "attorneys-in-fact," suing for themselves or others without special training.[18] After 1750, though, law was "professionalized," requiring educational and other prerequisites from which women were barred, and they were eliminated from the profession.

On the other side of the bar, women's rights depended on their marital status. Single women had similar legal rights to men: they could own property in their own names and manage it without male interference. Once they turned twenty-one, they kept any income they earned. They could not serve on juries, but they could sue or be sued. After marriage, women lost control over property. Some remarried widows managed to retain control of their property, but virtually the only rich women in British America were widows who remained single. Women could rarely start profitable enterprises: acquisitiveness, admired in men, was frowned upon in women. But women who tried to preserve or increase inheritances were respected.

Single women without property, or those whose husbands were sickly or failures or given to vice, had few options. A lucky few opened brokers' businesses or ran small shops. Women with husbands ran inns or brewed and sold ale and beer. With some training, a woman could become a milliner, mantua maker, or seamstress, or she could knit stockings at home to sell in town or to a factor. Educated women could run dames' schools for young children. Healthcare was universally given by women—midwives, wet-nurses, or nurses for the sick and old. But it was hard for women to survive without a household. Then, as now, women with children and no husbands lived marginally, and towns routinely refused to let them settle, fearing they would become public charges. A few spun and wove in public almshouses, which were hardly pleasant places.

The Puritans

Puritans certain of their own and their god's rightness felt no shame at exterminating Native Americans. Certain that god had predestined their fate before they were born, slotting them in heaven or hell, Calvinists knew their duty on earth was to examine their souls; good deeds had little weight in their value system. John Winthrop justified usurping Indian land on the grounds that the Indians had not "subdued" it, so had only a "natural," not a "civil" right to it. He dismissed a smallpox epidemic that wiped out Indians in 1633: "In sweeping away great multitudes of the natives . . . [God made] room for us here. . . . God hath thereby cleared our title to this place."

Puritan clergy cited Psalm 2: 8, "Ask of me and I shall give thee, the heathen for thine inheritance, and the uttermost parts of the earth for thy possession"; and Romans 13: 2, "Whosoever therefore resisteth the power, resisteth the ordinance of God: and they that resist shall receive to themselves damnation." Spaniards, French, and Puritans all worshiped a god whose grace extended only to their own sect, whose rightness guaranteed their own, vindicating their claim to supremacy.

Thousands of religious dissenters emigrated to New England in the Puritan Great Migration beginning in 1620. It ended in 1640, when civil war erupted in England. The Puritans, who won, no longer needed a refuge. The Massachusetts Bay colony spawned others—Plymouth, Connecticut, Rhode Island, and four New Hampshire towns— all of which were virtual Puritan theocracies. Believing with Calvin in a direct relation between man and god mediated by Scripture, they repudiated church hierarchy, icons, and priestly authority and urged each man to read Scripture for himself. They believed man could not strive for salvation, which was predestined by god, who alone chose the saved (the "elect"); conveniently, however, earthly prosperity indicated election. Making Congregationalism the official religion (only Rhode Island allowed freedom of worship), they taxed each household to build meetinghouses and pay ministers. Only male church members voted in colony elections; non-Puritan men seem to have voted in some town meetings. But no woman voted, Puritan or not. Law compelled people not to join the church but to attend Sunday worship. It fined them for irregular church attendance or vocal disapproval of ministers or independent preaching. Freedom was obedience to the "will of God."

Puritans tried to live honest, orderly lives and to force

everyone else to do the same.[19] They turned out hundreds of books prescribing the behavior god demanded from all humans in every situation. They were willing to endure harsh wilderness conditions to build a society based on their beliefs because of a religious certitude that offered them power. Men swore they and their families had faith in god, and then they required the families to keep their oath. Puritan minister John Cotton wrote, "We undertake to be obedient to [god] . . . in the behalfe of every soul that belongs to us . . . our wives, and children, and servants, and kindred, and acquaintance, and all that are under our reach, either by way of subordination, or coordination." Accordingly, the civil law enforced extreme marital dominance, wives' submission to husbands, and allowed widows less autonomy than English law. It exhorted parents to break children's spirits while they were young.

New England's climate was extremely healthful in comparison with the climate in English cities or the American South: compared to Englishmen's life expectancy, Chesapeake men lost ten years, while New England men gained ten. Even the first generation of New England immigrants who endured the hardship of the first winters lived to be sixty and older. The sex ratio was always even—they had migrated *en famille*. Together, husbands and wives carved out farms and towns, trying to realize a "Holy Experiment," a perfect godly commonwealth wedding church and state. Marriages lasted longer than in the South and produced larger families. Families owned their land and were motivated to work: if prosperity equalled salvation, hard work equalled godliness. Farmers replanted their fields, fertilizing rather than clearing land every few years. The good New England diet included meat, so colonists kept sheep and cattle. It was the need for grazing land that caused settlers to spread so swiftly, encroaching further on Indian land.

In the absence of traditional institutions, the family was the basic unit of social and political life. Puritans had grown up in nuclear families controlled (ideally) by fathers, but in England, nuclear families were enlarged by kin-networks. Severed from these contacts, colonial families were isolated. Men had the right to choose wives, and women the power to refuse, but both needed parental consent. Nearly 90 percent married but relatively late—women around twenty, men at twenty-seven or so—and in strict birth order, a sign of parental control. Children were tied to parents. Men needed land to marry; women needed dowries of household goods: both acquisitions could come only from fathers. Records show that long-lived fathers delayed handing property to sons, and married children often lived with fathers, who held them in tight control.

Puritan marriage was supposed to be based on ardent sexual love—a spouse's duty. But like their great poet John Milton, Puritans considered marriage a contract, not a sacrament, and held civil, not religious, ceremonies. Without derogating sexuality, they held it secondary to the ultimate relationship, man and god. They banned sex outside marriage for men and women, but records show that many babies were born to eighteenth-century couples who had been married less than nine months, so this rule may have eased. Puritan sexual mores were unique; other colonies had a double standard.

Divorce was easier in the colonies than in England, especially in New England, where marriage was a civil contract and either partner could sue for divorce for adultery, impotence, refusal of sex, or desertion. Puritans did not adopt English laws letting widows or married women keep or guard their property. Despite its ease, divorce was rare because it impoverished women, and despite equal sex rules, Puritans discriminated against women in law, church business and theology, education, and political and economic rights: the sexes were equal only in principle. Women were more dependent in marriage and widowhood under northern colonial law than in English or Chesapeake law.[20] Wives managing households were expected to help their husbands and act as their surrogates if necessary. Few tasks overlapped: gender roles remained consistent and distinct.

In the healthy environment the population surged, yet the sex ratio dropped to three men to every two women. Throughout the colonial period, New England women spent most of their lives pregnant or nursing, and one-fifth of them died in childbirth. Northerners typically bore a child every two years for twenty years; a woman who bore her first child at twenty-two and her last in her mid-forties had ten to eleven children, eight of whom might reach adolescence. If her last child left home at fifteen, she spent thirty-five years rearing children. About a quarter of children died before the age of five; two-thirds reached adulthood. But Ann Bradstreet was surely not the only woman whose eight children all lived to mature. Some New England towns had children's schools; other parents sent their children to live in households where a mother, usually, would teach them.

Not until emigration ended in 1640 did the native-born population begin to outnumber immigrants. Since northern colonial women married younger than Englishwomen, and colonial men lived longer than Englishmen, women were widowed later than in England. Judges awarded widows a minimum one-third of a husband's estate; if a couple had no children, she got half even if her man died intestate. New England men lived long enough to control their children. New England might be said to have "created" grandparents, since few Britons ever saw a grandchild. Puritans did not tolerate singleness—single people were forced to live with families or were fined and expelled.

Although New Englanders were the most educated of all colonists, only about a third of the women and half the men could sign their names in the 1600s. Puritan theology asserted that all souls were spiritually equal before god and that all believers should read the Scripture for themselves rather than passively bow to authority. Contrary to the colonial founders' intention, this sanctioning of women's thinking for themselves produced extraordinary women like the theologian Anne Hutchinson (1591–1643) and the poet Anne Bradstreet (1612–72). Sarah Harrison Blair, asked during her marriage ceremony in the 1690s to promise to obey her husband, replied "No obey." Repeated several times, the question earned the same response, so the ceremony proceeded without the promise.

Anne Hutchinson

In 1631 Roger Williams, a Separatist, migrated to Massachusetts Bay as assistant pastor at Salem. He began to express odd ideas, claiming that the English king had no right to give away Indian land, that the church and the state should be separate, and that Puritans had no right to impose their religious beliefs on others. Expelled from Massachusetts in 1635 for "dyvers newe & dangerous opinions, against the aucthoritie of magistrates," he continued to maintain cordial relations with John Winthrop. He founded Providence on Narragansett Bay, ensuring that it and other towns in Rhode Island colony allowed religious freedom and tolerated different religions, including Judaism. In 1638, he told Winthrop, "notwithstanding our differences concerning the worship of God . . . you hav bene always pleased lovingly to answer my boldnes in civil things."[21]

Anne Marbury Hutchinson was a different matter, and the fury of the vituperation heaped on her by the Puritan orthodoxy indicates the degree of their outrage and fear at being challenged by a woman. Massachusetts ministers considered females incapable of accomplishment or independence because, by nature, they lacked assertiveness and intellect. The only discourse available in Puritan colonies was religious; Hutchinson, a popular and skilled midwife, helped Boston women channel their anger and frustration into religious dissent.

Hutchinson began as a follower of Reverend John Cotton, who came to Boston in 1633. He believed in female inferiority and allowed women to speak in church only to confess a sin or sing hymns. But he stressed a Puritan doctrine, the "covenant of grace," the belief that god freely offered salvation to helpless, unworthy, human beings. From the first, the relative weight of good works (human effort) versus grace (godly effort) in salvation perplexed Puritans. Most ministers kept to a middle ground; Cotton's claim that good works were specious grounds of salvation, that god granted grace alone and unaided, upset a fragile ideological balance. Teaching that people could become conscious of the Holy Spirit in their souls, and urging his Boston congregation not to fear the word *revelation*, he ardently aroused some of his congregation, including Anne Hutchinson. This group set themselves to convert others to a belief in personal revelation—what Puritan divines pejoratively called Antinomianism, Opinionism, or Familism.

In 1636 Hutchinson began holding bi-weekly teaching sessions in her house, discussing sermons and interpreting Scripture, mainly with women. She argued that the elect could communicate directly with god and achieve certainty of salvation, instead of living in constant fear. Direct communication lessened one's need for an institutional church, just as Puritanism lessened the need for the priestly hierarchies of orthodox religions. Hutchinson's ideas appealed to women for a number of reasons. Women, who were not granted advanced

education, would appreciate Hutchinson's exalting of spiritual-
ity and denigration of formal learning.[22] Her ideas offered
"what the Reverend Tomas Weld called 'a faire and easie way to
heaven,' but they also provided her followers with a means of
challenging the increasingly repressive political and religious
orthodoxy that prevailed in Massachusetts Bay."[23] Women were
also drawn to Antinomianism because its claim that individuals could not achieve salvation paralleled their own inability to
achieve control in their lives. Antinomianism placed both sexes
vis-à-vis god in the same position that women held vis-à-vis
men in Puritan society, thereby extending female humility to
men.[24] A symbolic articulation of women's frustration at stifling
gender roles, Antinomianism gave them hope.

Unaware until too late of the political overtones of women's
revolt, Puritan ministers worried about Hutchinson's growing
following. Edward Johnson snarled that "the weaker Sex" had
set Hutchinson up as a "Priest, thronging after her"; John
Underhill complained that she made daily "clamor" that New
England men kept their wives in servile subjection; John
Winthrop warned she was causing "divisions between husband
and wife." An anonymous British pamphleteer described
Antinomianism as "somewhat like the Trojan horse for rarity,"
being covered with women's aprons. Pastors called Antinomians
"heretics of the worst and most dangerous sort" with "absurd,
licentious and destructive" views. Female challenge to the
Boston church reached its apex in 1636–37. Boston pastor
John Wilson was outraged that Hutchinson dared to interpret
and question his sermons. One day as he rose to preach she
publicly defied him by walking out of the meeting house—
followed by many other women.

What most disturbed Puritan men was the dissenters' sex: men
in patriarchies fear female uprisings as they do slave uprisings,

in terror of losing both their slaves and their undeserved supremacy. Cambridge minister Thomas Shepard berated Hutchinson severely, praising his own wife's "incomparable meekness of spirit, toward myself especially." Accusing Hutchinson of heresy, the Salem pastor Hugh Peter urged his daughter to see female meekness as "Womans Ornament"; another found Hutchinson a "charismatic healer, with the gift of fluent and inspired speech," but a rebel with a confused, bewildered mind like Joan of Arc (who was a devil to the English). Governor Winthrop, who strongly disapproved of intellect in women, denounced Hutchinson as "a woman of a haughty and fierce carriage, of a nimble wit and active spirit, and a very voluble tongue, more bold than a man, though in understanding and judgement, inferiour to many women." He later said that Ann Hopkins, the wife of Connecticut's governor, had lost her mind by reading and writing. All male Puritan leaders agreed that Hutchinson's followers were "a mob scrambling after God, and like all mobs quickly dispersed once their leaders were dealt with."

And deal swiftly with the leader they did, summoning her before a convocation of the clergy in 1636 to condemn her for failing in her ordained womanly role. Later, a synod of elders defined that role in religion: women might meet "to pray and edify one another," but if they resolved questions of doctrine or expounded Scripture "in a prophetical way," the meeting was "disorderly." Worried that other women would imitate Hutchinson, the authorities ordered further examinations. If they could catch her in a major theological error—heresy— they could publicly humiliate and punish her. Hutchinson brilliantly parried their attacks, retorting with questions that compelled them to justify their positions. Unable to refute her theological positions, the court discredited her on grounds of sex.

When Winthrop sneered, "We do not mean to discourse with those of your sex," she lost her temper, as they had hoped: "I know that for this you goe about to doe to me, God will ruine you and your posterity, and this whole State," she erupted, claiming to know this by "immediate revelation."

Bay Colony leaders called female Antinomian leaders "witches led by Satan" and aspersed the masculinity of Antinomian men, who supported "silly women laden with . . . lusts," unable to perform their female functions. Hutchinson had an abdominal mole and had suffered a stillbirth; the churchmen called them "thirty monstrous births" and a "monster" sent by god as punishment especially for female heresy.[25] Five men, including Hutchinson's brother-in-law, formally protested her admonition and excommunication. Cotton, who had first supported her but grew to resent her independence, silenced them by denouncing her and declaring male Antinomians exempt from blame since Antinomianism was "a woman's delusion." He split their group. Hutchinson regretted her errors of expression but admitted none of judgment. Wilson ordered her, "as a Leper to withdraw your selfe out of the Congregation." She rose, walked to the door, took her friend Mary Dyer's proferred hand, and, turning, said, "The Lord judgeth not as man judgeth, better to be cast out of the Church than to deny Christ."

Providence and Portsmouth offered religious freedom: both sexes had the right to teach, preach, and choose their church. The Hutchinsons went to Portsmouth, but there they became embroiled in a new controversy. The poor of the town, resenting the autocratic rule and land allotment policy of Judge William Coddington, tried to found a church that followed Massachusetts land policy. Hutchinson announced her support for passive resistance to authority, impugned the legitimacy of magistracy itself, and fomented a rebellion in 1639 with Samuel Gorton, a freethinker who defended justice for all, "rich or poore, ignorant or learned." Portsmouth citizens set up a new political body and threw Coddington out, replacing him with William Hutchinson. Rejecting magistracy per se, William refused the office. Coddington fled to Newport, where he claimed the judgeship by default. Massachusetts officials validated his claim and let him manage Rhode Island affairs from his new location. Gorton and others plotted an armed revolt against Coddington and were banished from the colony. Hutchinson broke with Gorton over his use of arms and went to Newport, where, in 1640, William died.

The Newport church dissolved and, in 1642, Hutchinson sought refuge in New Netherland (her trip is memorialized by the Hutchinson Parkway, the only one I know named for a woman). In 1643 Indians who were quarrelling with her Dutch neighbors took them for Dutch and killed her, her three daughters, two sons, and a friend, William Collins. Puritan divines rejoiced: god had taken vengeance on the "American Jezebel" and her children, the poisoned seed.

Hutchinson's expulsion did not end the Antinomian struggle: Massachusetts churchmen prosecuted female dissenters for years. The Boston church condemned Mary Dyer and Jane Hawkins, expelled Judith Smith, had Katherine Finch whipped, and excommunicated Phillipa Hammond, Sarah Keayne, and Joan Hogg. Other women entered the fray—Mary Drummer, Mary Oliver, and William Coddington's wife. Adopting Boston's method of dealing with assertive women, Salem excommunicated Jane Verrin, Mary Oliver, the servant Margery Holliman, and the widow Margery Reeves, who were all former followers of Roger Williams in 1636. Oliver was seen as dangerous for believing that anyone professing faith in Christ should be admitted to the church and its sacraments. A Salem magistrate enraged by her refusal to defer to his authority had her put in the stocks without trial. She sued him for false arrest and collected the minimum ten shillings damages. Between 1638 and 1850 she was summoned before magistrates six times, put in the stocks, lashed, jailed, and had a cleft stick stuck on her tongue.

Massachusetts divines felt that Hutchinson's death knelled the death of Antinomianism. Reporting on the Boston Antinomian controversy, they argued that her beliefs, activities, and rebelliousness, character and sex, threatened not only the family, state, religion, and hierarchy but also their status. In the first five years of Puritan settlement, women were convicted of only 1.7 percent of criminal offences; during and after the Antinomian controversy (1635–39), they were convicted of 6.7 percent, and from 1640 to 1644, of 9.4 percent. The Puritan campaign to eradicate Antinomians and Antinomianism succeeded: by 1650 it barely existed.

Anne Hutchinson's trial did not end with her death: historian Emery Battis tried her again in the 1960s. Granting her a prodigious memory and a keen mind, he nevertheless found her wracked with agonizing doubt because she lacked a male "mental director"—her husband lacked the power to guide her—and because of menopause.[26] Anthropological studies show that menopause psychically disturbs women only in cultures that demean menopausal women, but Puritan New England revered older women for supposedly vacating sex and let them act as deaconesses.[27] That Battis' judgment could be taken seriously in the 1960s is staggering: Does Hutchinson's intellectual independence threaten men three hundred years later?

The Society of Friends, or Quakers, was founded in England in 1648 during the Civil War, a time of innovative political ideas that briefly included women's suffrage.

The Quakers

Teaching that women subordinated by Eve's fall were redeemed and made men's equals by Jesus' sacrifice, the Quakers found biblical authority for their preaching and participating in all community affairs. Women drawn by this doctrine were among the first to preach the Quaker message, evangelizing beyond England in its early and most radical period and carrying Quakerism to Ireland, North America, and the Ottoman Empire. Ann Austin and Mary Fisher, who came to Boston in 1656 to bring Quakerism to the New World, were harshly whipped and deported under a 1637 law passed to deal with Anne Hutchinson and her followers. But three weeks later, more Quakers arrived, four men and four women, who were interrogated and taken before Governor John Endecott. Mary Prince denounced her interrogators as "hirelings, Baals and seed of the serpent"; fifty-nine more Quaker missionaries came to America between 1656 and 1663, twenty-six of them women, only four with husbands.

Quakers refused to take oaths and denounced liturgy, priesthood, and infant baptism, believing that adults should freely choose their religion. Quaker women, insisting that sex had no bearing on prophetic or teaching gifts, demanded equality in worship and church organization. Puritans persecuted their Quaker visitors. As Lydia Wardel watched them torture her husband and women in their group, she tore off her clothes and displayed herself before the Newbury congregation as a "naked sign." Both she and her husband were thereupon whipped. When Deborah Wilson walked through Salem as a naked sign, the Puritans tied her, her mother, and her sister to a cart and dragged them through town, whipping them.

But Quaker women later throve in New England. Mary Coffin, born in Massachusetts, moved at fifteen to Nantucket with her father, Tristram Coffin, who bought the island from Indians and settled on it in 1660–61. There she married Nathaniel Starbuck, a farmer involved in local politics, and had ten children. With her son, Nathaniel, she made Quakerism Nantucket's main religion and was prominent in its political affairs. So much public business was transacted at her house that it was called "Parliament House."

In later years, the Society of Friends slid into patriarchal attitudes, but women still influenced doctrine, church governance, and membership. After 1660, writes historian Mary Beth Norton, mothers, not fathers, linked church and family in Quaker Pennsylvania.[28] Motherhood gave Quaker women a public function: they oversaw family life, disciplined recalcitrant church members, mediated family disputes, organized charitable help for poor widows and children, and, along with men, approved marriages. As we will see, Quakerism profoundly affected later generations of American women whose ideas and confidence helped create the feminist movement.

Anne Bradstreet

Seeds of feminist consciousness were germinating in literature, too. Anne Dudley, born in England in 1612 to well-to-do Puritan parents and raised on the estate of the Earl of Lincoln, whose affairs her father managed, was educated by tutors and had access to a large library. She caught smallpox (which pocked her skin) when she was about fourteen and felt god had condemned her "carnal" heart. At sixteen she married Simon Bradstreet, a cultured Puritan Cambridge graduate of twenty-five. In 1630 they migrated to Andover, Massachusetts, enduring famine, illness, fiery summers, freezing winters, the wild alien land. Though she bore and raised to adulthood eight children, she made time to write poetry by scanting sleep and other "refreshment." A serious Puritan, she constantly examined her experience to find its religious meaning; her poetry grew from this inner questioning. She did not try to publish her work, but her brother-in-law had her poems, *The Tenth Muse, Lately Sprung Up in America*, published in London in 1650—without her knowledge, he said. It was a bestseller.

She merged great learning in literature and theology with domestic images, creating a sense of wholeness in her work. Although she says she accepts her lowly place—her "foolish, broken, blemish'd Muse," a talent "made . . . irreparable" by nature itself—she challenged female inferiority in an elegy for Queen Elizabeth:

> Nay masculines, you have thus taxed us long,
> But she, though dead, will vindicate our wrong.
> Let such as say our sex is void of reason,
> Know 'tis a slander now but once was treason.

In the Prologue to the *Tenth Muse*, she writes:

> I am obnoxious to each carping tongue
> Who says my hand a needle better fits,
> A Poets pen all scorn I should thus wrong,
> For such despite they cast on Female wits:
> If what I do prove well, it won't advance,
> They'l say it's stoln, or else it was by chance.

Bradstreet also wrote *Meditations Divine and Moral* and *Upon the Burning of Our House*. All but one of her children outlived her, and she, if often ill, lived to be sixty. She was the first American poet of excellence and her work remains vital and moving.

The Witch Trials of the 1690s

Despite—or perhaps because of—their religious certitude, Puritans seem never to have felt secure but continually threatened, needing to quash deviance, especially in females. The European witch craze found fertile soil in a New England alert to female dissent, and, between 1647 and 1700, 234 people were tried for witchcraft and 38 were executed. (The southern and middle colonies tried few witches and executed none.) The targets of persecution were ordinary women—women were about 75 percent of the accused and 70 percent of those executed. Achsah Young of Windsor, Connecticut, was the first person hanged for witchcraft, in 1647; Margaret Jones of Charlestown, the first executed in Massachusetts, declared her innocence as she mounted the gallows in 1648. In 1656 Ann Hibbins of Boston, the aged widow of a colonial official, a rich merchant whose reverses had left his wife with little, was found guilty of clairvoyance. Noting two of her accusers huddled in conversation, she charged them with talking about her. The Reverend John Norton remarked that she was killed "only for having more than her neighbors."

Connecticut hanged at least ten "witches"—eight women and the husbands of two. A couple condemned to ordeal by water (if you float, Satan is helping you; if you drown, you are innocent!) wisely disappeared from the colony. To try Mary Reeve Webster for witchcraft in 1683, Hadley, Massachusetts, officials dragged her from her house, hanged her almost to death, cut her down, and buried her in the snow. Surviving, she was acquitted and lived to old age. Boston authorities executed a woman in 1685, mainly for being Irish, Catholic, and speaking Gaelic. The poor soul, a washerwoman called Witch Glover, was blamed for fits that suddenly seized four formerly obedient children of a laborer in Cotton Mather's congregation. There were others—the 1692 witch craze was no sudden outburst but the peak of an intensifying paranoia.

In 1692 the daughter and niece of the Reverend Parris of Salem Village (now Danvers), Massachusetts, were taken with fits and other strange symptoms diagnosed as having been induced by witchcraft. Authorities charged Parris' West Indian slave, Tituba, and two other women marginal in Salem society. Under interrogation, Tituba confessed to being a witch, but officials searched for more, leading to widespread accusations and symptoms. In the next three years, 165 people (74 percent women) were accused as witches in Essex County; Salem executed fourteen women, six men, and two dogs (sex unknown) between March and September of 1692.

The victims came from every socioeconomic level; the only trait they shared was some personal eccentricity, flaw, or calling that distinguished them in the rigidly conformist Puritan society—having a bad temper, telling fortunes, being healers or wizened and old. Pipe-smoking Sarah Good, who looked seventy, was pregnant, Sarah Osburne was an invalid, Rebecca Nurse was seventy-one and almost deaf, Martha Carrier was thought to be a smallpox carrier, Bridget Bishop was a flashily dressed flirty tavern-keeper in middle age. George Burroughs and Sarah Wild were public scolds, generally disliked. The Puritans hanged John Proctor, but delayed killing his pregnant wife, Elizabeth, until she gave birth, loath to kill an unborn child. But they did not hesitate to jail and starve Sarah Good's six-year-old daughter, Dorcas, who went mad, remaining so for the rest of her life.[29] But when accusers began naming the colony's most distinguished men as witches, the governor disbanded the court and pardoned the remaining accused, including Elizabeth Proctor, four months away from childbirth.

Some historians claim that most accusers were adolescent girls whose neighbors supported their charges. Carol Karlsen suspects that persecution arose from the tension of contradiction in Puritan ideology, which praised women as godly helpmates yet scorned them as disorderly.[30] John Demos thinks witchcraft accusations were symbolic indictments of mothers.[31] But Mary Beth Norton asserts that most accusers were men, who charged females (mostly married) in mid-life (at the peak of their power over others, but on the brink of symbolically losing it with menopause) who tended to have turbulent family lives—noticeable in a society that demanded domestic stability under male control.[32] Since witches interfered with basic life processes, especially birth and the care and feeding of infants and animals, witchcraft crazes seem to express male uneasiness about, or fear of, women's resentment of their total subordination in the necessary—not unknown in New England.

For Norton, the witch hunt reflected extreme, pervasive anxiety over New England's political system, Indian wars, disastrous epidemics, and the disruption of an agrarian economy by new commercial ventures, but also sexual tensions as mechanisms designed to control women began to collapse. The persecution of Antinomian women in the 1630s and 1640s, and of Quaker women in the 1650s and 1660s, was followed by increased prosecutions for premarital pregnancy, fornication, and infanticide by single mothers. Such acts necessarily involve equal numbers of men and women, but authorities focused on the women. Before 1665, only about 20 percent of accused women were actually charged with fornication; by the 1690s, the number had risen to 63 percent. Free female sexuality is the most serious threat to patriarchy (which always makes female adultery a crime) because it defies male ownership of women's bodies. Females acting free, sexually, are insubordinate, indifferent to male heirs' legitimacy and the perpetuation of male-dominated lineages.

The 1690s witch hunt climaxed a history of male Puritan fear of female revolt. As an earlier generation of Puritans found Antinomian women more threatening than men, those of the 1690s found women the main source of disorder. The witch craze illustrates a pattern in societies that try to order themselves rigidly, allowing no foreign element to disturb their "purity." With no outlet for their own disruptive emotions, for unexpressed or unconscious rebellion, they seek it in women or in some other scorned group—blacks, Jews, or an ethnic minority. At least America killed a smaller percentage of its women than Europe did and ended its persecutions more quickly. By the early eighteenth century, Puritans, appalled at the excesses of the hysteria, declared a public day of fasting and prayer for divine guidance in Massachusetts. Some jurors and a judge publicly repented their part in the business and, gradually, prosecutors began to charge the sexes equally for fornication.

Men began to abandon religion after the witch hunt, turning their energies to more rewarding commerce. At the turn of the century, rich men used the church mainly to display wealth, buying reserved "family pews" from churches happy to profit from them. As male church membership in New England dropped, more women joined, making up 60–70 percent of new church members and eventually the majority in most congregations. Cotton Mather felt women's "difficulties both of *Subjection* and of *Child bearing*," made them more likely to experience "saving faith." Since women always bore children and Puritan women had always been subjected, this is an ahistorical explanation. I suspect women were drawn to the one arena in which they could now act.

Preachers focused sermons on their mainly female congregations. Mather, the first of a long series of American preachers who formally prescribed women's proper role in church and society, urged devotion to religious duty, submission to husbands, and watchfulness over children while teaching them religion. Ministers introduced domestic imagery into sermons, speaking of piety, tenderness, and love as exclusively female traits, rigidifying gender roles. More and more, society expected men to be ignorant of religion and women to uphold it. The "feminization" of religion in America had begun, though not in Anglican Southern churches, which were rarely arenas of overt political struggle.

The Eighteenth Century

When the Stuarts, with their Catholic sympathies, regained the English throne in 1660, many Anglican merchants migrated to New England. They disliked Puritanism and cared nothing about a "city on a hill." The feeling was mutual: Congregationalists refused to let them vote or practice their religion openly and inveighed against rising commercialism. Increase Mather, the father of Puritan minister Cotton Mather, reminded his congregation that "Religion and not the World was that which our Fathers came hither for." But merchants' money generated maritime trade and shipbuilding in New England, and by the 1670s, New England and other American colonies were part of an international trading network. Class stratification became more marked in towns, and between town and country. Black slavery was becoming the major form of labor on Southern plantations, and whites were rapidly encroaching on Indian lands, igniting sporadic conflicts. The sex ratio neared equality. Women married later and were widowed earlier in the North but later in the South, as death rates there fell—no one knows why.

The Stuart government designed the mercantile system to insure that only England profited from trade with its colonies. It decreed that only British or colonial merchants and ships could trade in its colonies, that certain products (the most profitable) must be sold to England, and that foreign goods intended for the colonies must be shipped through England, paying English import duty. Later laws barred colonies from making or exporting items competing with English goods like wool clothing, hats, and iron. (Such laws, which became common vis-à-vis colonies, contributed to the impoverishment of Ireland. Four hundred years later the Soviet Union adopted similar policies towards satellites like Poland.) But such laws were hard to enforce and prompted smuggling, so in 1696, over colonists' protests, Parliament established vice-admiralty courts to function without juries in America.

Governors and bicameral legislatures ruled American colonies: New England governors were elected by legislatures or by "the people" (that is, by white property-owning males); in Chesapeake, they were appointed by the king or by the proprietor. New England towns elected selectmen as managers until about 1700, when annual town meetings of adult white men began handling town affairs. County court judges and the parish vestry, a lay group, supervised both church and secular affairs in Chesapeake. By the late seventeenth century, American colonists were used to a fair amount of local political autonomy. Connecticut, Massachusetts, and Rhode Island were virtually independent, under direct authority of neither crown nor proprietor. White men with property over a stated minimum (which varied) expected a voice in government and taxes.

But local autonomy curtails a ruler's control, and James II tried to check the colonies' freedom, imposing uniformity on them. He was replaced in the Glorious Revolution by his daughter Mary and her husband, William of Orange, who, pursuing the same course, made Massachusetts a royal colony ruled by an appointee.

Everywhere, laws bolstered male domination. In some colonies, women could not keep their husbands from selling off parts of family estates. Intestacy laws, passed because few men wrote wills, favored oldest sons over wives and other children; men who wrote wills favored sons over daughters, who usually got half their brothers' portion—and in goods, not land. In the 1700s, men left widows with less control over family property than in the 1600s, enough to keep them off public assistance but not to live independently. Land was growing scarce, and men's hold on it made them powerful. Threats of disinheritance were formidable weapons of control.

By the end of the seventeenth century, American colonies were no longer remote settlements. Population had grown, swelling cities and making community surveillance harder. Colonial women's lives had changed subtly but significantly. More people worked in manufacturing, and more enjoyed prosperity and a better quality of life. Few early colonial families owned spinning, weaving, or dairy equipment; even in the mid-eighteenth century, only about half the Massachusetts households had spinning wheels, cheese molds, or butter churns, and fewer than 10 percent had wheels or looms for wool or flax. Chesapeake households were more likely to own such tools, worked by female slaves overseen by white mistresses. Female trading networks developed: a woman who made butter traded with one who made flax. Having a surplus to trade gave women a little more power at home, but only in German American families could they keep what they earned, a tradition based in a medieval right.

Once physical survival was less of a challenge, white women devoted time to domestic manufacture, earning money for amenities like knives, forks, pottery, and glassware. Tea-drinking was a new fad: almost no one in 1720s Virginia drank tea or owned tea-making equipment; by the 1770s, half the population did. Elsewhere, too, people drank tea and bought teapots, cups, kettles, and tea tables. Women with time for child-rearing considered their maternal responsibilities important, especially the Puritans and Quakers. Having gained standing as church members, women felt somewhat free of male authority.

Historians discuss whether America's loose social structure gave early colonial women freedom, but freedom is relative. Chesapeake women had a better chance of choosing their husbands and, if widowed, of being economically independent; New England women had better health, husbands nearer their own age, stabler marriages, and, possibly, more room for religious expression. One gauge of the influence of women is architecture—the arrangement of houses and towns. When women have a voice, they imprint it on the environment, especially the home. Seventeenth-century New England houses—larger, better built, with more efficiently arranged work spaces and more amenities like table linen—reflect greater female influence than Chesapeake's.

But still, the major fact in a woman's life was marriage. The only choice a girl had—if she had any—was a husband: to choose a husband was to choose a life. A woman was part of her husband: his status and finances determined her standing in the community, his emotional and sexual nature set the quality of her life, almost without exception. Englishwomen, who married later and lost their husbands earlier, were likely to live independent of paternal or marital households for as many years as their marriages lasted. They lived outdoors, trading goods and services with neighbors, working in shops with husbands or fathers, visiting kin. American women, in contrast, lived within nuclear families.

Some colonial wives acted as agents for their husbands, supervised a friend's business, or made contracts—responsibilities unheard of in England. What differed was the right to own property. English wives could not own property or make contracts even jointly with a husband or with his consent. Colonial women, however, especially in trading centers, could own property and make contracts. Letting women convey land was one of America's major contributions to raising women's legal status.[33] Colonial couples together executed the deed by which title passed; later, both had to acknowledge it. If a husband was absent, a wife was examined by a court to ascertain that her signature was voluntary and that her husband had exerted no undue pressure. New England court records contain land grants to wives whose husbands were still alive.

English common law held a husband responsible for supporting his wife and gave her a third of his estate, inviolate by creditors, on his death. But alive, he owned her wages and clothes, controlled and managed her property, and could use its profits without being held to account. Only a prenuptial contract both spouses signed legally protected a wife's property. The colonies encouraged prenuptial contracts that allowed wives to retain their property in their own names and dispose of it when and as they chose.

On average, colonists married three to five times. Since some couples stayed together all their lives, others married even more often. Divorce was possible but rare. Between 1620 and 1691 only six marriages were dissolved in Plymouth—five for adultery and one for desertion—yet, like Massachusetts Bay (where at least twenty-seven divorces were granted between 1639 and 1692, a period when England imposed Anglicanism on the colony), it had no divorce law. New Haven allowed divorce for adultery or desertion; Pennsylvania and New Jersey recognized legislative divorce. The South, faithful to the Church of England, granted none.

Indentured servants still emigrated to the colonies, many from Germany. Most female servants were teenagers planning to marry and live in America after service.[34] They were in such demand that owners—mainly middle- or upper-class families with large households—granted them shorter terms than men. Judges indentured native-born orphans and homeless girls, most to serve until they were twenty-one. A Virginia document reads: "Timothy Ryan being runaway, his children, viz. Mary aged eight, Martha, aged five, and Jeremiah, aged two, to be bound out." Poor folk bound their children into service, as a North Carolina woman did in 1702: "Martha Plato binds her daughter Hester Plato to Captain James Coles and Mary his wife till she comes of age or marries, she now being six years of age." Six-year-old girls spun flax, combed wool, wove, and did other farm or kitchen chores; boys helped make shoes or brooms, chopped wood, and did farm work. Boston built a workhouse in 1682 for boys and girls "who shamefully spend their time on the street."

Some widowers with young children bought wives. About 20 percent of female servants bore a child in service. If the father was unknown, or a servant under contract or who had absconded, courts usually added a year or two to the woman's term; if the father was known to be a local married man, judges might force him to support the child and pay a penalty to the servant's owner for his inconvenience. If the owner fathered the child, the case was murkier: some assumed that sexual service was included in women's contracts. Though without economic rights, servants had civil rights, including the right not to be raped. A court determined if a servant had willingly participated in intercourse, acceded under duress, or was raped (one can imagine the claims men made in such cases). If it deemed she had agreed, it usually added a year or two to her term or sold her contract to a third party, giving the proceeds to a local church. When her contract ended, she had to support herself and her child: this was considered equal justice. If it deemed the owner had forced himself on her, it usually reduced or voided her indenture, requiring him to support the child.

Only children of rich families might have more than a rudimentary education. Some women taught or tutored, but few schools existed and children had to learn at home. Able colonial women taught all their children to read, but few could write, and literate fathers taught only sons to write. Churches held people responsible for affirming their own faith and practice, so pious parents supervised their children's spiritual education. Both Puritans and Quakers were obsessed with child-rearing, but Quakers took a more nurturing approach. The Puritan John Cotton roared: "There is in all children . . . a stubbornness, and stoutness of mind arising from natural pride, which must, in the first place, be broken and beaten down; that so the foundation of their education being laid in humility and tractableness, other virtues may, in their time, be built thereon." Both sects were paying more attention to children, and thus to mothers. Yet child-rearing literature was aimed at fathers—and remained so until the nineteenth century.

This new attention to children was generated by religion in the North and by prosperity in the South. Successful planters hired servants or bought slaves to do domestic chores, freeing women to attend to their children. It was a mother's duty to socialize and teach her children basic literacy and religion. Janet Schaw, as she traveled in eighteenth-century North Carolina, noted a sharp contrast in manners between men and women and attributed it to daughters being raised in a more civil home environment while sons learned rough ways from their fathers in the woods or in business. The overriding concern of Southern colonial men was making a fast buck. The father of the country, George Washington, married Martha Custis, a seven-month widow, mainly for money.

After 1740, New England authorities prosecuted fewer women for infanticide, and convicted even fewer. They still prosecuted fornication, but more to assess the cost of rearing "illegitimate" children than to enforce community standards. In general, they were less likely to charge women with gender-based crimes, but treated both sexes equally in crime and in punishment. The New England elite had accepted changed female roles, in and out of families.[35]

But, from 1729 to 1745 in the North, and from the 1740s to 1760s in the South, religion swept the country in the first major American religious revival, "The Great Awakening." Revivals drew men and women, and the number of male converts grew dramatically, although women continued to make up the majority in Congregational churches. The Awakening attracted many poor people, including blacks and Indians, because it emphasized direct personal experience, the spoken rather than the written word, and was essentially anti-authoritarian. The idea that people convert themselves and have a direct relation with god legitimated oppressed people, who used it to further their own interests. Itinerant evangelists like Gilbert Tennant and George Whitefield held meetings in vast tents thronged with people. Both preacher and audience passionately shouted, wept, went into frenzies and trances, and

spoke in tongues. Conservative religious institutions condemned such behavior: an anti-revivalist minister, Charles
Chauncy, preached his alarm at "Female Exhorters" who,
against the Lord's commandment, encouraged "WOMEN, yea,
GIRLS to speak in assemblies for religious worship."

The Great Awakening admonished people to question
authority and to cherish feeling. Few revivalist preachers were
ordained, yet all claimed to know god better than ordained
ministers did. They taught congregations that emotion, not
learning, led to salvation. People now questioned social
orthodoxies. Awakened Baptists repudiated opulence as sinful,
questioning the highly conspicuous consumption of the plantation gentry. The Baptists rebuked fashionable clothes,
adopted simple dress, renounced dancing, gambling, and horse
racing, and called each other "brother" and "sister." Urging
equality in church, some even welcomed African Americans.

The Defeat of Native Americans

Native Americans recognized that whites threatened their existence, but could not imagine the eradication of their way of life
and never united against them. The tendency to see events from
a personal perspective in the moment seems universal. Even if
Native Americans (or Africans) had foreseen the destruction
whites would wreak on their societies and had immediately and
forcefully expelled them, it is doubtful whether, in the long
run, they could have prevailed against Western arms and
Europeans' drive for domination. Their failure in foresight par-
allels that of women: If they were central in society, why did
they allow their rights to be eroded?

While England and France struggled for nominal control
of North America, the Iroquois Confederacy actually controlled much of the continent. With no formal role, the skilled

diplomats of the Iroquois Council played Europeans against each other, refusing to commit themselves fully to anyone despite showers of "gifts." The council negotiated incessantly to win over western tribes from the French, whose Jesuit missions drew many Iroquois, draining their strength. It persuaded New York and Pennsylvania to create refuges for tribes broken by wars in Virginia, Connecticut, Maryland, and Massachusetts. After 1720, so many Europeans entered Pennsylvania that indigenous Indians could not survive.

War was constant. The Iroquois remained neutral in European wars that spread to North America: Queen Anne's War (the War of the Spanish Succession), 1702–13, and King George's War (the War of the Austrian Succession), 1744–48, which boosted American shipbuilding. They defeated the Catawba to gain control of the northern interior of Virginia and the Shawnee and Delaware alliances, pleasing the French.

Ohio Indians lived in Ohio Country, a region both the British and the French wanted, and in 1752 English fur traders penetrated the territory. It held the source of the Ohio River, which flowed past French trading posts on the Mississippi. British access to the area threatened French control of the Mississippi Valley fur trade, so in 1753, the French began to build forts along rivers in Ohio Country. Virginia's governor, claiming Ohio for England, sent militia to stop the French, but they were building Fort Duquesne at a strategic point where the Allegheny and Monongahela rivers form the Ohio (the site of present-day Pittsburgh). The milita was led by George Washington, a young, inexperienced colonel who foolishly attacked the French and got himself trapped at Fort Necessity. In one full-day battle, a third of his men were killed or wounded. He surrendered, and the French let the British return to Virginia. But, as historian Francis Jennings writes, Washington had started the first world war—the Seven Years' War (or, in American parlance, the French and Indian War).[36]

Native Americans had become too dependent on European goods to distance themselves from this conflict. The Iroquois read Washington's errors as a sign that the British would lose, so, for the most part, they switched their support to France. England did indeed lose every battle for the next three years. Fearing that France might retake Newfoundland and Nova Scotia (which it had earlier lost), England tightened its control over the region, forcibly expelling French Nova Scotians. The displaced Acadians wandered for years, and many ended up in Louisiana, where they were called Cajuns. In 1757 William Pitt, the British secretary of state, determined to win the war in North America and changed British colonial policy. Customarily, British military officers impressed recruits, commandeered supplies from American farmers and merchants, and usurped private houses to quarter their troops. Pitt urged them, instead, to cooperate with the colonists, to make localities responsible for recruiting soldiers, and to reimburse the expense. New colonist support enabled the British to recapture a fort at Louisbourg, break down Quebec's defences, and, after years of effort, to take Montreal, the last French stronghold. The British won the war.

The North American phase of the war ended in 1760, but it raged on in the Caribbean, India, and Europe until 1766. In 1763 France ceded all North American territories except Louisiana to Britain. Fearing a French presence in Louisiana, Britain forced France to yield it to Spain, which then ceded Florida to England. Jennings believes that the Seven Years' War, which spread across the world, was "as immense, complex, and in its own way as earthshaking as the Revolution." French and British armies and navies fought in Europe, Asia, the

Mediterranean, the Caribbean, the Atlantic, and the Pacific against Austria, Russia, Prussia, Spain, Native Americans, and colonists. And the conflict had profound consequences. Britain now dominated North America. The war removed France from the continent, and, after the war, Britain belittled American efforts, scoffing at the idea that the colonists had been any help. The colonists did not forget British arrogance or its arbitrary and high-handed actions. The most immediate and devastating results of the war fell, however, on Native Americans.

Northern Indians, who were daily losing ground, could no longer use European conflict as a tool in their fight to keep their lands. An earlier example conveys what this loss meant to them. From its founding, New York's most faithful allies were the Mohawks, who shunned the Iroquois League's treaties with Pennsylvania, yet lost their land. In 1753 Mohawk Chief Hendrick addressed Governor Clinton at a conference with the New York provincial council:

> Brother when we came here to relate our Grievances about our lands, we expected to have something done for us, and we have told you that the Covenant Chain of our Forefathers was like to be broken, and brother you tell us that we shall be redressed at Albany, but we know them so well, we will not trust to them, for they [Albany merchants] are no people but Devils, so we rather desire that you will say, Nothing shall be done for us; Brother By and By you will expect to see the Nations [of Iroquois] down [in New York City] which you shall not see, for as soon as we come home we will send up a Belt of Wampum to our Brothers the [other] 5 Nations to acquaint them the Covenant Chain is broken between you and us. So brother you are not to

expect to hear of me any more, and Brother we desire to hear no more of you.

The Indians lost their land and their way of life; humanity lost an admirable—and practical—set of attitudes to land and life.

The American Revolution

The war with France left Britain deeply in debt. George III's prime minister proposed repaying it by taxing the British colonies, and Parliament passed revenue-raising acts: the Sugar Act put new duties on imports and other provisions; the Currency Act outlawed paper money issued by colonies; and the Stamp Act required most printed matter to carry stamps sold for cash. These taxes hit an American economy already drained by the war. White property-owning men used to a voice in colonial matters would not accept imposed taxes, expecting to rule themselves (as well as women, Indians, and blacks).

Britain assumed absolute authority over all its colonies. But colonial leaders wary of government read British political writers' warnings that political power is always to be feared and that rulers always try to corrupt and oppress the people, and they deduced that they must be constantly vigilant.[37] One essay distinguished "dependence and inferiority" from "absolute vassalage and slavery," arguing that a superior did not have the right "to seize the property of his inferior when he pleases."[38] Thoughtful colonists sought rational bases for remaining part of the British Empire (no one yet dreamt of breaking away) while retaining control of internal affairs, especially taxation. But while the philosophical argument circled, a small group changed things by swift, inventive action.

In August 1765 the Loyal Nine, a Boston social club of

printers, artisans, and distillers, protested the Stamp Act by hanging an effigy of Andrew Oliver, the provincial stamp distributor, from a tree in Boston Common. That night they razed the proposed stamp office, burned the wood, beheaded and burned the effigy, broke Oliver's windows, and stoned officials who were trying to stop them. Oliver swore not to sell tax stamps. A few days later, a mob attacked the houses of customs officers and of the lieutenant governor, an act "respectable" citizens condemned. Middle-class protest was acceptable; working-class protest was not.

Class struggle pervaded the fight for independence in a highly stratified America. Colonists killed Indians for land, planters used humans as slaves, and both grew rich partly by exploiting poor whites. Between 1676 and 1760 blacks mounted six revolts from South Carolina to New York, and whites launched eighteen revolts and forty riots against colonial governments. To protect its wealth from Britain, the colonial elite had to unite people across class lines. It adopted the language of liberty and equality that had justified earlier middle-class revolutions. But despite their rhetoric, colonial leaders had no intention of ending slavery or the economic, political, and social inequality in their country.

Like England, the colonies had a tradition of street protest, and anti-Stamp Act mobs rose up—successfully—from Halifax, Nova Scotia, to Antigua in the Caribbean. By the date the law took effect, not one official was willing to sell the stamps. But middle-class men, uneasily imagining mobs turned on them, tried to focus resistance by creating an intercolonial association, the Sons of Liberty. By early 1766, merchants, lawyers, and prosperous men from South Carolina to New Hampshire had built a network, only to turn pale in horror when slaves paraded through the streets of Charleston also crying "Liberty!" Whites summoned the militia, warned of a possible plot, and banished a black man.

In March 1766 Parliament repealed the Stamp Act, but that summer a new British government took office. Determined to defeat the colonists, it taxed imports, including tea, to pay royal colonial officials and suspended the New York legislature for refusing to supply necessities like firewood and candles to British troops permanently stationed in America. Colonial assemblies' main weapon against the crown was the threat not to pay royal officials, and their members responded instantly in essays, letters, and debates. The Sons of Liberty and others tried to draw everyone into a resistance movement, even women, who were, of course, barred from politics.

Women's hostility to England paralleled or even preceded that of men.[39] Of forty newspapers published in the colonies in the revolutionary period, women owned at least six: of these, five supported the colonies.[40] Women formed clubs, refused to buy imported clothes, and planned boycotts during quilting bees. Young women calling themselves the Daughters of Liberty demonstrated in all the colonies, spinning publicly and fostering the use of homespun cloth to end dependence on English imports. Women marched solemnly through Wilmington, then burned their tea; in all the colonies, women swore off tea, traded recipes for tea substitutes, or drank coffee, boycotting English goods. Men were disunited on boycott: merchants who profited from selling imported goods opposed it; artisans whose own work would sell without British imports supported it. The women were effective: by 1769 they had made so much cloth that English imports fell. When colonists signed a Non-Importation Agreement, a British officer told Lord Cornwallis, "We may destroy all the men in America and we shall still have all we can do to defeat the women."

The next major clash between colonists and Britain occurred in Boston, the base for a British board of customs commissioners. These men were frequently attacked by mobs after they arrived in November 1767. When they seized John Hancock's sloop *Liberty* on suspicion of smuggling in June 1768, a mob rioted and wrecked their property. To "maintain order" in Boston, the British sent troops: highly visible in their red coats, they stopped people entering the city, checked their goods, roamed the streets at all hours harassing pedestrians, especially young women, and punished those who broke army rules by brutal public whippings. While soldiers paraded on the Common, they played booming martial music, constantly reminding colonists they were subjects. Off-duty soldiers took jobs from working-class men, who wrangled with them in taverns and streets. In March 1770 ship-rigging workers attacked soldiers seeking work, and the soldiers fought back. Three days later a mob threw hard-packed snowballs at Custom House sentries, who panicked and shot (against express orders), killing four and wounding eight.

The elite, who worried about but also incited political activism by the poor, seized on this event, called it the Boston Massacre, and mourned the dead "martyrs" for liberty. For their propaganda campaign, Paul Revere engraved a print of soldiers murdering a docile crowd. In 1770 a new British prime minister persuaded Parliament to repeal all duties except the tea tax. The colonial elite accepted the concession, wanting the thing done, especially after discovering that "patriots" like John Hancock had broken their vow not to import.

The resistance organized committees throughout the colonies, ordering a Committee of Correspondence (John Otis Jr., Samuel Adams, and Josiah Quincy Jr.) to prepare a statement of colonial rights. These committee men asserted absolute rights to life, liberty, and property, holding that it was "irreconcileable" with "the first principles of natural law and Justice . . . and of the British Constitution" for a British legislative body to grant American colonists their property. Another committee listed grievances like taxation without representation, unnecessary British troops and customs officers on American soil, and use of taxes to pay colonial officials. The political climate had changed: colonists were no longer seeking to reconcile themselves to British law, but demanded self-rule.

After 1770 the only new duty still in effect was the tax on tea, which some Americans still boycotted, though others had resumed drinking. Tea parties, the eighteenth-century version of cocktail parties, were important in colonial social life. In 1773, trying to save the East India Company from bankruptcy, Parliament passed a law to change the marketing of tea in the colonies, lowering the price. But colonists suspected a plot to force them to admit Britain's right to tax them, or a move towards giving the East India Company a monopoly on colonial trade. In the four cities appointed to receive the first shipments of tea, resistance members planned special receptions. Philadelphians persuaded the captain to return to England without unloading; in Charleston, local tradesmen had the tea unloaded and stored, then destroyed it; in New York, the ship arrived late, so nothing happened. And in Boston, 5000 people, almost a third of the population, met but could not agree on whether to accept the tea. That night sixty men disguised as Indians boarded the ships and dumped the tea into the harbor.

Acting swiftly, Parliament closed the port of Boston until the city paid for the £10,000 worth of dumped tea, altered the Massachusetts charter, banned all but necessary local trade and special town meetings, and strengthened the governor's power. It decreed that people accused of crimes in the colonies could be tried outside them and empowered military commanders to appropriate private houses for troops. Colonists called these laws the Coercive or Intolerable Acts. Parliament then turned to problems that had arisen in Quebec since Britain took that northern territory from France: it gave Catholics religious freedom and annexed land claimed by coastal colonies to Quebec, realizing the worst fears of the resistance. The Boston Committee of Correspondence urged a boycott of British goods. Other colonies, fearing such a drastic step, asked for another intercolonial congress.

In September 1774 fifty-five prominent colonial men convened the First Continental Congress in Philadelphia and agreed to boycott all goods from Britain, Ireland, and other British possessions and to ban exports to the British Empire—but not until that year's tobacco crop had been marketed. To enforce the boycott, it set up surveillance committees, which became complex networks of spies who reprimanded or punished people for dancing, gambling, "extravagance and dissipation," horse racing, attending town fairs, or killing lambs (wool was needed for clothing) and urged them to wear homespun. Spies, who inevitably become paranoiac, were soon listing people suspected of even minor misdemeanours to charge them with treason. Gradually extending their authority over almost all aspects of colonial life, the congress was able, by the spring of 1775, to challenge colonial governments.

As these governments disintegrated, the British decided to suppress the rebellion and, in January 1775, ordered General Gage to arrest the leaders at a provincial meeting in Boston. Gage got the letter after the meeting had dispersed, but sent troops to Concord to confiscate the colonists' military supplies. Messengers roused the villages around Boston, and seventy straggly militiamen met the British troops arriving at

Lexington. Seeing several hundred British, their leader ordered them to retreat, but someone fired and a battle broke out, killing eight and wounding ten colonists. The British went on to Concord, where they met a larger group; again shooting broke out, but the retreating colonists used guerrilla tactics, firing from concealed positions, and left the British with 202 wounded and 70 dead to the colonists' 93 losses.

In a week, local networks mustered about 20,000 colonial militiamen to the Boston area, who settled in siege lines around the city facing the British. In that position for two years (though many went home for the spring planting), they fought only once, at Breed's Hill (mistakenly called Bunker Hill). Battles occurred elsewhere: patriots took Fort Ticonderoga on Lake Champlain for its cannon; the British took cities. Having sent the largest single force they ever mustered—370 transport ships, 32,000 troops (thousands were German mercenaries), 73 ships with 13,000 sailors and tons of supplies, the British were convinced by their few casualties and their easy wins that they would swiftly win the war. But it continued.

Not everyone supported revolution. At least 20 percent—Anglican clergymen, people economically or emotionally loyal to Britain—actively opposed independence. But 40 percent, most of the northern colonial ruling class, were patriots. Pacifists like Quakers tried to stay neutral. Some shifted allegiance with the wind; others were indifferent. To patriots, neutrality or indifference were criminal, and they urged states to arrest and disarm "loyalists." A hundred thousand people were banished, their property confiscated.

Patriots feared that Indians and slaves might unite against them, but some blacks joined them, mainly New England freedmen, few of whom owned property. Blacks offered to fight for the British in return for freedom, fueling rumors of black rebellion. In oppressor paranoia, patriots used racism to promote their cause, identifying independence with white power. Slave owners in Southern states with as many or more blacks than whites joined the patriot side reluctantly: whites in the British West Indies dared not rebel against England for fear of an uprising by their black slaves, who outnumbered them by six or seven to one.

The loyalist governor of Virginia promised to free slaves who abandoned their owners to help Britain. Thousands dared to try and, for the first time, a large percentage of runaways were female, including thirteen of the twenty-three slaves who fled Thomas Jefferson's plantation, a slave owner who opposed slavery. They fled alone or with children, husbands, parents, or siblings. Five of the Norfolk Sawyer family, sold to three different owners, escaped and celebrated a reunion in British-held territory. Most runaways were captured and punished or died of camp fever or a smallpox epidemic that broke out in the ships housing them. But the British offer of freedom to slaves and a change in enlistment policy led the congress to end its ban on blacks in the Continental Army.

As the war dragged on, family men signed for short-term militia service. Only young single men were willing to serve the long army terms. Northern recruiters began to enrol blacks, free and slaves. About 5000 African Americans served in the revolutionary army, most of whom were freed as a result. They served beside whites, but were often given tasks white men disdained—cooking, foraging for food, driving wagons. Wives accompanying husbands did such tasks, and the army also hired poor soldiers' widows to cook, nurse, and launder for rations and a low wage.

Women in the Revolution

Given the settlers' treatment of Indians, most tribes symp-
athized with the British, who, after the Seven Years' War, tried
to protect Indian lands by creating firm boundaries around
them. Western colonists supported the revolution from fear of
Indian attack. Trying to take advantage of the war, some tribes
attacked marginal white settlements in Carolina and Virginia,
but, lacking allies, they were defeated. Most tribes chose to
remain outside the conflict.

The Iroquois were divided. Joseph and Mary Brant, the
children of a Mohawk sachem, were, respectively, a well-known
warrior and the common-law wife of Sir William Johnson, an
esteemed wealthy Indian superintendent. Mary helped him to
negotiate successfully with Indians and lived comfortably for
fifteen years as mistress of his estate. He acknowledged their
nine children as his natural issue, but, when he died, his legitimate son dispossessed Mary, who lived on land Johnson had
left her. Going west with Joseph, she convinced the Seneca,
Cayuga, and Mohawk to help an English military expedition.
Her influence with the tribes illustrates women's power among
the Iroquois. During the war, Mary gave the English food,
ammunition, and information on American troop movements.
But others in the Iroquois League sided with the patriots, so the
federation fought against itself.

Women joined the Daughters of Liberty or the Ladies
Association, raised money for the cause, boycotted tea and loyalist shops, and made homespun clothes. Southern women
publicly boycotted British imports and collected thousands of
dollars for the patriots through their churches. In Virginia,
Fredericksburg "ladies" worked in the gunnery, making about
20,000 bullet cartridges for the militias. Women nursed

Continental armies and acted as unpaid quartermasters. When British soldiers appropriated Virginia houses, the women parried to save their property, but not all of them succeeded.

Some women distinguished themselves. Twenty-four-year-old Molly "Pitcher" went to a New Jersey military camp with her husband to cook and wash for him and nurse the wounded. She got her nickname at the battle of Monmouth in 1778, when she brought spring water to the parched, exhausted soldiers; they said she loaded her husband's cannon until he was killed. George Washington personally thanked her, and the Pennsylvania legislature voted her a pension of $40 a year in 1822. At twenty-two, Deborah Champion rode for two days from her Connecticut home to Boston with urgent dispatches for Washington. In 1777 Sybil Ludington rode forty miles from Fredericksburg, New York, to summon Colonel Ludington's militiamen to drive newly arrived British troops back to their ships. South Carolinian Emily Geiger offered to deliver a message from General Nathaniel Greene asking General Thomas Sumter for help and reinforcements. Intercepted by the British and put under guard, she swallowed the note before they searched her. She was released, took a circuitous route, reached Sumter, and delivered the message orally.

Deborah Sampson, the most famous male impersonator of the revolution, was born in Massachusetts, indentured as a domestic servant from ten to eighteen, and taught for two months. But she wanted a more adventurous life. At twenty-one she stood at 5 feet 8 inches and, dressed in men's clothes and with bound breasts, she enlisted in the Continental Army as Timothy Thayer. She was discovered and ejected, but in 1782 she enlisted again as Robert Shurtleff and served eighteen months at West Point, fighting in several battles before being wounded at Tarrytown. When she contracted yellow fever, a hospital discovered her sex and she was dismissed from service. Sampson tried to support herself by lecturing about her experience but stayed poor even after 1792, when the Massachusetts General Court, deciding she "did actually perform the duty of a soldier," granted her £34 but no pension for past service. She married and had three children; after she died, Congress granted her husband a pension as a soldier's widower.

Most women at the front did arduous "women's" work. Sarah Benjamin's husband demanded that she come to serve him at Yorktown. She "busied herself washing, mending, and cooking for the soldiers," like other wives. One morning, after a terrific barrage, the officers cheered and swung their hats when the British surrendered. It meant nothing to the women, however. For them it was work as usual—breakfast for the men. Martha Washington was only one of many wives who suffered, along with their husbands, the hardship of the Valley Forge winter. Despite them, despite the female heroes and spies (Williams cites 160), the only female images of revolutionary virtue in the 1770s were mothers passively giving up their sons to war or helpless virgins abused by the enemy (a popular image in every war on every side).[41]

Victory

People disagreed on the purpose of the war. Even patriot leaders did not advocate seceding from the British Empire until January 1776, when Thomas Paine, a printer new to America, published *Common Sense,* an essay on freedom written in ordinary language with few classical allusions but familiar biblical references. Denouncing monarchy and aristocracy, he urged independence and a republic. The pamphlet sold wildly, was discussed everywhere, and changed the discourse: suddenly the unthinkable was possible. In June 1776 the Second Continental Congress declared the colonies independent of Britain and appointed Virginia lawyer Thomas Jefferson to draft a declaration of independence. He listed colonial grievances against George III (including the British introduction of slavery to America, which the Congress deleted), then stated the principle that still expresses the American ideal: "We hold these truths to be self-evident: That all men are created equal; that they are endowed by their Creator with certain inalienable rights; that among these are life, liberty and the pursuit of happiness."

France, smarting from defeat by Britain in the Seven Years' War, covertly sent the colonists weapons. After Benjamin Franklin went to Paris to ally formally with France, it recognized an independent America (1778) and sent troops, ships, clothing, and blankets as well as weapons. In 1779 Spain entered the war as an ally of France, not the colonists; the two powers fought the English from the West Indies, adding to Britain's headache. In the long dragged-out war, Britain's superiority in men and arms was offset by its strategic errors, the fact that colonists were fighting on their own soil, and sheer American endurance. England surrendered to America and France in October 1781, and Parliament ordered peace negotiation. But in the Carolinas and Georgia, the two sides fought for another year; mutual white and Indian raids kept the North at war too. The most brutal massacre of the war occurred after its formal end, in 1782 at Gnadenhuetten, Ohio. Militiamen pursuing Indians who had killed a frontier family came upon and slaughtered ninety-six Delaware, including children. Christian pacifists, the Indians did not resist as the whites tomahawked or burned them at the stake. Two months later, in reprisal, hostile Delaware captured and horribly tortured three militiamen.

Again, the real losers of the war were Indians: England ceded the colonists the land north to the current border between the United States and Canada, west to the Mississippi, and south to the thirty-first parallel, and returned Florida to Spain, simply ignoring its Indian allies. So did the colonists, who claimed the entire eastern half of the continent, ignoring Indian claims. War against Indians continued in one form or another. President John Quincy Adams declared Indians "destined to extinction" and, "as a race, not worth preserving," "not an improvable breed," and "their disappearance from the human family . . . no great loss." Later, he regretted his policy as "among the heinous sins of this nation, for which I believe God will one day bring [it] to judgement," wishing he could now assist "that hapless race of native Americans, which we are exterminating with such merciless and perfidious cruelty."[42] The war killed thousands, wrecked the economy, and uprooted thousands of families, forcing many into exile. It also established on paper—and in hearts—a new concept of government, people governing themselves for their own good. What was established was only an idea, because people argued about who "the people" were.

After the Revolution

The Middle Class: Women's Rights and Image

The men we exalt as the founders of this country had no difficulty in totally ignoring the rights of blacks, Indians, and women, although they were not blind to the injustice of the female plight. Thomas Paine, influenced by Mary Wollstonecraft, wrote an essay the year before he wrote *Common Sense*. Probably the first plea for equal rights published in the United States, it opened by saying that "man is the oppressor of woman."[43] And in 1776, when John Adams was in

Philadelphia at the Continental Congress preparing a new constitution, his wife, Abigail Adams, an astute and savvy woman, wrote an important letter:

> Remember the ladies . . . do not put such unlimited power into the hands of husbands. Remember all men would be tyrants if they could. If particular care and attention is not paid to the ladies, we are determined to foment a rebellion and will not hold ourselves bound by any laws in which we have no voice of representation. That your sex are naturally tyrannical is a truth so thoroughly established as to admit of no dispute.

Her husband tried weakly to gratify her, writing James Sullivan:

> Whence arises the right of the men to govern the women, without their consent? Why exclude women?

> You will say, because their delicacy renders them unfit for practice and experience in the great businesses of life, and the hardy enterprises of war, as well as the arduous cares of state. Besides, their attention is so much engaged with the necessary nurture of their children, that nature has made them fittest for domestic cares. . . . Your idea that those laws which affect the lives and personal liberty of all, or which inflict corporal punishment, affect those who are not qualified to vote, as well as those who are is just. But so they do women, as well as men; children, as well as adults. . . . Generally speaking, women and children have as good judgments and as independent minds, as those men who are wholly destitute of property; these last being

to all intents and purposes as much dependent upon others, who will please to feed, clothe and employ them, as women are upon their husbands, or children on their parents.

Abigail Adams (1744–1818), daughter of a liberal Congregational minister, Reverend William Smith, was a frail child who had been given no formal education. But her maternal grandmother Quincy, whom she visited often, gave her a love of learning, and she read widely in the parsonage library. She conversed vividly with the leading minds of her time. Her letters discuss subjects from wartime inflation to woman's place in society, showing a broad knowledge of history, Shakespeare, Dryden, Goldsmith, Pope, and Molière. Her husband was away from home almost continuously for a decade, and she raised their four children and managed the home and family finances. Until recently she was the only American mother and wife of a president—her husband, John, became president in 1797, and her son John Quincy Adams in 1825. Her strength in conversation is suggested by an insulting remark Albert Gallatin made about her influence over her husband: "Mrs. President not of the United States but of a faction."

Other contemporary women were equally accomplished.[44] Abigail Adams' good friend Mercy Otis Warren (1728–1814) was a prolific author of poetry, satirical plays, and a three-volume history of the American Revolution. Her history idealized neither the past nor any patriot, and included eyewitness accounts of war and political leaders, along with contemporary views of the Declaration of Independence and Indian policy. Warren even teased Abigail's husband, claiming that when John Adams became ambassador to England, he developed "a partiality for monarchy." He did not speak to her for seven years.

Warren was a Jeffersonian democrat: in the 1787 controversy over ratification of the Constitution, she anonymously wrote and circulated a pamphlet urging a strong Bill of Rights and criticizing the president's royal powers and the continuous re-election of senators and representatives.

Lucy Terry Prince (1730–1821), the slave who wrote a poem about the Deerfield massacre, married a free black who probably bought her freedom and moved with him to a farm in Vermont. A neighbor claimed part of their property, and Prince went to law and argued the case herself before the United States Supreme Court about 1800. After the revolution, she petitioned Williams College administrators to admit her son as a student, making a three-hour speech filled with legal arguments and biblical allusions. But it failed to move their bigoted hearts or minds.

Susannah Haswell Rowson (1762–1824), born in Plymouth, England, came to Massachusetts with her widowed father when she was six. She was a promising "little scholar" until 1775, when her father, an official in the British revenue service, was arrested, jailed, and had his property confiscated. After she returned to London, she was a governess for a time to the children of the Duchess of Devonshire, married, and wrote novels. *Charlotte Temple*, published in England in 1789 and Boston in 1790, became the first best-selling novel in America.

Despite such clever women, the new Constitution did not grant women citizenship or the vote—it did not mention them at all. States that had earlier allowed women to vote (see volume 3, chapter 5) rescinded the right one by one in this period. Only in New Jersey could single women with property worth £50 vote (and then only until 1807). Abigail Adams concluded that their lack of education was a great barrier to full equality for women, yet men did not need education for rights.

They were automatically citizens; to vote they needed money, not learning.

By the late eighteenth century, colonial men had settled into complacency about women. American women could no longer transfer property, sue or be sued, or give evidence against husbands as they had in seventeenth-century New England. No woman was charged with crimes committed in her husband's presence: he, not she, was responsible for her. Disciplines were professionalized and licensed only after special training, which barred women. In 1820 a Boston doctor put in writing what many had been saying for over fifty years: midwives must be replaced with well-trained men.[45] Women could not even do business in the community. Except during the Revolutionary War, woman's place was in the home: but home was no longer a center of production.

Before the revolution, commerce had created stratification and an elite: by the 1720s, men were building mansions equipped with crystal chandeliers, imported carpets, furniture, and silverplate. The elite adopted polite manners, Paris or London fashions, gave elaborate dinner parties, and imagined themselves part of an international "set." Men devoted to commerce worked away from home, making women responsible for child-rearing, the household, and the emotional support of men. Work and responsibilities men had formerly taken or shared now devolved on women alone; households once centers of production now only consumed. Women doing housework, not production, hired fewer servants and began to limit family size.

Fathers gave children (especially sons, but daughters too) more freedom in choosing mates. Men's wills often allowed children to plan their future independently; as young people gained autonomy, rates of premarital pregnancy rose. Such wills often had negative consequences for widows, so some states revised laws to give widows more control over inheritances. Many legalized divorce, which hosts of women and men swiftly sought, but post-revolutionary courts were less open-minded about separation than colonial courts. Seventeenth- and eighteenth-century courts in all colonies regularly protected wives' and children's financial interests without forcing divorce and notoriety. Nineteenth-century judges disliked separation, feeling it allowed people's judgment to infringe on the judicial power to supervise marriage.

Eighteenth-century judges gave widows less control of property, even reducing a widow's portion if she remarried; men less often named wives as executors or willed land to daughters. Susannah of New Kent married Isles Cooper in 1717. She had property, not he, but when he deserted her three years later, her property was seized to pay his debts.[46] She struggled alone for years to support her son, finally accumulating more property. But as a married woman, she could not sell it or sue her tenants for defaulting on rent or will her assets to her son. In 1744, however, the unusually resourceful Cooper persuaded the General Assembly to pass a law letting her exercise property rights.

The law placed no restraints on men's cruelty and limited only the degree of abuse. Wife beating was legal if a man used a switch no thicker than his thumb (the "rule of thumb"). Newspapers were strewn with notices of runaway wives and slaves. Widows had serious problems. The sex ratio in the South had evened out, making remarriage more difficult, especially for older widows, but women had even fewer ways to support themselves in the South than in the North. Seventeenth-century county welfare rolls were lists of orphans; in the eighteenth century they swelled with women.

Women, having supported a revolution for freedom and equality, could not but notice their lack of both. Revolutionary intellectual and social ferment gave middle-class women a new perspective. They read more political works, thought, argued, and worked to advance or impede independence, as part of the dialogue and the action. Their effort in the war forced men to reconsider their exclusion from both the public sphere and civic education. The rhetoric of the new republic insisted that all citizens contributed to the nation's well-being, but men, loath to see any change in women's position, countered women's demands with debate, not about women's rights, but Woman's Nature and intellectual capacity. Men felt forced to redefine Woman: what she should be, and the proper aims and content of her education. This war was waged mainly in literature; new ideas came from English essays, novels, and manuals until colonial men (and then women) offered their own views.

The popular image of Woman was frivolous. Etiquette books and magazines constantly admonished young women to avoid "feminine" follies and deviousness. The male myth holds that virtuous women want only what men want. Even animals have desires, but women, not having selves, lack will and gratefully accept whatever they are given, obediently maintaining "purity." But moralists found women artful, foolish, vain, immodest, frivolous, easily seduced by flattery, self-indulgent, and luxury loving. (Men have, spend, and waste hugely more than women, yet our exemplars of profligate luxury or extravagance are often women like Imelda Marcos or Leona Helmsley.) Such weak, infantile creatures must, in reason and justice, be controlled and supervised by men.

Late eighteenth-century moralists wanted women to remain confined to the home despite its diminished role in production, but had to justify this restriction by giving women something to do there. Creating a prescriptive literature on Woman's Place, they revalorized the place, redefining children as blank tablets to be filled in. Guidebooks began to stress the unique importance of the maternal role, deploring wet-nursing and claiming that maternal nursing (newly characterized as exquisite pleasure) positively affected the baby psychologically. Domestic medical manuals spread good advice—loose clothes instead of swaddling, cleanliness, exercise, special diet, and feeding on demand rather than on schedule. Manuals aimed at women, who were often uneducated, included practical information on tools, money, basic reading, arithmetic, biography, art, history, geography, and science. Motherhood, an involuntary and casual function, became in this new view a role of world-historical import, a vehicle for women to wield broad social and political influence: "The hand that rocks the cradle rules the world." Now, wives had a beneficent influence: after more than seventeen hundred years of Christian depictions of women as bestial and licentious, they were suddenly pure, asexual, self-controlled paragons.

Before the revolution the little written in America about mothers or mothering was usually disparaging. Didactic and sentimental literature offered two ideal female images: the helpmate (the sensible, industrious, submissive wife) and the ornament. Eighteenth-century writers who saw women as men's helpmates urged education to improve their housewifery; those who saw them as ornaments urged music, drawing, and French lessons to heighten their charm, modesty, and refinement. Puritans never idealized motherhood, considering childbirth god's special curse on Eve's daughters; they treated it mainly in connection with the risk of death. Some discussed breastfeeding, or, more likely, failure to breastfeed, which they thought a vain, sinful, slothful offence against divine intention.

Puritan ministers even censured mothers' fondness for their children and accused them of engulfing children with their embraces. But because they believed infants were depraved, Puritans wrote a great deal on children's education.

Most of these works assumed that fathers were children's primary caretakers or at least equally responsible with mothers—early colonial fathers worked close enough to home to be actively engaged in child-rearing. Clergymen like Cotton Mather portrayed mothers as inferior parents compared to fathers, hinting that the biblical injunction to honor them was a considerable trial, especially for boys. But if parenting was not women's main responsibility, neither was it their main occupation. Many parents saw children largely in economic terms and were somewhat cavalier about them.

Moralists' attention to mothering gave it status and value. As clergymen increasingly assumed men's absence from church, moralists increasingly assumed their absence from the home and directed their advice to mothers. Since men had a corner on moral and intellectual superiority, female piety and emotions were discovered to be special qualifications for rearing children. Mothers might spoil children, but their tenderness could correct fathers' newly recognized harshness. In the fiction of the era, many cruel fathers force children into unhappy marriages.

The first major American theorist on women's education was the patrician Benjamin Rush. His 1787 essay argued that women should be prepared for three major responsibilities, all within the home. First, women must be trained to manage servants, who in America did not know their place. Second, although he found no reason even for upper-class women to learn foreign languages or musical instruments, he asserted that all female education should include useful literature,

Christianity, penmanship, and bookkeeping, so wives could keep their husbands' accounts and "be stewards and guardians of their husbands' property." Third, they should learn to rear children without men's help and "instruct sons in the principles of liberty and government."

The most important essay on women in this period was written by Mary Wollstonecraft (1759–97), who had been raised in some comfort and educated before her physically abusive father frittered away his inheritance. Destitute at seventeen, Wollstonecraft supported herself as a seamstress, governess, schoolteacher, and writer. Although she scandalously refused to tend her two younger sisters, she promised to support them by her pen—and she did. Influenced by Enlightenment thinking, she treated religion, morality, education, and politics from a female perspective in *Thoughts on the Education of Daughters* (1786) and the pious *Original Stories from Real Life* (1788). She socialized with Dissenters, Protestants hostile to the Church of England and sympathetic to egalitarianism. The French Revolution inspired her to go to France to see a society based on equality and fraternity—as, over a century later, people went to the USSR. After refuting Burke's *Reflections: The Vindication of the Rights of Man* (1791), she wrote her masterwork, *The Vindication of the Rights of Woman* (1792).

Defying convention, Wollstonecraft became the lover of the American Gilbert Imlay, with whom she had a daughter in 1794. When he abandoned her, she considered suicide, but instead made a business trip for him through Scandinavia (where "the men stand up for the dignity of man, by oppressing the women") and published her letters from the journey. Wollstonecraft's last work, a novel, *Maria, or The Wrongs of Woman*, traces two women, Maria, a middle-class woman, and Jemima, a worker. Despite class difference, they live parallel lives and suffer terribly, mainly because they are "women, the *outlaws* of the world." *Maria* portrays the social realities of women's lives, their pain and thwarting by male dominance, for which Wollstonecraft blamed social conditions and institutions. She did not finish *Maria*: she fell in love with the philosopher William Godwin, married him (though they lived apart), and died at thirty-eight giving birth to a daughter, Mary (who went on to marry Shelley and wrote *Frankenstein*).[47]

The Vindication of the Rights of Women (published in America in 1793) is considered the founding text of feminism. It thrust the demand for female emancipation into mainstream English politics, linking women's emancipation to that of common people and to abolition of class privilege, especially of the clergy and the nobility.[48] The work concentrates on female education, with an analysis that adumbrates the current distinction between sex and gender: we are born with sex; society creates gender. Conceding female inferiority, Wollstonecraft attributes it to education and culture, not nature or biology. Humans are made "feminine" by being warped. Scornful of the vapidity, flirtatiousness, and obsession with fashion she saw in elite women, she recommended Jean Jacques Rousseau's regimen of education for them.

But Rousseau had pointedly excluded girls, finding them frivolous and vain. Because they were born to please men, he said, they did not need education. Wollstonecraft accepted that women's destiny was to rear children, "laying a foundation of sound health both of body and mind in the rising generation." But she argued that, to fulfill this role properly, women needed education. Fear of fashion made women weak and dependent, yet intelligent adults capable of independent action needed an education that imbued them with proper values. As adults, women, like men, could claim inalienable rights. (Decades later, George Sand refused to support suffrage for French women until they were educated and owned property, and became more than their husbands' puppets.) Most radically, Wollstonecraft suggested that the male world would benefit from an infusion of feminine values.

Educated people earnestly discussed Wollstonecraft's ideas. A few women followed her example and took up writing as a career, apologizing for their presumption by claiming they were writing only for other women. But after Wollstonecraft died, Godwin published her unfinished novel and her passionate letters to Imlay, full of anguish at his desertion. As a result, for a century afterwards, people dismissed Wollstonecraft as a tainted woman, seduced and abandoned with a bastard. Her ideas were evidence of the maddening fate of women who dared to be radical.

Yet her work spread the idea that some traits were acquired, not inborn, and "sentimental" novels popular with women began to stretch the usual female stereotypes. But such literature could not change female roles because, in literary convention, virginity was crucial to female virtue. Women's only form of "honor" was virginity before marriage, fidelity after it. Married women were defined by their husbands, so novels focused on girls, who could not do very much. Girls concerned with guarding their hymens cannot move around freely in a world where men treat women as prey.

Almost everything defined women as subordinate. Education was geared to class and sex. Men enjoyed writing about their ideal woman, assuming that women would fit their molds.[49] Visual art expressed similar notions: a 1777 British engraving, *The Old Maid*, portrays an ill-tempered, homely creature. A needlework picture stitched in 1775, "The First, Second, and Last Scene of Mortality," depicts a woman's life from cradle to grave: the entire sequence takes place in one crowded room.

In colonial portraits after 1670, boys wore petticoats until about six, then adopted adult male trousers and shirts. Girls' gowns were altered as they grew. After 1770, boys wore long trousers until they were fourteen, and girls wore frocks until they were twelve, when both adopted full adult dress. Eighteenth-century girls did not dress like miniature women; rather, women, infantilized, dressed like large children.[50]

The colonies had few basic schools for either sex, but many colleges to train men as ministers: Harvard was chartered in 1636, William and Mary in 1693 (opening in 1726), and Yale in 1701. Princeton opened in 1747, Columbia in 1754, Brown in 1765, and Rutgers in 1766, to train clergymen for Presbyterian, Anglican, Baptist, and Dutch Reformed churches, respectively; Dartmouth was chartered in 1769 to convert Indians to Christianity. But after 1800, boys abandoned the ministry for medicine, law, or business.

All colleges excluded women. The idea of liberty and equality as promised by the revolution must have been inconceivable to women of the period. Without reliable birth control, having coitus with a man meant to risk having a child. To be independent and self-supporting was nearly impossible for a sex with few property rights and, in paid work, half the wages of men; to support oneself and a child was beyond imagining. It is still hard to raise children alone, to tend them and work for pay. Understandably, early nineteenth-century middle-class women took what they could—a newly valorized role that made the best of things.

American republicanism needed a role for women. All republican traditions defined public virtue as inherently masculine, granting women rationality only in personal virtues—charity, faith, prudence, and temperance.[51] In the 1780s–'90s, women began to be presented not as patriots but promoters of patriotism in men: they were now Republican Mothers. Middle-class American women were to be bulwarks of civic virtue, responsible for inculcating piety, self-control, and high ideals in children. They would serve the state by producing good sons. This role emphasized the cruel paradox of traditional gender roles—the powerless are made responsible, while the powerful are free of responsibility. But American and British moralists insisted that influence over men gave women power to reform the manners and morals of society.

Wollstonecraft's ideals were shrunk to size: girls' schools were founded, expanding female educational opportunities. Women with leisure, who had done political work in the revolutionary period, formed benevolent and reform societies to work with other women. Young educated women formed deep bonds with each other, creating female worlds. The Constitution having decreed the separation of church and state, churches lost state help (were disestablished) in the 1780s–'90s and needed new sources of revenue. Women's first voluntary associations were founded to raise money for churches in sewing circles and charities. After a second "Great Awakening" (1790–1840), these groups multiplied and became major movements in the nineteenth century. Urban philanthropies grew into welfare agencies. The temperance and abolition movements and feminism itself were rooted in this first tentative step—the creation of sisterhood, of female solidarity.

Middle-class women barred from professions, commerce, and politics became the nation's conscience. Women were expected to maintain republican commitment to the well-being of all society.[52] This new role was the cornerstone of a society rigidly segregated by sex; when manufacturing moved from homes to factories in the nineteenth century, women's role was already fixed. The new myth idealized mothers, mother love, and egalitarian companionate marriage and created a new ideal, the "lady." Yet, paradoxically, the rate of childbirth dropped as women managed conception or did not marry. Before, women took subordinate roles complementary to men's; now, as many women no longer did production, the roles grew asymmetrical, and the private and public spheres became separate.

Philosophers bolstered women's new role. British Enlightenment thinkers had defined "the moral sense" as a masculine rational faculty. Now some argued that emotion was not subordinate to reason but expressed "an instinct toward happiness" and that the moral sense depended on parental nurturance. Urging noncoercive child-rearing, John Locke and the Scots defined children as corruptible but not corrupt, possessing moral sense and innate reason which, nurtured, could make a man virtuous. Concerned only with males, they wrote for educators and fathers, but their sense of the importance of early childhood education fed the new didactic and medical literature on motherhood. Philosophers were also changing their definitions of Man and revalorizing avarice (a sin for the Christian era) as rational "interest."[53] Rationality, a male trait, was tied to self-interest; emotion, a female characteristic, to morality. After 2500 years of being linked to beasts, women were promoted—not to equality, but to superiority! Women were now the incarnation of virtue, linking men and the angels.

Urban Poor Women

Middle-class women freed from the onus of sexuality molded themselves into ideal mothers, but the unsavory traits traditionally associated with females had to live somewhere, so were dumped on working women with no time for republican motherhood. Massachusetts divorce records show that eighteenth-century sexuality was far freer than it was later. Their picture of the family mocks our pious image of Puritans and patriots.[54] Hannah Wales did not prevent her four-year-old daughter from seeing a man lying "on the bed with her mamma, and she saw her thighs, and the man told her to lay up higher," her servant reported. Mary Higerty of Salem, a sailor's wife, did not hide her sexual affair from her fourteen-year-old son or end it when he threatened to tell his father. One wonders how many fathers "violated the chastity" of a daughter, as did Stephen Temple of Upton. In 1772 he raped his fourteen-year-old daughter, sick in bed, and "afraid of him and thought I must obey him."

People of both sexes seized sexual freedom, but only one sex and class was held responsible for this "decline." As middle-class women agitated for rights to education and political participation, men increasingly associated lower-class women with social anarchy and sexual license.[55] Lanah Sawyer, a seventeen-year-old seamstress, was walking one evening when Harry Bedlow, introducing himself as Lawyer Smith, asked to take her out. She agreed. One night after they toured the Battery eating ice cream, Bedlow forced Sawyer into a bawdy house and sexual "connection." Sawyer charged Bedlow with rape. He claimed she seduced him.

This case is worth rehashing for what it reveals about attitudes towards women. That Sawyer was raped seems unquestionable—she would not have brought charges if she were a prostitute. But neither her rape nor Bedlow's guilt or innocence was an issue in the trial: the issue was Sawyer's awareness of sex and class codes. As still occurs in rape trials, Sawyer, not Bedlow, was tried—not for past immorality or seductiveness but naiveté.

Bedlow's lawyers browbeat Sawyer, arguing she could not

be so stupid as to imagine that a man of his class would pay attention to her, a seaman's daughter and a seamstress, except for sex. Sawyer's neighbors testified to her good character and the unlikelihood of her willingness to fornicate, but they were women—the defence impugned the validity of female testimony by intimating that females were sexually loose. Fewer women than men were asked to appear as witnesses in divorce cases; wives needed male testimony because their sex was not taken seriously in court.[56] After deliberating for fifteen minutes, the jury acquitted Bedlow. A riot ensued; 600 friends of Sawyer's father vandalized the brothel where Bedlow took her, then other brothels, before the militia stopped them. Her father swore that if she was wrong, "he would turn her out."

Only one person supported Sawyer, a woman who wrote to a newspaper as "Justitia" to condemn Bedlow. Offering her regrets to male citizens grieving over the attack on the brothels, "considering what comfortable hours they have passed in these peaceful abodes far from the complaints of a neglected wife," she suggested that brothels would be better policed if magistrates did not patronize them. Again, accusation was reversed: just as Sawyer was tried instead of Bedlow, Justitia was attacked and her charges ignored. Letters poured into the newspaper: no respectable woman could know of such things, so she could not be respectable; her identity was hinted at, her intelligence belittled, her writing style scorned, and her honor questioned. Men considered "weak-mindedness" and promiscuity implicit in females.

Yet men were far more sexually unbridled. "Bloods" in fancy dress, with a patrician manner—languorous, bored, superior—idled on city streets harassing passing women, barring the path, loudly evaluating women's appearance obscenely, cat-calling, and hooting. Philadelphia ladies did not walk abroad unescorted.

Men charged with wife beating, rape, and murder justified their acts. Prescriptive literature of the period treated sexual war complacently, portraying courtship as a war of wits in which each sex manipulated the other, and marriage as an extended siege by wily females trying to undermine male authority. Poor, uneducated women bore the old association of females with sex.

But poor women had too many other problems to protest this treatment. Landless people thronged to cities to find a living, swelling New York from 60,000 people in 1800 to 123,000 in 1820, Boston to 17,000, and Philadelphia to 13,000. In cities, the poor seeking work encountered manufacturers seeking cheap labor, and, by the early 1800s, poverty was intrinsic to wage labor—manufacturers paid workers too little to live. Urban working-class families always teetered on the edge of destitution—one stroke of bad luck could send them over it. In Philadelphia, the average wage of male workers did not provide a family with the bare necessities; wives and children had to work for wages.

Half of eighteenth-century free women were illiterate. After 1750, many girls' schools opened, but they taught only three subjects—dancing, fancy needlework, and maybe French. Women with a smattering of education opened schools. Some women managed to go into business and certain jobs were usually female—midwifery, dressmaking, millinery (milliners often sold other small items—snuff, schoolbooks, spices, pudding pans). Women dominated inn-, tavern-, and brothel-keeping. They needed licenses, but unlicensed female innkeepers in Petersburg outnumbered the licensed two to one. Women were a third of the dealers in illegitimate liquor. Such work, which required little capital or skill yet could support them, drew more women than any but millinery and prostitution.

Women were healers—there, at least, one could became

wealthy. Some inherited men's businesses. Clementina Rind, the wife of a Williamsburg public printer, had five children when her husband died in 1773. She took over the *Virginia Gazette*. When a rival newspaper printed an exposé of some well-known locals, Rind refused to print it. Accused of partiality, she retorted that the anonymous author of the article acted from personal malice and offered to print the piece if the writer admitted authorship. A few months later the assembly voted her as public printer in her own name. A Richmond woman ran a wireworks and stonecutters, making screens and grindstones for milling grain; two women were millers; one ran a tanyard, one made shoes, and another ran the Henrico County jail.

One general history of the United States, *A People and a Nation*, quotes a letter from a young man who had left the family farm for Providence, full of "Noise and Confusion and Disturbance . . . the jolts of Waggons, the Ratlings of Coaches, the crying of Meat for the Market, the Hollowing of Negros and the ten thousand jinggles and Noises, that continually Surround us in every Part almost of the Town."[57] Cities were filthy, teeming with people, activity, disease, and accidents. Wastes were poured into gutters, and the poor sanitation and terrible crowding led to epidemics: Boston, New York, and Philadelphia endured sieges of smallpox and yellow fever. Families with two rooms rented boarders floor space to sleep in. Streets and docks crowded with horses and wagons were dangerous and, since medical knowledge was primitive, a simple injury, a broken limb or cut, could cripple a person permanently. Infections and respiratory disease were rampant in this age of tuberculosis.

Still, in cities, people could buy food and wood at a market and cloth at a dry goods shop. Well-to-do urbanites had leisure to read, to walk around town, to take a carriage ride to the country, and to play cards or go to dances, plays, concerts. By 1750 most colonial cities had theaters and assembly halls, and they all had at least one weekly newspaper. City women with husbands who earned steady wages might keep a kitchen garden, chickens, or a pig in their backyards (or foraging in the streets) and make some product themselves. And there was the fun of eavesdropping on neighbors.

People lived so close together and walls were so thin that Mary Angel could not help hearing Adam Air beat his wife and her screaming—often.[58] Passing his house with a friend one day, Angel saw Air, through a window, having sex with Pamela Brichford. She and her friend went in, watched the pair for a time, then asked if Air "was not Ashamed to act so when he had a Wife at home." He stood up naked and replied coolly that one woman was as good as another to him. The Jameses and McCarthys lived under the same roof in Boston in 1754–55 and found it "no matter" that lodger William Stone slept in the same room as Daniel McCarthy's wife, Mary, because there were two beds. Then Ann James spilled the beans that Mary and William slept in one bed while Mary's sisters and Ann slept in the other!

William Chambers did not fret about his wife, Susanna, while he was at sea because she slept with thirteen-year-old Mary Salmon. But on four nights the bed had a third occupant, Sergeant George Hatton, and, by the third, Mary could not help noticing that "Mrs. Chambers lay in the middle at which time it appeared to me . . . that Sergeant Hatton had carnal knowledge of Mrs. Susanna Chambers. [She] gave me three coppers and charged me to tell nobody what I saw." Captain Peter Staples lodged with the Hammets, sleeping two feet from their bed, and regularly climbed into bed with Abigail after Thomas rose in the morning.

For working people, marriage was an economic contract

between a husband, who agreed to provide a wife with food, clothing, and shelter, and a wife, who agreed to manage his home frugally, serve him obediently, and submit to his rights over her body. Most wives suing for divorce charged desertion or nonsupport or both, sometimes along with adultery, bigamy, or cruelty. Women wanted financial support; men wanted service (a form of support)—and a third of men claimed desertion. Some blamed wives for wasting provisions, poor household management, or robbing them. Male wage-earners had strong feelings about their rights. Women who had gathered for the lying-in of the wife of Laurence Bracken, woodworker, said that, six hours after the birth, he burst into the room, saw her lying in *his* bed, seized her hair, and dragged her naked to the floor. George Hart's common-law wife took four shillings from his pocket, probably to buy food. After beating her to death, he told his neighbors she had her just desserts: "I will serve any damned whore so who robs me of my money." Sailor John Banks quarreled with his common-law wife about marketing, smashed her with a shovel, slit her throat with a razor, and declared, "I would kill a dozen like her, for she was a dam'd bitch."

Marital conflict was worse for women than for men, not just because men forcibly expressed their conviction that they owned women's bodies and service but because women usually kept the children and their married status limited their ability to earn a living. By common law, husbands owned wives' personal property, earnings, and the use and profit of their real estate. Without a husband's consent, a married woman could not make contracts or sue to collect debts; no matter how shifty a husband, a wife could not run a business while she was married to him. Henrietta East Caine ran a fashionable Boston millinery shop before she married. When her bigamist husband deserted her, no one would supply her with goods to do business. Inept or wastrel husbands dragged well-to-do wives into destitution: Bostonian Mary Hunt's husband beat her, went through her fortune of £1500, then left her with three children to support. Many women complained to courts that their husbands did not pay support, but there was no remedy for it. Not until the late eighteenth century did people sue for divorce on the grounds that affection between a couple had died. Many suits substantiated charges of adultery.

It is clear why most of the poor were women. Widowhood was virtually synonymous with poverty: men abandoned wives or died in the revolution or the War of 1812. Most destitute wives were domestic servants. The very rich liked to hire black women—blackness was associated with slavery, which conveyed status. A woman with a room could earn a few pence a week from a lodger who slept on the floor. Laundry work, dependable all year round, was hard and low-paid; many free black women did laundry, one of few jobs they could get. Female hucksters sold vegetables, fruit, cakes, or candies door to door or on busy streets near docks or countinghouses; women who were black, very poor, or too frail to be servants hawked foods and supplies in the streets, but peddling, the only work open to them, could not keep them alive.

Women with a bit of money, often widows, had stands in frequented corners of cities, rented stalls in public markets to sell produce or dairy food, or sold food or drink from their homes. A few owned little food markets—in 1805, 18 of New York's 793 grocers were women. The first female New York charity, the Society for the Relief of Poor Widows, which helped widows start businesses, resolved in 1804 to help no one who sold liquor, but that was where the money lay. About the only way a woman could earn a decent living was to run a disorderly or bawdy house selling cheap liquor to lower-class men—journeymen, apprentices, free blacks, and sailors, and to "loose" women (those not tied to men), runaway wives, girls seeking husbands, and prostitutes. Black and white women ran "groceries," places to relax and chat or brothels renting rooms for sex: both had racially mixed clienteles.

Women could support themselves "respectably" only as craftswomen, shopkeepers, midwives, or nurses. The only women artisans in New York in 1805, a shoemaker and a hatter, probably learned the craft helping their husbands. Denied formal training in craft shops, women worked in them marginally. Only in the sewing trades were they a substantial presence, following the traditional sequence of apprentice, journeywoman, then mistress in dressmaking and millinery. In 1805 New York, women made up 31 of the seamstresses, 51 of 59 mantua (dress) makers, and 22 of 166 tailors.

Few women were hired to produce commodities; most who did worked in the putting-out system. After the revolution, entrepreneurs began to travel the eastern seaboard seeking housebound women who could process raw materials into goods ready for sale—spin flax and wool, weave yarn into cloth and stockings, seam stockings, braid straw into hatmakings, bind shoes, or sew gloves and shirts for tiny wages. As in Europe, men viewed spinning as a panacea for poor women, even though it paid too little to support them. The first city poorhouse opened in 1734 (and closed in 1812); it was filled with spinning wheels that charitable benefactors donated for poor women to earn their keep. But after 1820 even that "solution" ended, for spinning was then done in textile mills.

As marginal workers, women did what they could when they got it. They worked seasonally, traveling to rural Connecticut, New Jersey, New York, or Long Island at harvest to reap or preserve food. They held several jobs: two women accused of keeping disorderly houses in 1820 also washed and sewed; food hawkers did laundry; and laundresses did put-out work in freezing weather. Desperate women asked the city for relief (cash, wood, or food) or went to the almshouse or the over-crowded dismal hospital. Once in the almshouse, few old women ever left, but younger women lacking fuel or warm clothes took refuge there in winter or when their men were away.

Ezra Stiles Ely met such a woman in 1811. A poor Irish emi-grant, she had a fever and was taking her four children to the almshouse to a ward aswarm with other women and children equally hard up. Her husband had deserted the family for the camaraderie of the tavern the winter after the family arrived in New York. Ely met her and her children again at the Battery, searching for her husband, who had signed on to a ship; she hoped to get half his salary so they could leave the almshouse. Her children were sick—public shelters spread disease—and she wanted to take them to fresher air where she believed they would recover. She failed and returned to the almshouse, where a child died. She left that spring, but a chilly, windy, wet May made her ill again and, when Ely met her next, she was returning.

Women in the South

By the eighteenth century, long-settled regions of Virginia were rich. Southern wealth came from land, not commerce, and cre-ated a landed aristocracy. Some benefits of wealth filtered to women, but their status and control over property had declined and they were less active in public life.[59] Stratification had occurred in the South too—the rich were richer, the poor poorer, and the gap between them widened as it became harder to get rich. Only men with huge landholdings and money to invest heavily in slaves and to absorb losses profited from slavery.

In the 1600s a farm woman boiled dinner in her one pot; by 1700 she had a skillet and spit. Most people had two rooms, a separate kitchen, and household amenities like candlesticks; middle-level Virginia houses might have a seventeen-foot (5.2 meters) ceiling in the first story, with a study, ballroom, separate dining rooms for adults and children, bedsteads, bureaus, mirrors, dining linens, clocks, silver, and china. Wealth increased women's work. Dinner on big plantations meant culinary exhaustion. A plantation mistress noted in her diary: "For dinner boil'd a ham, goose, turkey, tongue, turtled head, pigeon pye, saucege & eggs, vegetables, mince pye, jelly, custards, plumbs, almonds, nuts, apples, &c." Another day she served "drest turtle, cold turkey, rost beef, stued fish, tongue, sturgeon cutlets, citron pudding, potatoe pudding, cheese-cakes, custards, plenty of asparagus every day." In the late 1700s Virginia women boycotted British imports and made their own linen and wool cloth, which they decorated with fancy needlework.

Women living in plenty had less personal freedom than their grandmothers. Even their dress was more constricting. The stiff ruffs and tight bodices of the sixteenth century relaxed in the seventeenth to loose easy gowns and simple hairstyles, but discomfort returned with a vengeance in the eighteenth century. Girls were laced tightly into corsets with whalebone stays to minimize their waistlines, and they wore hoopskirts six feet wide stiffened by whalebone. Walking through a doorway was a project, and stairs were perilous. Ladies' appearance advertised men's wealth: clothes made for immobility screamed idleness; while hair frizzed, oiled, swept up straight from the forehead into a very high tower, combed over wires or pads, and adorned with baubles required a maid.

Marriage was "civil death" for women. A woman's property

became her husband's once she was married—earnings, wealth, or labor. Women could not transact business, pursue court cases, buy, sell, or free a slave, do business for others, or make or serve as executor of a will or as legal guardian for her own children. Husbands decided where a couple lived. Women, white and black, bore an average of six to nine children, whom white husbands owned absolutely. If a husband fell into debt, the property his wife had brought to the marriage could be seized and sold to repay it.

Women pioneers lived on frontiers, which were constantly advancing; lines of appropriation of Native American territory were in dispute. In the 1600s farmers used slaves to raise tobacco in the piedmont frontier. Settlers spread to the Shenandoah Valley, where tobacco did not thrive, and grew wheat and hemp: slavery did not take hold there. In the 1700s English, French, and Indians warred over the Ohio Valley: France ceded its claim at the end of the Seven Years' War, but the Indians kept up guerrilla warfare.

Female pioneers were tough. William Byrd, exploring the North Carolina frontier in 1710, met Mrs. Jones, "a very civil woman [who] shews nothing of ruggedness or Immodesty in her carriage, yett she will carry a gunn in the woods and kill deer, turkeys, &c., shoot doun wild cattle, catch and tye hoggs, knock down beeves with an ax and perform the most manfull Exercises as well as most men in those parts." Such women did lonely drudgery in one-room houses. Byrd sheltered in one, sharing its single room with eight people. Surveying the Shenandoah Valley in 1748, George Washington derided "barbarians" who "lay down before the fire upon a little hay, straw, fodder, or bearskin . . . with man, wife, and children like a parcel of dogs and cats."[60]

In 1755, when Mary Ingles' husband was away in the fields

near the present town of Blacksburg, Virginia, Shawnee raiders seized her and her two sons, along with her sister, Betty Draper. The Shawnee forced the captives west, but were not unkind. They let Ingles carry her sons on horseback and they allowed her to gather herbs alone in the woods for medicine for Draper, who had been hurt in the attack. She repaid them by making them shirts after they met French cloth traders. When the Shawnee sent her boys away to be raised by other Indians, however, she decided to escape and, with a German woman captive, asked permission to gather grapes. Taking a blanket and a tomahawk, they found the Ohio River and followed it, seeking the Kanawha and New Rivers, their passage home. They skirted Indian villages, walked miles out of their way to find fords over streams, and, starving, ate unknown roots. The German broke from the strain and threatened to kill Ingles, who fled. After 500 miles (805 kilometers) over forty-two days of travel, she reached a farm—emaciated, frostbitten, and almost naked. She returned home, had four more children, and lived to be eighty-three. One of her kidnapped sons died and the other came back after thirteen years, but was uneasy in white society, having been raised Indian. The German woman too found her people. Draper was returned after six years.[61]

CHAPTER 7

BLACK EXPERIENCE
IN NORTH AMERICA

S LAVERY WAS COMMON IN AFRICA before European intrusion, and some historians compare the "benign" African form to the malign New World variety. Although no slavery is benign, New World slavery was far more cruel. In Africa, slaves represented wealth—people who followed a rich man and whom he supported. Large followings of people, especially women, proclaimed status and wealth. African societies tended to assimilate slaves, gradually incorporating them in the local culture, in a place befitting their lineage, age, and sex. In Africa, slave and free women did virtually the same work and had similar lives, but slaves were vulnerable to sexual exploitation and could be sold. Only in gold or salt mining did Africans exploit slaves on purely economic grounds.

The development of sugar plantations on Caribbean islands provided the impetus to transport Africans to the New

World. There was massive importation of African slaves after 1570, but technical innovations in sugar production and a rise in sugar prices increased the numbers dramatically after 1630. Between 1640 and 1800, the height of the Atlantic trade, 4.5 million slaves were exported from the coast of West Africa to the Americas. Of the 4 million whose origins are known, over half (56 percent) came from regions dominated by the new African states. American Africans came from varied backgrounds. Among the women, for example, Muslim Hausa women from northern Nigeria had been secluded, barred from direct participation in economic or political life. Women from Ghana, Sierra Leone, and the Ivory Coast were traders and farmers. Women from centralized societies like Yorubaland were used to woman chiefs on all governing councils. Igbo women from eastern Nigeria were accustomed to a political system with parallel sexual hierarchies of chiefs.

Most slaves were captured—seized, marched in chains to the coast, sold to European or American traders, and placed in holding pens until a shipload had been collected, then herded aboard and jammed body to body below decks with ceilings so low they could barely sit up. Males were chained, but females might be put on the quarterdeck, where they had fresh air and freedom of movement—and were available to the crew for rape. The voyage, called the Middle Passage, took at least six weeks, and one-fifth of the captives died during the voyage. Survivors were driven naked onto the deck and sold like animals. We have only whites' accounts of this process. As slave trader Alexander Falconbridge testified before Parliament in 1788:

> [On one] voyage we were obliged to confine a female Negro of 23 yrs on her becoming a lunatic. She was afterwards sold during one of her lucid intervals. . . .

Frequently Negroes on being purchased become raving mad and many die in that state, particularly the women. One day at Bonny, a middle-aged, stout woman who had been brought down from a fair the preceding day was chained to the post of a black trader's door in a state of furious insanity. On board ship was a young Negro woman chained to the deck who had lost her senses soon after being purchased and taken on board. . . . A young female Negro became despondent; it was judged necessary, in order to attempt her recovery, to send her on shore to the hut of one of the black traders. Elated at the prospect of regaining her liberty she soon recovered, but hearing, by accident, it was intended to take her on board the ship again, the young woman hanged herself.

New Englanders had only a few hundred slaves in 1680. Perhaps for this reason, owners were rather casual and laws less harsh. In 1638 Samuel Maverick of Boston had three black slaves, one "a queen in her own country." In 1641 John Winthrop wrote that "a Negro woman" became a full member of the First Church of Boston. In 1705 Sarah Kemble Knight saw owner families and slaves eating together at the dinner table. Arbitrating a dispute between a Connecticut owner and his slave, a judge found against the owner and made him pay the slave and apologize. Northern blacks were treated like indentured servants, except that their status was permanent and passed to their children.

A few slaves were freed, like Boston poet Phillis Wheatley (1753–84). Shipped as a slave from Africa to Boston in 1761, she was bought by John Wheatley. Educated by his daughter Mary, she soon showed talent and the family urged her to stop housework when she needed to write. Like a family member, she chatted with their friends in Boston society, joined their church, and used their libraries. She was sickly and the family doctor advised an ocean voyage. They sent her to England, where she became a sensation and stayed with the Countess of Huntingdon, who had one of her poems published, and then a book of her poetry. Thomas Paine, George Washington, John Hancock, and Lord Dartmouth all praised her work; her literary gift, learning, and exotic beauty made her a darling of English aristocrats. When Mrs. Wheatley fell ill, she returned to Boston, but wife and then husband soon died. Phillis Wheatley married and had a baby, but her husband deserted them. The only work she could find to support her infant and herself was housework in a cheap boarding house. Both Wheatley and her child died in Boston in 1784: she was only thirty-one.

Never more than 3 percent of the population of the North as a whole, slaves in the eighteenth century comprised 8 percent of the population of Boston, 8 percent of New Jersey and Pennsylvania, and 14 percent of New York, which had more African slaves than any other northern colony. Most lived in New York City, where they represented 15 percent of the population. But in 1760 the South (Maryland, Virginia, North Carolina, South Carolina, Georgia), with a total population of one million, had 350,000 slaves—a third of them female. There were great differences in numbers among these colonies: the population of North Carolina was 25 percent slaves; of South Carolina, over 60 percent.[1]

In the early years most slaves worked one to a household, with no fellow African for company; for decades, buyers imported mainly men, so woman slaves were even more isolated. Plantations used three forms of labor: indentured servitude, slavery, and wage labor. Believing the hard work needed in early colonies had to be coerced, planters preferred bonded labor. At first, slavery and indenture were both seen as temporary and the two kinds of workers were treated alike—Richard Ligon, a visitor to Barbados, thought that slaves were treated better than servants. When tobacco prices fell, wiping out small Caribbean planters, large owners bought their land and required more slaves. Then, when Britain's economy improved, fewer indentured servants emigrated. Planters feared they would lose their workforce, so decided to use color to justify bondage.

By 1660 large planters dominated the islands and passed laws fixing slave status. Africans were soon identified by law and practice with chattel slavery and plantation production: dark skin meant slave, and vice versa. Barbadians, black and white, were the exception, for they raised livestock, which did not require slave labor. Ironically, free black Barbadians were among South Carolina's first settlers.[2] While Virginia courts held that slaves were "not only property, but . . . rational beings . . . entitled to the humanity of the courts, when it can be executed without invading the rights of property," laws criminalizing the killing of a slave were not enforced.

Life was usually harder for Southern slaves, partly because of its economy and climate. A quarter died during their first year in Virginia. On North American plantations, slaves lived on empty land some distance from the main house and were only sporadically supervised. Many specialized in a trade or a skill like hunting. Black and Indian slaves shared quarters and were drafted into militias to repel Indian raids. Africans were experienced in raising rice, so, among many experimental crops, it became South Carolina's major crop. Workers were increasingly separated by race after 1695, and certain tasks—producing rice and indigo, collecting and disposing of garbage—were left to Africans. Laws increasingly prescribed the kind and quality of clothing slaves should wear and the amount of food they should be given (in general, it was half to three-quarters of white diets, even though they worked far harder). They were restricted to the plantation and, in 1712, were forbidden to hunt beyond plantation borders.

In the last decades of the seventeenth century all ranks of Virginia workers were wretched enough to foment chronic disruption. Blacks and whites conspired in Bacon's rebellion in 1676, a mini-civil war. In the 1670s the Southern middle class saw their whole workforce as a threat to "social order"; by the 1690s Africans were blamed as the main source of disruption. Tobacco prices rose in 1684, and prosperous white farmers bought more land and more Africans to work it, pushing Native Americans even further west. By 1700 Virginians had replaced white servants with African slaves. A new hierarchy emerged—white planters at the top, then lower-echelon white overseers, bookkeepers, and artisans, then poor whites, and then slaves—both men and women.

In 1690 Africans made up about 15 percent of Virginians; by 1775 they were about half. At mid-century nearly half of them worked on plantations with twenty or more slaves, and women and men were nearly equal in number. As their numbers grew and they began to share language, they developed the skills that whites required; however, they also created their own community and culture. Whites had a rigid sexual division of labor: men were blacksmiths, carpenters, valets, gardeners, and shoemakers; women were dairymaids, seamstresses, cooks, and midwives (for both black and white women). A Louisiana cotton planter punished slave men by making them do laundry. Africans passed their skills on to their children—a native-born artisan class. Some Chesapeake mistresses let female slaves raise chickens to trade or sell for extra clothes or blankets. Most indigo and rice plantations operated on a task system: if slaves finished their daily tasks, they could work for themselves, cultivating their own rice or indigo. So South Carolina slaves earned their own money. Maryland and Virginia owners hired their slaves out, giving them some of the wages they earned.

Plantation slaves were ranked. The elite were male distillers, stockmen, wainmen (carters), watchmen, factory workers; male and female drivers, headpeople, and house slaves—who were often female Creoles (native born) or mulattoes. Beneath them were craftsmen, cooks, other servants, and hospital workers. Apart from house service, status jobs (cook, healer) went only to incapacitated or old women no longer able to do field work. The bottom class, field workers, was filled with women: 80 percent of women were field workers, grouped by age and strength into gangs often headed by men. Low-status field work was identified with women and new arrivals, but most slaves were field workers. Women picked cotton better than men and a great many plowed. The strongest or most valued field hand on a plantation was often a woman. Many women preferred "men's" jobs like plowing, proud of their physical strength and skill. They were ditch diggers, lumber jacks, and logrollers; they performed heavy labor in textile, hemp, and tobacco works, sugar refineries, rice and lumber mills, transportation, coal mines, and iron foundries; and they built railroads, levees, and canals, haltered like animals to pull trams and canal boats.

Women worked harder than men because they, too, worked from sunrise to sunset, but also had to cook, tend children, and rise first in the morning to make breakfast. They got pregnant, gave birth, and nursed. Visiting an eighteenth-century plantation, Fanny Kemble noted that women slaves, but not middle-aged men, looked overworked. Harrison

Beckett of Texas remembered his mother returning exhausted from the fields and having to cook for her children and husband, so tired she went to sleep without eating anything herself. Driven by need, women worked into the night, spinning thread, weaving, making quilts, mattresses, and candles, sewing whatever clothing the family owned, tending the garden (if there was one), and washing. Women's work was endless and more time consuming than men's. Eugene Genovese quotes a report from the period: "The women are required, when work is done in the field, to sweep their houses and yards and receive their supper (communally prepared) at the call of the cook, after which they may sew or knit but not leave their houses otherwise."[3]

Slaves did not control where they lived, the work they did, the pace at which they worked, the food they ate, the clothes they wore, or their own bodies. Owners gave slaves so little clothing that many were nearly naked, then blamed women's nudity for men's lust; they lashed, tortured, and killed slaves, and used female slaves sexually. The only area of life slaves had some control over was in their own enclave, where they chose their own customs and favored settled unions: marriage if a woman became pregnant, and fidelity in married partners. They made incest taboo. Slaves lived in equality with each other; whites did not. Historians see their creation of families as an act of rebellion. When people are without rights, collective action is subversive. In building families and kin networks, slaves created a power base. Owners helped reinforce men's power within households, for they believed that men who dominate wives and children had an investment in maintaining patriarchal mores. But they also denied slaves legal marriage, recorded only the mothers of slave children, and sold mates or the young away from plantations with impunity.

The family was the heart of slave life. Not just an instrument for rearing children, it kept alive a sense of self as a person, the necessary root of dignity and satisfaction in any life. Family bonds gave slave existence whatever meaning and pleasure it had; the family was also the locus of resistance. Women, the core of this locus, made it all happen. Whites differentiated between the sexes in promotion and in status, but in the fields they saw everyone as a mere beast of burden. However demeaning or exhausting their job, slave women challenged oblivion by shifting into another gear at home and in the community, to act like women. They never internalized white's denial of their sex by denying their womanhood among their own people.

The family was also the site of protest. Kin asked to live together, protested excessive punishment of relatives, and often asked special treatment for a child. Even arrogant, harsh owners could be swayed by eloquence. On one Virginia plantation, a slave woman arranged for a certain black doctor to treat her sick daughter; a man persuaded his owner to let his daughter live with her stepmother. Black men risked owners' retaliation by interposing between wives or daughters and white men who threatened them, often killing, beating, or driving off overseers who were whipping women they loved.

Genovese writes about a slave man who attacked an overseer trying to rape his wife. The furious man was killing the white until the wife pleaded with her husband and the overseer promised not to punish him. But once freed, the overseer had him seized, lashed a hundred times, and nailed his ear to the whipping post before cutting it off. The man's son, Josiah Henson, recalled his father as "a good humored . . . lighthearted man, the ringleader in all fun at corn-huskings and Christmas buffoonery. His banjo was the life of the farm, and all night long at a merrymaking would he play on it while the other Negroes danced. But from this hour he became utterly changed. Sullen, morose, and dogged, nothing could be done with him." Defying his owner's threat to sell him, he was sold in Alabama and never saw his family again. White failure to honor promises or repay debts to slaves is a recurring theme in slave narratives.

When the slave trade ended, owners tried to breed their "stock." Laws required them to lighten women's work in the last month of pregnancy and give them a month to recover after birth, but many did not—against their own interest—and underfed, overworked, and humiliated slave women died as a result of childbirth or bore deformed infants. African women must have been very hardy, for their birth rates were higher than those of contemporary white women. But some, refusing to produce slave children, aborted or killed them. In 1822 some white citizens of Virginia petitioned the courts to spare the life of a slave condemned to death for killing her baby. The woman said she would not have killed a black child, but her baby was white, sired by a "respectable" married white man. A former slave described how slaves protected a woman who poisoned her baby: her children had been sold away from her, one after the other, and she wanted no more.

Owners needed new workers, yet kept women from nursing their babies: they might let them leave the fields to nurse three times a day (hardly enough), or punish them for persuading overseers to give them more breaks. West Africans tried to maintain their tradition of nursing for two or three years. The love between slave mothers and their children was intense: Genovese writes that children's love of mothers shines through all slave narratives (even owners noted it). Fannie Moore of South Carolina recalled, "My mammy she work in de field all day and piece and quilt all night. . . . I never see how my mammy stand such hard work. She stand up for her chillen though. De old overseer he hate my mammy, 'cause she fought him for beatin' her chillen. Why she get more whippin' for dat dan anythin' else." Selma Williams cites the diary of William Byrd, a planter in the early eighteenth century, which offers a painful picture of an owner's treatment of slaves. He often casually whipped female slaves for small faults, some simply because they were present when he quarreled with his wife.[4]

About a century later, in the 1820s, Basil Hall, a British Navy captain, called on a rice plantation on a sea island off Charleston and watched slaves (whom he found highly intelligent) do backbreaking work. Women carrying baskets of earth on their heads were building a dam to hold back a river that was inundating the rice fields. The hot, damp climate was unhealthy and they worked in fields that were alternately flooded and dried. He lamented that "the negroes are perpetually at work, often ankle-deep in mud, with their bare heads exposed to the sun."

In the 1850s Frederick Law Olmsted visited a plantation on a tributary of the Mississippi which was serviced only by an occasional steamboat. The man who owned it as an investment visited it twice in five years. It consisted of four contiguous farms, each with an overseer, stable, and slave quarter. All produce was sent to a gin- and warehouse supervised by a bailiff, who managed the whole estate. Its slaves made up about a twentieth of the population of a predominantly black county. The only whites on the estate, the overseers and the bailiff, were terrified (fear and paranoia are the price of domination) and believed it necessary to treat the slaves cruelly. Since slave testimony against whites was not accepted in court, they were not restrained by fear of the law.

Slave families on these plantations lived in large well-built cottages, two rooms and a loft, with galleries in front; single slaves and the overseers had small, mean log huts. African families built fowl-houses and pigsties, where they kept fowl and swine with corn "stolen" from the estate cornfields. They cultivated vegetable gardens and sold or ate their eggs, fowl, bacon, and crops. Bailiffs oversaw drivers who distributed to each family head carefully measured allotments of food every week: three pounds of pork, a peck of meal per person, and, from January to July, a quart of molasses; each month they received a pound of tobacco and four pints of salt. Most families bought a barrel of flour a year and trapped game—raccoons, rabbits, and turkeys. They drank water. They were given work clothes twice a year, summer and winter. Most got clothes—calico dresses or handkerchiefs—as holiday gifts, and, if they could, they also bought clothes for themselves.

The estate had a large smithy and wheelwright shop, and a loom-house where Olmstead saw a dozen Africans making shoes and coarse cotton for clothes. These workers were impaired—chronic invalids, cripples, or people too old for field work. One was insane. The manager almost never called a doctor for them: people not visibly ill were considered shirkers. The workday began before sun-up and ended after sunset. Around eight in the morning slaves could stop briefly for breakfast, and at noon they were given half an hour to an hour for dinner—which they had to prepare. Women "very well performed" plowing, with single and double mule teams. Olmstead felt slaves were driven harder in the southwest than in eastern or northern states.

Slaves who had been whipped were usually angry and often ran away, but they had nowhere to go. They hid in swamps, slipping home at night for food, but seldom stayed away for more than a fortnight. There was indeed nowhere for them to go. They were whipped on their return. Some determined never to let a white whip them and resisted: "Of course you must kill them in that case," the manager remarked. Each overseer had over a hundred slaves in his power. Olmstead found most overseers "passionate, careless, inefficient men, generally intemperate and totally unfitted for the duties of the position," and he was shocked by the savage whipping one of them gave a girl suspected of shirking. Noting one girl with pale white skin and light straight hair, Olmstead opined she could escape. Her language and manners would give her away, the overseers said: "a slave girl would always quail when you looked in her eyes."

Emily Burke, a white teacher working in Georgia in the 1830s and 1840s, wrote that owners give slaves "one coarse torn garment a year . . . hardly food enough of the coarsest kind to support nature," and a rough blanket that they carry with them always, so they can sleep wherever they are when night falls:

> The huts of the field servants [lay] . . . at considerable distance from the master's residence, yet not beyond the sight of his watchful and jealous eye. These . . . huts were arranged with a good deal of order . . . each slave had his small patch of ground adjacent to his own dwelling, which he assiduously cultivated after completing his daily task. I have known the poor creatures, notwithstanding "tired nature" longed for repose, to spend the greater part of a moonlight night on these grounds. In this way they often raise considerable crops of corn, tobacco, and potatoes, besides various . . . garden vegetables. Their object . . . is to have something with which to purchase tea, coffee, sugar, flour, and . . . articles of diet . . . not provided by their masters, and clothing.

But the best descriptions of slavery come from slaves themselves. Solomon Northup, born free in New York, was drugged and kidnapped by white men and sold to a Louisiana cotton planter. A stranger to agriculture and slavery, hired out as a field hand on a sugar plantation, Northup observed closely:

> When a new hand, one unaccustomed to the business, is sent for the first time into the field, he is whipped up smartly and made for that day to pick as fast as he can possibly. At night it is weighed so that his capability in cotton picking is known. He must bring in the same weight each night following. If it falls short, it is considered evidence that he has been laggard and a greater or less number of lashes is the penalty.

Corn was hoed four times, the last in early July, when it was about a foot (0.3 meters) high. "The space between the rows is plowed, leaving a deep water furrow in the center. During the hoeings, the overseer or driver follows the slaves on horseback with a whip. The fastest hoer takes the lead row. He is usually about a rod in advance of his companions. If one of them passes him, he is whipped. If one falls behind or is a moment idle, he is whipped. The lash is flying from morning until night, the whole day long." Men and women plowed with oxen and mules, and the women fed and cared for their teams "in all respects doing the field and stable work, precisely as do the plowboys of the north." A woman, Patsey, the most remarkable cotton picker on his plantation, "picked with both hands and with such surprising rapidity that five hundred pounds a day was not unusual for her."

Hands had to be in the field at light, and had ten or fifteen minutes at noon "to swallow their allowance of cold bacon."

> They are not permitted to be a moment idle until it is too dark to see, and when the moon is full, they often

times labor till the middle of the night. They do not dare to stop even at dinner time, nor return to the quarters, however late, until the order to halt is given by the driver. . . . No matter how fatigued and weary he may be—no matter how much he longs for sleep and rest—a slave never approaches the gin-house with his basket of cotton but with fear. If it falls short in weight—if he has not performed the full task appointed him, he knows that he must suffer. If he has exceeded it by ten or twenty pounds, in all probability his master will measure the next day's task accordingly. After weighing follow the whippings.

Even then the slaves could not rest, for they had chores: they fed the pigs or mules, cut wood, or packed cotton by candlelight. Reaching their cabins exhausted, they still had to kindle a fire, grind corn in a handmill, and prepare supper and the next day's dinner. On this plantation they were given only corn and bacon—no tea, coffee, sugar, or salt—and in some respects were treated worse than the animals: "Master Epps' hogs were fed on *shelled* corn—it was thrown out to his 'niggers' in the ear." Few slaves had knives (none had forks) and they had to cut the bacon with the woodpile ax. They lay on foot-wide wood planks, a stick of wood for a pillow, covered with one coarse blanket, and as anxious as they had been at the gin-house—if they overslept, they were punished by a minimum of twenty lashes. The log cabin had a dirt floor and no windows. Chinks between logs let in light, air, and rain during storms. After a few hours' rest, the slaves were wakened by a horn an hour before sunrise, to live again a day like the one before.

I believe that cruelty is difficult for human beings; as proof, I submit that no humans have ever upheld a cruel system without a vindicating ideology. To present slavery as a "good," Frederick Cooper explains, Southern slave owners depicted their society as a medieval Christian divine order in which everything had a place and was related to everything else.⁵ Owners owed their slaves care, and slaves owed their owners labor. White owners thought of themselves as benevolent *paterfamilias* of extended black and white families and complacently contrasted a hospitable, gracious South with a competitive, individualistic North, where employers exploited workers impersonally. But, Cooper writes, feudal images did not fit the competitive commercial economy of the South, where the state protected white autonomy and rights. Moreover, by the end of the eighteenth century, Africans were the largest racial or ethnic group entering the colonies (over 95 percent in perpetual bondage) and they represented a majority in many Southern states. Owners had to create an apparatus of control directed specifically at slaves—they had to create racism.

Early colonists saw Africans as different from themselves, but also, as Peter Kolchin writes, as different from each other in national origin, just like whites.⁶ Colonial society had gradations of bound, semifree, and free workers and did not segregate Africans. Like Indians, Africans hunted, trapped, and fished; they were sailors and guides, and several times they were sent into battle against Indians. In early Virginia, the underclass mingled black, white, slave, servant, and ex-servant.

To create racism, slave owners emphasized difference: in 1758 a South Carolina official admitted that "it has been allways the policy of this government to create an aversion in them [Indians] to Negroes," to prevent them from making common cause. Slave owners rarely hired poor whites, yet they appealed to them as a racial group distinct from Africans. In the late seventeenth century, law after law was passed barring slaves from voting, marrying, and testifying in court. Superiority requires inferiority, and whites buttressed their dominance with biological and scientific proof of Negro infantilism, laziness, and innate intellectual inferiority. The framers worded the Constitution so that Congress could not end the slave trade until 1808. When laws barred the importing of slaves, authorities helped traders to defy them. Together, they created a racism we still live with today. This racism, which causes all Americans to suffer immeasurably, was intended to justify a social-economic system that, happily, no longer exists.

The Effect of Slavery on White Women

The big house—the center of authority for slaves, the showplace for the vaunted values of plantation aristocrats, the nursery of those values in the young, and the arena for enacting gender roles—was inhabited by women, white and black. Blacks maintained it with their work, whites with their manners. White women's behavior and status testified to the cultural, legal, and economic dominance of white men. Slavery provided white women and white men with an unearned and factitious superiority that boosted their self-esteem.

While teenaged slaves labored, the teenaged Gertrude Clanton rose leisurely to a day of reading, visiting, or shopping. Elizabeth Fox-Genovese describes her dressing, arranging her room, gathering roses, mending her kid gloves, and fixing her hair for the evening.[7] Some days she did nothing whatever. White girls received almost no academic and little household education. They married young into households run by slaves and controlled by husbands, so many never grew up at all. In Christine Stansell's words, "This was a class of daddy's girls, set up, ironically, to rule over, goad and torment a race of women who saw motherhood, not daughterhood, as the essence of their collective identity, and labor, not leisure, as the keystone of women's self-esteem." As a slave, Harriet Jacobs worked unceasingly for a mistress she described with a pseudonym:

> Mrs. Flint, like many Southern women, was totally deficient in energy. She had not strength to superintend her household affairs; but her nerves were so strong, that she could sit in her easy chair and see a woman whipped, till the blood trickled from every stroke of the lash. She was a member of the church; but partaking of the Lord's supper did not seem to put her in a Christian frame of mind. If dinner was not served at the exact time on that particular Sunday, she would station herself in the kitchen, and wait till it was dished, and then spit in all the kettles and pans that had been used for cooking. She did this to prevent the cook and her children from eking out their meagre fare with the remains of the gravy and other scrapings.[8]

White mistresses often avenged their husbands' abuse of them on female slaves. In an 1848 Virginia divorce case cited by Jaqueline Jones, a witness testified that Mr. N. told his slave concubine to sit down with him and his wife at the breakfast table one morning.[9] His wife protested, threatening to punish her severely. "Her husband replied 'that in that event he would visit [Mrs. N] with a like punishment.' The wife burst into tears and asked 'if it was not too much for her to stand.'" Slave owner Mary Chesnut noted, "There is no slave, after all, like a wife."

Rich white women had nothing to do: slaves managed the house, did the work, and slept with their men. Slaves had to do these things, but white women blamed the slaves, not the system or men. They tortured slaves with pins and needles, had them whipped, forced them to nurse white babies instead of their own and ignore their own children for white ones, and often worked them to death. If they were less cruel than men—who branded slaves, tortured them in farm machines, pulled out toenails, castrated men—it was probably because they had fewer means. Women had few perquisites of domination, but clearly felt its burden. When slaves were emancipated, one white woman wrote "Free at last!" Another wrote "Our burden of work and responsibility was simply staggering. . . . I was glad and thankful on my own account when slavery ended, and I ceased to belong body and soul to my negroes."[10]

The white men who controlled this society were also brutalized by slavery. Even kindly owners who drank with male slave buddies and never used a whip were demoralized by it: superiority isolates and constricts. They also lived in constant terror of black rebellion. Whites saw black uprisings everywhere.

Always on guard against any sign of vulnerability, wary of possible insubordination, elite men laid some of the brunt of their misery on wives already demoralized by their humiliating position. Women, too, feared slave revolt, but feared contamination more. Only women could be contaminated: white men could have many liaisons with black women, but for white women responsible for the "purity" of "the family," even looking at black men was unthinkable. As men in horticultural societies imagine themselves undone by a drop of menstrual blood, so slave holders would be ruined by a black gene. No one ever admitted that a "lady" could be drawn to a black man, but white ladies, writes Fox-Genovese, "rarely ventured beyond the household without male escort" or spoke even to poor whites. Slave worlds imprison everyone.

Rebellion and Revolt

Slaves whose skin color stood out had nowhere to flee. All paths of escape traversed a white world, and slavery was legal in all the British colonies. South Carolina runaways headed for (and hundreds reached) the only haven, Spanish Florida; thousands joined the British in the American Revolution. But most flight was individual, local, and temporary: slaves fled to visit friends or relatives on distant plantations or to escape work for a time. They had to come back and face punishments often worse than whipping. And once blackness *meant* slave, no free black went unchallenged.

Slave women resisted and subverted as they could. They bravely hid runaways from other plantations, stole food to carry to them, lied, and maintained their lies under the whip. They slowed their work pace, sabotaged tools or projects, faked illness, stole, and fiercely fostered African community life. Defying owners' whips, they sneaked off to visit nearby plantations or woods for secret ritual or social gatherings. Some retaliated against cruel owners, beating mistresses, starting fires, and poisoning masters, which was easier to do than to detect.

Just maintaining personal dignity was to resist. An ex-slave, Cornelia, described her mother, Fanny, an enormously energetic and dignified woman. Fanny, "the smartest black woman in Eden," Tennessee, quick and competent at every task—cooking, washing, ironing, spinning, nursing, and fieldwork—was independent and high-spirited, but fierce. Cornelia pitied her father and their owners, the Jennings, who suffered from Fanny's temper. A powerfully loving mother to her four children, Fanny regularly told her children that slavery was cruel, but the six-year-old Cornelia thought her mother, not slavery, was cruel and found Fanny "mean" to their owners. In her enterprising family, Pa grew vegetables, raised chickens, and traded produce with local whites, neighboring free blacks, and the hotel owner in Eden. He hid booty from his "hunting" trips under planks in their cabin floor and, at specified times, Fanny cooked great feasts for free blacks who "would steal to our cabin" restaurant. The pair was so adept and skilled that the Jennings overlooked their enterprise— besides, Pa was Jennings' drinking companion.

One day, Mrs. Jennings hit Fanny with a stick—Cornelia never knew why. Fanny went crazy, struck the woman back, and they wrestled for half an hour. Terrified, Mrs. Jennings ran out onto the road; Fanny followed and tore the woman's clothes off. She was nearly naked when a storekeeper ran up, pulled Fanny off, and asked what she was doing. "Why I'll kill her, I'll kill her dead if she ever strikes me again!" she cried. Mr. Jennings said that the law required that Fanny be whipped and, two days later, two men came to the gate, one carrying a long lash. Cornelia hoped her mother had hidden, but she appeared and ran straight at the man, grabbing his beard with one hand, and seized the whip with the other. The other man drew his gun, but Jennings pulled her off. Fanny yelled, "Use your gun, use it and blow my brains out if you will!" The men left, but that evening Mrs. Jennings came to the cabin to say she would have to send Fanny away. "You won't be whipped, and I'm afraid you'll get killed." Fanny retorted: "I'll go to hell or any-where else, but I won't be whipped." She was to be hired out and, Mrs. Jennings said, without her baby.

That night, Cornelia heard her parents talking. Pa insisted on going with Fanny to Memphis. Ordering "Puss"—her name for Cornelia—never to let herself "be abused," Fanny told her she had to leave. Sobbing without stop, Cornelia suddenly saw the cruelty of slavery. The morning they were to go, Fanny held the baby under her arm like a bundle of rags. When Mr.

Jennings arrived, he calmly ordered her to leave the baby, at which "Ma took the baby by its feet, a foot in each hand, and with the baby's head swinging downward, she vowed to smash its brains out before she'd leave it. Tears were streaming down her face. It was seldom that Ma cried, and everyone knew that she meant every word. Ma took her baby with her." Their hire ended a year later and they returned, Pa drinking more than ever, and Fanny with new clothes and earrings but worked out. She gave birth to a new baby and went to bed, saying that "she had brought five children in the world for the Jennings and that was enough." Predicting she would die at eight o'clock, she summoned Jennings and asked him to hire Cornelia out "among ladies, so she can be raised right . . . A funny look came over [his] face," he bowed his head, and she died.[11]

Slaves usually fled in outrage because of unjust punishment or a white breaking his own rule. Only one of ten runaways was female: most slave women were mothers unwilling to abandon their children. To take them along made escape incredibly harder. One who tried, Margaret Grant, whose owner said she always was "an artful hussy," disguised herself as a male valet to a white indentured servant posing as free. Harriet Jacobs succeeded in escaping and wrote a book about it. So pervasive is racism in America that, until the 1980s, literary people asserted that the account was too well written to be the work of a black woman. In her book, Jacobs called herself Linda Brent and her mistress, Mrs. Flint. Jean Fagan Yellin, who proved Jacobs' authorship, restored the real names.[12]

Jacobs' parents were North Carolina slaves, her father a carpenter whose mistress, knowing his intelligence and skill, let him work for himself and pay her $200 a year. Yearning to buy his children out of slavery, he saved his money and tried several times, but she refused him. Jacobs became aware that she was a slave at six, when her mother, Delilah, died. When her father died, her owner, Margaret Horniblow, refused to let her go to his burial, insisting that she gather flowers for a party. When Horniblow died, she willed Harriet to her niece, the five-year-old daughter of Dr. James Norcom of Edenton. Horniblow's will did free Harriet's grandmother, Molly, who opened a bakery. Harriet often stopped for food, and Molly also made her clothes. Norcom treated his slaves cruelly, barely feeding or clothing them. He regularly locked the family cook away from her nursing infant for over a day. She never sent a dish to the dining room without fear, because he was fussy about food (Jacobs kindly calls him an epicure). If Norcom found it wanting, he had her whipped or forced her to bolt down the entire dish in front of him.

When Harriet entered puberty, Norcom harassed her unremittingly. Feeling desire, he did not have her whipped but made her life wretched. His wife turned jealously on Harriet instead of helping her evade her husband. (Many Horniblow black women had been raped by white men: Molly was light, and Harriet almost white.) Harriet saw a slave girl die after giving birth to a near-white child, while her mistress, who had seven children, cursed her to hell. She writes, "Southern women often marry a man knowing that he is the father of many little slaves. They do not trouble themselves about it. They regard such children as property, as marketable as the pigs on the plantation." And she blesses two wives who pressured their husbands to free their slave children.

As Norcom harassed her, a young white lawyer, Samuel Tredwell Sawyer, seduced Harriet. She had two children with him. Writing in an era that demanded "sexual purity" in women, Jacobs expresses deep shame for engaging in sex without marriage and blames her "weakness"; not until late in the book does she mention Sawyer's promises. Outraged, Norcom threatened that she would become his lover or become a field hand on one of his plantations. She refused, so he sent her to Auburn, several miles from town. Her children, Norcom's legal property, could be freed by their father, but he failed to do so. Norcom threatened to send them to the plantation to be trained as slaves. This made Harriet desperate and she considered fleeing: "I could have made my escape alone; but it was more for my helpless children than for myself that I longed for freedom. Though the boon would have been precious to me, above all price, I would not have taken it at the expense of leaving them in slavery." She made a plan.

She arranged to appear to disappear, though in fact she was hiding, with help from sympathetic friends, white and black. For seven years she lived in a tiny crawlspace over a storeroom under the tin roof of her grandmother's house. Suffering intense heat in summer, cold and chilblains in winter, she could not stand up or barely even move, and she nearly lost the use of her limbs. She bored a hole in the wall to watch her children in the house, sewed clothes for them, practiced the writing she learned as a child, and read. In time, she escaped. She removed her children after their father, Sawyer, broke his promise to free them. The family reached the North but lived in fear because the Fugitive Slave Act required northern states to return runaway slaves and Norcom wouldn't give up. He haunted her and her children. She wrote her life story secretly, hiding it from her employer, whose attitudes she did not trust. Eventually Norcom died, but his daughter took up the search, wanting money for the slave. Jacobs was freed only when a friendly white woman bought her. She was grateful, but mortified.

At first, no one would publish her account. Then a

publisher in England (and in America in 1862) brought out *Incidents in the Life of a Slave Girl*. Critics praised "Brent" for portraying slavery with restraint and describing some whites favorably. One added, "Her chief persecutor, a physician in good repute and practice, seems to have been subjected to all restraints that Southern public opinion can put upon a professional man. . . . A few sentences in which the moral is rather oppressively displayed, might have been omitted with advantage." Whites read Jacob's book not for a great story (which it is) or to learn a slave's perspective or experience, but to find whites exonerated.

In the autobiography, Jacobs' courage, spirit, resilience, and unremitting work and devotion to her children outweigh her devastating ordeal. And, for once, a life has a happy ending: Jacobs' children are free, her loving daughter by her side; her brother travels across the country giving anti-slavery lectures. Jacobs uses her earnings to work with fugitive slaves behind Union Army lines and with Quakers in the anti-slavery movement, distributing clothing and supplies, and organizing orphanages, schools, and nursing homes. Yellin points to the importance female solidarity had for Jacobs: black women and men who dared to help her risked terrible reprisals; white women risked ostracism, betraying "allegiances of race and class to assert stronger allegiance to the sisterhood of all women."

Armed slave rebellion was rare: blacks had difficulty finding arms or a haven. Uprisings of ten or more slaves did occur but were quickly squelched—only a handful reached more than local proportions. Nat Turner led the most effective slave revolt in American history. A Virginia slave who believed he had a divine mission to deliver his people from bondage, he persuaded seventy other slaves to march through Virginia in 1831. Sparing poor whites, they carefully chose the sixty people they killed before they were stopped. Whites retaliated, massacring them along with scores of innocent slaves. Turner, caught months later, was executed, but the South, haunted for decades by "Nat Turner's Rebellion," used it to justify terrifying search-and-seizures right up to the Civil War. Before the 1850s, hundreds of slaves fought alongside the Seminoles in Florida. Northern abolitionists broke the law to start an Underground Railroad (a secret abolitionist network) to transfer fugitive slaves to freedom in Canada or the West.

Harriet Tubman, a slave in Maryland, always wore a turban to hide a deep scar on her skull: an irate overseer had thrown an iron weight at her when she was fifteen, leaving her with periodic unconscious spells for the rest of her life. She married a free black but remained a slave, as did her two children. Her owner died in 1849; hearing that his heir planned to sell her out of state, she begged her husband to flee with her and the children. When he refused, she went alone and reached Pennsylvania. In the next two years she made the risky trip back to Maryland twice to free her children, sister, mother, brother, and his family. Later she made nineteen trips into slave states as a "conductor" on the Underground Railroad, freeing over three hundred people. African Americans called her Moses. Whites put a price of $40,000 on her head, but she was never caught and never lost a "passenger." Some attributed her success to mysterious powers, but acquaintances stressed her intelligence and foresight. During the Civil War she worked as a Union scout and nurse but ended up impoverished. Congress voted her a $20-a-month pension when she was eighty.

In 1780 Jefferson wrote: "The whole commerce between master and slave is a perpetual exercise of the most boisterous passions, the most unremitting despotism on the one part, and degrading submission on the other. Our children see this, and learn to imitate it. . . . The man must be a prodigy who can retain his manners and morals undepraved by such circumstances." Some feel his statement expresses more concern for whites than for slaves, but his point is essential: slavery damages owners as much as slaves. He knew this, yet he did not free his slaves.

Free African Americans

Before the Civil War, few blacks in the United States were free. An early move to free them increased the number of free Africans by 82 percent in one decade (1790–1800) and 72 percent in the next. Colonial governments then hindered manumission. Little research has been done on free ante-bellum blacks, but they probably lived in anxiety. Freedom was tenuous—even legally free Africans (like Molly Horniblow and Solomon Northup) could be kidnapped, sold, and enslaved. The free blacks who ate at Fanny's restaurant had to sneak to visit their slave friends. Unlike whites, free blacks were whipped for offences. Only in St. Augustine, settled by Spaniards and Africans, were they seen as human beings. Today, archaeologists are excavating Florida for information about its black culture—its carpenters, ironsmiths, and fort-builders. Scholars are studying free blacks elsewhere: Suzanne Lebsock, for example, investigated Petersburg, Virginia, a town of some consequence in 1820, with the highest proportion of free blacks in America—1000 of 7000 people—and almost one-third of its free people.[13]

The blacks of 1820s Petersburg, emancipated after the American Revolution, were the first free generation of their families in America. Women headed half the households: white male historians called the arrangement "matriarchy" and pronounced it pathological. Lebsock comments that men call women matriarchs when their power, relative to men in their own group, is in any way greater than society considers appropriate. Many people call any woman living with no man present to supersede her authority over her children a matri- arch—although the word is parallel to "patriarch" and means domination of the opposite sex in a society.

The family was the center of slave culture, and women were central to slave families. Because black women worked like men, and black men did not own property through which they could control women, black women had authority in the fam- ily. And women had borne a heavier burden in slavery, main- taining their own families, often being sexually appropriated, and bearing white men's children. Some whites freed slaves when they were too old to work and could no longer support themselves. A few freed the children along with a mother, spar- ing her the ordeal of trying to save enough to buy them herself. But the family left with only the rags on their backs. These women had to find a way to feed, house, and clothe a family of one to five children.

In 1820, eastern Virginia had 100 free black adult women to every 85 freed black men. For work, they all flocked to Petersburg, which had 100 women to every 64.5 men. Until the Virginia legislature barred manumission in 1806, 173 Petersburg slaves were freed. Over half of these freed slaves were women, most probably white men's daughters or sexual part- ners. It cost an owner less to free a female slave than a male slave because women were paid less than men, and hired-out slave women suffered from this universal discrimination. By hard work and strict saving, blacks themselves redeemed about a sixth of the freed slaves; about half the emancipators were women, but no woman could liberate more than one slave until after 1820.

Many enterprises failed in the panic of 1819. Indebted

whites had to sell off their slaves at low prices, and many free blacks bought their relatives. Although black people too were hurt by the recession, many black women first appeared on the tax rolls in 1819, usually for owning a slave. Poor as free black women were, they were better off within their own communities than white female heads of household. In 1820 black women represented 40 percent of the free blacks with property; they made up two-fifths of black taxpayers and paid two-fifths of the revenue collected from blacks. White women, in contrast, made up 12.8 percent of white taxpayers but paid only 3.5 percent of revenue collected from whites. Black women were not economically better off than white women, but had more parity with black men. Single women and widows had the same property rights and obligations as men, and black women tended to remain single (though not chaste): the law prevented their marrying white men; slaves could not legally marry; and free black men were scarce. For all these reasons, black women more often than white women owned property.

Most free black women in Petersburg worked, though they endured severe discrimination in the work they were allowed to do. The majority were child-tenders, seamstresses, cooks, and cleaners, and a few were midwives, nurses, and entrepreneurs. The Petersburg Grand Jury charged at least five with keeping "tippling houses"—selling liquor without a license. The main business for women was prostitution, the only trade in which women have historically been able to wrest a living wage from men.

The most successful black woman in Petersburg was Elizabeth Allerque. The local French community patronized a store she opened in 1801, and historians believe she had come from St. Dominique. Five years later she began investing in real estate and did well in that. "Madame Betsy," as she was called, bought slaves and was well-off at her death in 1824, with land and six slaves.

Free black women bore great responsibilities. They maintained more than half the free blacks and nearly 60 percent of black children in Petersburg. There was no typical free black household: most women lived alone or with children. Less common were adult couples with children, and 10 percent were childless couples. Although whites also lived in varied arrangements, between 1810 and 1820 almost 85 percent of white families had male heads and a greater percentage of children under sixteen.

Most of what we know about free blacks of this period concerns property. In addition, we know that a free black Baptist church and Sunday school flourished, teaching both girls and boys. We know that even propertied blacks were demeaned: a middle-aged free black propertied woman, arrested for stealing cabbages from a white man's vegetable patch in 1853, was sentenced to thirty-nine lashes. Such punishment was inconceivable for a white: Eliza Gallie hired lawyers to urge that she be tried as a white, but they failed. She was whipped.

Blacks freed before the Civil War made up the core of the black middle class that emerged after abolition. E. Franklin Frazier believes that many free blacks were mulattoes freed by their white fathers, estimating that, in 1850, mulattoes made up 37 percent of free blacks and 8 percent of slaves.[14] Slaves who could work on their own after completing their slave labor and keep some or all of the wages from "hiring their time" bought their freedom. Most free Africans left plantations for cities, to live at bare subsistence level, but some bought land and became prosperous independent farmers or worked as mechanics or artisans. In New Orleans and Charleston, free blacks who accumulated wealth bought plantations and slaves of their own and eagerly absorbed European culture and manners. When the Civil War broke out, half the 500,000 free blacks in the United States lived in the South.[15]

CHAPTER 8

THE FRENCH REVOLUTION

THE FRENCH ENLIGHTENMENT, an eighteenth-century philosophical movement, introduced a new idea in political discourse—human rights, the belief that humans are, by nature, free and equal. Colonists in America, embroiled in a primarily economic dispute with England, gave their rebellion a moral ground by basing it on this idea. The terms *liberty* and *equality* were waved like banners over a war incited mainly by white landowning men, a tiny percentage of the population, against a British government that ruled to benefit an elite class of aristocrats and royalty. The white landowners of America had no thought of extending the equality they demanded to the lower classes of their own country, yet they adopted a rhetoric that would seduce everyone to work and sacrifice for a war that, in the end, benefited only them. The situation in France was similar: men who resented the privileges and irresponsibility of an elite class of nobles and churchmen used similar terms to inspire an entire populace. The French Revolution, however, was fuelled by the rage of poor people in extreme economic hardship.

In the 1780s, heavily in debt from both the Seven Years' War and the American Revolution, France spent half its budget on interest on the national debt. Government efforts to increase revenue were blocked by the elite—the still feudally organized aristocracy and clergy who fiercely defended their traditional exemption from many taxes. The brunt of the tax burden fell on small farmers, tenant farmers, and peasants.

Small landowners, tenant-farmers, and day laborers had to pay tithes to the church and a levy on what they produced. They worked to feed society, paid taxes on what they produced, and did corvée on roads. They had to pay wealthy landlords for using mills, wine presses, and other facilities and for transferring land. The state-owned salt monopoly required each person to buy seven pounds of salt a year at fifty or sixty times its value. Peasants could not hunt—hunting was the prerogative of aristocrats.

As ever, women worked harder than men. They plowed, reaped, threshed, collected and spread dung, tended poultry, and made butter, cheese, soap, and candles; they preserved meat, fruit, and vegetables, made cloth, sewed and washed the family clothing, baked bread and prepared meals daily, oversaw servants, and tended children. The poorest women mowed, reaped, or sheared sheep for better-off farmers at half of men's wages. Women gave birth, ate less, and died younger than men, most before they were thirty. Few people lived past forty.

Urban poor women were worse off. The main job open to them was domestic service, which provided little more than a bed and a scanty diet; female servants saved for years just to buy linen for their dowries. Older women did the most menial work: carrying heavy loads like night soil, collecting refuse, sifting cinders, sorting rags, and helping masons and bricklayers, always at half-wages—and in jobs where men earned barely enough to sustain themselves. Poor urban women with children had the hardest time: they spun linen and cotton, sewed, made lace or hats for the female garment trades, earning a pittance. Many women in these painstaking jobs ended up blind. Impoverished middle-class women could be governesses or ladies-in-waiting earning little beyond a room and food.

Any blow could push the poor over the edge. During hard times in the 1740s and 1770s, many men abandoned their families. Women did not: in 1740 a curé lamented being overwhelmed by the numbers of women who came begging bread, weeping that their husbands threatened to leave unless they let their youngest child die. In 1770 a Tours curé described a "hierarchy of hunger": women, he wrote, do not die of hunger first but feel it first, because they give their food to their children and husbands.[1] By will and work, paid or not, mothers kept families alive; when mothers died or were incapacitated, families collapsed into indigence. Serious crop failures in 1785 and 1789 sent bread prices soaring; bread alone cost the poor 50 percent of their income in 1788. Peasants thronged to cities seeking work, but things were worse there. Dearth affected everything. By 1789, bread cost 80 percent of a low income.

Yet the Catholic Church, which was ruled in France by aristocratic clergy, paid no tax on huge revenues from property it had inherited over the centuries or on tithes of 10 percent or more of the harvest on all cultivated land. Most of the income went to monastic orders and to ranking clerics who held many posts simultaneously but lived secular lives; the least went to hardworking parish priests. Aristocrats, too, had traditional "liberties" to live without interference or taxation. But nobles were divided: the *noblesse de la race* (who traced their titles back to the Middle Ages) left the overseeing of their estates to bailiffs and spent their time at court in Versailles and their energy in frivolity. Wanting to impede the *noblesse de la robe* (whose titles had been bought in recent generations), they pushed through a law in 1781 which limited the sale of military commissions to men whose noble lineage harked back at least four generations. As a result, nobles *de la robe* favored reform.

The bourgeoisie—bankers, merchants, professionals, government officials, and artisans with master status and their own shops—could, if they were rich enough, rise into the nobility by buying a title or marrying daughters of poorer nobles. The obstacle created by the nobles *de la race* affected them deeply because, without titles, they had no voice in society and could not hold high political office or vote in any but local elections. Together, the more recent nobles, and merchants who wanted greater access to privileges, rebelled against the absolute monarchy. Many became revolutionaries and saw themselves as "the people," struggling for *liberté, égalité, et fraternité* (liberty, equality, and brotherhood, clearly excluding women).

When the nobles refused to pay more taxes even in the face of a bankrupt government, the king convened the Estates General (a body including men from all three "estates"— church, aristocracy, and bourgeoisie) for the first time in 150 years. Knowing that the First Estate and the Second Estate had allied against it in the past, the Third Estate now demanded twice as many delegates to give it a voice against the clerical and secular aristocrats. In the nearly six months the king took to agree, the bourgeoisie lost faith in him.

King Louis XVI was a dense flounderer who believed in his "divine" right to rule and his own "natural" superiority. But the rebels blamed him far less than his queen, Marie Antoinette. As silly and arrogant as he, but with less power, she was blamed for his vacillations. We don't know the dynamic between them—perhaps she did dominate the king—but he had the legitimate power and thus the responsibility. However, it is easier to rebel against a woman in high position than against a father figure, and in June 1789, declaring themselves "everything," even the state itself, the bourgeoisie left the Estates General *en masse*. They formed a new body, the National Assembly, and promised to draft a constitution for France. Cowed, the king acceded and ordered the other two estates to meet with the Third.

During the hard winter of 1788–89, local assemblies had collected *cahiers de doléances*, grievance lists. The National Assembly proposed reforms based on men's grievances—the state's financial chaos, the privileges of the First and Second estates, the exclusion of the Third Estate from political power. Women drew up their own cahiers and submitted them unofficially. Illiterate women dictated their complaints to scribes: destitution, grain speculators causing price rises in bread, tax collectors, and hospitals that jammed children four to a bed and spread contagion. Working women lamented the erosion of guilds and increasing male competition in the female trades. All complained of the lack of police protection. Middle-class women wanted equal treatment at law, access to education, and protection against men's abuse of their bodies and their dowries. Their lists contained matters more life-threatening than men's, but no one paid any attention to them.

The electors (the voters in the Third Estate) decided to form a municipal government to keep order, fearing the *sans-culottes* (literally, "without breeches," a reference to working-class men's trousers) as much as the nobles did. But as the price of bread spiralled out of control, rumors flew that the king planned to starve Paris and the Third Estate into submission. Seeking arms, people marched to the Bastille, a prison they thought housed an armory. Throngs of women in the huge crowd demanded that the governor of the Bastille surrender the arms to them. He ordered an attack, which killed ninety-eight people. The crowd lunged, captured the fort, released its seven prisoners, and decapitated the governor. Across France, similar groups took over several key cities. Defeated, the king and nobles accepted the National Assembly as the legislative body of the nation.

Peasants, suspecting that middle-class revolution might not help them, rioted throughout the country, burning nobles' manors, demolishing monasteries and bishops' houses, and killing nobles who resisted. Panicked, the Assembly swiftly ended tithes, serfdom, corvée, monopolies, and nobles' prerogatives and issued the Declaration of the Rights of Man and of the Citizen. This declaration proclaimed that sovereignty lay in the people, who have the right to depose governments that abuse their power. Asserting citizens' natural rights to property, liberty, security, and to resist oppression, it decreed freedom of speech, religion, and the press inviolable and guaranteed citizens equal treatment in court and freedom from imprisonment, except after due process of law. Women were not citizens, so were omitted in this document: but they now demanded direct democracy, the right to join the National Guard and to recall unpopular deputies, and they protested that suffrage depended on wealth. They gathered in their neighborhoods, agitating for direct democracy; they spoke at meetings and organized marches.

In October, the market women woke to a Paris without bread. They thronged to the streets, then marched to the Hôtel de Ville (City Hall). Forcibly barring men, they hunted for ammunition and for administrative records, swearing that all the revolution had accomplished so far was paper work. Proclaiming they had the power and the right of insurrection, they drummed the *générale* (a military call to arms) to recruit other women. Responding to the tocsin declaring an insurrection in progress, thousands marched to the Champs Élysées, where an observer saw "detachments of women coming up from every direction, armed with broomsticks, lances, pitchforks, swords, pistols and muskets." Led by drummers, they marched the twelve miles (19 kilometers) to Versailles to protest directly to the king.

They broke through the palace gates, demanding that the king hear them and return to the city. A group of women granted an audience with Louis conveyed his avowed good intentions. The mass of women in the courtyard forced them to go back and get his signature on a document promising bread in Paris. It took Louis a day to agree to sign and the women triumphantly escorted the royal family to Paris, led by a National Guard sympathetic to them. But Louis broke his promise. Paris officials decreed martial law after a group of women lynched a baker for reserving bread for Assembly deputies, while others exposed hundreds of deputies who sold out the public good for private interest. Six months later, market woman Reine Audu went to prison for a year for leading the march.

In November the National Assembly ordered church lands to be confiscated and used as collateral for paper money it hoped would solve the economic crisis. It put the French church under state control in 1790, making priests and bishops elected by "the people" subject to state law and paid from the public treasury. Women, relegated to the galleries of assemblies, yelled their demands. Their revolutionary clubs exerted strong pressure on men's political clubs, which were the equivalent of political parties. In 1791 the Dutch revolutionary Etta Palm addressed the

National Assembly, urging equal education for girls and equal rights for women: "You have restored to man the dignity of his being in recognizing his rights," she said; "you will no longer allow woman to groan beneath an arbitrary authority."[2]

But the new constitution, while limiting the monarchy, gave most of the power to rich men. It granted civil rights to all *citoyens* (male citizens), but extended suffrage only to men who paid a given minimum in taxes. About half of adult Frenchmen owned enough property to qualify to vote for electors, department officials, and legislative delegates. The constitution ignored women.

Prices fluctuated, though they were usually on the rise. Women rioted, demanding cheaper bread and an end to inflation; they looted, petitioned as *citoyennes* for the right to bear arms, and demanded the overthrow of the government. The king dithered, and the queen wrote to her brother, Leopold II of Austria, asking for his help to escape from France and for support from the other European monarchies for a counter-revolution. In June 1791 the royal family tried to flee from France but was caught at the border in Varennes and brought back to Paris. The bourgeoisie now governed France.

Intellectuals across Europe were jubilant at the toppling of absolutism and privilege; Thomas Paine, for instance, endorsed the revolution in *The Rights of Man* (1791–92). Strikes and rebellions flared elsewhere, as Germans and Belgians imitated the French, but monarchists, aghast at the arrest of a "divine" king, were terrified by fleeing French aristocrats who warned that the revolution might spread. Edmund Burke, a great British orator and politician who had supported the American Revolution, condemned this one as a barbarous crime against the social order. He idealized the French royal family and won sympathy for it throughout Europe. One after another, fearful of revolution at home, nations declared war on France or provoked it to declare war on them: once at war with France, they could define their counterrevolution and repressions as loyalty and patriotism. The French, too, hoped that war would unite the country: the new ruling class, merchants called Girondins (named for a French *département*), hoped it would bolster their shaky hold, while radicals hoped that war losses would discredit the Girondins and sweep their group into power.

The radicals won. When the French army barely resisted Prussian and Austrian armies advancing towards Paris, people believed that the invasion had come at Louis' behest to recoup his absolute power. Incensed, they stormed the palace and killed the royal guards: Louis took refuge in the National Assembly. Radicals overthrew the Paris municipal government, created a revolutionary Commune, and demanded that the Assembly surrender the king and his party. The faction in control, the Jacobins (named for a political club), who were bourgeois like the Girondins but more liberal, supported civil and political equality, universal male suffrage, and state aid to the poor. They held an election to name delegates to a National Convention to draft a new republican constitution, and this convention governed the country for the next three years. But during the election in September 1792, the country was convulsed: massacres occurred in Paris, Lyon, Orleans, and elsewhere; mobs hauled political prisoners before kangaroo courts that condemned them to death, killing over a thousand people in a few days. The convention declared France a republic, condemned the king, and, in January 1793, beheaded him.

By February, Britain, Holland, Spain, and Austria were at war with France. Meanwhile at home, the convention was busy: it reorganized the army; it abolished Christianity, slavery in French colonies, and primogeniture; it banned imprisonment for debt; and it confiscated "enemy" property and broke it into lots to sell cheaply to the poor.

Throughout the turmoil, women were strongly nationalistic; even before the war they asked to bear arms and train with men, and some of them did. A few men singled out for special praise for bravery were even found to be women in disguise. The playwright Olympe de Gouges wrote political tracts praising the revolution and the king; inspired by the Declaration of the Rights of Man, she produced *The Declaration of the Rights of Woman and the Female Citizen*. She demanded education and equal rights in marriage for women, arguing that women with the right to mount the platform to the guillotine had the right to mount political platforms—a sad prophecy of her own fate. Wollstonecraft's *Vindication of the Rights of Women* bolstered their cause in 1792, and in 1792–93 the Republic granted women equal rights to divorce, with custody of infants and daughters, equal inheritance rights, and a share of family property. It later ordered compulsory, free, sexually segregated primary schools for all children, though they were never established. But it did not grant women political rights. Women therefore began to form their own political clubs.

Organized women became a major force in early 1793, when Claire Lacombe and Pauline Léon formed the Society for Revolutionary Republican Women, the first female interest group in Western politics.[3] Hundreds of women joined, some of whom were linked to radical local men, the Enragés. The Society helped to eject the Girondins from the National Convention and pressured it to restrain aristocrats more forcefully, to support the revolutionary army, and to grant women the right to bear arms to fight for France. Asserting not *fraternité* but sisterhood among all members of society, it urged price controls to help poor women. Poor women in turn lobbied the National Convention to lower the price of bread and soap. Instead, the convention adjourned. The women stood in the corridors bitterly complaining, "We are adjourned until Tuesday; but as for us, we adjourn until Monday. When our children ask us for milk, we don't adjourn them until the day after tomorrow."[4] The convention thereupon ordered women to disband the Society.

Claiming a war emergency, the convention deferred introducing universal male suffrage. In its place it named a twelve-man Committee of Public Safety to rule the nation and keep inflation down. The committee was dominated by men who accepted terror as a means of control, including Jean Paul Marat, Georges Jacques Danton, and Maximilien Robespierre. Holding total power, they inevitably saw enemies everywhere and feared overthrow by the Girondins. Danton and Marat launched the Terror, seizing and executing everyone who was said to be counterrevolutionary; Robespierre extended it, killing almost 1300 people in his last six weeks of life. All told, they killed about 20,000 people, and more of them were peasants or laborers than nobles. In the end these three men all died violently: Marat was stabbed by the young Girondin Charlotte Corday, and Danton and Robespierre were guillotined.

Groups of women who supported the Terror patrolled the streets in trousers, with pistols stuck in their belts, and were attacked by the Girondins. In October 1793 the Committee of Public Safety forbade women from political clubs or educational improvement projects, barring them, in effect, from any political activity, even from meeting on the street in small groups. The committee justified this action by blaming women's moral weakness, lack of political education, and nervous excitability in a "full-blown misogynist theory of the biological, psychological, and moral determinants of women's incapacities for political action."[5]

Declaring that "a woman should not leave her family to meddle in the affairs of government," the committee jailed and publicly whipped some women suspected of political action. Among the many they guillotined were Marie Antoinette, Olympe de Gouges (for royalist sympathies), and Manon Roland, the wife of a government minister, who had run a liberal salon. Her crime, Marat said, was influencing her husband. She mounted the scaffold, crying "Liberty, what crimes are committed in thy name!" but newspapers condemned her as a mother who "sacrificed nature by desiring to rise above herself" out of a "desire to be learned." As Wollstonecraft wrote in *Maria*, "women [are] the *outlaws* of the world. Since they are excluded from the law's benefits, they really have no country."

When Robespierre was guillotined, the Terror ended—but so did price controls. Most political thinkers had been executed, and only "moderates" remained—men who were indifferent to poverty. Inflation eroded the Paris poor. Whole families leaped into the Seine, preferring to drown than to starve. The daily bread ration fell from six to four to two ounces. Women demonstrated and rioted. In May 1795 they met in the street, called men from work to follow them, forced shops to close, and marched through the city beating drums to call people to arms. Surging into Convention Hall, they shouted "Bread and the Constitution of 1793!" Many thousands strong, they marched again the next day. The convention temporized, then ordered the army to surround Saint-Antoine, a poor neighborhood at the heart of the revolt, and starve it into submission. The next day it decreed that all women were disturbers of the peace and that they must stay inside their homes: gatherings of more than five would be dispersed by force.

The revolution was over. The political visionaries who had created the Terror were devoured by their own instrument. Only the Girondins tried to continue the war and to control inflation. Undoing the work done by Jacobins, they let the aristocrats return. The middle class, which was now stronger than the aristocracy, continued to oppose capitalist industrial development in France. Bowed by continuing war and money problems, however, they threw the country into the lap of Napoleon. In his fifteen years of rule, despite constant war, he created enduring institutions, including a centralized police and bureaucracy and an educational system. But he reversed every gain women had won. The Napoleonic Code made women noncitizens, subject to fathers and husbands; it barred them from practicing law or being guardians; and it forbade investigation of paternity—henceforth, single mothers were held solely responsible for their offspring and punished severely. Women retained only a right to divorce, but in 1815, when the Bourbons were restored to the throne, women lost that option too.

Yet the French Revolution is a major event in women's history: it represents the first mass protest by women as a caste. Individual women and small groups of women had remonstrated their lot in the past, but never before had large numbers of women protested their treatment by men as a caste to demand political and social rights. Men went on ignoring and resisting their demands for the next 150 years, but after the French Revolution, women were never again silent. Moreover, taking part in the revolution taught women new ideas of popular sovereignty, citizenship, and political legitimacy. The very people who were denied citizenship redefined it.[6]

The sole ground of female solidarity is that women as a caste are oppressed by men. To end their subjection, women must grasp this fact, but male rhetoric is designed to divide them. Dorinda Outram shows how the language of the French Revolution split women and incidentally subverted its own cause.[7] For eighteenth-century French revolutionaries, "virtue," or "the general will," meant masculine reason. Their favorite image of virtue was Brutus the Elder, who put the state above his feelings and family by executing his sons for betraying the Roman Republic. Their favorite image of vice was Marie Antoinette: indeed, they defined monarchy as a structure corrupted by women, blaming Louis' weakness and arrogance on "boudoir politics." To get rid of the monarchy was to get rid of women in politics. (We have noted before that women have power in monarchies because they have power in families. The structure in which they have least power is oligarchy, rule by a group of unrelated men, the form of government that is most common in the world today.)

Marie Antoinette was tried in 1793 for plotting the invasion of France and abetting the king's flight to Varennes, but also for sexual perversion and incest, for supposedly sexually corrupting the Dauphin, the heir to France, and corrupting the body politic as she had corrupted the body of her son. Blaming women for the power and abuses of the *ancien régime,* revolutionaries used an anti-female rhetoric that absolved men from responsibility for the monarchy's weakness or its overthrow.

The American and French revolutions were "modern" wars in that leaders had to persuade masses of people of the rightness of their cause. French propagandists did so by presenting a complex power struggle as a moral conflict between the powerful, seen as totally evil and contaminating, and the powerless. Such myths imply that a state can function without domination and will if the rebels win. Desirable as such a state might be, there is no structure yet designed that can express it. Whoever wins becomes the new elite; and, lacking a new structure, all elites oppress, using power for private advancement—whatever the rhetoric.

A man who inspired the revolution, Jean-Jacques Rousseau, stirred the world by writing "Man was born free, and everywhere he is in chains."[8] Yet in his novel *Émile*, Rousseau shows his hero, Émile, enriched by education, while his heroine, Sophie, pursues luxury, pleasure, and sexual freedom. The Jacobins accepted Rousseau's idea of virtue, insisting that women be subordinate to men and confined in the domestic sphere (partly to compensate men for losing authority over other men).[9] Men equated chastity, the only virtue of which women were capable, with male virtue—valuing the good of the state above personal or sectional interests—and female sexual freedom with the collapse of the state. Revolution was possible only if women were utterly excluded from power.

Women who wanted a political voice, who refused to be excluded, had trouble finding language in a male revolutionary discourse. Men defined women's role in the revolution as teaching their children "to speak the male language of liberty." Male revolutionaries regularly contrasted the good of the state with women's sphere of home and family. To defend nutritive values, they said, was to be against revolution. This conflict came to a head when the Committee of Public Safety abolished Christianity because its rhetoric expressed different values.

The Catholic Church controlled education in France, and the parish church was central to the lives of the people, who respected and deferred to their curés. Despite its greed, elitism, and exploitation of the common folk, the church exalted nurture and valued the contribution of women. Counterrevolution therefore thrived in rural France among women. As Dorinda Outram points out, the church offered the only other discourse available in the period. Revolutionary discourse excluded women; the discourse of religion exalted their sacrifice, humility, and love. Since women who opposed the revolution used religious language, women were identified with conservative anti-revolutionary doctrines.

In later decades, Rousseau's ideas were the bases of campaigns urging French (and English and American) women to become good mothers and to nurse their babies. Female novelists swallowed the new program, making their heroines models of virtue and domesticity. Yet they also stretched the role, defying cultural mores by writing and arguing for women's education and dignity in work. Germaine Necker (Mme de Staël) used her salon to foster intellectual and political opposition to Napoleon, and was damned as a "mannish" hermaphrodite and exiled. Revolutionary women's actions, Wollstonecraft's *Vindication of the Rights of Women*, and women's continuing interruption into public debate horrified men on both sides of the Atlantic. Edmund Burke associated feminism with political radicalism and damned it as derived from "the revolutionary harpies of France, sprung from night and hell."[10]

AFTERWORD

THE FRENCH REVOLUTION marked a change in human affairs. Whether that change had occurred in people in general or in a critical mass, ordinary men and women began to believe they had some control over their lives and were entitled to a voice in society. The nineteenth and twentieth centuries are rife with efforts at radical change—peaceful attempts to build utopian communities, the forming of political parties proposing experiments in social structure, and major uprisings and rebellions worldwide. Western women were exceedingly vocal in demanding that any social change alter their situation, and the idea that women's lives had to be improved was implicit in most European proposals. Even men who essentially ignored women's particularities, like Karl Marx (although not Frederick Engels), were aware of women's plight.

The fact is that European and American women were more powerless in the nineteenth century than they had ever been throughout history. Local traditions, which had often granted women some small right, were now subsumed in national law, under which women were mainly invisible. In Europe and the Americas, women were property, men's slaves, although rhetoric granted them the status of angels. For most women, life was hard to impossible, since they lacked economic rights. Planners of utopias tried to ameliorate women's lives in their schemes, but few seemed to notice how much women's labor underlay men's work and living arrangements. The only utopian communities that gave women political power equally were those founded by women.

Consequently, women found they had to start a movement of their own. Earlier women's movements had focused primarily on a religion, the abolition of slavery, temperance, or socialism infused with women's passion for their own liberation, but in 1848 some American women decided to slough off other causes and fight for themselves. They were followed by movements in England, Germany, and eventually, in the later twentieth century, the entire world.

The third and final volume in this history focuses on the nineteenth and twentieth centuries and represents a shift in tone. Because so little was recorded about women, most of what we know about them in early periods comes from men's laws constricting them, records of law courts, and an occasional preserved letter or diary. After the French Revolution, women become the authors of their own lives, speaking and writing publicly, acting for themselves, and recording their participation in revolutions and political movements. No longer must the historian describe them as primarily acted upon, but as actors in their own play. Consequently, the tone of this work can shift to a guarded optimism, and even exhilaration, at being able to hope for the future.

NOTES

INTRODUCTION

1 It is often the mother-in-law who actually performs the murder.

2 Frans de Waal is the leading expert on chimpanzee society. See *Chimpanzee Politics* (New York: Harper & Row, 1982); *Good Natured* (Cambridge, Mass.: Harvard University Press, 1996); *Our Inner Ape* (New York, N.Y.: Riverhead Books, 2006).

3 This information comes from Jane Goodall. See *In The Shadow of Man* (Boston: Houghton Mifflin, 1971), *The Chimpanzees of Gombò Cambridge* (Mass.: Belknap Press of the Harvard University Press, 1986); *Through a Window* (London: Weidenfeld & Nicolson, 1990).

4 Frans de Waal, *Primates and Philosophers* (Princeton, N.J: Princeon University Press, 2006).

5 For descriptions of these cultures, see Richard B. Lee and Irven deVore, ed., *Kalahari Hunter Gatherers* (Cambridge, Mass; Harvard University Press, 1981), Colin Turnbull, *The Forest People* (New York: Simon & Schuster, 1961); and Richard A. Gould, *Yiwara* (New York: Scribner, 1969).

6 Some of their marvelous sculptures are on exhibit in the Archaeological Museum in Konya.

7 Catal Hüyük was discovered and described by James Mellaart. See his Catal Hüyük, *A Neolithic Toiwn in Anatolia* (New York: McGraw-Hill, 1967)

8 Even as late as the composition of the Jacob cycle of stories in Genesis, the writer did not understand how young were conceived, and imagines conception in sheep is influenced by what the ewe sees as it drinks.

9 For the political ramifications of religious prejudice against women, see my *The War Against Women*.

10 Ann Jones, *Winter in Kabul* (New York: Picador, 2006).

CHAPTER 1

1 Biographies of Eleanor of Aquitaine include Marion Meade, *Eleanor of Aquitaine: A Biography* (New York: Hawthorne Books, 1977), and R. Pernoud, *Eleanor of Aquitaine* (London: R. Hale, 1977).

2 Susan Stuard, "The Dominion of Gender: Women's Fortunes in the High Middle Ages," in *Becoming Visible: Women in European History*, ed. Renate Bridenthal, Claudia Koonz, and Susan Stuard (Boston: Houghton Mifflin, 1987).

3 *A History of Their Own*, ed. Bonnie S. Anderson and Judith P. Zinsser (New York: Harper & Row, 1988).

4 Christiane Klapisch-Zuber, *Women, Family and Inheritance in Renaissance Florence*, trans. Lydia Cochrane (Chicago: University of Chicago Press, 1985).

5 Barbara Hanawalt, *The Ties That Bound: Peasant Families in Medieval England* (New York: Oxford University Press, 1986).

6 Eileen Power, *Medieval People* (Garden City, NY: Doubleday, 1954).

7 Jo Ann McNamara, personal communication.

8 Hanawalt, *The Ties That Bound*.

9 McNamara, personal communication.

10 Asunción Lavrin describes seventeenth- and eighteenth-century beguinages in Mexico City that became great banking institutions, investing in property, loans, and mortgages at 5 percent. Lavrin, "Women in Convents: Their Economic and Social Role in Colonial Mexico," in *Liberating Women's History*, ed. Berenice A. Carroll (Urbana: University of Illinois Press, 1976).

11 Works by women like Tibors, Clara d'Anduza of Languedoc, Alamanda, and Beatriz, Countess of Dia, are collected and available. See Meg Bogin, *The Women Troubadours* (New York: W.W. Norton, 1976).

12 See Joan Kelly-Gadol, "Did Women Have a Renaissance?" in *Becoming Visible*, ed. Bridenthal, Koonz, and Stuard.

13 For further information about Joan of Arc, see Frances Gies, *Joan of Arc: The Legend and the Reality* (New York: Harper & Row, 1981); Régine Pernoud, *Joan of Arc, by Herself and Her Witnesses*, trans. Edward Hyams (London: MacDonald, 1964); and Ingvald Raknem, *Joan of Arc in History, Legend, and Literature* (Oslo: Universitets-forlaget, 1971).

14 Stuard, "The Dominion of Gender."

15 This sentence was later commuted to three beatings because of her age and misery. Margaret Wade LaBarge, *A Small Sound of the Trumpet: Women in Medieval Life* (Boston: Beacon Press, 1986).

16 Stuard, "The Dominion of Gender."

17 Ibid.

18 Ibid.

19 Linda Mitchell was my research assistant on medieval women, and Christine Gailey consulted on Germanic and Celtic peoples for this section. Sources not already cited in the text are A. Abram, "Women Traders in Medieval London," *Economic Journal* (London) 26 (June 1916): 276–85; *Women from the Greeks to the French Revolution*, ed. Susan Groag Bell (Stanford: Stanford University Press, 1973); William Boulting, *Women in Italy* (London: Methuen, 1910); Kathleen Casey, "The Cheshire Cat: Reconstructing the Experience of Medieval Women," in *Liberating Women's History*, ed. Carroll; Stanley Chojnacki, "Dowries and Kinsmen in Early Renaissance Italy," in *Women in Medieval Society*, ed. Susan Stuard (Philadelphia: University of Pennsylvania Press, 1976); Alice Clark, *Working Life of Woman in the Seventeenth Century* (1919; New York: A.M. Kelley, 1968); Barbara Ehrenreich and Deirdre English, *For Her Own Good* (Garden City, NY: Doubleday, 1979); Christine Faure, "Absent from History," trans. Lillian S. Robinson, *Signs* 7, 1 (1981): 71–86; Viola Klein, "The Historical Background," in *Women: A Feminist Perspective*, ed. Jo Freeman (Palo Alto, Cal.: Mayfield, 1979); Paul Lacroix, *A History of Prostitution*, trans. Samuel Putnam (New York: Covici-Friede, 1926); Ernest W. McDonnell, *Beguines and Beghards in Medieval Culture* (New Brunswick, NJ: Rutgers University Press, 1954); Jo Ann McNamara and Suzanne F. Wemple, "The Power of Women through the Family in Medieval Europe: 500–1100," in *Clio's Consciousness Raised*, ed. Mary S. Hartman and Lois Banner (New York: Harper & Row, 1974); Jo Ann McNamara, "Victims of Progress: Women and the 'Civilizing' of Europe," St. Gertrude's Symposium, Copenhagen, Denmark, August 1986; E. William Monter, "The Pedestal and the Stake: Courtly Love and Witchcraft," in *Becoming Visible*, ed. Bridenthal and Koonz (1977 edition); Viana Muller, "Kin Reproduction and Elite Accumulation in the Archaic States of Northwest Europe," in *Power Relations and State Formation*, ed. Thomas C. Patterson and Christine W. Gailey (Washington, DC: American Anthropological Association, 1987); Julia O'Faolain and Lauro Martines, *Not in God's Image* (London: Temple Smith, 1973); Mosei Ostrogarski, *The Rights of Women* (New York: Scribner's, 1893); Eileen Power, "The Position of Women," in *The Legacy*

of the Middle Ages, ed. C.G. Crump and E.F. Jacob (Oxford: Clarendon Press, 1962); Doris Mary Stenton, *The English Woman in History* (New York: Schocken Books, 1977); Laurence Stone, *The Family, Sex, and Marriage, 1500–1800* (New York: Harper & Row, 1977); *Women in Medieval Society*, ed. Susan Stuard (Philadelphia: University of Pennsylvania Press, 1976); Keith Thomas, *Religion and the Decline of Magic* (New York: Scribner's, 1971); Suzanne F. Wemple, "Sanctity and Power: The Dual Pursuit of Medieval Women," in *Becoming Visible*, ed. Bridenthal, Koonz, and Stuard.

CHAPTER 2

1 After millennia, these communities are being wiped out by economic exploitation by male-dominated fishing associations and a new dependence on wet suits, which produce a painful muscular condition that is treated with addictive painkilling drugs. See Georgia Dullea, "In male-dominated Korea, an island of sexual equality," *New York Times*, July 9, 1987. The women are paid so little for their dangerous work that daughters are deserting their mothers' skill to farm, which is easier and better paid.

2 The word for empress—*nakatsu-sumera-mikoto*—may be translated as "the august medium who transmits the mi-koto of the heavenly kami" (mi-koto = divine word; kami = sacred spirits, female, male, or neuter, animal, vegetable, or mineral; Shintoism is "the way of the kami"). Later, empress is translated as "one who carries on the imperial duty between the death of her husband and the accession of the next emperor."

3 Karen A. Smyers, "Women and Shinto: The Relation between Purity and Pollution," *Japanese Religions* 12, 4 (1983): 7–18.

4 Carol Hochstedler, a consultant on Japan for this project. She is the author of *The Tale of Nazame* (Ithaca: Cornell University East Asian Papers, 1979).

5 Joyce Ackroyd, "Women in Feudal Japan," *Transactions of the Asiatic Society of Japan*, Third Series, 7 (November 1959): 31–68.

6 Ackroyd, personal communication.

7 Ackroyd, "Women in Feudal Japan."

8 From Mi no Katami, c. 1427.

9 Basil Hall Chamberlain, *Things Japanese* (London: John Murray, 1905).

10 Hochstedler, personal communication.

11 Sources not listed in the notes above include W.G. Aston, *Nihongi: Chronicles of Japan from the Earliest Times to A.D. 697* (Rutland, Vt: Tuttle, 1972); *Kojiki*, material on Japanese myth from Donald Philippi (Tokyo: University of Tokyo Press, 1969); and Sharon L. Sievers, "Women in China, Japan, and Korea," in *Restoring Women to History*, ed. Renate Bridenthal, Claudia Koonz, and Susan Stuard (Bloomington, Ind.: Organization of American Historians, 1988). For Japanese verse, see Geoffrey Bownas and Anthony Thwaite, *The Penguin Book of Japanese Verse* (London: Penguin Books, 1964). For further information on *The Great Learning for Women*, see Basil Hall Chamberlain, *Things Japanese* (London: John Murray, 1905). Also consulted were Enchi Fumiko, *Nihon joseishi jiten* [Dictionary of Japanese Women's History] (Tokyo: Sanseido, 1984); Jonathan Norton Leonard, *Early Japan* (New York: Time-Life Books, 1968); Ivan Morris, *The World of the Shining Prince: Court Life in Ancient Japan* (New York: Alfred A. Knopf, 1964); and George Sansom, *A History of Japan, 1334-1615* (Stanford, Cal.: Stanford University Press, 1961).

CHAPTER 3

1 Sven Lindqvist, *Exterminate All the Brutes* (New York: The New Press, 1996), points out that the Chinese discovered gunpowder in the tenth century and cast a cannon in the mid-thirteenth, but never attempted to use these weapons. In contrast, sixteenth-century Europe, backward and poor, "acquired a monopoly on ocean-going ships with guns capable of spreading death and destruction across huge distances." The unique feature of cannon was to kill before an enemy's weapons could return the fire.

2 Carolyn Merchant, *The Death of Nature: Women, Ecology and the Scientific Revolution* (New York: Harper & Row, 1979).

3 Natalie Zemon Davis, *Society and Culture in Early Modern France* (Stanford, Cal.: Stanford University Press, 1975).

4 E. William Monter, "Protestant Wives, Catholic Saints, and the Devil's Handmaid: Women in the Age of Reformations," in *Becoming Visible: Women in European History*, ed. Renate Bridenthal, Claudia Koonz, and Susan Stuard (Boston: Houghton Mifflin Co., 1987).

5 Davis, *Society and Culture*.

6 Ibid.

7 John Gillis, *For Better, For Worse: British Marriages 1600 to the Present* (New York: Oxford University Press, 1985).

8 Ibid.

9 Alan J. Macfarlane, *Love and Marriage* (Cambridge: Cambridge University Press, 1986).

10 Michael MacDonald, *Mystical Bedlam* (Cambridge: Cambridge University Press, 1981).

11 Michel Foucault calls the workhouse "a central instrument of stabilization in the bourgeois absolute state."

12 Paul Lacroix, *History of Prostitution*, trans. Samuel Putnam (New York 1931), 861.

13 Davis, *Society and Culture.*

14 The entire text of the *Malleus Maleficarum* is available in Alan C. Kors and Edward Peters, *Witchcraft in Europe, 1100–1700: A Documentary History* (Philadelphia: University of Pennsylvania Press, 1972).

15 Keith Thomas, *Religion and the Decline of Magic* (New York: Scribner's, 1971).

16 Ibid.

17 Monter, "Protestant Wives," and "The Pedestal and the Stake: Courtly Love and Witchcraft," in *Becoming Visible*, ed. Bridenthal, Koonz, and Stuard (1977 edition).

18 Olwen Hufton, "Early Modern Europe," *Past and Present* 101 (November 1983): 125–40.

19 Glückel of Hameln, *Memoirs*, trans. Marvin Lowenthal, intro. Robert S. Rosen (New York: Schocken Books, 1977).

20 Richard T. Vann, "Towards a New Lifestyle: Women in Preindustrial Capitalism," in *Becoming Visible,* ed. Bridenthal, Koonz, and Stuard (1977 edition).

21 For a more detailed survey of woman scholars and writers of this period, see Bonnie S. Anderson and Judith P. Zinsser, *A History of Their Own: Women in Europe from Prehistory to the Present* (New York: Harper & Row, 1988).

22 See Louise Labé, *Sonnets*, trans. Graham Dunstan Martin, Edinburgh Bilingual Library 7 (Austin: University of Texas Press, 1972).

23 Tilde A. Sankovitch, *French Women Writers and the Book* (Syracuse, NY: Syracuse University Press, 1988).

24 Carolyn C. Lougee, *Le Paradis des Femmes: Women, Salons, and Social Stratification in Seventeenth-Century France* (Princeton: Princeton University Press, 1976).

25 Elizabeth Fox-Genovese, "Women and the Enlightenment," in *Becoming Visible*, ed. Bridenthal, Koonz, and Stuard.

26 Claudia Koonz was consultant for this segment. Besides the sources noted above, I used the following texts: *Connecting Spheres: Women in the Western World, 1500 to Present*, ed. Marilyn J. Boxer and Jean H. Quataert (New York: Oxford University Press, 1987); Angeline Goreau, *Reconstructing Aphra* (New York: Dial Press, 1980); *Women and Work in Preindustrial Europe,* ed. Barbara Hanawalt (Bloomington: Indiana University Press, 1986); Sarah Hanley, "Family and State in Early Modern France: The Marriage Pact," in *Connecting Spheres*, ed. Boxer and Quataert; Olwen Hufton and Frank Tallett, "Communities of Women, the Religious Life, and Public Service in Eighteenth-Century France," in *Connecting Spheres*, ed. Boxer and Quataert; Joan Kelly-Gadol, "Did Women Have a Renaissance?" in *Becoming Visible*, ed. Bridenthal, Koonz, and Stuard, and "Early Feminist Theory and the Querelle des Femmes, 1400–1789," *Signs* 8, 1 (1982): 4–28; Christiane Klapisch-Zuber, *Women, Family, and Ritual in Renaissance Italy*, trans. Lydia Cochrane (Chicago: University of Chicago Press, 1985); Abby Kleinbaum, "Women in the Age of Light," in *Becoming Visible*, ed. Bridenthal, Koonz, and Stuard (1977 edition); Steven Ozment, *When Fathers Ruled* (Cambridge, Mass.: Harvard University Press, 1983); Joan Wallach Scott, "The Modern Period," *Past and Present* 101 (November 1983): 141–57; Doris Stenton, *The English Woman in History* (New York: Macmillan, 1957); Merry Wiesner, "Women's Work in the Changing City Economy, 1500–1650," in *Connecting Spheres*, ed. Boxer and Quataert; Sherrin Marshall Wyntjes, "Women in the Reformation Era," in *Becoming Visible*, ed. Bridenthal, Koonz, and Stuard (1977 edition).

CHAPTER 4

1 There are five language sets in Africa today; they include the following languages:

Afro Asiatic: Amhara, Arabic, Beja, Berber, Hausa, Galla, Somali, and Tuareg. Area: North Africa, and the Horn of Africa to Uganda and Kenya.

Nilotic: Dinka, Luo, Maasai, and Nuer. Area: one area of east Africa.

Khoisan: Khoi Khoi and the San peoples of South Africa. These speakers were largely exterminated by whites in the seventeenth and eighteenth centuries.

Bantu: Knogo, Herero, Bemba, Yao, Swahili, Nyamwezi, Ganda, Kikuyu, and Zulu. Area: most peoples of southern Africa.

Malagasy: related to Southeast Asian languages, and spoken on islands in the Indian Ocean.

Other: West Africa and North-Central Africa have distinct languges: Mene, Wolof, Malinke, Fulani, Mossi, Akan, Yoruba, Kanuri, Fur, Nuba, Banda, and Azande.

2   Marcia Wright was a consultant on Africa for this project.

3   Jeanne K. Henn, "Women in the Rural Economy: Past, Present, and Future," in *African Women South of the Sahara*, ed. Margaret Jean Hay and Sharon Stichter (New York: Longman, 1984).

4   Niara Sudarkasa, "The Status of Women in Indigenous African Societies," *Feminist Studies* 12, 1 (1986): 91–103.

5   John K. Thornton, *The Kingdom of Kongo: Civil War and Transition, 1641-1718* (Madison: University of Wisconsin Press, 1983).

6   Marjorie Mbilinyi, personal communication. Mbilinyi was a consultant to this project.

7   David Sweetman, *Women Leaders in African History* (London: Heinemann, 1984).

8   Ibid.

9   Rosalyn Terborg-Penn, "Women and Slavery in the African Diaspora: A Cross-Cultural Approach to Historical Analysis," *Sage* 3, 2 (1986): 11–15.

10 Marcia Wright, personal communication, 1986.

11 In 1983 a United Nations mission to Mauritania found 100,000 blacks still enslaved to Arabs; the last public auction of slaves in Mauritania, where slaves are still sold privately, occurred in 1978; males cost R177, and females capable of reproducing, R3550.

12 Marie Perinbaum described this myth in a lecture given at Spelman College in Atlanta, Georgia, in 1969. It is cited by Joyce A. Ladner, "Racism and Tradition: Black Womanhood in Historical Perspective," in

Liberating Women's History, ed. Berenice A. Carroll (Urbana: University of Illinois Press, 1976), 182.

13 Marjorie Mbilinyi, "Wife, Slave and Subject of the King: The Oppression of Women in the Shambala Kingdom," *Tanzania Notes and Records* 88–89 (1982).

14 Robin Law, "Dahomey and the Slave Trade: Reflections on the Historiography of the Rise of Dahomey," *Journal of African History* 27 (1986): 237–67, and "Slave-Raiders and Middlemen, Monopolists and Free-Traders: The Supply of Slaves for the Atlantic Trade in Dahomey c. 1715–1850," *Journal of African History* 30 (1989): 45–68.

15 I.A. Akinjogbin, *Dahomey and Its Neighbors, 1708–1818* (Cambridge: Cambridge University Press, 1967).

16 Karl Polanyi with Abraham Rotstein, *Dahomey and the Slave Trade: An Analysis of an Archaic Economy* (Seattle: University of Washington Press, 1966).

17 Christine Gailey, personal communication; Gailey was a consultant to this project on Dahomey.

18 Edna G. Bay, "Servitude and Worldly Success in the Palace of Dahomey," in *Women and Slavery in Africa*, ed. Claire Robertson and Martin Klein (Madison: Wisconsin: University of Wisconsin Press, 1983).

19 Thomas Birch Freeman, in a typescript for the Methodist Missionary Society Archives, n.d., cited by Bay, "Servitude," 359.

20 E. Chaudoin, *Trois mois de captivit au Dahomey* (Paris, 1891), cited by Bay, "Servitude," 358.

21 In addition to Marcia Wright, Christine Gailey, and Marjorie Mbilinyi, Susan Hall was a consultant for this section. Sources not already noted in the text are Susan Herlin Broadhead, "Slave Wives, Free Sisters: Bakongo Women and Slavery c. 1700–1850," in *Women and Slavery in Africa*, ed. Robertson and Klein; George E. Brooks, "African 'Landlords' and European 'Strangers': African-European Relations to 1870," in *Africa*, ed. Phyllis M. Martin and Patrick O'Meara (Bloomington: Indiana University Press, 1986); Graham Connah, *African Civilizations: Precolonial Cities and States in Tropical Africa: An Archaeological Perspective* (Cambridge: Cambridge University Press, 1987); *Women in Africa: Studies in Social and Economic Change*, ed. Nancy J. Hafkin and Edna G. Bay (Stamford, Cal.: Stamford University Press, 1976); *African Women South of the Sahara*, ed. Margaret Jean Hay and Sharon Stichter (New

York: Longman, 1984); M. Kwamena-Poh et al., *African History in Maps* (London: Longman, 1982); *Slavery in Africa: Historical and Anthropological Perspectives*, ed. Suzanne Miers and Igor Kopytoff (Madison: University of Wisconsin Press, 1977); Christine Qunta, "Outstanding African Women, 1500 BC–1900 AD," in *Women in Southern Africa*, ed. Christine Qunta (London: Allison & Busby, 1987); *Women and Slavery in Africa*, ed. Robertson and Klein; Karen Sachs, *Sisters and Wives: The Past and Future of Sexual Equality* (Westport, Conn: Contributions in Women's Studies 10, 1979).

CHAPTER 5

1   Howard Zinn writes that what Columbus did to the Arawak of the Bahamas, Cortés did to the Aztec of Mexico, Pizarro to the Inca of Peru, and English settlers of Virginia and Massachusetts to Powhatans and Pequots. See Zinn, *A People's History of the United States* (New York: Harper & Row, 1980).

2   Ibid.

3   Tzvetan Todorov, *The Conquest of America* (New York: Harper & Row, 1984).

4   Ibid. This remark was reported by Columbus' son, Ferdinand.

5   Cited by Todorov, *The Conquest of America*, 47–49.

6   Fray Bartolomé de Las Casas, *History of the Indies* (1552).

7   Cortés had three Mexican lovers besides Malintzin, a Spanish wife in Cuba who died in 1522, and a lover who bore him a daughter but whom he abandoned in Cuba. On returning to Spain in 1530, he was ennobled and married Doña Francisca de la Cueva, a young virgin and the niece of a duke, who went with him to Guatemala to share his duties as captain-general.

8   Juan Bautista Pomar, *Relación de Texcoco* (1582).

9   The first plague, smallpox, was brought by one of Narváez' soldiers.
    Because Indians had no remedy for smallpox, wrote Motolinía, and had the bad habit of bathing frequently, whether well or ill (unlike Europeans), they died in heaps like bedbugs. Jonathan Kandell notes in *La Capital: The Biography of Mexico City* (New York: Random House, 1986), that Spanish disparagement of bathing brought Indian hygiene down to European levels, making epidemics even more lethal. Some people died of starvation because everyone fell ill at once, leaving no one to

feed or nurse them. Whole families were wiped out, and the stench of bodies was terrible. There were so many dead they could not be buried, and survivors simply razed houses over the dead as tombs.

The second plague were the massive killings during the conquest, especially around Mexico City. The third was a great famine that occurred just after the Spanish took Tenochtitlan. Farmers had to fight in the war and could not sow; the Spaniards destroyed all crops, so even they had trouble finding corn—a situation, Todorov writes, that says everything. The fourth was the *calpixques*, overseers who brutally abused Indians by taking them far from their land and overworking them until many of them died. The fifth plague were the great taxes and tributes. When the people had no gold left, Motolinía writes, they sold their children; when they had no more children, they had nothing to offer but their lives; when these did not suffice, they died, "some under torture and some in cruel prisons, for the Spaniards treated them brutally and considered them less than beasts."

The sixth plague were the gold mines, in which it was "impossible to count the number of Indians who have died." Seventh was the building of the city of Mexico: Indians died during construction, crushed by beams, fallen from heights, caught beneath buildings being torn down, "especially when they tore down the principal temples of the devil." Not only were Indians not paid or fed during this work, but they had to provide the building materials. Since they could not work in construction and in the fields simultaneously, they went hungry, which tended, Todorov remarks, to increase "labor accidents."

The eighth plague was enslavement, used to force Indians to work in the mines. First the Spanish used Aztec slaves, then any who showed signs of insubordination, and finally all they could catch. The ninth plague was the work in the mines: heavily laden Indians had to travel 60 leagues or more from home carrying provisions that were often insufficient, particularly when the workers were kept for several days to remove ore or build houses. "When their food gave out they died, either at the mines or on the road, for they had no money to buy food and there was no one to give it. Some reached home and died soon after." The bodies of those who died in the mines "produced such a stench it caused a pestilence, especially at the mines of Guaxaca. For half a league around the mines and along a great part of the road one could scarcely avoid walking over dead bodies or bones, and flocks of birds and crows came to feed on the corpses and were so numerous they darkened the sun so that many villages along the road were deserted." The tenth and final plague were factions among the Spaniards in Mexico, divisions that spilled over onto Mexicans, whom the Spaniards executed in great numbers.

The consequences, Las Casas wrote, were that "husbands and wives were together only once every eight or ten months and when they met they were so exhausted and depressed on both sides . . . they ceased to procreate. As for the newly born, they died early because their mothers, overworked and famished, had no milk to nurse them, and for this reason, while I was in Cuba, 7000 children died in three months. Some mothers even drowned their babies from sheer desperation . . . husbands died in the mines, wives died at work, and children died from lack of milk. . . . In a short time this land which was so great, so powerful and fertile . . . was depopulated. . . . My eyes have seen these acts so foreign to human nature, and now I tremble as I write." Pregnant women sometimes took herb potions to induce stillbirth.

10 Ann M. Pescatello, "Latina Liberation: Tradition, Ideology, and Social Change in Iberian and Latin American Cultures," *Liberating Women's History*, ed. Berenice A. Carroll (Urbana: University of Illinois Press, 1976).

11 Todorov, *The Conquest of America*.

12 Quoted from Zinn, *A People's History of the United States*.

13 Kandell, *La Capital*.

14 In *Peter Martyr*, VII, 4, the Dominican Tomás Ortiz wrote: "On the mainland they eat human flesh. They are more given to sodomy than any other nation. There is no justice among them. They go naked. They have no respect either for love or for virginity. They are stupid and silly. They have no respect for truth, save when it is to their advantage. They are unstable. They have no knowledge of what foresight means. They are ungrateful . . . changeable . . . brutal. They delight in exaggerating their defects. There is no obedience among them, or deference on the part of the young for the old, nor of the son for the father. They are incapable of learning. Punishments have no effect upon them. . . . They eat fleas, spiders, and worms raw, whenever they find them. They exercise none of the human arts or industries. When taught the mysteries of our religion, they say that these things may suit Castilians, but not them, and they do not wish to change their customs. They are beardless, and if sometimes hairs grow, they pull them out. . . . I may therefore affirm that God has never created a race more full of vice and composed without the least mixture of kindness or culture. . . . The Indians are more stupid than asses."

15 Bartolomé de Las Casas, the Dominican bishop of Chiapas.

16 According to a 1556 letter by Archbishop Montúfar.

17 Personal communication, Ann Farnsworth, Duke University.

18 Rhoda E. Reddock, "Women and Slavery in the Caribbean: A Feminist Perspective," *Latin American Perspectives* 12, 1 (1985): 63–80.

19 Richard Ligon, "A Sugar Plantation in Barbados," from *A True and Exact History of the Island of Barbadoes in Africans Abroad*, ed. Graham Irwin (London: Moseley, 1657; reprint, London: Frank Cass, 1970).

20 Lucille Mathurin, "The Arrival of Black Women," *Jamaica Journal* 9, 2–3 (1975).

21 Barbara Bush, "Towards Emancipation: Slave Women and Resistance to Coercive Labor Regimes in the British West Indian Colonies, 1790–1838," in *Abolition and Its Aftermath: The Historical Context*, ed. David Richardson (London: Frank Cass, 1985).

22 Reddock, "Women and Slavery in the Caribbean."

23 Bush, "Towards Emancipation," and "White 'Ladies', Colored 'Favorites' and Black 'Wenches': Some Considerations on Sex, Race and Class Factors in Social Relations in White Creole Society in the British Caribbean," *Slavery and Abolition* 2, 3 (1981): 245–62.

24 For example, the Carmichaels, who bought an estate in Trinidad, felt so harassed by the resentment, grumbling, and lies of mainly female slaves that they sold it.

25 Bush, "Towards Emancipation."

26 Jean Rhys describes this revolt in *Wide Sargasso Sea* (New York: W.W. Norton, 1992).

27 Bush, "Towards Emancipation."

28 Quoted in Irene Silverblatt, "Andean Women under Spanish Rule," in *Women and Colonization*, ed. Mona Etienne and Eleanor Leacock (New York: Praeger, 1980).

29 James Lockhart, *Spanish Peru, 1532–1556* (Madison: University of Wisconsin Press, 1968).

30 Marysa Navarro, personal communication. Marysa Navarro was a consultant for this section.

31 Bush, "Towards Emancipation."

32 Several poems written by Spanish women of the fifteenth and sixteenth centuries are laments about father-daughter incest.

33 Bush, "Towards Emancipation."

34 The convents were La Encarnación and Santa Catlina.

35 A.J.R. Russell-Wood, "Female and Family in the Economy and Society of Colonial Brazil," in *Latin American Women: Historical Perspectives*, ed. Asunción Lavrin (Westport, Conn.: Greenwood Press, 1978).

36 Maria Dundas Graham, *Journal of a Voyage to Brazil and Residence There during Part of Three Years, 1821, 1822, 1823* (New York: Praeger, 1969).

37 Marysa Navarro, private communication.

38 *A Narrative Compendium of the Pilgrim in America* (1760).

39 Russell-Wood, "Female and Family in the Economy and Society of Colonial Brazil."

40 Kandell, *La Capital.*

41 *A Sor Juana Anthology*, trans. Alan S. Trueblood (Cambridge, Mass.: Harvard University Press, 1989). Octavio Paz is largely responsible for the current re-evaluation of Sor Juana's work, but his interpretation is distorted—like some evaluations of Emily Dickinson—by his insistence that a woman poet's life must have a male center. Paz refuses to accept that Sor Juana probably loved women. For a more balanced view of Sor Juana, see Electa Arenal, "Comment on Paz's Juana Ramirez," *Signs* 5, 3 (1980), and "The Convent as Catalyst for Autonomy," in *Women and Hispanic Literature: Icons and Fallen Idols*, ed. Beth Miller (Berkeley: University of California Press, 1983).

42 Kandell, *La Capital.*

43 Jean Franco was the consultant for this section. Sources not listed above in the notes are Mary Beth Norton et al., *A People and a Nation: A History of the United States* (Boston: Houghton Mifflin Company, 1986); Ann Pescatello, *Power and Pawn: The Female in Iberian Families, Societies, and Cultures* (Westport, Conn.: Greenwood Press, 1976); and Rosalyn Terborg-Penn, "Women and Slavery in the African Diaspora: A Cross-Cultural Approach to Historical Analysis," *Sage* 3, 2 (1986).

CHAPTER 6

1 John White, later governor of Virginia, wrote a history of the colony, with sixty-three watercolor sketches of New World natives, flora, and fauna. See Selma R. Williams, *Demeter's Daughters: The Women Who Founded America, 1587–1787* (New York: Atheneum, 1976).

2 Edmund Morgan, *American Slavery, American Freedom: The Ordeal of Colonial Virginia* (New York: W.W. Norton, 1975).

3 Jan Noel, "New France: Les Femmes Favorisées," *Atlantis* 6, 2 (1981): 80–98.

4 Williams, *Demeter's Daughter*.

5 Carol Devens, "Separate Confrontations: Gender as a Factor in Indian Adaptation to European Colonization in New France," *American Quarterly* 38, 3 (1986): 461–80.

6 Kirsten Fischer, personal communication, June 1990.

7 The Dutch also imported three African women in 1628.

8 Williams, *Demeter's Daughter*, cites the oath: "I do further swear I will not . . . trouble, molest, or discountenance any person whatsoever in the said province professing to believe in Jesus Christ, and in particular no Roman Catholic, for or in respect of his or her religion, nor his or her free exercise thereof within the said province, so that they be not unfaithful to his said Lordship or molest or conspire against the civil government established under him."

9 Alice Kessler-Harris, *Women Have Always Worked* (Old Westbury, NY: The Feminist Press, 1981).

10 A servant taken to Virginia against her will wrote that she had pulled plow and cart, carried faggots on her back, was starving, clad in clothes worn thin, and slept on a bed made of straw. She laments:

Since that I first came to this Land of Fame
Which is called Virginny, O,
The Ax and the Hoe have wrought my overthrow,
When that I was weary, weary, weary, O.

For the complete poem, see *Root of Bitterness: Documents of the Social History of American Women*, ed. Nancy Cott (New York: E.P. Dutton, 1972), 31.

11 Julia Cherry Spruill, *Women' s Life and Work in the Southern Colonies* (New York: W.W. Norton, 1972).

12 Francis Jennings, *Empire of Fortune: Crowns, Colonies and Tribes in the Seven Years War in America* (New York: W.W. Norton, 1988). William Bradford, governor of Plymouth colony, wrote: "Those that scaped the fire were slaine with the sword; some hewed to peeces, others rune throw

with their rapiers, so as they were quickly dispatchte, and very few escaped. It was conceived they thus destroyed about 400 at this time. It was a fearful sight to see them thus frying in the fyer, and the streams of blood quenching the same, and horrible was the stincke and sente there of, but the victory seemed a sweete sacrifice, and they gave the prayers thereof to God, who had wrought so wonderfully for them, thus to inclose their enemise in their hands, and give them so speedy a victory over so proud and insulting an enimie." William Bradford, *History of the Plymouth Plantation, 1620–1646*, ed. William T. Davis (New York: Charles Scribner's Sons, 1908).

13 Russell Bourne, *The Red King's Rebellion: Racial Politics in New England, 1675–1678* (New York: Atheneum, 1990).

14 Sylvia Van Kirk, *Many Tender Ties: Women in Fur Trade Society in Western Canada, 1700–1850* (Norman: University of Oklahoma Press, 1983).

15 The historian was the nineteenth-century William Fowler, *Woman on the American Frontier* (1878).

16 Laurel Ulrich, *Good Wives: Image and Reality in the Lives of Women in Northern New England* (New York: Oxford University Press, 1982).

17 Williams, *Demeter's Daughters*.

18 Gerda Lerner, *The Majority Finds Its Past: Placing Women in History* (Oxford: Oxford University Press, 1979).

19 Edmund S. Morgan, *The Puritan Family: Religion and Domestic Relations in 17th-Century New England* (New York: Harper & Row, 1966).

20 Marylynn Salmon, *Women and the Law of Property in Early America* (Chapel Hill: University of North Carolina Press, 1986).

21 Mary Beth Norton, *Founding Mothers and Fathers: Gendered Power and the Forming of American Society* (New York: Alfred A. Knopf, 1996).

22 Ibid., 368.

23 Ibid., 366.

24 Lyle Koehler, "The Case of the American Jezebels: Anne Hutchinson and Female Agitation during the Years of Antinomian Turmoil, 1636–1640," *William and Mary Quarterly* 31 (1974).

25 She had an odd growth, which was later diagnosed by Dr. Paul A. Younge as probably a uterine hydatidiform mole, which often accompanies menopause.

26 Emery Battis, *Saints and Sectaries: Anne Hutchinson and the Antinomian Controversy in the Mass Bay Colony* (Chapel Hill: University of North Carolina Press, 1962).

27 Joan Solomon, " Menopause: A Rite of Massage," *MS.* 1 (1972): 18.

28 Mary Beth Norton, "The Evolution of White Women's Experience in Early America," *American Historical Review* 89, 3 (1984): 593–619.

29 All the material is from Williams, *Demeter's Daughters*.

30 Carol Karlsen, "The Devil in the Shape of a Woman: The Witch in Seventeenth-Century New England" (PhD dissertation, Yale University, 1980).

31 John Demos, *Entertaining Satan: Witchcraft and the Culture of Early New England* (New York: Oxford University Press, 1982).

32 Norton's *Founding Mothers* observes that 73 percent of women charged with witchcraft elsewhere were married, compared with only 52 percent of the Salem accused, a difference caused mainly by the fact that 30 percent of the Salem women were young, most of them related to older suspects.

33 Williams, *Demeter's Daughters*.

34 Edwin J. Perkins, *The Economy of Colonial America* (New York: Columbia University Press, 1988).

35 Norton, *Founding Mothers and Fathers*.

36 Jennings, *Empire of Fortune*.

37 John Trenchard and Thomas Gordon, *Cato's Letters* (1720–23).

38 Daniel Dulany, *Considerations on the Propriety of Imposing Taxes on the British Colonies* (London, 1766).

39 Williams, *Demeter's Daughters*.

40 These female publishers are described ibid.

41 Ruth H. Bloch, "The Gendered Meanings of Virtue in Revolutionary America," *Signs* 13, 1 (1987): 37–58.

42 Noam Chomsky, *World Orders Old and New* (New York: Columbia University Press, 1996), 30–31.

43 Tom Paine, "Occasional Letter on the Female Sex," *Pennsylvania Magazine*, March 1775. Cited by Sally Roesch Wagner, "The Root of

Oppression Is the Loss of Memory: The Iroquois and the Early Feminist Vision," paper delivered at the 1988 Champlain Valley History Symposium, Plattsburgh, NY.

44 Williams, *Demeter's Daughters*, provides comprehensive information on women of accomplishment in all areas of American colonial life.

45 Ibid.

46 Suzanne Lebsock, *A Share of Honor: Virginia Women, 1600–1945* (Richmond: Virginia State Library, 1987).

47 Mary Wollstonecraft's ideas are discussed further in volume 3, chapter 3.

48 Barbara Taylor, *Eve and the New Jerusalem: Socialism and Feminism in the Nineteenth Century* (New York: Pantheon Books, 1983).

49 Ann D. Gordon and Mari Jo Buhle, "Sex and Class in Colonial and Nineteenth-Century America," in *Liberating Women's History*, ed. Berenice A. Carroll (Urbana: University of Illinois Press, 1976).

50 Karin Calvert, "Children in American Family Portraiture, 1670 to 1810," *William and Mary Quarterly* 39 (1982), 111–12.

51 Ruth Bloch, "American Feminine Ideals in Transition: The Rise of the Moral Mother, 1785–1815," *Feminist Studies* 4 (1978): 101–26, writes that in classical republican constitutional theory, a government preserves liberty by sharing powers among levels of society. A free republic was marked by divided powers and an autonomous legislature with taxing power; sustaining it required a large base of arms-bearing freeholders and relatively equal and independent male property owners.

52 Norton, "The Evolution of White Women's Experience."

53 Albert O. Hirschman, *The Passions and the Interests: Political Arguments for Capitalism before Its Triumph* (Princeton, NJ: Princeton University Press, 1977).

54 Nancy Cott, "Eighteenth-Century Family and Social Life Revealed in Massachusetts Divorce Records," *The Journal of Social History* 10 (fall 1976): 20–43.

55 Christine Stansell, *City of Women: Sex and Class in New York, 1789-1860* (New York: Alfred A. Knopf, 1986).

56 Cott, "Eighteenth-Century Family and Social Life Revealed in Massachusetts Divorce Records."

57 Mary Beth Norton et al., *A People and a Nation: A History of the United States* (Boston: Houghton Mifflin Company, 1986).

58 Cott, "Eighteenth-Century Family and Social Life Revealed in Massachusetts Divorce Records."

59 Lebsock, *A Share of Honor.*

60 See Spruill, *Women's Life and Work in the Southern Colonies*, 41.

61 Lisa Norling did research for this section. Other sources not already mentioned in the notes above are Karen Anderson, "Commodity Exchange and Subordination: Montagnais-Naskapi and Huron Women, 1600–1650," *Signs* 11, 1: 48–62; Linda Briggs Biemer, *Women and Property in Colonial New York: The Transition from Dutch to English Law, 1643–1727* (Ann Arbor, Mich.: UMI Research Press, 1983); Judith K. Brown, "Iroquois Women: An Ethnohistoric Note," in *Toward an Anthropology of Women*, ed. Rayna R. Reiter (New York: Monthly Review Press, 1975); *Liberating Women's History: Theoretical and Critical Essays*, ed. Berenice A. Carroll (Urbana: University of Illinois Press, 1976); Lee Virginia Chambers-Schiller, *Liberty, a Better Husband—Single Women in America: The Generations of 1780–1840* (New Haven: Yale University Press, 1984); Linda Grant De Pauw, "Native American Women," in her *Founding Mothers: Women in America in the Revolutionary Era* (Boston: Houghton Mifflin, 1975); *Women and Colonization*, ed. Mona Etienne and Eleanor Leacock (New York: Praeger, 1980); Linda K. Kerber, "Separate Spheres, Female Worlds, Woman's Place: The Rhetoric of Women's History," *Journal of American History* 75, 1 (1988): 9–39; Edmund S. Morgan, *The Puritan Family: Religion and Domestic Relations in 17th Century New England* (New York: Harper & Row, 1966); Mary Beth Norton, "'My Resting Reaping Times': Sarah Osborn's Defense of Her 'Unfeminine' Activities, 1767," *Signs* 2, 2 (1976): 515–29; Edwin J. Perkins, *The Economy of Colonial America* (New York: Columbia University Press, 1988); Peggy Reeves Sanday, *Female Power and Male Dominance* (Cambridge: Cambridge University Press, 1981); Carole Shammas, Marylynn Salmon, and Michel Dahlin, *Inheritance in America from Colonial Times to the Present* (New Brunswick, NJ: Rutgers University Press, 1987).

CHAPTER 7

1 Winthrop D. Jordan, *White over Black* (Chapel Hill: University of North Carolina Press, 1968).

2   Judith Byfield, consultant to this project.

3   Eugene Genovese, *Roll, Jordan, Roll* (New York: Pantheon Books, 1974).

4   See Selma R. Williams, *Demeter's Daughters: The Women Who Founded America, 1587–1787* (New York: Atheneum, 1976).

5   Frederick Cooper, "Islam and Cultural Hegemony: The Ideology of Slaveowners on the East African Coast," in *The Ideology of Slavery in Africa*, ed. P. Lovejoy (Beverly Hills, Cal.: Sage Publications, 1981).

6   Peter Kolchin, *Unfree Labor: American Slavery and Russian Serfdom* (Cambridge, Mass.: Harvard University Press, 1987).

7   Elizabeth Fox-Genovese, *Within the Plantation Household: Black and White Women of the Old South* (Durham: University of North Carolina Press, 1989).

8   Harriet A. Jacobs, *Incidents in the Life of a Slave Girl*, ed. Jean Fagan Yellin (Cambridge, Mass.: Harvard University Press, 1987).

9   Jacqueline Jones, "'My Mother Was Much of a Woman': Black Women, Work, and the Family under Slavery," *Feminist Studies* 8, 2 (1982): 235–69.

10 Cited by Erlene Stetson, "Studying Slavery," in *But Some of Us Are Brave*, ed. Gloria T. Hull, Patricia Bell Scott, and Barbara Smith (Old Westbury, NY: The Feminist Press, 1982).

11 This account appears in the "Unwritten History of Slavery: Autobiographical Accounts of Negro Ex-Slaves," ed. Ophelia Settle Egypt, J. Masuoka, Charles S. Johnson, in Social Science Documents 1 (Nashville, Tenn.: Fisk University, Social Science Institute, 1945), bound typescript, 284–91. It also appears in *Black Women in White America*, ed. Gerda Lerner (New York: Pantheon Books, 1972).

12 Jacobs, *Incidents in the Life of a Slave Girl*.

13 Suzanne Lebsock, *A Share of Honor: Virginia Women, 1600–1945* (Richmond: Virginia State Library, 1987).

14 E. Franklin Frazier, *Black Bourgeoisie* (New York: The Free Press, 1957).

15 Judy Byfield did research for this section. Sources not noted in the text above include *A Documentary History of Slavery in North America*, ed. Willie Lee Rose (New York: Oxford University Press, 1976), containing selections from Frederick Law Olmsted, *A Journey in the Back Country, 1860*; Basil Hall, *Travels in North America in the Years 1827 and 1828*

(Philadelphia: Carey, Lea & Carey, 1829); Solomon Northup, *Twelve Years a Slave: Narrative of Solomon Northup, a Citizen New York, Kidnapped in Washington City in 1841, and Rescued in 1853, from a Cotton Plantation near the Red River in Louisiana* (Auburn, NY: Derby and Miller, 1853); and Emily P. Burke, *Reminiscences of Georgia* (Np: James M. Fitch, 1850); Eleanor Flexner, *Century of Struggle* (Cambridge, Mass.: Harvard University Press, 1980); Lucille Mathurin, "A Historical Study of Women in Jamaica" (PhD dissertation, University of the West Indies Press, 1986); Christine Stansell, review of Elizabeth Fox-Genovese, *Within the Plantation Household, The Nation*, March 27, 1989; Rosalyn Terborg-Penn, "Women and Slavery in the African Diaspora: A Cross-Cultural Approach to Historical Analysis," *Sage* 3, 2 (1986): 11–15; and C. Vann Woodward, "The Lash and the Knout," review of Peter Kolchin, *Unfree Labor: American Slavery and Russian Serfdom, The New York Times Book Review*, November 19, 1987.

CHAPTER 8

1   Both curés are cited by Olwen Hufton, "Women in Revolution 1789–1796," *Past and Present* 53 (November 1971): 93.

2   Richard J. Evans, *The Feminists* (London: Croom Helm, 1977).

3   Darline Gay Levy, Harriet Branson Applewhite, and Mary Johnson, *Women in Revolutionary Paris, 1789–1795* (Urbana: University of Illinois Press, 1979), 62, 75.

4   Bonnie S. Anderson and Judith P. Zinsser, *A History of Their Own* (New York: Harper & Row, 1988).

5   Levy, Applewhite, and Johnson, *Women in Revolutionary Paris.*

6   Ibid.

7   Dorinda Outram, "Le langage mâle de la vertu: Women and the Discourse of the French Revolution," in *The Social History of Language*, ed. Peter Burke and Roy Porter (New York: Cambridge University Press, 1987).

8   Rousseau's long-term lover, Thérèse, bore him four children, whom he took from her and turned over to a foundling home.

9   Elizabeth Fox-Genovese, "Women and the Enlightenment," in Bridenthal, Koonz, and Stuard, *Becoming Visible.*

10 Besides the sources already given in the notes, this discussion is indebted

to Ruth Graham, "Loaves and Liberty: Women in the French Revolution," in Renate Bridenthal, Claudia Koonz, and Susan Stuard, *Becoming Visible: Women in European History* (Boston: Houghton Mifflin, 1987); and Edward NcNall Burns et al., *World Civilizations* (New York: W.W. Norton, 1986).

SELECTED
BIBLIOGRAPHY

Abram, A. "Women Traders in Medieval London." *Economic Journal* 26 (June 1916): 276–85.

Ackroyd, Joyce. "Women in Feudal Japan." *The Transactions of the Asiatic Society of Japan*, Third Series, 7 (Nov. 1959): 31–68.

Addams, Jane. *Twenty Years at Hull House.* First published 1910. New York: Macmillan, 1981.

Akinjogbin, I.A. *Dahomey and Its Neighbors, 1708–1818.* Cambridge: Cambridge University Press, 1967.

Allen, Paula Gunn. *The Sacred Hoop: Recovering the Feminine in American Indian Traditions.* Boston: Beacon Press, 1986.

Anderson, Bonnie S., and Judith P. Zinsser. *A History of Their Own.* New York: Harper & Row, 1988.

Anderson, Karen. "Commodity Exchange and Subordination: Montagnais-Naskapi and Huron Women, 1600–1650." *Signs* 11, 1 (1986): 48–62.

Anton, Ferdinand. *Woman in Pre-Columbian America.* New York: Abner Schram, 1973.

Ardrey, Robert. *African Genesis.* New York: Dell, 1963.

Ayalon, David. *The Mamluk Military Society.* London: Galliard, 1979.

Babatunde, Agiri. "Slavery in Yoruba Society in the 19th Century." *The Ideology of Slavery in Africa,* ed. P. Lovejoy. Berkeley, Cal.: Sage Publications, 1981.

Battis, Emery. *Saints and Sectaries: Anne Hutchinson and the Antinomian Controversy in the Mass Bay Colony.* Chapel Hill: University of North Carolina Press, 1962.

Battuta, Ibn. *The Travels of Ibn Battuta, A.D. 1325–1354*, ed. H.A.R. Gibb. Cambridge: Cambridge University Press, 1962.

Bay, Edna G. "Servitude and Worldly Success in the Palace of Dahomey." In *Women and Slavery in Africa*, ed. Claire Robertson and Martin Klein. Madison: University of Wisconsin Press, 1983.

Berger, Iris. "Women of Eastern and Southern Africa." In *Restoring Women to History*, ed. Renata Bridenthal, Claudia Koonz, and Susan Stuard. Bloomington, Ind.: Organization of American Historians, 1987.

Biemer, Linda Briggs. *Women and Property in Colonial New York: The Transition from Dutch to English Law*. Ann Arbor, Mich.: UMI Research Press, 1983.

Bloch, Ruth H. "American Feminine Ideals in Transition: The Rise of the Moral Mother, 1785–1815." *Feminist Studies* 4 (1978): 101–26.

— "The Gendered Meanings of Virtue in Revolutionary America." *Signs* 13, 1 (1987): 37–58.

Bogin, Meg. *The Women Troubadours*. New York: W.W. Norton, 1976.

Bottigheimer, Ruth B. *The Bible for Children: From the Age of Gutenberg to the Present*. New Haven: Yale University Press, 1996.

Boulting, William. *Women in Italy*. London: Methuen, 1910.

Bourne, Russell. *The Red King's Rebellion: Racial Politics in New England, 1675–1678*. New York: Atheneum, 1990.

Boxer, Marilyn J., and Jean H. Quataert. *Connecting Spheres: Women in the Western World, 1500 to Present*. New York: Oxford University Press, 1987.

Bridenthal, Renate, Claudia Koonz, and Susan Stuard. *Becoming Visible: Women in European History*. Boston: Houghton Mifflin, 1987.

Broadhead, Susan Herlin. "Slave Wives, Free Sisters: Bakongo Women and Slavery c. 1700–1850." In *Women and Slavery in Africa*, ed. Claire Robertson and Martin Klein. Madison: University of Wisconsin Press, 1983.

Brooks, George E., Jr. "African 'Landlords' and European 'Strangers': African-European Relations to 1870." In *Africa*, ed. Phyllis M. Martin and Patrick O'Meara. Bloomington: Indiana University Press, 1986.

— "The Signares of Saint-Louis and Gore: Women Entrepreneurs in Eighteenth-Century Senegal." In *Women in Africa: Studies in Social and Economic Change*, ed. Nancy J. Hafkin and Edna G. Bay. Stanford, Cal.: Stanford University Press, 1976.

Brophy, Julia. "Custody Law, Childcare, and Inequality in Britain." In *Child Custody and the Politics of Gender*, ed. Carol Smart and Selma Sevenhuijzen. New York: Routledge, 1989.

Brown, Judith K. "Iroquois Women: An Ethnohistoric Note." In *Toward an Anthropology of Women*, ed. Rayna R. Reiter. New York: Monthly Review Press, 1975.

Brun-Gulbrandsen, Sverre. "Sex Roles and the Socialization Process." In *The Changing Roles of Men and Women*, ed. Edmund Dahlstrom. London: Duckworth, 1967.

Brundage, Burr Cartwright. *The Fifth Sun*. Austin: University of Texas Press, 1979.

Bullough, V., and B. Bullough. *Sin, Sickness, and Sanity*. New York: The American Library, 1977.

Burke, Emily P. *Reminiscences of Georgia*. First published 1850. Savannah: Beehive Press, 1978.

Burkett, Elinor C. "Indian Women and White Society: The Case of Sixteenth-Century Peru." In *Latin American Women*, ed. Asuncion Lavrin. Westport, Conn.: Greenwood Press, 1988.

Bush, Barbara. "Towards Emancipation: Slave Women and Resistance to Coercive Labor Regimes in the British West Indian Colonies, 1790–1838." In *Abolition and Its Aftermath: The Historical Context*, ed. David Richardson. London: Frank Cass, 1985.

Caldecott, Leonie. "At the Foot of the Mountain: The Shibokusa Women of Japan." In *Keeping the Peace*, ed. Lynn Jones. London: The Women's Press, 1983.

Calvert, Karin. "Children in American Family Portraiture, 1670 to 1810." *William and Mary Quarterly* 39 (1982): 111–12.

Chamberlain, Basil Hall. *Things Japanese*. London: John Murray, 1905.

Chambers-Schiller, Lee Virginia. *Liberty, a Better Husband. Single Women in America: The Generations of 1780–1840*. New Haven: Yale University Press, 1984.

Chomsky, Noam. 1975. *World Orders Old and New*. New York: Columbia University Press, 1996.

Clark, Alice. *Working Life of Woman in the Seventeenth Century*. First published 1919. New York: A.M. Kelley, 1968.

Connah, Graham. *African Civilizations: Precolonial Cities and States in Tropical Africa: An Archaeological Perspective*. Cambridge: Cambridge University Press, 1987.

Cooper, Frederick. "Islam and Cultural Hegemony: The Ideology of Slaveowners on the East African Coast." In *The Ideology of Slavery in Africa*, ed. P. Lovejoy. Beverly Hills, Cal.: Sage Publications, 1981.

Cott, Nancy. "Eighteenth-Century Family and Social Life Revealed in Massachusetts Divorce Records." *The Journal of Social History* 10 (fall 1976): 20–43.

Creevy, Lucy E. "The Role of Women in Malian Agriculture." In *Women Farmers in Africa: Rural Devlopment in Mali and the Sahel*, ed. Lucy E. Creevy. Syracuse, NY: Syracuse University Press, 1986.

Cutrufelli, Maria Rosa. *Women of Africa: Roots of Oppression*. London: Zed Press, 1983.

Davidson, Basil. *The Story of Africa*. London: Mitchell Beazley, 1984.

Davis, Angela Y. *Women, Race, and Class*. New York: Random House, 1981.

— "The Role of Black Women in the Community of Slaves." *The Black Scholar* 3, 4 (1971).

Davis, Fanny. *The Ottoman Lady: A Social History from 1718 to 1918*. Westport, Conn.: Greenwood Press, 1986.

Davis, Natalie Zemon. *Society and Culture in Early Modern France*. Stanford, Cal.: Stanford University Press, 1975.

DeBerg, Betty A. *Ungodly Women: Gender and the First Wave of American Fundamentalism*. Minneapolis: Fortress Press, 1990.

De Pauw, Linda Grant. "Native American Women." In *Founding Mothers: Women in America in the Revolutionary Era*, ed. Linda Grant De Pauw. Boston: Houghton Mifflin, 1975.

De Tott, Baron. *Memoires sur les Turcs et les Tartares*. Paris 1789.

Degler, Carl N. "The Changing Place of Women in America." In *The Woman Question in American History*, ed. Barbara Welter. Hinsdale, Ill.: The Dryden Press, 1973.

Demos, John. *Entertaining Satan: Witchcraft and the Culture of Early New England*. New York: Oxford University Press, 1982.

Devens, Carol. "Separate Confrontations: Gender as a Factor in Indian Adaptation to European Colonization in New France." *American Quarterly* 38, 3 (1986): 461–80.

Douglas, Ann. *The Feminization of American Culture*. New York: Alfred A. Knopf, 1977.

Dulany, Daniel. *Considerations on the Propriety of Imposing Taxes on the British Colonies*. London: Reprinted for J. Almon, 1766.

Duley, Margot I., and Mary I. Edwards, eds. *Cross-Cultural Study of Women*. New York: The Feminist Press, 1986.

Etienne, Mona, and Eleanor Leacock. *Women and Colonization*. New York: Praeger, 1980.

Fabbro, David. "Peaceful Societies: An Introduction." *Journal of Peace Research* 15 (1978): 1.

Fanon, Frantz. *The Wretched of the Earth*, trans. Constance Farrington. New York: Grove Press, 1963.

— *A Dying Colonialism*, trans. Haakon Chevalier. New York: Grove Press, 1967.

Faure, Christine. "Absent from History," trans. Lillian S. Robinson. *Signs* 7, 1 (1981): 71–86.

Foucault, Michel. *Power/Knowledge*, ed. Colin Gordon. New York: Pantheon, 1980.

— *Discipline and Punish: The Birth of the Prison*, trans. Alan Sheridan. New York: Pantheon Books, 1977.

Fox, Robin Lane. *Pagans and Christians*. New York: Alfred A. Knopf, 1987.

Fox-Genovese, Elizabeth. *Within the Plantation Household: Black and White Women of the Old South*. Durham: University of North Carolina Press, 1989.

Franco, Jean. "The Incorporation of Women: A Comparison of North American and Mexican Popular Narrative." *Studies in Entertainment*, ed. Tania Modleski. Bloomington: Indiana University Press, 1985.

Frank, Douglas W. *Less than Conquerors: How Evangelicals Entered the Twentieth Century*. Grand Rapids, Mich.: W.B. Eerdmans, 1986.

Franklin, Frazier, E. *Black Bourgeoisie*. New York: The Free Press, 1957.

French, Marilyn. *Beyond Power*. New York: Summit Books, 1985.

Genes and Gender VI: On Peace, War, and Gender, ed. Anne E. Hunter. New York: The Feminist Press, 1993.

Genovese, Eugene. *Roll, Jordan, Roll: The World the Slaves Made*. New York: Random House, 1974.

Giddings, Paula. *When and Where I Enter*. New York: William Morrow, 1984.

Gillis, John. *For Better, For Worse: British Marriages 1600 to the Present*. New York: Oxford University Press, 1985.

Gordon, Ann D., and Mari Jo Buhle. "Sex and Class in Colonial and Nineteenth-Century America." *Liberating Women's History*, ed. Berenice A. Carroll. Urbana: University of Illinois Press, 1976.

Graham, Maria Dundas. *Journal of a Voyage to Brazil and Residence There during Part of Three Years, 1821, 1822, 1823*. New York: Praeger, 1969.

Grant, Jacqueline. "Black Women and the Church." In *Some of Us Are Brave*, ed. Gloria T. Hull, Patricia Bell Scott, and Barbara Smith. Old Westbury, NY: The Feminist Press, 1982.

Gross, Susan Hill, and Marjorie Wall Bingham, eds. *Women in Latin America*. St. Louis Park, Minn.: Glenhurst Publications, 1969.

Gutman, Herbert. *The Black Family in Slavery and Freedom, 1750–1925*. New York: Pantheon, 1976.

Hafkin, Nancy J., and Edna G. Bay, eds. *Women in Africa: Studies in Social and Economic Change*. Stanford, Cal.: Stanford University Press, 1976.

Hahner, June, ed. *Women in Latin American History: Their Lives and Views*. Los Angeles: UCLA Latin American Center Publications, 1976.

Hall, Basil. *Travels in North America in the Years 1827 and 1828*. Philadelphia: Carey, Lea & Carey, 1829.

Hall, Jacqueline Dowd, Robert Korstad, and James Leloudis. "Cotton Mill People." *American Historical Review* 91, 2 (1986): 245–85.

Hanawalt, Barbara. *The Ties That Bound: Peasant Families in Medieval England*. New York: Oxford University Press, 1986.

Hanley, Sarah. "Family and State in Early Modern France: The Marriage Pact." In *Connecting Spheres: Women in the Western World, 1500 to Present*, ed. Marilyn J. Boxer and Jean H. Quataert. New York: Oxford University Press, 1987.

Henn, Jeanne K. "Women in the Rural Economy: Past, Present, and Future." In *African Women South of the Sahara*, ed. Margaret Jean Hay and Sharon Stichter. New York: Longman, 1984.

Herlihy, David. "Land, Family, and Women in Continental Europe, 701–1200." In *Women in Medieval Society*, ed. Susan Mosher Stuard. Philadelphia: University of Pennsylvania Press, 1976.

Hess, Beth, and Myra Marx Ferree, eds. *Analyzing Gender*. Beverly Hills, Cal.: Sage, 1987.

Hewitt, Nancy A. "Friends: Agrarian Quakers and the Emergence of Woman's Rights in America." *Feminist Studies* 12, 1 (1986): 28–49.

Hilton, Anne. *The Kingdom of Kongo*. Oxford: Clarendon Press, 1985.

Hobsbawm, E.J. *The Age of Revolution: Europe 1789–1848*. London: Cardinal, l988.

Horton, Robin. "African Traditional Thought and Western Science." *Africa* 37 (Jan. 1967).

Hufton, Olwen. "Early Modern Europe." *Past and Present* 101 (Nov. 1983): 125–40.

— "Women in Revolution, 1789–1796." *Past and Present* 53 (Nov. 1971): 90–108.

Huston, Nancy. "The Matrix of War: Mothers and Heroes." In *The Female Body in Western Culture: Contemporary Perspectives*, ed. Susan Suleiman. Cambridge, Mass.: Harvard University Press, 1986.

Jacobs, Harriet A. *Incidents in the Life of a Slave Girl*, ed. Jean Fagan Yellin. Cambridge, Mass.: Harvard University Press, 1987.

Jennings, Francis. *Empire of Fortune: Crowns, Colonies and Tribes in the Seven Years' War in America*. New York: W.W. Norton, 1988.

Johnson, Cheryl. "Class and Gender: A Consideration of Yoruba Women during the Colonial Period." In *Women and Class*, ed. Claire C. Robertson and Iris Berger. New York: Africana Publishing Co., 1986.

Jones, Jacqueline. "'My Mother Was Much of a Woman': Black Women, Work, and the Family under Slavery." *Feminist Studies* 8, 2 (1982): 235–69.

— *Labor of Love, Labor of Sorrow: Black Women, Work, and the Family from Slavery to the Present*. New York: Basic Books, 1985.

Jordan, Winthrop D. *White over Black*. Chapel Hill: University of North Carolina Press, 1968.

Joseph, Gloria I. "Sojourner Truth: Achetypal Black Feminist." In *Wild Women in the Whirlwind: Afra-American Culture and the Contemporary*

Literary Renaissance, ed. Joanne M. Braxton and Andrée Nicola McLaughlin. New Brunswick, NJ: Rutgers University Press, 1990.

Kalpisch-Zuber, Christiane. *Women, Family, and Ritual in Renaissance Italy*, trans. Lydia Cochrane. Chicago: University of Chicago Press, 1985.

Kandell, Jonathan. *La Capital: The Biography of Mexico City*. New York: Random House, 1986.

Karlsen, Carol. "The Devil in the Shape of a Woman: The Witch in Seventeenth-Century New England." PhD dissertation, Yale University, 1980.

Katzman, David. *Seven Days a Week: Women and Domestic Service in Industrializing America*. Chicago: University of Illinois Press, 1981.

Keen, Benjamin, and Mark Wasserman. *A Short History of Latin America*. Boston: Houghton Mifflin, 1984.

Kelly-Gadol, Joan. "Early Feminist Theory and the *Querelle des Femmes*, 1400–1789." *Signs* 8, 1 (1982): 4–28.

Kerber, Linda K. "Separate Spheres, Female Worlds, Woman's Place: The Rhetoric of Women's History." *Journal of American History* 75, 1 (1988): 9–39.

Kessler-Harris, Alice. *Women Have Always Worked: A Historical Overview*. New York: The Feminist Press, 1981.

Klapisch-Zuber, Christiane. *Women, Family and Inheritance in Renaissance Florence*, trans. Lydia Cochrane. Chicago: University of Chicago Press, 1985.

Klein, Viola. "The Historical Background." In *Women: A Feminist Perspective*, ed. Jo Freeman. Palo Alto, Cal.: Mayfield, 1979.

Knauss, Peter R. *The Persistence of Patriarchy*. New York: Praeger, 1984.

Koehler, Lyle. "The Case of the American Jezebels: Anne Hutchinson and Female Agitation during the Years of Antinomian Turmoil, 1636–1640." *William and Mary Quarterly* 31 (1974): 55–78.

Kolchin, Peter. *Unfree Labor: American Slavery and Russian Serfdom*. Cambridge, Mass.: Harvard University Press, 1987.

Kors, Alan C., and Edward Peters. *Witchcraft in Europe, 1100–1700: A Documentary History*. Philadelphia: University of Pennsylvania Press, 1972.

LaBarge, Margaret Wade. *A Small Sound of the Trumpet: Women in Medieval Life*. Boston: Beacon Press, 1986.

Labé, Louise. *Sonnets*, trans. Graham Dunstan Martin. Edinburgh Bilingual Library 7. Austin: University of Texas Press, 1972.

Lacroix, Paul. *History of Prostitution*, trans. Samuel Putnam. New York: P. Covici, 1926.

Ladner, Joyce A. "Racism and Tradition: Black Womanhood in Historical Perspective." In *Liberating Women's History*, ed. Berenice A. Carroll. Urbana: University of Illinois Press, 1976.

Lavrin, Asunción. "Women in Convents: Their Economic and Social Role in Colonial Mexico." In *Liberating Women's History*, ed. Berenice A. Carroll. Urbana: University of Illinois Press, 1976.

Law, Robin. "Dahomey and the Slave Trade: Reflections on the Historigraphy of the Rise of Dahomey." *Journal of African History* 27 (1986): 237–67.

— "Slave-Raiders and Middlemen, Monopolists and Free-Traders: The Supply of Slaves for the Atlantic Trade in Dahomey c. 1715–1850." *Journal of African History* 30 (1989): 45–68.

Lebsock, Suzanne. *A Share of Honor: Virginia Women, 1600–1945*. Richmond: Virginia State Library, 1987.

Lenero, Elu de. "Women's Work and Fertility." In *Sex and Class in Latin America*, ed. June Nash and Helen I. Safa. New York: Praeger, 1976.

Lerner, Gerda. *The Creation of Patriarchy*. New York: Oxford University Press, 1986.

Levy, Darlene, Harriet Applewhite, and Mary Johnson. *Women in Revolutionary Paris, 1789–1795*. Urbana: University of Illinois Press, 1979.

Lewis, Diane K. "The Black Family: Socialization and Sex Roles." *Phylon: The Atlanta University Review of Race and Culture* 36, 3 (1975): 221–37.

Ligon, Richard. "A Sugar Plantation in Barbados," from *A True and Exact History of the Island of Barbadoes* in *Africans Abroad*, ed. Graham Irwin. First published 1657. London: Frank Cass, 1970.

Lindqvist, Sven. *Exterminate All the Brutes*. New York: The New Press, 1996.

Lockhart, James. *Spanish Peru, 1532–1556*. Madison: University of Wisconsin Press, 1968.

Lougee, Carolyn C. *Le Paradis des Femmes: Women, Salons, and Social Stratification in Seventeenth-Century France.* Princeton: Princeton University Press, 1976.

MacDonald, Michael. *Mystical Bedlam.* Cambridge: Cambridge University Press, 1981.

Macfarlane, Alan J. *Love and Marriage.* Cambridge: Cambridge University Press, 1986.

Mann, Kristin. *Marrying Well: Marriage, Status and Social Change among the Educated Elite in Colonial Lagos.* Cambridge: Cambridge University Press, 1985.

Marsden, George M. "Defining American Fundamentalism." In *The Fundamentalist Phenomenon,* ed. Norman J. Cohen. Michigan: William B. Eerdmans Publishing, 1990.

Mathurin, Lucille. "The Arrival of Black Women." *Jamaica Journal* 9, 2–3 (1975).

Mbilinyi, Marjorie. "'City' and 'Countryside' in Colonial Tanganyika." *Economic and Political Weekly: Review of Women Studies* 20, 43, Oct. 26, 1985.

— "Wife, Slave and Subject of the King: The Oppression of Women in the Shambala Kingdom." *Tanzania Notes and Records* 88–89 (1982).

McBride, Theresa. "The Long Road Home: Women's Work and Industrialization." In *Becoming Visible: Women in European History,* ed. Renate Bridenthal and Claudia Koonz. First ed. Boston: Houghton Mifflin, 1977.

McDonnell, Ernest W. *Beguines and Beghards in Medieval Culture.* New Brunswick, NJ: Rutgers University Press, 1954.

McLaughlin, Andrée Nicola. "Black Women, Identity, and the Quest for Humanhood and Wholeness: Wild Women in the Whirlwind." In *Wild Women in the Whirlwind: Afra-American Culture and the Contemporary Literary Renaissance,* ed. Joanne M. Braxton and Andrée Nicola McLaughlin (New Brunswick, NJ: Rutgers University Press, 1990).

McNamara, Jo Ann. "*Matres Patriae/Matres Ecclesiae*: Women of the Roman Empire." In *Becoming Visible: Women in European History,* ed. Renata Bridenthal, Claudia Koonz, and Susan Stuard. Boston: Houghton Mifflin, 1987.

— *A New Song*. New York: Haworth Press, 1983.

— *Sisters in Arms: Catholic Nuns through Two Millennia*. Cambridge, Mass: Harvard University Press, 1996.

McNamara, Jo Ann, and Suzanne F. Wemple, "The Power of Women through the Family in Medieval Europe, 500–1100." In *Clio's Consciousness Raised*, ed. Mary S. Hartman and Lois Banner. New York: Harper & Row, 1974.

Mill, J.S. *On the Subjection of Women*. London: Everyman, 1965.

Moers, Ellen. *Literary Women*. New York: Doubleday, 1977.

Montagu, Mary Wortley. *The Complete Letters of Lady Mary Wortley Montagu*, vol. 1, ed. Robert Halsband. Oxford: Clarendon Press, 1965.

Morgan, Edmund S. *The Puritan Family: Religion and Domestic Relations in 17th Century New England*. New York: Harper & Row, 1966.

— *American Slavery, American Freedom: The Ordeal of Colonial Virginia*. New York: W.W. Norton, 1975.

Muller, Viana. "Kin Reproduction and Elite Accumulation in the Archaic States of Northwest Europe." In *Power Relations and State Formation*, ed. Thomas C. Patterson and Christine W. Gailey. Washington, DC: American Anthropological Association, 1987.

Nash, June. "The Aztecs and the Ideology of Male Dominance." *Signs* 4, 2 (1978): 349–62.

Noble, David F. *A World without Women: The Christian Clerical Culture of Western Science*. New York: Random House, 1992.

Noel, Jan. "New France: Les Femmes Favorisées." *Atlantis* 6, 2 (1981): 80–98.

Northup, Solomon. *Twelve Years a Slave. Narrative of Solomon Northup, a Citizen of New York, Kidnapped in Washington City in 1841, and Rescued in 1853, from a Cotton Plantation near the Red River in Louisiana*. Auburn, NY: Derby and Miller, 1853.

Norton, Mary Beth. "The Evolution of White Women's Experience in Early America." *American Historical Review* 89, 3 (1984): 593–619.

— *Founding Mothers and Fathers: Gendered Power and the Forming of American Society*. New York, Alfred A. Knopf, 1996.

— "'My Resting Reaping Times': Sarah Osborn's Defense of Her 'Unfeminine' Activities, 1767." *Signs* 2, 2 (1976): 515–29.

Norton, Mary Beth, et al. *A People and a Nation: A History of the United States*. Boston: Houghton Mifflin Company, 1986.

O'Faolain, Julia, and Lauro Marinte. *Not in God's Image*. London: Temple Smith, 1973.

O'Flaherty, Wendy Doniger. *Women, Androgynes, and Other Mythical Beasts*. Chicago: University of Chicago Press, 1980.

Obbo, Christine. *African Women*. London: Zed Press, 1980.

Oboler, Regina Smith. *Women, Power, and Economic Change: The Nandi of Kenya*. Stanford Cal.: Stanford University Press, 1985.

Okonjo, Kamene. "Sex Roles in Nigerian Politics." In *Female and Male in West Africa*, ed. Christine Oppong. London: George Allen & Unwin, 1983.

Outram, Dorinda. "Le Langage Mâle de la Vertu: Women and the Discourse of the French Revolution." In *The Social History of Language*, ed. Peter Burke and Roy Porter. New York: Cambridge University Press, 1987.

Ozment, Steven. *When Fathers Ruled*. Cambridge, Mass.: Harvard University Press, 1983.

Patterson, K. David, and Gerald W. Hartwig, "The Disease Factor: An Introductory Overview." In *Disease in African History: An Introductory Survey and Case History*, ed. David Patterson and Gerald W. Hartwig. Durham, NC: Duke University Press, 1978.

Perkins, Edwin J. *The Economy of Colonial America*. New York: Columbia University Press, 1988.

Pescatello, Ann M. "Latina Liberation: Tradition, Ideology, and Social Changes in Iberian and Latin American Culture." In *Liberating Women's History*, ed. Berenice A. Carroll. Urbana: University of Illinois Press, 1976.

— *Power and Pawn: The Female in Iberian Families, Societies, and Cultures*. Westport, Conn.: Greenwood Press, 1976.

Peterson, Frederick A. *Ancient Mexico*. New York: G.P. Putnam's Sons, 1959.

Polanyi, Karl, with Abraham Rotstein. *Dahomey and the Slave Trade: An Analysis of an Archaic Economy*. Seattle: University of Washington Press, 1966.

Pomar, Juan Bautista. *Relación de Texcoco* (1582).

Porter, Gina. "A Note on Slavery, Seclusion and Agrarian Change in Northern Nigeria." *Journal of African History* 30 (1989): 487–91.

Power, Eileen. "The Position of Women." In *The Legacy of the Middle Ages*, ed. C.G. Crump and E.F. Jacob. Oxford: Clarendon Press, 1962.

— *Medieval People*. Garden City, NY: Doubleday, 1954.

Qunta, Christine N. "Outstanding African Women, 1500 BC–1900 AD." In *Women in Southern Africa*, ed. Christine Qunta. London: Allison & Busby, 1987.

Rapp, Rayna. "Household and Family." In *Examining Family History*, ed. Ellen Ross Rapp and Renate Bridenthal. *Feminist Studies* 5 (spring 1979).

Rathbone, Eleanor. *The Disinherited Family*, republished as *Family Allowance*. London: Allen and Unwin, 1949.

Reddock, Rhoda E. "Women and Slavery in the Caribbean: A Feminist Perspective." *Latin American Perspectives* 12, 1 (1985): 63–80.

Reed, Evelyn. *Women's Evolution: From Matriarchal Clan to Patriarchal Family*. New York: Pathfinder Press, 1975.

Rogers, Barbara. *The Domestication of Women: Discrimination in Developing Societies*. London and New York: Tavistock, 1980.

Salmon, Marylynn. *Women and the Law of Property in Early America*. Chapel Hill: University of North Carolina Press, 1986.

Sánchez-Korrol, Virginia. "Women in Nineteenth- and Twentieth-Century Latin America and the Caribbean." In *Restoring Women to History*, ed. Renata Bridenthal, Claudia Koonz, and Susan Stuard. Bloomington, Ind.: Organization of American Historians, 1987.

Sandelowski, Margarete J. "Failures of Volition: Female Agency and Infertility in Historical Perspective." *Signs*, 15, 3 (1990).

Sankovitch, Tilde A. *French Women Writers and the Book*. Syracuse, NY: Syracuse University Press, 1988.

Schama, Simon. *Landscape and Memory*. New York: Vintage Books, 1996.

Scott, Joan Wallach. "The Modern Period." *Past and Present* 101 (Nov. 1983): 141–57.

Scott, Joan W., and Louise A. Tilly. *Women, Work and Family*. New York: Holt, Rinehart and Winston, 1978.

Scott, Russell. *The Body as Property*. New York: Viking Press, 1981.

Shammas, Carole, Marylynn Salmon, and Michel Dahlin. *Inheritance in America from Colonial Times to the Present*. New Brunswick, NJ: Rutgers University Press, 1987.

Sievers, Sharon L. "Women in China, Japan, and Korea." In *Restoring Women to History*, ed. Renata Bridenthal, Claudia Koonz, and Susan Stuard. Bloomington, Ind.: Organization of American Historians, 1987.

Smyers, Karen A. "Women and Shinto: The Relation between Purity and Pollution." *Japanese Religions* 12, 4 (1983): 7–18.

Spender, Dale. *Invisible Woman: The Schooling Scandal*. London: Wirters & Readers, 1982.

Spruill, Julia Cherry. *Women's Life and Work in the Southern Colonies*. New York: W.W. Norton, 1972.

Stack, Carol. *All Our Kin: Strategies for Survival in a Black Community*. New York: Harper & Row, 1974.

Stampp, Kenneth M. *The Peculiar Institution*. New York: Random House/Vintage Books, 1956.

Stansell, Christine. *City of Women: Sex and Class in New York, 1789–1860*. New York: Alfred A. Knopf, 1986.

Stenton, Doris Mary. *The English Woman in History*. New York: Schocken Books, 1977.

Stetson, Erlene. "Studying Slavery." In *But Some of Us Are Brave*, ed. Gloria T. Hull, Patricia Bell Scott, and Barbara Smith. Old Westbury, NY: The Feminist Press, 1982.

Stone, Laurence. *The Family, Sex, and Marriage, 1500–1800*. New York: Harper & Row, 1977.

Sudarkasa, Niara. "The Status of Women in Indigenous African Societies." *Feminist Studies* 12, 1 (1986): 91–103.

Sweetman, David. *Women Leaders in African History*. London: Heinemann, 1984.

Swerdlow, Amy, and Phyllis Vine. "The Search for Alternatives: Past, Present, and Future." In *Household and Kin*, ed. Amy Swerdlow et al. New York: The Feminist Press, 1981.

Terborg-Penn, Rosalyn. "Women and Slavery in the African Diaspora: A Cross-Cultural Approach to Historical Analysis." *Sage* 3, 2 (1986): 11–15.

Theweleit, Klaus. *Male Fantasies*, vol. 1: *Women, Floods, Bodies, History*. Minneapolis: University of Minnesota Press, 1987.

Thomas, Keith. *Religion and the Decline of Magic*. New York: Scribner's Sons, 1971.

Thornton, John K. *The Kingdom of Kongo: Civil War and Transition, 1641–1718*. Madison: University of Wisconsin Press, 1983.

Tilly, Louise A., and Joan W. Scott. *Comparative Studies in Society and History*, vol. 17. Cambridge: Cambridge University Press, 1975.

— *Women, Work & Family*. New York: Holt, Rinehart and Winston, 1978.

Todorov, Tzvetan. *The Conquest of America*. New York: Harper & Row, 1984.

Tovar, Federico Ribes. *The Puerto Rican Woman: Her Life and Evolution throughout History*. New York: Plus Ultra Books, 1972.

Ulrich, Laurel Thatcher. *Good Wives: Image and Reality in the Lives of Women in Northern New England, 1650–1750*. New York: Knopf, 1982.

Van Kirk, Sylvia. *Many Tender Ties: Women in Fur Trade Society in Western Canada, 1700–1850*. Winnipeg: Watson & Dwyer, 1980.

Wagner, Sally Roesch. "The Root of Oppression Is the Loss of Memory: The Iroquois and the Early Feminist Vision." Paper delivered at the Champlain Valley History Symposium, Plattsburgh, NY, 1988.

White, E. Frances. "Creole Women Traders in the Nineteenth Century." *Working Papers No. 27,* African Studies Center, Boston University.

— *Sierra Leone's Settler Women Traders: Women on the Afro-European Frontier*. Ann Arbor: University of Michigan Press, 1987.

— "Women of Western and Western Central Africa." In *Restoring Women to History*, ed. Renata Bridenthal, Claudia Koonz, and Susan Stuard. Bloomington, Ind.: Organization of American Historians, 1987.

White, Landeg. *Magomero: Portrait of an African Village*. Cambridge: Cambridge University Press, 1987.

Wiesner, Merry. "Spinning Out Capital: Women's Work in the Early Modern Economy." In *Becoming Visible: Women in European History*, ed. Renate Bridenthal, Claudia Koonz, and Susan Stuard. Boston: Houghton Mifflin, 1987.

Williams, Selma R. *Demeter's Daughters: The Women Who Founded America, 1587–1787*. New York: Atheneum, 1976.

Wright, Marcia. "Technology, Marriage and Women's Work in the History of Maize-Growers in Mazabuka, Zambia: A Reconnaissance." *Journal of African Studies* 10, 1(1983): 71–85.

Zinn, Howard. *A People's History of the United States*. New York: Harper & Row, 1980.

WORLD MAP: PETERS PROJECTION. English version by Oxford Cartographers Ltd. Copyright Akademische Verlagsanstalt. Used by permission. Distributed in North America by

INDEX

wealth
    in Africa, 176–77
    in colonial America, 351
    from Latin America, 199–200
    in medieval Europe, 38
    slaves as, 161
    and women's work, 352
weaving, 282
    in Africa, 149, 156
    in colonial America, 306
    in Europe, 114, 117
    in Japan, 93
Webster, Mary Reeve, 300
weddings, 110–11, 207, 250
West Africa, 148–49, 151. *See also indi-*
    vidual states and peoples
    Europeans in, 156, 157
    slave trade in, 165, 167, 218, 364
West Indies. *See* Caribbean islands
wet-nurses
    in colonial America, 285, 335
    in Europe, 34–35, 115
    in Japan, 69
Wheatley, John, 357–58
Wheatley, Mary, 357
White, John, 249
Whitefield, George, 311
Whydah, 178, 180, 185
widows
    in Africa, 145, 159, 161–62
    children of, 119
    in colonial America, 266, 270–71,
        284–85, 287, 289, 306–7, 308,
        332–33
    in early modern Europe, 113–14,
        119, 120, 134, 203
    as entrepreneurs, 36, 41, 125
    in Japan, 77–78, 81, 85, 87
    in Latin America, 231, 232, 239–40
    in medieval Europe, 30–31, 36, 37,
        41, 63
    persecution of, 121
    poverty of, 349–50
    remarriage of, 119, 162, 237

    in United States, 349–50, 383
Wiesner, Merry, 115
wife-beating
    in Africa, 147
    in the Americas, 239, 345
    in Japan, 75–76
    punishment for, 75, 108
William III of England, 306
Williams, Roger, 290, 295
Williams, Selma, 365
Williams College, 331
Wilson, Deborah, 297
Wilson, John, 292, 294
Winthrop, John, 276, 285, 290,
    292–94, 357
witches, 54, 120–21
    in colonial America, 124, 258,
        300–304
    in Europe, 54, 60, 120–24
    in Latin America, 245
Wittgenstein, Ludwig, 58
wives. *See also* husbands; polygyny; wid-
    ows
    abuse of, 75–76, 116, 147, 234, 239,
        345–49
    in Africa, 148, 157, 176
    in the Americas, 229–30, 229–30,
        234, 237–38, 239, 287, 289, 345,
        349
    behavior expected of, 39–40, 43,
        237–38
    in Europe, 23–24, 203
    impressed, 267
    indentured servants as, 309
    in Japan, 86
    oppression of, 23, 116
    power-sharing by, 23–24, 25
    as property, 176
    punishment of, 23, 87, 102, 108–9
    rights of, 176, 333
    of soldiers, 323
"wives of the king", 180–81, 182,
    185–86

The Feminist Press at the City University of New York is a nonprofit literary and educational institution dedicated to publishing work by and about women. Our existence is grounded in the knowledge that women's writing has often been absent or underrepresented on bookstore and library shelves and in educational curricula—and that such absences contribute, in turn, to the exclusion of women from the literary canon, from the historical record, and from the public discourse.

The Feminist Press was founded in 1970. In its early decades, the Feminist Press launched the contemporary rediscovery of "lost" American women writers, and went on to diversify its list by publishing significant works by American women writers of color. More recently, the Press's publishing program has focused on international women writers, who remain far less likely to be translated than male writers, and on nonfiction works that explore issues affecting the lives of women around the world.

Founded in an activist spirit, the Feminist Press is currently undertaking initiatives that will bring its books and educational resources to underserved populations, including community colleges, public high schools and middle schools, literacy and ESL programs, and prison education programs. As we move forward into the twenty-first century, we continue to expand our work to respond to women's silences wherever they are found.

For a complete catalog of the Press's 250 books, please refer to our web site: www.feministpress.org.